ACTIVITIES 1939–1945

The Collected Writings of John Maynard Keynes

Keynes with his books

THE COLLECTED WRITINGS OF
JOHN MAYNARD KEYNES

VOLUME XXII

ACTIVITIES 1939-1945

INTERNAL WAR FINANCE

EDITED BY
DONALD MOGGRIDGE

MACMILLAN
CAMBRIDGE UNIVERSITY PRESS
FOR THE
ROYAL ECONOMIC SOCIETY

Published for the Royal Economic Society by

THE MACMILLAN PRESS LTD

London and Basingstoke
Associated companies in Delhi Dublin Hong Kong Johannesburg Lagos
Melbourne Singapore Tokyo

THE SYNDICS OF THE CAMBRIDGE UNIVERSITY PRESS
32 East 57th Street, New York, N Y 10022, U.S.A.

Macmillan ISBN 0 333 10732 2 excluding U.S.A. and Canada
CUP ISBN 0 521 21876 4 U.S.A. and Canada only

Printed in Great Britain at the
University Press, Cambridge

CONTENTS

GENERAL INTRODUCTION

This new standard edition of *The Collected Writings of John Maynard Keynes* forms the memorial to him of the Royal Economic Society. He devoted a very large share of his busy life to the Society. In 1911, at the age of twenty-eight, he became editor of the *Economic Journal* in succession to Edgeworth; two years later he was made secretary as well. He held these offices without intermittence until almost the end of his life. Edgeworth, it is true, returned to help him with the editorship from 1919 to 1925; Macgregor took Edgeworth's place until 1934, when Austin Robinson succeeded him and continued to assist Keynes down to 1945. But through all these years Keynes himself carried the major responsibility and made the principal decisions about the articles that were to appear in the *Economic Journal*, without any break save for one or two issues when he was seriously ill in 1937. It was only a few months before his death at Easter 1946 that he was elected president and handed over his editorship to Roy Harrod and the secretaryship to Austin Robinson.

In his dual capacity of editor and secretary Keynes played a major part in framing the policies of the Royal Economic Society. It was very largely due to him that some of the major publishing activities of the Society—Sraffa's edition of Ricardo, Stark's edition of the economic writings of Bentham, and Guillebaud's edition of Marshall, as well as a number of earlier publications in the 1930s—were initiated.

When Keynes died in 1946 it was natural that the Royal Economic Society should wish to commemorate him. It was perhaps equally natural that the Society chose to commemorate him by producing an edition of his collected works. Keynes himself had always taken a joy in fine printing, and the Society, with the help of Messrs Macmillan as publishers and the Cambridge University Press as printers, has been anxious to give Keynes's writings a permanent form that is wholly worthy of him.

The present edition will publish as much as is possible of his work in the field of economics. It will not include any private and personal correspondence or publish letters in the possession of his family. The edition is concerned, that is to say, with Keynes as an economist.

Keynes's writings fall into five broad categories. First there are the books which he wrote and published as books. Second there are collections of articles and pamphlets which he himself made during his lifetime (*Essays in Persuasion* and *Essays in Biography*). Third, there is a very considerable volume of published but uncollected writings—articles written for newspapers, letters to newspapers, articles in journals that have not been included in his two volumes of collections, and various pamphlets. Fourth, there are a few hitherto unpublished writings. Fifth, there is correspondence with economists and concerned with economics or public affairs.

This series will attempt to publish a complete record of Keynes's serious writing as an economist. It is the intention to publish almost completely the whole of the first four categories listed above. The only exceptions are a few syndicated articles where Keynes wrote almost the same material for publication in different newspapers or in different countries, with minor and unimportant variations. In these cases, this series will publish one only of the variations, choosing the most interesting.

The publication of Keynes's economic correspondence must inevitably be selective. In the day of the typewriter and the filing cabinet and particularly in the case of so active and busy a man, to publish every scrap of paper that he may have dictated about some unimportant or ephemeral matter is impossible. We are aiming to collect and publish as much as possible, however, of the correspondence in which Keynes developed his own ideas in argument with his fellow economists, as well as the more significant correspondence at times when Keynes was in the middle of public affairs.

Apart from his published books, the main sources available to those preparing this series have been two. First, Keynes in his will made Richard Kahn his executor and responsible for his economic papers. They have been placed in the Marshall Library of the University of Cambridge and have been available for this edition. Until 1914 Keynes did not have a secretary and his earliest papers are in the main limited to drafts of important letters that he made in his own handwriting and retained. At that stage most of the correspondence that we possess is represented by what he received rather than by what he wrote. During the war years of 1914–18 Keynes was serving in the Treasury. With the opening in 1968 of the records under the thirty-year rule, many of the papers that he wrote then and later have become available. From 1919 onwards, throughout the rest of his life, Keynes had the help of a secretary—for many years Mrs Stevens. Thus for the last twenty-five years of his working life we have in most cases the carbon copies of his own letters as well as the originals of the letters that he received.

There were, of course, occasions during this period on which Keynes wrote himself in his own handwriting. In some of these cases, with the help of his correspondents, we have been able to collect the whole of both sides of some important interchange and we have been anxious, in justice to both correspondents, to see that both sides of the correspondence are published in full.

The second main source of information has been a group of scrapbooks kept over a very long period of years by Keynes's mother, Florence Keynes, wife of Neville Keynes. From 1919 onwards these scrapbooks contain almost the whole of Maynard Keynes's more ephemeral writing, his letters to newspapers and a great deal of material which enables one to see not only what he wrote but the reaction of others to his writing. Without these very carefully kept scrapbooks the task of any editor or biographer of Keynes would have been immensely more difficult.

The plan of the edition, as at present intended, is this. It will total twenty-nine volumes. Of these the first eight are Keynes's published books from *Indian Currency and Finance*, in 1913, to the *General Theory* in 1936, with the addition of his *Treatise on Probability*. There next follow, as vols. IX and X, *Essays in Persuasion* and *Essays in Biography*, representing Keynes's own collections of articles. *Essays in Persuasion* differs from the original printing in two respects: it contains the full texts of the articles or pamphlets included in it and not (as in the original printing) abbreviated versions of these articles, and it also contains one or two later articles which are of exactly the same character as those included by Keynes in his original collection. In *Essays in Biography* there have been added a number of biographical studies that Keynes wrote both before and after 1933.

There will follow two volumes, XI–XII, of economic articles and correspondence and a further two volumes, already published, XIII–XIV, covering the development of his thinking as he moved towards the *General Theory*. There are included in these volumes such part of Keynes's economic correspondence as is closely associated with the articles that are printed in them.

The next thirteen volumes, as we estimate at present, deal with Keynes's *Activities* during the years from the beginning of his public life in 1905 until his death. In each of the periods into which we divide this material, the volume concerned publishes his more ephemeral writings, all of it hitherto uncollected, his correspondence relating to these activities, and such other material and correspondence as is necessary to the understanding of Keynes's activities. These volumes are edited by Elizabeth Johnson and Donald Moggridge, and it is their task to trace and interpret Keynes's activities sufficiently to make the material fully intelligible to a later generation. There will be a further volume printing his social, political and literary writings and a final volume of bibliography and index.

Those responsible for this edition have been: Lord Kahn, both as Lord Keynes's executor and as a long and intimate friend of Lord Keynes, able to help in the interpreting of much that would be otherwise misunderstood; Sir Roy Harrod as the author of his biography; Austin Robinson as Keynes's co-editor on the *Economic Journal* and successor as Secretary of the Royal Economic Society, who has acted throughout as Managing Editor.

Elizabeth Johnson has been responsible for the *Activities* volumes xv–xviii covering Keynes's early life, the Versailles Conference and his early post-1918 concern with reparations and international finance. Donald Moggridge has been responsible for the two volumes covering the origins of the *General Theory* and for all the *Activities* volumes from 1924 to the end of his life in 1946.

The work of Elizabeth Johnson and Donald Moggridge has been assisted at different times by Jane Thistlethwaite, Mrs McDonald, who was originally responsible for the systematic ordering of the files of the Keynes papers and Judith Masterman, who for many years worked with Mrs Johnson on the papers. More recently Susan Wilsher, Margaret Butler and Leonora Woollam have continued the secretarial work. Barbara Lowe has been responsible for the indexing. Susan Howson undertook much of the important final editorial work on these volumes.

EDITORIAL NOTE

In this volume, the first of three concerning Keynes's involvement in the problems of financing Britain's war effort after 1939, the concentration is on internal financial policies. Later volumes will deal with the external aspects of Britain's war finance including lend lease. A further three volumes will be devoted to Keynes's efforts to shape the post-war world.

For Keynes's efforts to shape opinion through contributions to the Press, the main source is the series of scrapbooks which, as explained in the General Introduction, his mother carefully maintained (with Keynes's assistance) throughout his working life. For correspondence and memoranda, we are dependent on his surviving papers, materials available in the Public Record Office and the papers of colleagues and friends, in particular Professor J. R. N. Stone, to whom Keynes passed his working files concerning the national income exercise that accompanied the 1941 Budget. Where the material used has come from the Public Record Office, the call numbers for the relevant files appear in the List of Documents Reproduced following page 487.

In this and the succeeding wartime volumes, to aid the reader in keeping track of the various personalities who pass through the pages that follow, we have included brief biographical notes on the first occasion on which they appear. These notes are designed to be cumulative over the whole run of wartime volumes.

In this, as in all the similar volumes, in general all of Keynes's own writings are printed in larger type. All introductory matter and all writings by others than Keynes are printed in smaller type. The only exception to this general rule is that occasional short quotations from a letter from Keynes to his parents or to a friend, used in introductory passages to clarify a situation, are treated as introductory matter and are printed in the smaller type.

Most of Keynes's letters included in this and other volumes are reprinted from the carbon copies that remain among his papers. In most cases he has added his initials to the carbon in the familiar fashion in which he signed to all his friends. We have no certain means of knowing whether the top copy, sent to the recipient of the letter, carried a more formal signature.

PART I
SHAPING OPINION

Chapter 1

THE BEGINNING

On 15 August 1939 Keynes left England for a fortnight's holiday at Royat. He expected an international crisis in the next month, but as he told Richard Kahn[1] on 14 August:

> I shall be most surprised if it ends in war. It seems to me that Hitler's argument is unanswerable that he must get Danzig, because it matters so little to him or to anyone else. They will fix up some formula by which Danzig becomes part of the Reich, with no substantial change in the actual situation, e.g. by making it a demilitarised zone. So do not break your holiday, whatever you read in the papers until the last extremity.

He expressed similar views on 25 August.

The outbreak of war on 3 September saw him back in England. At the time he expected that he would 'come up here [to King's] to run a good part of the bursary of the College, the *Economic Journal,* and teaching in the Economics Faculty, which...[would] in due course release more active people' (Letter to R. F. Harrod, 7 September 1939). He told Lord Stamp on 15 September that 'Committee work, which would involve quiet drafting in my own room and occasional visits to London, would be the sort of thing I might be fit for'.

However, by that time he had already turned his mind to the economic problems of the war. On 14 September, talks in London had led him to his first contribution, which he sent to Lord Stamp,[2] H. D. Henderson,[3] R. F. Kahn and the Treasury a day later.

[1] Richard Ferdinand Kahn (b. 1905), Life Peer 1965; Fellow of King's College, Cambridge; temporary civil servant in various government departments, 1939–46; Professor of Economics, University of Cambridge, 1951–72.

[2] Josiah Stamp (1880–1941), K.B.E. 1920, 1st Baron 1938; Inland Revenue Department, 1896–1919; Chairman, L.M.S. Railway, 1926–41; Director, Bank of England, 1928–41; member, Economic Advisory Council, 1930–9; Chairman, Committee on Economic Information, 1931–9; Chairman, Survey of Financial and Economic Plans (attached to Cabinet Office), 1939–41.

[3] Hubert Douglas Henderson (1890–1952), Kt. 1942; Editor, *The Nation and Athenaeum,* 1923–30; Joint Secretary, Economic Advisory Council, 1930–4; Economic Adviser, Treasury, 1939–44; member, Survey of Financial and Economic Plans, 1939–41; Drummond Professor of Political Economy, Oxford, 1945–52; Fellow of All Souls College, Oxford, 1934–52.

PRICE POLICY

A large number, but not all, of the raw material controls have, as a temporary measure, fixed prices substantially at the pre-war figure. For a preliminary period of, say, a month this may do no harm. But before the separate controls can develop a more permanent price policy, it is evident that general decisions must be taken governing price policy as a whole. It is out of the question for the different controls to be settling the matter in isolation and without reference to a general principle of policy.

To establish a general principle of price policy, applicable at any rate for the rest of this year, is therefore one of the most urgent and important matters for the Home Cabinet. The following notes are intended to indicate some of the relevant points. The suggestions thrown out are mere possibilities, and it does not follow that the writer himself is in favour of all of them.

1. The sterling exchange has fallen nearly 15 per cent in relation to the dollar; to which has to be added the increased costs of freight and war risk. Thus if the international prices of raw commodities were unchanged, the delivered cost in sterling would probably rise by not less than 20 per cent on the average.

In fact international prices have risen sharply. Some of these rises seem to be beyond all reason and must be due to a wave of speculation or a hasty stocking up by manufacturers. Thus some reaction is to be expected; indeed it has already begun in the case of some commodities compared with the highest point reached last week. On the other hand, many pre-war prices were unduly low both in relation to the level of activity already reached and to the cost of production. For example, it would require a rise of nearly 15 per cent to bring the Board of Trade wholesale index for July 1939 up to the level of July 1937; and the same was true of the United States index. Thus a fairly substantial rise of a more permanent character is to be expected. At any rate for some months;— a more considerable reaction is possible after there has been time for new productive capacity to be set in motion.

At the present time (Sept. 13) Moody's daily index of staple commodity prices in the U.S.A. is 22 per cent above what it was a month ago. It follows that the average sterling costs in the United Kingdom of goods imported from U.S.A. is now about 46 per cent higher than a month ago.

Thus it is fanciful to suppose that the prices of imported goods can be maintained much longer in the neighbourhood of pre-war levels. To do so would throw most private importers out of business. The Government would have to take over the importation of almost everything and then sell the stuff at a stupendous loss to the Treasury.

Of course it does not follow that the delivered U.K. prices of commodities produced within the Empire have risen, or need rise, nearly so much. (See § 7 below.)

2. Apart from the increased cost of imported goods, it is actually desirable that the British price of such goods should rise relatively to the price of home-produced goods. We want to divert consumption away from imported goods. If they remain as cheap as before, it would require an extremely complicated and complete system of rationing to effect this object.

3. The previous paragraph aims at influencing the direction of domestic consumption. But what about the domestic producer? We want him, in the case of essential commodities, to *increase* his output considerably in conditions of some difficulty where his costs are likely to rise quite apart from the cost of imported material. Will he do this if he is limited to a pre-war selling price which will very probably involve him in a loss?

The most obvious example is that of agriculture. In the case of livestock there is probably a high elasticity of supply in response to a wholesale price rise of say 15–20 per cent. But pre-war prices were already unsatisfactory to the farmer, and the recent announcement fixing the prices of sheep and pigs at the pre-war level is already having a disastrous effect on his policy. One might have hoped that he would now set out to increase his breeding stock. But at a sale of young breeding sows held in my neighbourhood yesterday the prices were disastrous and below the pre-war level. The farmers were simply not buying. They say, with reason, that the price fixed for bacon is one at which they cannot afford to produce. Yet we are told that bacon is one of the very few foodstuffs which may have to be rationed very shortly owing to shortage. It is a sad waste of time to discourage farmers from breeding. I believe that the market for store cattle is also weak.

4. The aspect of higher prices as an instrument of revenue is not to be overlooked. Direct taxation can scarcely do all that is wanted. A tax on consumption will be required in some shape or form. The policy of a somewhat higher price level combined with provisions for diverting to the Treasury directly or indirectly a large proportion of any resulting profits deserves to be considered.

In those cases where the Government itself undertakes importation, it would be better to make a substantial profit on selling than to make a substantial loss. Let me take what is very likely a bad example. It may be that the state of stocks of petrol absolutely requires the stringent rationing recently announced. If so, the Treasury will have to face a heavy loss of revenue from motor and petrol taxes. If not, the necessity to economise petrol should be harmonised as far as possible with the interests of the Treasury. For example, the existing small ration might be supplied at 1s 6d and moderate, but more substantial amounts obtainable at, say, 2s 6d. This might be more efficient administratively and more productive to the Treasury than the endless wangling now in prospect to get additional rations at 1s 6d on more or less plausible pretexts,

6

the real validity of which there will be no time to examine. It might be sounder in every way to make motoring expensive than to make it the subject of wangling;—it might even save more petrol. I mention this because of its particular interest to the Treasury (with the present ration the cost per mile including car-tax and insurance is prohibitive). But it is easy to think of less controversial examples.

5. If a higher price level is inevitable, it will be better to bring it about by a deliberate act of policy at an early date than to allow prices to drift gradually upwards as a result of the necessities of individual control bodies.

6. The above relates to wholesale prices. The primary object of price control is presumably to prevent retail prices from rising to a level which will make a movement for higher wages irresistible. Thus we have to think how best to adjust the necessities of the situation to this primary object.

There is no reason why retail prices should rise nearly as much as wholesale prices. We must be prepared to simplify enormously the machinery of distribution, with a consequent reduction of costs. There should be a drastic curtailment in variety and in consumer's choice and all the frills of distribution, advertising, expensive systems of delivery and so forth, should be dispensed with. There is no reason why the costs of distribution, instead of going up should not be substantially reduced. (We may even learn a good deal which may be useful when peace returns.)

Some such price scheme as the following might be practicable. Let the wholesale price level rise on the average by about 25 per cent, imports prices rising as a rule by more than this, home produce by less. With a proper system of distribution this should be compatible with a rise in the cost of living (which includes rents) of 10 per cent at the outside and it might well be less. Even a rise of 10 per cent would make the cost of living only 7 per cent above the level of the autumn of 1937 when wages (Oct. 1937) were 3½ per cent below what they are now; so that the reduction in the hourly real wage below what it was in 1937 would be only 3½ per cent. It is absurd to suppose that a war can be waged without *any* reduction in anyone's standard of life. Yet allowing for an increase in employment and in the length of the working week, the rise suggested above might involve virtually no reduction below the 1937 level. If the working week is increased by 3½ per cent with hourly wage rates unchanged, i.e. if men work on the average a quarter of an hour more a day, their real weekly wages would remain at the 1937 level.

All these figures are, of course, not much more than for purposes of illustration. But they show that a rise in the wholesale price-level of the order of 25 per cent could be allowed without creating any reasonable claim for a rise in the hourly rate of wages.

7. The task of keeping the price-rise of imported goods within narrow limits is closely bound up with arrangements with the Dominion and Colonial Administrations for the limitation of prices and the maximum degree of self-sufficiency within the Empire.

There are many substantial groups of imported goods where the supply available within the Empire would be wholly or almost sufficient for our needs. It might be advisable for the Government to enter into arrangements with the Dominion Administrators to purchase all we require of their surplus output at a fixed price in sterling for the period of a year.

It would not be advisable, any more than in the case of home producers, that this fixed price should be the pre-war price. As a general average I suggest that home and Empire producers of staple raw commodities should alike receive a price about 20 per cent above the pre-war level; which, allowing for freights and war-risk, would mean a greater c.i.f. cost for Empire than for home goods.

A plan on these lines would be immensely helpful in solving

the exchange problem. It would also facilitate orderly transport arrangements.

The following are some prominent examples of commodities which could be covered by this scheme:

Wheat, meat, butter, cheese, sugar, tea, oilseeds, copra,
wool, jute, rubber, copper, lead, zinc, tin, nickel.

8. To sum up: the task of preventing any price rise is
impracticable. To attempt it will lead to chaos, delay and
waste. A 20 per cent rise in wholesale prices is the *least* we can
expect. A prudent policy will aim at a deliberately considered
price-level within the limits which are practicable.

14 September 1939   J. M. KEYNES

His price policy memorandum led him into discussions with Sir Richard
Hopkins and Sir Frederick Phillips[4] and a request from Phillips for his ideas
on exchange control, which he sent to Phillips and H. D. Henderson on
24 and 25 September respectively.[5]

NOTES ON EXCHANGE CONTROL

1. In the last war there was no exchange control as such, apart
from import licences, restrictions on foreign investment etc.
The procedure adopted was analogous to that of the Exchange Equalisation Fund just before the war. That is to say,
there were free dealings over the exchange at a rate which
was 'pegged' by the Treasury, unlimited dollars being supplied at this rate. The only difference was that the pegging
was done in New York and not in London, the dollars being

[4] Sir Richard Hopkins (1880–1955); member, Board of Inland Revenue, 1916;
Chairman, Board of Inland Revenue, 1922; Controller of Finance and Supply
Services, Treasury, 1927–32, Second Secretary, 1932–42, Permanent Secretary,
1942–5.
  Sir Frederick Phillips (1884–1943); entered Treasury 1908, Under-Secretary,
1932; represented Treasury in U.S.A., 1940–3.
[5] He followed this up on 27 September with a letter to Phillips suggesting that
payments for interest and sinking fund due in terms of sterling might prove a
useful source of black sterling. This idea had resulted from a note by P. Einzig
in *The Financial News*. Paul Einzig (1897–1973); financial and political journalist
and prolific author; Political Correspondent for *The Financial News*, 1937–45.

supplied by Morgans as our agents. E. C. Grenfell would come round to the Treasury each morning with a pink cable in his hand, showing what had been paid out on the previous day.

Complete control was so much against the spirit of the age that I doubt if it ever occurred to any of us that it was possible. But the absence of it made my task of preparing a monthly budget of the dollar position very precarious. I used to obtain each month an estimate from the various departments and from the allies both of their total outstanding dollar commitments and of the amounts which they expected to mature in each month. To this, if I remember rightly, I added my own estimate of the probable requirements of the 'free exchange'. On the other side, our dollar assets, actual and prospective, were set out in the shape of gold and securities and the proceeds of loans. But the requirements of the 'free exchange' would come irregularly in great rushes, just like the demands on the Equalisation Fund, largely depending on the nature of the war and political news. I remember in particular a terrific run at the end of 1916, when the daily requirements (if my memory is correct) ran for a short time in excess of $5 million, which in those days we considered simply terrific. Chalmers and Bradbury never fully confessed to Ministers the extent of our extremity when it was actually upon us, though of course they had warned them, fully but unavailingly, months beforehand of what was coming. This was because they feared that, if they emphasised the real position, the policy of the peg might be abandoned, which, they thought, would be disastrous. They had been brought up in the doctrine that in a run one must pay out one's gold reserve to the last bean. I thought then, and I still think, that in the circumstances they were right. To have abandoned the peg would have destroyed our credit and brought chaos to business; and would have done no real good. I recall an historic occasion a day or two after the formation of the second coalition Government at the end of 1916. The position was very bad. We in the Treasury were all convinced that the only hope was to pay out and trust that the drain would suddenly dry up as it had on previous occasions. But we had no confidence in the understanding of Ministers. Chalmers went over to Carson's room (my memory tells me that it was in the War Office; but was it?) to report to the newly formed War Cabinet. 'Well, Chalmers, what is the news?' said the goat. 'Splendid,' Chalmers replied in his high quavering voice, 'two days ago we had to pay out $20 million; the next day it was $10 million; and yesterday only $5 million.' He did not add that a continuance at this rate for a week would clean us out completely, and that we considered an average of $2 million very heavy. I waited nervously in his room, until the old fox came back triumphant. In fact the drain did dry up almost immediately and we dragged along with a week or two's cash in hand until March 1917 when U.S.A. came in and that problem was over. So far as I know, the Germans were totally unaware of our financial difficulties. But the American Government, of course, knew them. It has been an important part of the case of the recent Nye Committee for denying credits to belligerents that Mr Page cabled to his government as follows on 5 March 1917: 'I think that the pressure of this approaching crisis has gone beyond the ability of the Morgan financial agency for the British and French Governments. Perhaps our going to war is the only way in which our present prominent trade position can be maintained and panic averted.'

On the other hand, my monthly estimates were saved by the fact that, as a result of delays in deliveries, the departments and the Allies never succeeded anywhere near in spending up to their forecasts. At the end of the war quite a significant part of the orders placed by Ll. G. and Russia in the summer of 1915, were still undelivered; and there were still hundreds of millions of dollars of these old orders outstanding when we were cleaned out in March 1917 and the American Treasury had to foot the bill.[6]

2. These reminiscences are not meant to be wholly irrelevant. It is true that in one important respect our problem then was different. Foreign balances in London were insignificant and were greatly outweighed by what foreigners owed us on acceptance credits. The financial crisis of 1914 was due, not to our being unable to pay what we owed abroad, but to foreigners being unable to pay us. It was not sterling which crashed in that month, but the dollar (which went temporarily over 6 to the £). But by 1916 the difference between the position then and the position now was not so fundamental.

It is, therefore, well to remember that we did get through after a fashion without blocking the exchanges; and this policy was not without considerable advantages of simplicity and efficiency.

Our international position is so totally different from Germany's that their technique does not offer a good model for us. I have not reached a decided opinion on the point. But there is much to be said against blocking up *all* the loopholes and crevices. Not all the money which slips through is 'lost'. There is a good deal of business which does us no harm and is better allowed which, nevertheless, one cannot make into a precedent by giving it official approval. There is a case for controls which those in charge know to be imperfect and incomplete and deliberately leave so; especially in England. It is far more trouble than it is worth to be too logical about controls. (I remember how the day after I had established the principle that the Russian credits should be for munitions only, M. Routkowsky came round for my initials to a Bond Street bill for a Grand Duchess's underclothing; and there was the case of the beeswax for the Little Fathers.)

I am therefore, doubtful if it is practicable or advisable to close down too completely the black exchange. It has its uses

---

[6] I have depended wholly on my memory unrefreshed by documents in writing the above, and it is probably inaccurate in detail.

within limits. One could see to it that it did not cost too much *net*. I can even imagine occasions when it might be worth the while of the Treasury to give it covert support. It is probably on a relatively small scale and is a useful safety valve. It is not advisable to render literally impossible all those transactions which the Treasury cannot afford formally and publicly to approve.

I suggest therefore, that the main transactions should be canalised and that the rest should be left to themselves. My main criticism of the measures put into force too quickly by the Board of Trade etc. is that they seem to flow from the belief that there is no middle course between complete *laissez-faire* and complete totalitarianism. I feel that it would be more in accordance with the traditions of the Treasury to be cautious and cagey with its control-system, and to cultivate turning a blind eye with the other one wide open. It looks, indeed, as if wisdom of this kind has been already at work. I return to the details later.

3. If we were to attempt complete exchange control on the German model, the position of the Dominions would offer to us an additional complication. It would be very undesirable to treat their bank accounts as blocked foreign balances. Canada is establishing an exchange control, and other Dominion Governments are likely to follow suit. But the details of management are not likely to be the same in each case.

4. For complete exchange control, it would be necessary that each individual foreign account should be blocked and only made available for specific approved purposes. This would not increase our popularity with neutrals and would involve an enormous amount of red-tape over London's international relations. It is undesirable if it can be avoided.

5. It is arguable, therefore, that a moderate development on the lines of what we are doing already would be best. The following is an outline of what might be necessary:

(1) The most important step forward is to require that

British exporters should hand over the foreign currency they earn.[7] Apart from deliberate evasions, the machinery for this should not be difficult. This is obvious and does not need emphasising.

(2) It is also desirable for the Treasury to acquire the cash equivalent of as much as possible of our invisible exports. These fall mainly under the following heads:–

(i) dividends and interest;

(ii) unearned income from foreign trusts, real estate etc. (American heiresses);

(iii) net shipping earnings;

(iv) insurance earnings;

(v) royalties, copyright, films etc.;

(vi) tourists;

(vii) income of resident aliens, and expenses of foreign businesses domiciled here which are received from abroad.

Some people believe that there is already a regulation relating to (i) but not relating to (ii). I am not aware of any present regulations affecting the other items. (iii) and (iv) present no difficulties because only a limited number of large well-known concerns are involved. (i), (ii) and (v) could be dealt with by requiring all foreign income to be turned over for official exchange into sterling. Some existing contracts under (v) are expressed in sterling. Perhaps it is enough to say that all further contracts should be expressed in foreign currency. (vi) and (vii) might be left unregulated, sterling for such purposes being purchased over the free exchange if so desired.

6. This would mean that the free exchange would be mainly concerned with capital transactions in sterling between foreigners, supplemented by leakages and permitted receipts under (vi) and (vii) above; though it would also cover all sorts of oddments which one cannot think of beforehand.

It will save a world of red-tape and trouble to allow such

[7] Contracts can still be made in terms of sterling, provided actual payment is made in foreign currency.

14

a free exchange on a modest scale. A modest discount below the official exchange will encourage foreigners to pay their sterling debts, and the amount of foreign money in London anxious to escape will gradually diminish. I would even go so far as to give covert support to the free exchange on a moderate scale if the discount widened too much. A free exchange, which is not much below the control price even when the foreign news is not satisfactory, will be good for our credit.

7. There remains the difficult problem of how to regulate the provision of foreign exchange for the private purchase of imports. In the last war (unless my memory is at fault) we depended solely on import licences and an arrangement by which the banks had to be satisfied that the exchange was required for a normal and proper purpose. There was, I think, a large volume of such normal transactions over the free exchange; but then we did not commandeer the proceeds of private exports.

Now import licences are usually given chiefly with reference to the usefulness of the goods and the shipping problems involved. It is difficult for an exchange controller to have the necessary knowledge to divert the demand from one source to another where exchange difficulties are less.

If trade can be left uncontrolled within the Empire, that would be a great simplification. But I do not see my way through the rest of this part of the problem.

24 September 1939   J. M. KEYNES

Also, from 20 September, Keynes, in the course of his few days a week in London, began to act as host to the 'Old Dogs'—First World War officials not (with the exception of H. D. Henderson at the Treasury) as yet involved officially in the war effort—H. D. Henderson, Sir Arthur Salter, Sir William Beveridge and Sir Walter Layton.[8] Inevitably, they discussed

[8] Sir Arthur Salter (1881–1975), K.C.B. 1922, 1st Baron of Kidlington, 1953; Independent M.P. for Oxford University, 1937–50; Conservative M.P. for Ormskirk, 1951–3; entered Admiralty, Transport Department, 1904; Director of Ship

their attempts to influence the management of the war—air raid precautions (A.R.P. to contemporaries), dispersion, blockade policy, war aims.

From the discussions of this group—and, inevitably, discussions with others—came several memoranda. First, there was one memorandum on blockade policy, which he sent to Sir Frederick Leith-Ross.[9] This led to a meeting with Leith-Ross on 26 October, but the suggestions did not affect official policy.[10]

THE FINANCIAL PRINCIPLES OF THE BLOCKADE

The proposal for a limitation of the blockade, so as to free certain classes of food, would fit in well with a certain broad conclusion as to the best technique for our economic warfare. It will be most useful, perhaps, that I should elaborate this conclusion in general and not merely with reference to the above conclusion.

Requisitioning, 1917; Secretary of Allied Marine Transport Council, 1918; member, Supreme Economic Council, 1919; General Secretary, Reparations Commission, 1920–2; Director, Economic and Financial Section of League of Nations, 1922–31; Chairman, Railway Staff National Tribunal, 1936–9; Parliamentary Secretary to Ministry of Shipping, 1939–41; Joint Parliamentary Secretary to Ministry of War Transport, 1941; Head of British Merchant Shipping Mission, Washington, 1941–3; Senior Deputy Director-General, UNRRA, 1944; Gladstone Professor of Political Theory and Institutions, Oxford, 1934–44.

Sir William Beveridge (1879–1963), 1st Baron 1946; Liberal M.P. for Berwick, 1944–5; 1st Chairman of Employment Exchanges Committee, 1905–8; Board of Trade, 1908–16; Director of Labour Exchanges, 1909–16; Assistant General Secretary, Ministry of Munitions, 1915–16, Ministry of Food, 1916–19; Director, London School of Economics, 1919–37; Vice-Chancellor, London University, 1926–8; Master of University College, Oxford, 1937–45; member, Royal Commission on Coal Industry, 1925; Chairman, Unemployment Insurance Statutory Committee, 1934–44, Imperial Defence Committee on Food Rationing, 1937, Committee on Skilled Men in Services, 1941–2; member, Fuel Rationing Enquiry, 1942.

Sir Walter Layton (1884–1966); Lecturer in Economics, Cambridge, 1912–19; Member of the Munitions Council responsible for Requirements and Statistics, Ministry of Munitions, 1916–18; Editor, *The Economist*, 1922–8; Director-General of Programmes, Ministry of Supply, 1940–2, Chairman of Executive Committee, Ministry of Supply, 1941–1; Chief Adviser, Programmes and Planning, Ministry of Production, 1942–3; Head of Joint War Production Staff, 1942–3.

[9] Sir Frederick Leith-Ross (1887–1968); entered Treasury, 1909; Deputy Controller of Finance, 1925–32; British representative on Finance Board of Reparation 42;Commission, 1920–25; Chief Economic Adviser to Government, 1932–46; Director-General, Ministry of Economic Warfare, 1939–42; Chairman, Inter-Allied Committee on Post-War Requirements, 1941–3; Deputy Director-General, UNRRA, 1944–5; Chairman, European Committee of Council, UNRRA, 1945–6.

[10] W. N. Medlicott, *The Economic Blockade*, vol. I (London, 1952), 39, 250 ff.

16

In the last war, both sides made the mistake of concentrating too much on specific goods and too little on money, which is generalised purchasing power and available for any goods. Germany started her unrestricted U-boat campaign within a few weeks of the date of the exhaustion of our finances in U.S.A. and without any reference to that vital fact (and, probably, without any knowledge of it). Our blockade was carried on to the grave impairment of our own financial resources and was apparently based on the assumption that the purchasing power of the enemy in the countries of the neighbouring neutrals was inexhaustible.

I lay down the following proposition as being, at the least, highly probable. Germany will succeed in spending all the foreign purchasing power she can acquire, and will not end the war with substantial foreign cash in hand. If this proposition is accepted, three important conclusions follow from it.

I. It should be our principal object to guide as much as possible of Germany's purchasing power towards goods which are not of absolutely the first order of necessity for winning the war. This is what in the last war I used to call 'the temptation policy', though I was never successful in persuading the Blockade Ministry of its importance.

If Germany's controls were to work with perfect coordination, efficacy and wisdom and with complete freedom from departmental jealousy, they would be able to resist the temptation policy. In fact we can hope that departmental zeal in the provision of particular commodities will often cause them to succumb to temptation, just as it would here. Every mark which we can induce Germany to spend on what is not absolutely essential is so much stolen from what is required for the most efficient prosecution of a long war.

We should, therefore, take the utmost pains to distinguish between what is essential to the German machine and what is merely useful, and concentrate all our blockade efforts on the former.

Let us now apply this principle to the important case of

17

food. Can Germany *afford* to buy any material quantity of food in excess of the amount with which in any case we have no power to interfere? Are we not, perhaps, wasting our effort and our money if, on this occasion, we attempt a *complete* blockade of food?

Is there not some reason to think that the scale of rationing already enforced in Berlin is stricter than is required by the blockade we have enforced or are likely to be able to enforce, and that the German authorities are deliberately economising on food purchases in order to keep their resources for still more essential purposes? Are we blockading (e.g.) sugar? Yet I have read that Germany is actually trying to export sugar to Holland in exchange for zinc.

If so, we are allowing them to put on our blockade the odium of restrictions which they would think it prudent to enforce in any case.

Moreover, if we were to remove from the contraband list selected foodstuffs, our relations with neutrals would be made much easier and we could effectively concentrate larger resources on hindering really essential imports.

II. It is almost as useful to force Germany to pay a high price for her imports as to prevent her from getting them. Thus it is desirable to force up the prices of what she wants in the neighbouring neutrals, even when we allow her to make the final successful bid. In the last war we signally failed to use this tactic and insisted on never being the under-bidder even when we had forced up the price to an uneconomic figure.

It is a tactic which needs much skill and finesse. But if one is taking a long view, nothing is cleverer than to allow her to buy *very dear*.

The great danger in a Ministry of Economic Warfare is excessive zeal on the part of officials who are dealing exclusively with particular commodities. It is safe to assume that Germany will manage to use her purchasing power *somehow*, that one cannot prevent this, and that one's prime object, therefore, is to make her use it inefficiently and to the least possible advantage.

III. It is just as important to interfere with Germany's export trade as with her imports. Perhaps more important. Since she will know how best to use her foreign purchasing power, it is more important to curtail her purchasing power than to impede her in the exercise of it in particular directions.

Thus, corresponding to the policy of forcing her to buy her imports dear, there should be a policy of forcing her to sell her exports cheap by methods of cut-throat competition.

This requires exact knowledge of what she is exporting and at what prices and a careful organisation of our own exporters. We should flood the neighbouring neutrals with cheap exports of the same general character as the German exports. A convenient way of helping our own exporters in this direction might be to buy from them the foreign currency proceeds of their sales at a very favourable rate of exchange. The fact that we shall need such currency to pay for our own official purchases offers a sufficient excuse for this.

Money will be better spent in flooding the neighbouring neutrals with our own exports at bargain prices than in buying from them at very high prices commodities which the Germans are quite likely better off without. For example, if it turns out that Germany can spare any material quantity of coal for export, we should not seek to prevent her, which is probably impossible, but should ourselves offer coal to Scandinavia on terms which would reduce the Scandinavian price for that commodity to a very unremunerative level. On the same principle we should be more concerned to raise the price of Swedish ore than to attempt the impracticable task of entirely preventing its shipment. If we can double the price of Swedish ore in terms of German coal, we shall be at the same time very popular in Scandinavia and highly efficient in the conduct of economic warfare. This is a policy for which we can expect covert Scandinavian cooperation!

In the last war our Ministry of Blockade came to the rescue of the German Treasury, just as their U-boat campaign came to the rescue of our Treasury. There are, of course, arguments on both sides. But the considerations here emphasised should not be lost sight of.

8.10.39   J. M. KEYNES

The second memorandum, also on food blockade, arose from conversations with Sir William Beveridge, to whom Keynes sent the memorandum on 15 October. He also sent it to the Foreign Office and the Ministry of Economic Warfare.[11]

WHEAT AS CONTRABAND

It is suggested that the following arguments for choosing a suitable moment to remove wheat from the list of contraband deserve consideration:–

1. It would be a genuine step, similar to the decision to refrain from bombing the civilian population except in reprisal as a last resort, to do a little towards the humanising of war; and is, therefore, desirable for its own sake unless there are clearly sufficient arguments to the contrary.

2. For this reason, its effect on neutral opinion would be favourable, and a regular item of German propaganda would be deprived of its sting.

3. In so far as starvation and short rations continue to

[11] Keynes also tried it on Churchill in conversation but met with great discouragement.

Winston Spencer Churchill (1874–1965); Conservative M.P. for Oldham 1900–4; Liberal M.P. for Oldham, 1904–6, for N.W. Manchester, 1906–8, for Dundee, 1908–22; Conservative M.P. for Epping, 1924–45, for Woodford, 1945–64; Parliamentary Under-Secretary of State for Colonies, 1906–8; President, Board of Trade, 1908–10; Home Secretary, 1910–11; First Lord of Admiralty, 1911–15; Chancellor of Duchy of Lancaster, 1915; Minister of Munitions, 1917–19; Secretary of State for War, 1919–21, for Air, 1919–21, for the Colonies, 1921–2; Chancellor of the Exchequer, 1924–9; First Lord of Admiralty, 1939–40; Prime Minister, 1940–5, 1951–5.

prevail in Germany, the odium of this state of affairs in the eyes of the German population would be removed, in part at least, from ourselves to where it properly belongs, namely the German Government. The decision to starve the part of the civilian population which has no military value would be seen clearly as their decision and not ours.

4. For the odium which we are at present bringing on ourselves in the eyes of the German public and before some sections of neutral opinion may be serving a very negligible military purpose. It is unlikely that German supplies of food, actual and potential, are so short as to justify so low a civilian ration as that which is already enforced. It is probable that a better supply of food is already available, but that the German authorities prefer to use their limited resources for more essential military purposes. If this is true, we are allowing them to throw on us an odium which belongs elsewhere. It is for us to expose this situation; which we can do by removing wheat, and wheat only, from the contraband list. For no one need starve if abundant wheat is available.

5. It is a fallacy to conduct our blockade policy as though the enemy's purchasing power were unlimited. We need to concentrate on depriving him of first essentials, and even to tempt him to purchase what is not a first essential. A concentration of the blockade on a limited range of articles will render it more effective, financially cheaper to us and financially more exhausting to the enemy, than if we spread ourselves ineffectually and expensively, with the maximum of machinery and friction, over every conceivable thing; and it will greatly ease our relations with the neighbouring neutrals.

6. It is true that wheat can be turned into alcohol or acetone and can be used, either directly or by substitution, or by exchange, as a feeding stuff for animals. But it is expensive and relatively inefficient for these purposes. There should be better ways in which Germany is free to spend her

limited supplies of foreign exchange; though it would be necessary to enquire into Germany's holdings of blocked exchange in (e.g.) the Argentine and what opportunities there are for her to use it otherwise.

We cannot prevent Germany from spending her foreign exchange on something, and it is futile to attempt it. Our efforts should be directed to diverting her money towards relatively inefficient and expensive purchases and, above all, to interfere with her ability to acquire money by exporting. We need subtler methods than that of attempting the impracticable task of a hundred per cent blockade, in which everything is treated as equally important.

7. It is not suggested that we should demand any kind of reciprocity from Germany. We should not get reciprocity if we asked for it, and we should lose the psychological gain that we are seeking of showing the neutrals that we behave differently from Germany.

Finally, there was a memorandum intended for President Roosevelt drafted for discussion with Sir George Schuster[12]. Mr Leonard Elmshirst[13] and Schuster had been encouraging Keynes to write the note three or four weeks previously, as well as to go to America to present the ideas directly to Roosevelt. Keynes expressed some interest in going to America in the late spring of 1940.

Elmshirst and Schuster also discussed similar ideas with Hoare, Halifax, Waley and Ashton-Gwatkin,[14] but Keynes urged delay until conditions

[12] Sir George Schuster (b. 1881); National Liberal M.P. for Walsall, 1938–45; member, Advisory Committee to Treasury, 1921–2; Financial Secretary to Sudanese Government, 1922–7; Economic and Financial Adviser to Colonial Office, 1927–8; Finance Member, Executive Council of Viceroy of India, 1928–34; member, Select Committee on National Expenditure, 1939–45.

[13] Leonard Elmshirst (1893–1974); Founder and Chairman, Dartington Hall Trust, 1925; Director, Institute of Rural Reconstruction, Bengal, 1921–4; President, International Conference of Agricultural Economists, 1930–61; Chairman, Political and Economic Planning, 1939–53; Agricultural Adviser, Government of Bengal, 1944–5.

[14] Samuel Hoare (1880–1959), 2nd Baronet, Viscount Templewood, 1944; Conservative M.P. for Chelsea, 1910–44; Secretary of State for Air, 1922–4, 1924–9; Secretary of State for India, 1931–5; Secretary of State for Foreign Affairs, 1935, resigned over the Hoare–Laval Plan designed to solve the Italo–Abyssinian crisis; First Lord

made American assistance seem more necessary. As a result, the memorandum never became the basis of action until events in the spring of 1940 made it, and a Keynes visit to America, redundant.[15]

NOTES ON THE WAR FOR THE PRESIDENT

These notes are based on the assumptions

that the United States really intends to remain entirely aloof from the hostilities of the war by land, sea and air;

that there is a predominant, and even a passionate, desire that the Anglo–French cause should be victorious; and that the slippery path of giving this cause as much practical assistance as possible, compatibly with the above, will be cautiously explored.

Their object is to make suggestions about practical assistance. But I should like to preface that with a few words on the larger problem.

of the Admiralty, 1936; Home Secretary, 1937; Lord Privy Seal and member of War Cabinet, 1939; Secretary of State for Air, 1940; Ambassador to Spain, 1940–4.

Edward Frederick Lindley Wood (1881–1959), 1st Baron Irwin, 1925, 3rd Viscount Halifax, 1st Earl, 1944; Parliamentary Under-Secretary of State for Colonies, 1921–2; Viceroy of India, 1926–31; President, Board of Education, 1932–5; Secretary of State for War, 1935; Lord Privy Seal, 1935–7; Lord President of the Council, 1937–8, 1940; Secretary of State for Foreign Affairs, 1938–40; British Ambassador, Washington, 1941–6.

Sigismund David Waley (1887–1962), K.C.M.G. 1943; as Sigismund Schloss (until 1914) entered Treasury, 1910; Assistant Secretary, 1924; Principal Assistant Secretary, 1931; Third Secretary, 1946–7; European Recovery Department, Foreign Office, 1948.

Frank Trelawney Arthur Ashton-Gwatkin (b. 1889); Second Secretary, Foreign Office, 1921; First Secretary, 1924; Acting Counsellor, British Embassy, Moscow, 1929; First Secretary, Foreign Office, 1930, Counsellor, 1934; Policy Adviser, Ministry of Economic Warfare, 1939; Assistant Under-Secretary, Foreign Office, 1940; Senior Inspector of Diplomatic Missions (with rank of Minister), 1944.

Ashton-Gwatkin passed the memorandum to Sir Horace Wilson (1882–1972), K.C.B. 1924; entered Civil Service, 1900; Principal Assistant Secretary, Ministry, of Labour, 1919–21, Permanent Secretary, 1921–30; Chief Industrial Adviser to Government, 1930–9; seconded to Treasury for service with the Prime Minister, 1935; Permanent Secretary of Treasury and Head of the Civil Service, 1939–42.

[15] Some time after drafting the memorandum, Keynes made some pencil alterations to passages on page 27. These changes are reproduced in footnotes.

I

There is great confusion of mind everywhere about this war. The muddled and tortuous diplomacy which introduced it, the superficial but deeply misleading resemblance to the last war, and the tendency to think of peace aims in terms of avoiding last time's mistakes prevents much of what is being said and written to-day by sensible and well-intentioned persons from striking deeply. What our hearts know is but slowly penetrating our brains. It is still too soon for most Englishmen to know in clear cut shape what they think and feel. Perhaps it is easier for Americans to see the case objectively. The deepest reflections on the war which I have read anywhere have been written by two American journalists, Walter Lippmann and Dorothy Thompson[16]. It is not necessary, therefore, that we should try to explain ourselves to you. You can explain us much better than we can. I will, therefore, make one comment only, and I will make that for the sake of its corollary.

Of all the wars which have ever been waged there never was one more purely a war of religion. Our most genuine object, our deepest wish is not to conquer Germany, but to convert her. We seek nothing but her return into the bosom of western civilisation. We should do almost anything for her if we were convinced of her change of heart. Her lapse is partly our fault. For twenty years we have behaved like asses. But today our consciences are clear and our motives honourable. There never was a plainer case of war with genuine, universal reluctance, without the slightest hope of getting anything out of it. This war is, as has been well said, nearer in spirit to the American Civil War than to the imperialist wars of the past.

[16] Walter Lippmann (1889–1974); journalist and author; specialist writer for the *New York Herald Tribune*, 1931–62, for the *Washington Post* and other newspapers, 1963–74.
  Dorothy Thompson (1894–1961); newspaper columnist, *New York Herald Tribune*, 1936–41, Bell Syndicate, 1941–58.

What is the religion which is in danger and for which there is a duty to fight? I accept Dorothy Thompson's definition: 'It is the synthesis of three things: the Christian ethic; the scientific spirit; and the rule of law.' And this is my corollary. America shares this religion with us. It would be intolerable for America and a cause of unappeasable shame if this cause were to be overwhelmed. For this reason my third assumption above is sure to turn out a big understatement. Perhaps nearly half America sees the issue at least as clearly as we do. But half the other half is deceived by the superficial resemblance to the last war and walk like blind men. Thus the national intention is unclear and it is difficult for the Administration to move fast enough. So it may be useful to be ahead, rather than behindhand, with a suggestion. Whatever anyone may intend and with whatever firmness they may intend it, the only way of keeping America out of the war is to make sure that France and Great Britain do not get into difficulties. The whole issue is whether public opinion will allow the Administration to apply half measures of assistance at the right date when, both psychologically and materially, they will make all the difference.

II

Except in case of circumstances which cannot be foreseen and do not now seem likely, the first assumption—that America will not join in the war—is not questioned in what follows. But in these days there are several kinds of neutrality, just as there are several degrees of being at war. 'Neutrality' (modern style) is inconsistent with joining in hostilities, but it is not inconsistent with taking sides. If my fundamental assumptions are right, it is fair to ask America deliberately and in set terms to take sides. My proposals may be far-reaching but they are simple.

(1) The United States should break off diplomatic relations with Germany and declare a state of non-intercourse. This

step should not be taken immediately, but Germany should be informed now that it will be taken if Germany breaks any of the undertakings she has given for the humanisation of war, in particular her recent promise to the President about the bombing of civilians from the air, and her undertaking about the use of poison gas. Non-intercourse would include the prohibition of imports of German origin. This threat is a real one because there is at present no blockade or other interference with the export of German goods to America in neutral ships. It would be still better if the United States could form a bloc for this purpose of all American countries. The main importance of this measure would be of course, psychological. Done at the right moment, its effect in this kind might be crushing.

(2) Unless the war is a short one, financial assistance from the United States is sooner or later indispensable. Never before has this been considered inconsistent with neutrality. Our default on last time's war debts is presumably the real reason why the present law prohibits credits. The other ostensible grounds are not convincing. Nevertheless it cannot be reasonably defended except by those who reject the fundamental assumptions set forth above. The moral to be drawn from last time's experience (and as one who was particularly intimate with the details of that occasion this, and no other, is the moral which with untroubled conscience I draw) is that the arrangements for the credits should be quite different, and should take the following form.

(a) All credit transactions should be from the outset between governments alone (private credit transactions remaining prohibited) and, so far as munitions are concerned, should be expended by a joint purchasing board for the proper regulation of prices and profits.

(b) The credits should carry no interest.

(c) They should be repayable by annual instalments over a short period of years, but they should not be repayable to the United States. They should constitute a part of the contribution of the United States to the post-war reconstruction of Europe. The instalments of repayment should be allocated, that is to say, to the countries which have to be reconstituted after the war[17], to Poland, Bohemia and Slovakia, to Germany herself and Austria. (This time it must be clear from the beginning that the indemnity is paid by the victor to the vanquished.)

These instalments should make up a part, but not the whole, of America's contribution to the Reconstruction Fund. On the assumption that the war lasts a year and a half to two years, let us suppose that the United States Government advances $2,000 million to the British and French Governments, repayable in ten annual instalments without interest. On the conclusion of the war the United States Government would allocate to the Reconstruction Fund the benefit of these instalments (which would be collectible, not in cash, but only in the exports of the countries discharging the debt), and in addition a further $2,500 million[18] in gold out of its lunatic and redundant stock to provide the bank reserves in the countries to be reconstructed. The detailed allocation of these funds between the recipients would be settled by the United States herself.

(3) This participation by the United States in the task of reconstruction makes essential, what would be desirable without it, namely some measure of responsibility by the United States for the terms of peace. The nature of this

---

[17] After completing the first draft Keynes changed the words: 'To Poland, Bohemia...annual instalments without interest', in the following manner: 'That is to say, to all the countries which have to be reconstituted after the war. That is to say, they should be paid to the credit of a Reconstruction Board which would be concerned with the financial side of the reparation of damage and the rehabilitation of financial credit in all the allied and associated countries.

(d) These instalments should make up part, but not whole, of America's contribution to the Reconstruction Fund. Let us suppose that the United States Government advances $5,000 million to the British and French Governments, repayable in annual instalments without interest.'

[18] Keynes changed the figure $2,500 million to $5,000 million and the word 'lunatic', in the same line, to 'useless', after completing the original draft.

responsibility and of these terms lies outside the scope of these notes. I find it difficult myself to concentrate at this stage on the political and constitutional issues, on frontiers and disarmament and the future government of Europe, not because these issues are not of the first importance but because there are too many unknowns yet to be disclosed. I am more exercised over a preliminary anxiety. If this war is fought to a finish, nothing is more likely than that it will end in a Communist revolution in Germany. What will happen then to the plans of us liberals and federalists?

The important thing—and this is my last plea to the President—is that, the minute after the Hitler gang seems ripe for disappearance, the President should instantly intervene with a view to the offer of peace terms of unprecedented generosity (in which the Reconstruction Fund would play a prominent part).

This leads up to a word about timing. It is evident that the time for American financial assistance on these lines is not yet. British and French financial resources are still largely intact; there are no present difficulties and the true character of the war itself is not yet disclosed; and public opinion in the United States has not yet had time to settle down after the bitterness of the recent debate. What is important to the conduct of the war is that the British Treasury should have some assurance that they will not have to depend indefinitely on their own resources. I am afraid, however, that there is no possibility of giving them such an assurance at present and they must be asked to budget on faith. When will the time come? Only events can show. But I suggest that the order of events may perhaps turn out roughly as follows. First of all, on the assumption that all goes fairly well: (1) It is useless to discuss peace until the balance of forces has disclosed itself more clearly than at present. (2) It is useless to discuss peace until the prestige of the Hitler régime is suffering eclipse in Germany itself. (3) As soon as these two conditions are satisfactorily settled, generous peace terms should be offered on lines which the President approves and the President should take that opportunity of announcing the alternative to their acceptance, which should include financial assistance on the above lines. Secondly on the assumption that all does not go well. (1) In this case a somewhat rapid change is possible in American public opinion. (2) This movement should be accelerated by a more explicit statement of war aims and peace terms, made after consultation with the President. (3) On the assumption that these aims and terms are acceptable to American opinion, the President should stake his authority on securing powers for non-intercourse and financial assistance.

Our prime purpose must be to prevent the disappearance of the few stable elements in German life which still remain. If they can be rallied and supported, the evil of the post-war years may yet be undone and Western civilisation reprieved. If they are submerged, all the fine plans for the future boundaries and government of Europe will belong, in spite of our resounding victory, to a world which has disappeared.

2.11.39   J.M.K.

However, all of Keynes's early war activities were not as 'private' as those already outlined. Thus Keynes wrote to *The Times* on the first war budget.

To the Editor of The Times, *28 September 1939*

Sir,

That part of the cost of the war which we meet by parting with gold and foreign assets, by borrowing abroad, by using up stocks of materials, and by failing to make good physical deterioration in houses and other capital goods at home, must necessarily fall on posterity. The nation will emerge from the war that much poorer, and the loss can only be made good by future efforts. In the aggregate these items will amount to a very large sum. This part of the cost of war it is clearly right to borrow.

The remaining part of the cost can only be met by increased

current effort and diminished current consumption, and, taking the nation as a whole, must necessarily fall on us here and now. But the Treasury have the choice between bringing the contributions to account against individual taxpayers either forthwith or by instalments.

The following figures show that the level of the rate of interest is overwhelmingly important in deciding between these alternatives. The Chancellor proposes this year to raise £107 million extra by taxation and to borrow £938 million. Next year the heavier taxes, apart from the excess profits tax, will yield £226 million, and substantially more than £1,000 million is likely to be borrowed. The effect of these loans on future Budgets, taking the annual sinking fund at, say, ½ per cent compound, will depend on the rate of interest payable. Thus the future burden of £1,500 million borrowed at 2½ per cent will be the same as the burden of £1,280 million borrowed at 3 per cent and of £1,000 million borrowed at 4 per cent, since in each case the annual service of the loan including sinking fund will be £45 million per annum. That is to say, the gain of borrowing at 3 per cent rather than 4 per cent is greater than the whole of the proceeds of the new rates of taxation in a full year; and the gain of borrowing at 2½ per cent rather than 3 per cent would help the Treasury as much as would doubling all the increases announced yesterday.

I suggest that it will cause less disturbance, injustice, and suffering to find methods of borrowing during the war at an average rate of interest not exceeding 2½ per cent, than will be caused by any other fiscal expedient open to us which is of equal financial efficacy. Indeed to restrict the rate of interest on current savings to 2½ per cent will cause no disturbance, injustice, or suffering worth mention.

The reader should not infer that I consider the new burdens excessive. Quite the contrary. What strikes me about this Budget is the utter futility of the old imposts to solve the problem, even when pushed almost to the limits of endurance. Apart from the excess profits tax, the increased taxation comes to less than 5 per cent of our pre-war income. But our national income should increase in due course, through greater employment, longer hours, and the bringing in of women and others not previously available for employment, by some 10 per cent–20 per cent, at pre-war wages and prices. Thus the purchasing power left in the hands of the public after deducting the new taxation will be considerably more than before.

In these circumstances the idea apparently prevalent in government circles that prices can be kept more or less at pre-war levels is fanciful and highly unrealistic. The sterling exchange has depreciated about 15 per cent; world prices have risen, and so have the costs of shipping goods here; purchasing power is certain to increase, while supplies will be diminishing. In a free community a deliberate price rise on a reasonable scale, which leaves the consumers' choice as much unimpeded as possible, is the right solution. An average increase of 20 per cent at least in wholesale prices, which would mean a much smaller increase in the cost of living, is necessary and desirable; and would greatly facilitate the Treasury's task. This brings us to the excess profits tax, which in the long run is the most interesting and important of the Chancellor's proposals. The rest, however appalling it may seem to individuals, is chicken-feed to the dragons of war.

Yours, etc.,

J. M. KEYNES

This led to a letter from Professor J. R. Hicks[19] suggesting that Keynes was unfair to Sir John Simon[20] in his emphasis on the problems of voluntary

[19] John Richard Hicks (b. 1904), Kt. 1964; Lecturer, London School of Economics, 1926–35, Cambridge, 1935–8; Professor of Political Economy, Manchester, 1938–46; Official Fellow, Nuffield College, Oxford, 1946–52; Drummond Professor of Political Economy, Oxford, 1952–65.

[20] Sir John Simon (1873–1954), 1st Viscount 1940; Liberal M.P. for Walthamstow, 1906–18, for Spen Valley, 1922–3, as Liberal National, 1931–40; Solicitor-General, 1910–13; Attorney-General, 1913–15; Home Secretary, 1915–16; Foreign Secretary, 1931–5; Home Secretary and leader of the House, 1935–7; Chancellor of the Exchequer, 1937–40; Lord Chancellor, 1940–5.

savings and the aftermath, as well as a letter from Mrs F. D. V. Narborough and Mrs F. E. Bennett of St Saviour's Church Council, Southwark asking for an increase in pensions. To these Keynes replied on 3 October.

To the Editor of The Times, *3 October 1939*

Sir,

Professor Hicks is content with the yield of Sir John Simon's taxes, but 'would feel more convinced of my prescription of low interest rates' for borrowing the balance required if it were not for 'the problem of the aftermath'. We must be at cross-purposes. My point is that low interest rates will alleviate the problem of the aftermath, compared with high interest rates, as effectively as a very high burden of immediate taxation. He does not want more taxes, and he clearly cannot mean that high interest rates will help. So I am perplexed.

He is content with the yield of the new taxes because he estimates the yield of the excess profits tax in a full year at £240 million, merely as a result of the increase in the national income and without any help from rising prices. I doubt if the Treasury shares his optimism. And, although I am very hopeful of the yield of the tax, this seems to me to be an extravagant estimate. It assumes that the whole of the increase of non-working-class income falls within its scope without any offsets or deductions whatever.

Your correspondents from St Saviour's Church Council must distinguish between a rise in wholesale prices and a rise in the cost of living. A rise of 20 per cent in the former means in itself a rise of only 6–7 per cent in the latter; not that this disposes of their reasonable plea for the case of old-age pensioners in so far as the cost of living does rise.

I take this opportunity to emphasise the conclusion that if working-class incomes are to rise by 10 to 20 per cent and the taxes they pay by only 5 per cent, either their real consumption must rise appreciably above the pre-war standard or they must save a large proportion of the increase in their incomes, or prices must rise. This is the human and political problem which we are, and are likely to remain, very reluctant to face. It is an aspect which, perhaps, you will allow me to develop on another occasion.

Yours, etc.,

J. M. KEYNES

This letter led to a further exchange of letters with Professor Hicks.

From J. R. HICKS, *4 October 1939*

Dear Keynes,

I feel I must rather apologise to you for butting in to The *Times*, particularly since it is clear I have done it so badly! I now feel it would have been much better to have written to you privately; at least so far as the present matter is concerned. On the other hand, I shall no doubt have benefitted from a little experience in the difficult art of newspaper correspondence; perhaps I may do it better another time.

May I now try to explain my difficulties more fully? They are not by any means 100 per cent divergences from your position, but rather particular difficulties, which I think you might be able to help me out of. I dare say they are partly due to my lack of opportunity for discussing these matters up here; but I expect there are other people in the same position as myself.

I do of course altogether appreciate the force of the dilemma as you put it in your second letter—if incomes are increased and supplies diminished either there must be taxation, or saving, or a rise in prices. What I find disturbing is your apparent acceptance of the third alternative as if it were a solution. I simply cannot see how we can expect that organised labour (in its present frame of mind—there are already demands for wage increases) will possibly be persuaded to content itself with a fall in the standard of living induced in that way. Surely they will say: we know the answer to that—wages must go up with the cost of living. And, although I know there are qualifications, surely you will agree that that must mainly defeat the aim of the price rise. It seems to me that it will defeat it more quickly than in the last war.

Some solution has certainly to be found; my own preference would be to go as far along each of the three channels as may be necessary. I welcomed the Budget, as being a bolder movement along the first than I had expected, and being (I still think) likely to be sufficient for the present —that is to say, until there is opportunity for a further large revision of financial policy (I did not mean for the duration of the war). I do think we can reckon on some very considerable assistance under the head of

33

saving, and I welcome the extension of rationing and so on, as a means of getting more under that head. Surely people are much readier to put up with rationing than with profiteering (it will still be profiteering even with E.P.T.)—and I think they ought to be, in wartime.

I wish I was clear why you choose to lean so heavily on the price alternative, and give the others such a back seat. Surely prices will rise enough to keep industry busy—in any case.

My point about the aftermath was evidently too elusive. It is not the long-run problem which troubles me—there I am of course completely in agreement with you. What I am bothered about is the *immediate* post-war problem, the problem of the post-war boom. The more saving and the less private investment there is in wartime, the greater will be the release of effective demand the moment the war is over; there is every reason to expect this to happen long before public expenditure can be contracted very vigorously. This is the stage when (am I right?) even you become a deflationist, for it is at this stage, when people are naturally impatient of controls, that the danger of really runaway inflation is much the most serious.

Although I am quite in agreement with you about the *pros* of keeping interest rates down during the war, I cannot help feeling that that policy has the considerable disadvantage of piling up liquid funds in the hands of the public, which is likely to make the problem of controlling the post-war boom even more intractable. I probably rate this danger higher than you do, but I do not think you will deny its existence. I am not saying that this is a decisive argument against the policy of low interest rates—I do not regard it as such myself. But I do feel (as I said in my letter) that the low interest policy would be more convincing if it were combined with some prescription for this particular trouble which it is likely to induce. I do not doubt that a remedy might be found, probably in the field of special taxation, capital levy or perhaps some more easily workable alternative.

You may say (though I do not think you will) that this is looking too far ahead. I cannot feel that it is, because I feel sure that no remedy will be applicable unless it has been prepared in advance. It is perhaps too early for the technical and administrative preparation, but it is not too early to get our minds up on the subject.

Of course I kicked myself for allowing you to score a point on the yield of E.P.T. I didn't really mean £240 million, I had something of the sort of £200 million in mind; but I now realise that even that is probably a good deal too much. What I did want to emphasise was that it is likely to be a big part of the budget levy.

Yours sincerely,

J. R. HICKS

To J. R. HICKS, *7 October 1939*

My dear Hicks,

It is certainly not the case that it is my idea to depend entirely on a rise in prices to produce equilibrium. On the contrary, I should aim at preventing, if possible, a rise in the cost of living which would make a demand for higher money wages irresistible. But we have depreciated the exchange 15 per cent, and international prices have risen substantially. I am not in favour of putting on the Treasury the huge burden of selling many imported articles below cost price. Moreover, it seems to me quite sufficient, in the circumstances, if we can maintain the real weekly wage. I have calculated that, if, on the average, everyone would work half an hour more a day, this would maintain the real weekly wage in face of the rise in wholesale prices which I advocate.

But, of course, this by itself may be insufficient to produce equilibrium. For it is quite doubtful whether we can hope to maintain the pre-war standard of weekly real wages, if the war continues for a long time. For that reason, I am also in favour of heavy taxation, and also for special measures of an unorthodox kind. As to the latter, I have not quite made up my mind what is least objectionable.

The main point is that I consider an attempt to stabilise the cost of living at the pre-war level, with the result that the real weekly wage will rise quite materially, a hopeless proposition. Yet, up to date, that is what in fact the Government (as distinct from the Treasury) have been trying to achieve.

About the problem of the aftermath, I am still perplexed as to what you mean. The amount of effective demand released after the war would not, I should have thought, be materially affected by the question whether what had been borrowed during the war had been borrowed at a high or a low rate of interest. If you are right in expecting a post-war boom like last time, the long-term rate of interest will be for the time being of only secondary importance. Whether or not, however, you are right in expecting such a boom, I should

35

be inclined to predict that it would only be an event of a few months and that our real post-war problem would be inadequate effective demand. The difficulty will be to find any continuing successor to war expenditure. That indeed is an important part of the reason why I want to end up the war with a low rate of interest. During the war this policy will limit the burden we put on the future tax-payer and, after the war is over, it will facilitate the transition to peace-time capital expenditure.

The problem of how to control a short time immediate post-war boom, due to replenishments of stocks and restoration of damage, appears to me to lie largely outside this problem.

Yours sincerely,
[copy initialled] J. M. K.

On 12 October, Keynes was awarded a medal by the Swedish Academy of Science for his 'valuable contributions to the evolution of economic theories and their application to international problems of the greatest importance.'

In the next fortnight the editor of *The New Statesman* drew Keynes's ire in the form of two letters. The first arose from a letter from Bernard Shaw[21] urging Britain to give up the pretence of war and leave Russia and Germany to come to terms. Keynes had advised the editor, Kingsley Martin,[22] not to publish the letter. When the letter was published with one small deletion, much correspondence followed before Keynes weighed in.

To the Editor of The New Statesman, *14 October 1939*

Sir,

The intelligentsia of the Left were the loudest in demanding that the Nazi aggression should be resisted at all costs.

---

[21] George Bernard Shaw (1856–1950); author, playwright and publicist.
[22] Basil Kingsley Martin (1897–1969); Student and Fellow, Magdalene College, Cambridge, 1918–23; Assistant Lecturer, London School of Economics, 1923–7; on the editorial staff, *Manchester Guardian*, 1927–31; Editor, *The New Statesman and Nation*, 1931–60, Editorial Director, 1960–2.

When it comes to a showdown, scarce four weeks have passed before they remember that they are pacifists and write defeatist letters to your columns, leaving the defence of freedom and of civilisation to Colonel Blimp and the Old School Tie, for whom Three Cheers.

J. M. KEYNES

To the Editor of The New Statesman, *21 October 1939*

Sir,

You ask the Prime Minister to make his peace terms precise. But I notice that you yourself are as chary as he is to do so in practice; perhaps wisely.

To a *jusqu'á-boutist* who is determined to achieve the ideal peace at whatever sacrifice, or to a defeatist who is prepared to accept forthwith Hitler's *fait accompli* in central Europe, there is no insuperable difficulty in being precise. But I infer that you yourself belong to neither of these extremes, but are prepared for a compromise peace on terms that are reasonably satisfactory. If so, I suggest that for the Government to state rigid terms now would be both unrealistic and a possible obstacle to peace hereafter; though this does not preclude useful discussion by less responsible people. For a compromise peace must depend on circumstances which we cannot anticipate, the future concealing too many unknowns.

For myself, I am not yet ready to rule out the ideal peace. It may fall within our grasp in ways we cannot yet foresee. More unlikely things have happened before now. If, on the other hand, events prove that it is beyond our attainment, it is utterly impossible to say now what sort of compromise will be wise and feasible.

J. M. KEYNES

The early stages of the war also saw a parliamentary by-election for Cambridge University owing to the illness, and eventual death, of Sir John Withers, one of the sitting members. Mr A. B. Ramsay, Master of

Magdalene and Chairman of the University Conservative Committee, on the instruction of his members approached Keynes with the offer of the nomination. Given the party truce the Conservative Committee held the nomination, but it was understood that all three parties would sign the nomination papers and that Keynes's position would be that of an independent.

Keynes, although hesitant, obviously found the offer attractive, for he consulted, not only his doctor, Professor J. Plesch, but also Sir William Beveridge, Sir Walter Layton and H. D. Henderson. However, he eventually declined the offer on 23 November. Two letters to Plesch and to Ramsay set out his position well (a view he held to when Ramsay approached him again in December).

To A. B. RAMSAY, *24 November 1939*

My dear Master,

I have seen Dr Plesch and he confirmed to me what he had told you. His forecast of what my health should be in nine months time I accept confidently. But when he thinks that an immediate activity of this kind will do me no harm, I am much more doubtful. I don't think he knows how fully I am using up all the powers I have.

Nevertheless, if it was only a question of health, I should take the risk, after what he said, without hesitation. But in the week since I saw you I have been giving deep reflection to the matter apart from questions of health. I have never had a more difficult decision to make and have been torn both ways to a truly tormenting degree. But gradually a clear and final decision has risen to the surface. The active political life is not my right and true activity. I am indeed an extremely active publicist. And that is just the difficulty. I am on lines along which I can only operate usefully and have my full influence if I am aloof from the day to day life of Westminster. I have become convinced that that would be actually destructive to my present usefulness and embroil me in the kind of controversy where my powers and my habitual line of approach to public matters would be at a disadvantage.

I feel ashamed to write to you to this effect after all you

have done and your extreme kindness and goodness in the matter. I ought not—I now see clearly—to have kept you so long indecisively. But the truth is that I was so convinced until I saw you last week that my doctor would disagree with your proposal that I did not give it the deep and continuous thought which I ought to have given it before and have given it now. Forgive me for all this tergiversation—though, as you will have judged from our conversations, there were strong forces holding me back all the time, and I could not persuade you to take No for an answer.

Yours ever,
[copy initialled] J. M. K.

From a letter to PROFESSOR J. PLESCH, *24 November 1939*

I am writing a letter today to the Master of Magdalene saying 'no'. But, after what you told me, I am not taking this decision on grounds of health. It has been a tormenting decision to make, but gradually a clear and final conclusion has risen to the surface. I am, as you know, a pretty active publicist, but it appears to me rather definitely that I can only operate usefully and have my full influence on my own peculiar lines if I am aloof from the day to day life of Westminster. I am sure that the latter would be actually destructive to my present usefulness. While they are naturally hesitant to urge one to refuse, some conversations I have had this week with friends whom I trust most, show that this is their real instinct. Sorry to have given everyone so much trouble about it.

Chapter 2

HOW TO PAY FOR THE WAR

Although in his letter to Professor Hicks of 7 October[1] Keynes had not yet made up his mind completely as to the best way of obtaining real resources for war, he was moving quickly toward a solution. On 20 October he gave a lecture to the Marshall Society, the undergraduate economics society at Cambridge, entitled 'War Potential and War Finance'. In the days following, he worked it up for publication in *The Times* under the title 'The Limitation of Purchasing Power: High Prices, Taxation and Compulsory Savings'. Keynes sent copies of the draft to Sir John Simon, Mr Attlee,[2] Lord Stamp, R. H. Brand,[3] and H. D. Henderson (who was a member of the Stamp Survey of Economic and Financial Plans) for comment on 24 October, as well as offering it to *The Times*, whose editor agreed to print it after Keynes had completed his initial discussions. He also spoke on the subject to a dinner of officials, Ministers and M.P.s on 27 October.

Initial reactions proved encouraging. As Keynes told Geoffrey Dawson[4] on 4 November:

> The result of my correspondence with eminent persons has been reasonably encouraging. Stamp is enthusiastic and says that it fits in extremely well with the recommendations he will be making himself. The Chancellor of the Exchequer is, of course, as guarded as usual.[5] But I

---

[1] Above, p. 35.

[2] Clement Richard Attlee (1883–1967), 1st Earl 1955; Labour M.P. for Limehouse, 1922–50; Leader of the Opposition, 1935–40; Lord Privy Seal, 1940–2; Secretary of State for Dominion Affairs, 1942–3; Lord President of the Council, 1943–5; Deputy Prime Minister, 1942–5; Prime Minister, 1945–51; Minister of Defence, 1945–6; Leader of the Opposition, 1951–5.

[3] Robert Henry Brand (1878–1963), 1st Baron, 1946; Director, Lazard Bros, merchant bankers; served in South Africa under Lord Milner, 1902–9; Imperial Munitions Board, Canada, 1915–18; Financial Adviser to Lord Cecil at Peace Conference, 1919; member, Macmillan Committee on Finance and Industry, 1930–1; Head of British Food Mission, Washington, 1941–4; Treasury Representative in Washington, 1944–6; Chairman, British Supply Council in North America, April–November 1942, June 1945–March 1946; U.K. delegate, Bretton Woods and Savannah Conferences.

[4] Geoffrey Dawson (1874–1944); as Geoffrey Robinson (until 1917), joined Colonial Office, 1898; Private Secretary to Lord Milner in S. Africa, 1901–5; Editor, *The Times*, 1912–19, 1923–41.

[5] 'I rather think he welcomes kite-flying on my part to see how public opinion takes it.'

have had a long talk with Hopkins about it,[6] who is sending the scheme to Inland Revenue to be considered from their point of view. This scheme does not obviate other useful measures. But the more I think of it, the more convinced I am that something of the kind is an essential ingredient in any sound and workable scheme for war finance.

In revising his paper for publication in *The Times*, Keynes lengthened it to two articles to improve the exposition and balance, modified points of detail and, on the advice of Henry Clay,[7] removed a proposal to guarantee the purchasing power of compulsory savings because it would draw discussion away from his main proposal. In this revised form, the articles appeared on 14 and 15 November.[8]

From The Times, *14 and 15 November, 1939*

PAYING FOR THE WAR

The control of consumption

Nothing is more certain than that the wages bill of this country will increase. More men will be employed, and sometimes, as a result of 'dilution', at a higher grade of work than that to which they are accustomed; they will work longer hours and at overtime rates; and it is to be expected that a demand for labour in excess of the supply will result in sporadic, and perhaps widespread, increases in wage rates themselves by at least some figure such as 5 or 10 per cent. Already in October coalminers, textile workers, agricultural labourers, and (in prospect) railway workers were given a rise. An increase in the purchasing power of wage earners by at least £500 million a year is to be expected; and by the time

---

[6] On 1 November. The meeting, over lunch at Gordon Square, had been arranged before Keynes sent his scheme to the Treasury. However, the Chancellor expected Hopkins and Keynes to discuss the scheme (Simon to Keynes, 29 October 1939).

[7] Sir Henry Clay (1883–1954); Ministry of Labour, 1917–19; Stanley Jevons Professor of Political Economy, Manchester, 1922–7; Professor of Social Economics, 1927–30; Economic Adviser to bank of England, 1930–44; member, Royal Commission on Unemployment Insurance, 1931; member, Stamp Survey of Financial and Economic Plans, 1939–41; Warden, Nuffield College, Oxford, 1944–9.

[8] The *Frankfurter Zeitung* carried them on 7 November on the basis of proofs from a neutral correspondent.

we have reached our maximum effort a much larger increase than this would be inevitable. Failing special measures to the contrary, a substantial proportion of this sum will be spent in the shops and elsewhere.

It is the declared policy of the Government to keep the prices of consumption goods as near as they can to the pre-war level. If they succeed, it follows that the purchasing power of the working classes will command in the aggregate substantially more goods than before, even if a general rise of wages is avoided. And if a further rise of wages is allowed, to compensate for any higher cost of living resulting from this expansion of demand, the situation will be correspondingly aggravated. For all that the outside observer can observe, the problem thus created—the central problem of the home economic front, a problem which requires for its solution the coordination of price policy, budget policy, and wages policy —has not yet been faced.

It is arguable that the present rate of Government expenditure of (say) £2,500 million a year is compatible with the maintenance of something not much worse than the pre-war standard of working-class consumption. At least it will be so arguable when we are no longer reducing our productive capacity by an extravagant A.R.P. policy out of proportion to the protection gained. But no one can suppose that we can afford an appreciable improvement over the pre-war standard. And any further increase towards our maximum war effort must be at the expense of pre-war standards of consumption.

Thus the working classes will have a substantially larger money income than before, but they must not, at the best, consume any more than they did. For the wise and just solution of this problem the leaders of the working class must be taken into earnest and sincere consultation. An economist may be able to help by indicating the alternatives which are open to us. But the choice between them must depend on political and human considerations about which every one is entitled to his opinion.

There are three genuine ways of reaching equilibrium, and two pseudo-remedies. The first pseudo-remedy is by rationing. If there is so great a relative lack of an essential article of consumption that a reasonable rise in price cannot restore equilibrium between supply and demand, we must have recourse to rationing. But against a general increase of purchasing power rationing is useless. It merely serves to divert demand from the rationed to the unrationed article. Rationing is always a bad method of control because it has to go on the assumption that everyone normally spends the same amount on a given article; and, even apart from the intolerable bureaucratic burden which is involved, this characteristic puts out of court a system of universal rationing applied to all articles. The second pseudo-remedy is an anti-profiteering measure, which exalts into undue prominence the least significant cause of rising prices. Therefore those whose first thoughts run to rationing and anti-profiteering have not begun to discern the real nature of the problem—namely, that the aggregate of purchasing power is increasing faster than the available supply of goods.

Let us turn to the three genuine remedies. All of them will have to be applied in some measure, but the degree to which we depend on each it is more difficult to decide. The first is to allow prices to rise. Some rise in prices is inevitable. Indeed, in spite of all efforts to the contrary, the cost of living has risen by 6½ per cent in the first month of the war. But some rise is also desirable. For otherwise, as a result of the depreciation of the exchange, the increased cost of transport and insurance, and the rise of prices abroad, the goods would have to be sold at a loss, quite apart from higher costs at home. There is an important distinction between a higher price corresponding to the higher world prices and a still higher price which is out of relation to the rest of the world. It is unlikely that we can avoid some further rise up to (say) 20 per cent above pre-war, due to both causes. But if we were to depend on this remedy alone, the rise in prices sufficient to restore equilibrium would be beyond all reason and endurance. The yield of the excess profits tax would gain, but most of the other consequences would be bad. We cannot avoid the 'vicious spiral' of rising prices and wages merely by attending to the cost of living; for the first step of the spiral's ascent can begin just as well at the wages end, and this, perhaps, is what happens more often. But an excessive rise of prices will assuredly set such a process in motion. Apart from this, there are grave disadvantages in this method, except in strict moderation. A rising cost of living puts an equal proportionate burden on every one, irrespective of his level of income, from the old-age pensioner upwards, and is a cause, therefore, of great social injustice. Moreover it is largely futile unless we recast our wages system. The rise in prices helps only to the extent that it is greater than the rise in wages. But there are today many wage rates linked by agreement with the cost of living, so that the two move together.

The second genuine remedy is taxation. But to help solve our present problem it must involve taxation of the working classes. Three-fifths of the net expenditure on consumption (after deducting normal saving and taxation) is by those whose incomes are less than £250 a year, and it is this class whose incomes are likely to rise by upwards of 15 per cent.

Not much more can be expected from the existing indirect taxes. A general turnover tax seems to be the only unexplored source of substantial revenue from working-class incomes. A turnover tax on non-essentials deserves closer examination than it has yet received. But not too much must be hoped from it. It would be a heavy administrative task to introduce it for the first time in a war when the bureaucratic machine already creaks and groans. Like a rise in prices, a general turnover tax falls with equal proportionate weight on all levels of income, and must, if it is to yield enough, fall with intolerable severity on the lower levels. So far as revenue from staple goods is concerned, the best and easiest plan is for the Government to resell at prices which yield a profit some at least of those articles of which it is monopolising the distribution. Whether this be regarded as remedy by price-raising or remedy by taxation, the benefit will accrue to the Treasury with the least possible addition to the existing machinery and without leakage.

The price remedy and the taxation remedy are alike in depriving the working class of any benefit from their increased earnings. Yet a large portion of the earnings now in question represents increased effort on their part. The third remedy is free from this objection.

It is conventional nowadays to talk about the justice and wisdom of paying for a war almost entirely out of current taxation without borrowing. We all know that such a thing is impossible; but many people seem to think that it would be just and wise to do it if we could. The argument is that the major part of the expenditure has to be met out of increased current effort and diminished current consumption, so that for the community as a whole it makes no real difference how it is financed, while the method of taxation avoids future complications. But a little reflection will show that the reason why it is impossible entirely to refrain from borrowing is also a reason why it would not be just and wise to do so. It makes all the difference in the world to each individual personally whether the excess of his income over his consumption is taken from him by tax or by loan. To him personally Government stock is an addition to his wealth, to his security, and to his comfort in facing the future. It gives him a claim over the future resources of the community. Someone will have to meet this claim. But this someone is not necessarily himself, and, even if it were, it may suit him better and involve less

45

sacrifice to part by instalments with his personal resources and to possess meanwhile a title to wealth which he can realise in case of need. Moreover, even in war we cannot afford to dispense altogether with the economic incentive to effort— which a too exclusive financing by taxation would involve. We have already got dangerously near to this in the case of the entrepreneurs and we must not make the same mistake with the working classes. There is a fatal family resemblance between bureaucracies in Moscow, Berlin and Whitehall; and we must be careful.

The community at war cannot allow the individuals of the working class to make a greater immediate demand on the national resources than hitherto; and it may have to ask of them a reduction. But that is no reason why they should not be rewarded by a claim on future resources. For the individual that is what wealth is. If it is physically impossible to reward the labour of the working class by immediate consumption, we should welcome and not reject the opportunity thus given to make its members individually wealthier.

The third remedy, therefore, is to distinguish two kinds of money-rewards for present effort—money which can be used, if desired, to provide immediate consumption, and money the use of which must be deferred until the emergency is over and we again enjoy a surplus of productive resources—that is to say, current cash on the one hand and on the other a blocked deposit in the Post Office Savings Bank. This is the general idea behind the third remedy. Part payment by the second kind of money is, during the emergency, the only way by which the real earnings of the working class can be increased. Can their leaders be made to see clearly this elementary fact? To the details of a proposal on these lines I will proceed in a second article.

Compulsory savings

At the end of our first article we were left with the conclusion that the working class, taken as a whole, can only enjoy an increase in real earnings if they are prepared to accept deferred payment. Each individual may dislike postponing his own consumption, but he will gain from a similar postponement by his fellows. If every one spends, prices will rise until no one is better off. The increased earnings of the working class will not have benefited them one penny, but will have escaped through higher prices and higher profits, partly into taxation and partly into the savings of the entrepreneur class. Here, therefore is the perfect case for compulsion; for general compulsion will benefit all its victims alike. A chance is given us to use the opportunity of war finance—an opportunity always missed hitherto—to increase the individual resources of the working class and not merely of the entrepreneur class.

The following are the details of my proposal:–

1. A percentage of all incomes in excess of a stipulated minimum income will be paid over to the Government, partly as compulsory savings and partly as direct taxes. The percentage taken will rise steeply as the level of income increases.

2. The following table illustrates the kind of scale which might be proposed, though it would have to be more complicated so as to avoid sudden jumps:–

The stipulated income, which would be free of the levy, might be 35s a week for an unmarried man, 45s for a married man, with an addition of 7s 6d a week for each child. Thus an unmarried man with 40s a week would contribute 1s a week, while a married man with two children would pay nothing until his income was above 60s a week. There might also be a provision similar to that in the most recent Finance Act to provide mitigation or exemption where a man's income had fallen substantially below its pre-war level.

47

Annual income (£) not exceeding	Per cent of the excess over a stipulated income
150	20
150– 250	25
250– 500	30
500– 1,000	35
1,000– 2,000	40
2,000– 5,000	50
5,000–10,000	60
10,000–20,000	70
above 20,000	80

3. A part of this amount will be credited to the individual as a deposit in the Post Office Savings Bank. The balance will be used to discharge his income tax and surtax, if any. The percentage of the levy credited as a savings deposit will fall, and the percentage taken as taxes will obviously rise, as the level of income increases. For example, if we take the level of income tax and surtax which will be in force in 1940–41 for a married man with two children, whose income is earned, with £300 a year or less, the whole of what he pays will be credited to him in the Post Office Savings Bank and will remain his property. At £500 the total levy will be £105, of which £77 10s will be credited to him and £27 10s retained to pay his income tax. Thereafter the percentage of the levy which is credited to him falls steadily, until at an income level just over £20,000, out of a levy of £16,000 only £3,000 (in round figures) is credited to him and £13,000 is taken in taxes.

The following are further illustrations. An unmarried man with 50s a week will have to save 3s a week; a married man with two children and £5 a week must save 10s and pays no income tax, and with £1,000 a year he must save £107 10s a year and pays £180 income tax. These do not seem to be extravagant demands in time of war and may be not al-

48

together to his disadvantage. If his life is insured or if he owes instalments to a building society the above demands will be reduced correspondingly, as is explained below.

4. The sums credited in the Savings Bank, which will carry 2½ per cent interest, will be blocked for the time being, and will not be available, generally speaking, for current expenditure or as security against loans. But the holder will be allowed to use them to meet pre-war commitments of a capital nature, such as instalments to a building society, or for hire-purchase, or to meet insurance premiums. He can also use them, with the approval of a local committee, to meet exceptional and unavoidable expenses, arising, for example, out of illness or unemployment. They would be available to meet death duties.

5. The deposits will be unblocked and made freely available to the holder, probably by a series of instalments, at some date after the war. The appropriate date for release would have arrived when the resources of the community were no longer fully engaged. Such releases would help us through the first post-war slump, and would give us time to concert more permanent plans. There would be perfect efficiency in this. The people could enjoy the consumption to which their war efforts had entitled them at a time when this would cost the community nothing, since the resources required would otherwise be running to waste.

6. The machinery for collection would be the same as for National Insurance in the case of wage earners, with employers stamping Post Office Savings books at a rate appropriate to the week's earnings, subject to quarterly adjustment by the Post Office should the earnings have fluctuated; and the same as for income tax in the case of others, the total lump sum due under the above scale for both purposes being deducted at source at the standard rate of income tax (i.e. 7s 6d in the £), subject to subsequent adjustment by the

Revenue in the individual case exactly as at present for the purposes of allowances and surtax. Thus no new machinery would be required.

7. I am not able to estimate accurately the amount of the compulsory savings which would result. The figures given above, which are only for illustration, might bring in a yield of at least £400 million over and above income tax and surtax, a yield which may seem less than one would have supposed at first sight. This is because so large a part of working-class incomes is exempt even under this proposal. A stiffer scale would bring in a correspondingly large return. But it is not suggested that the problem of purchasing power can be solved by this means alone. It is a proposal supplementary to the other remedies—more efficacious than any conceivable increase in taxation, and nearly as good as a 10 per cent fall in real wages, while doing no lasting injury to working-class consumption. Above all, it is a new fiscal resource capable of further extension if our exigencies increase.

8. This scheme would not obviate a programme of normal borrowing out of voluntary savings additional to the above. For resources will accrue in the hands of banks, insurance offices, and the like; and Government loans can be subscribed out of company reserves, out of unexpended depreciation moneys, out of sinking funds and sundry repayments, and out of capital released by the sale of foreign investments, and the reduction of stocks, none of which will be subject to the levy. To some extent the levy will obviously come out of income which would be saved in any case. No more can be claimed for it than that it would appreciably ease the Treasury's task.

9. It might be thought fair that those serving with the Forces should be credited with additional pay by the same method. We cannot afford to pay them more now, but we can afford them the reward of deferred consumption.

I see much social justice and social efficiency in this system.

At present our resources of production fall short of our needs; the time will come when the position will be reversed; and it is therefore only sensible to reward current effort out of future surplus capacity. Meanwhile we retain a reasonable incentive to present effort, and the commitments of the community among its own members are spread a little more equally.

In judging this scheme critics must compare it with the alternatives. The income group between £3 and £10 a week is scarcely touched by direct taxation and cannot be relied on to restrict its consumption when its incomes are increasing. Some method must therefore be found for restricting the use of purchasing power on present consumption, which covers this group. Are there any alternatives except those which we have considered? The method of compulsory saving is incomparably better for the class with incomes below £500 than to deprive them of their reward by high prices or taxing, while for the higher incomes the practicable limit of direct taxation is already reached. Moreover there will be great social advantages in spreading the inevitable increase in the National Debt widely among every class in the community.

All methods of war finance are open to objections. But this new one offers some positive advantages on the other side which will not go unnoticed, I hope, by the leaders of the Labour Party. If the Chancellor of the Exchequer does not deliberately choose a positive method he will inevitably slip into inflation merely by hesitating.

The day after his second article in *The Times* Keynes sent Sir Richard Hopkins and Lord Stamp 'the statistical background out of which the particular magnitude of my proposals emerges' (Letter to Hopkins, 16 November 1939). The document was the first draft of an article for the December *Economic Journal*.

From The Economic Journal, *December 1939*

THE INCOME AND FISCAL POTENTIAL OF
GREAT BRITAIN

The capacity of the country to meet the Government's increased demands depends on three factors—the *liquidation* of existing assets, the *expansion* of output and the *diversion* of output. The expansion of output depends on the greater intensity of work by the existing labour force and on the increase of the labour force from the ranks of the unemployed and from those not previously on the labour market; whilst the diversion of output has to be considered under the heads of the previous capital output which is not essential and of the possible reduction of consumption.

The statistics on which to base an estimate of the income potential of the country and of the proportion of it which can be made available to the Government are very inadequate. But it may be helpful to attempt a rough approximation, at any rate, of the order of magnitude of the quantities involved. A better guess should become possible as time goes on and further evidence accumulates. The following figures are mainly based on the work of Mr Colin Clark[9], brought up to date where necessary by Mr E. Rothbarth[10], who gives his sources in detail in appendix II to this article. The national income of the financial year, 1 April 1938 to 31 March 1939 is expressed in terms of the prices of that year, and no allowance has been made for the effect of any later change of prices in the forecast for the subsequent period.

[9] Colin Clark (b. 1905); economist; Staff of Economic Advisory Council, 1930–31; University Lecturer in Statistics, Cambridge, 1931–7; Under-Secretary of State for Labour and Industry, Director of Bureau of Industry and Financial Adviser to the Treasury, Queensland, 1938–52; Director of Institute for Research in Agricultural Economics, Oxford, 1953–69.

[10] Erwin Rothbarth, Keynes's statistical assistant in these early exercises in social accounting, was born in Frankfurt in 1913. He came to England in 1933 and became an undergraduate at the London School of Economics. After graduating with first class honours in 1936, and a period of research in London, he came to Cambridge in 1938 as Assistant in Statistical Research. When he was allowed to in 1944, he joined the army and was killed in action in Holland in December 1944.

In the year ending 31 March 1939, the gross income of the country, including income received from abroad, can be put at £5,700 million. Of this aggregate, £420 million was devoted to making good wastage and depreciation of existing assets so as to maintain our previous capital intact, £250 million to increasing our capital equipment in the shape of buildings, transport and equipment, and £1,300 million to government expenditure, central and local, including 'transfer' incomes such as pensions, unemployment relief, and the interest on the national debt, including £50 million (net) which was borrowed from the public. One might call this £5,700 million the gross taxable income of the country. It is the sum of what individuals and incorporated bodies think of as their income. For various reasons, in particular the inclusion of wastage and depreciation and of 'transfer' incomes, it is considerably larger than the net income of additional values created by the effort of the year. But it is the most useful concept for our present purpose.

In order to arrive at the amount left over, after meeting their direct taxes and putting aside their net savings, which the public spent on the current expenses of life—in the shops, for travel and amusement, to pay their rent and rates and so forth—we have to include not only the cost of making good wastage and depreciation of existing capital assets, but also indirect taxes and rates, since these items have to be covered by the retail prices charged to consumers. Consumption expenditure thus calculated might be put very roughly at £4,350 million. A considerably larger proportion of this figure than of the gross income of £5,700 million was at the disposal of the wage-earning and salaried classes with incomes of less than £250 a year. If we put the savings of this income-group at £60 million a year, their consumption expenditure may have been about £2,800 million, or nearly two-thirds of the whole.

What are the sources from which the outlay on the war,

over and above the previous government expenditure, can be met?—

(1) A contribution of £250 million p.a. might be found from abroad by selling gold and foreign investments. Indeed, if we put our more liquid foreign assets at not less than (say) £1,000 million, an annual contribution considerably larger than the above could be found over a period of two years without an excessive depletion of our ultimate reserves. For the next year at least, the only borrowing on which we can rely will probably take the form of increased balances held in London by the Dominion and other banks as a result of the large contracts which have been placed for the purchase of raw materials within the Empire. Let us put this contribution at £100 million. The above is another way of saying that we can finance a deterioration in our balance of trade, due to an increase of imports over exports, by some such figure as £350 million per annum.

(2) Out of the £420 million devoted to maintaining capital assets at home, perhaps £150 million might be diverted to government purposes, after allowing for any new private investment; and, in the first year, at least another £50 million by running down stocks, etc., although so large a contribution could not be maintained over a longer period.

(3) A lengthening of working hours by half an hour a day would give an increase of about 7½ per cent; and much more overtime than this can and will be worked in many cases. Unemployment during our base year amounted to 12·75 per cent; whilst the workers who can be brought in from outside the insured population, including boys, women and retired or unoccupied persons, should considerably exceed in number those within it who must be written off as incapable. On the other hand, there will be increasing withdrawals to the armed forces and other government services, whose output should be measured, presumably, by the cost of their pay, allowances and keep. At a very rough guess an increase

of output worth between £500 million and £1,000 million should be possible without any far-reaching disturbances or reorganisation of our existing ways of life.

(4) Let us begin with the assumption—to be reconsidered later—that aggregate consumption remains the same, in spite of the aggregate of income having been increased by from £500 to £1,000 million.

We can sum up the above by saying that there is sufficient margin to increase the real expenditure of the Government, measured in pre-war prices, by £1,500 million a year without great difficulty; that an increase of £2,000 million may approach or exceed the limit of what can be accomplished by more or less normal methods; and that an increase of £2,500 million or more would require drastic and extraordinary measures. The present increase of government expenditure may be somewhere in the neighbourhood of £1,500 million a year. It should be emphasised that these figures assume no increase in prices or wages. Since this assumption is not likely to be satisfied in practice, the actual increase in government expenditure in terms of money is likely to be materially greater than the above at each stage of expansion.

So far, the result of our calculation may seem satisfactory. Unfortunately it assumes that the most difficult part of the problem has been already solved. For we are supposing that there is no increase in consumption, although the incomes available for such expenditure have been increased by from £500 to £1,000 million per annum, or an increase ranging from (say) 15 to 20 per cent. There is little or no evidence on which to estimate the marginal propensity to consume. But it is safe to say that a considerable proportion of this increase, the greater part of which will accrue to the income-group having £10 a week or less,[11] will be expended, unless special measures are applied to prevent it.

[11] No adequate data exist for any precise estimate, but the proportion accruing to the income group having £5 a week or less might be roughly guessed at 50 per cent of the total increase of the national income.

Let us resume the argument in even rounder figures than before. Out of an increase in government expenditure ranging between £1,500 million and £2,000 million a year, about half can be found out of the realisation and diversion of existing capital resources (foreign assets, borrowing, depreciation and sinking funds, depletion of stocks and the reduction of normal capital development), and about half out of increased output, provided that this increased output is not accompanied by any increase in private consumption. The fiscal problem, therefore, is how to permit an increase of incomes by 15 to 20 per cent without any of this increase being spent on increased real consumption.

Retaining for the moment our assumption of no change in prices, this increase of £750 to £1,000 million in current incomes can only be prevented from resulting in increased consumption if it is handed back to the Treasury in the shape either of taxes or of savings, voluntary or involuntary. It is not easy to estimate the increased yield of the taxes on the basis which the Chancellor of the Exchequer has proposed for 1940–41, since his own estimates do not take account, I think, of an increase on the above scale in the national income. Moreover, they relate to the taxes to be collected in that year rather than to the taxes accruing in respect of the income of that year. I propose, therefore, to reach a rough-and-ready estimate by a simple formula which can be easily adjusted to different specific figures. I assume (1) that the higher level of taxation will yield 4 per cent of the former net national income, (2) that we are successful, one way or another, in keeping consumption at its previous figure, so that the yield of indirect taxes is not increased by reason of increased consumption, and (3) that the yield of direct taxes is increased by 12 per cent of the increased income, though, owing to time-lags, by no means the whole of this sum would be collected within the year. Taking the mean figure of £825 million for the increase of income and £5,000 million for the former net income, this formula yields exactly £300 million for increased taxation in the year 1940–41 compared with the year 1938–9, leaving £525 million still available for increased consumption.

It is not easy to guess how much of this balance would be voluntarily saved. But since by far the greater part of the increased taxes will fall on the higher income groups, it is probable that practically the whole of the net increment of income, which remains after payment of the increased taxes and subtraction of the amount equal to normal saving, will accrue in the hands of those with less than £10 a week. If they were voluntarily to save £125 million out of the £525 million in addition to their quite substantial normal savings for which we have allowed already, perhaps they would have done pretty well. Certainly they will not save the whole of it!

I conclude that we can get nowhere near the solution of the problem by depending on the existing and projected taxes together with voluntary saving. So far the Chancellor of the Exchequer has not given us the slightest hint of his own solution. But he will have, sooner or later, to choose from amongst the following alternatives. Moreover, he will have to remember that no expedient will really help him which does not restrict the consumption of those who have less than £10 a week. We have become so accustomed to think of taxation as a means of redressing the inequality of incomes that we do not easily adjust our minds to a state of affairs where it does not fulfil its purpose unless it restricts the outlay of the main body of consumers.

His first alternative is to increase taxation. In view of the income group the expenditure of which must be reduced, no new taxes deserve serious consideration except a wages tax coupled with a large reduction in income tax allowances or a sales (or turnover) tax. Both these types of tax may deserve a closer examination than they have yet received. A wages tax if it is to be adequate to the situation, would have to be of the order of 2*s* in the £, if it were to be over all, and of 3*s* in the £ if it were to apply to wages in excess of prescribed minima. It is hard to see how a tax of this magnitude could be made either to be or to appear in accord with social justice; whilst a smaller tax would raise acute political difficulties without solving the problem.

A sales tax applied to all retail sales would be acutely regressive, since it would fall with equal proportionate weight on all incomes, from those of old-age pensioners upwards. It would have to be limited, therefore, to non-essentials. It is not easy to estimate the possible yield of so vague a proposal, but I should suppose that a sales tax on non-essentials would have to be of the order of at least 25 per cent to produce an adequate yield, if we were relying on it as our main solution. I do not reject such a tax, the case for which must depend on a comparison between its yield and the difficulty of rapidly creating the necessary bureaucratic machinery. But I should expect that in practice it might, at the best, be a source of (say) £50 to £100 million additional revenue, which would be a good help, but not by itself a solution.

The Chancellor's second alternative is to do nothing and to allow nature's remedy, so to speak, which is a rise of prices sufficient to divert real resources out of the pockets of the main body of consumers into the pockets of the entrepreneurs and thence to the Treasury, partly in the shape of a higher yield from existing taxes, particularly excess profits tax, and partly in contributions to loans out of the increased savings and reserves of the entrepreneurs. But even nature's remedy will not work smoothly if *nothing* is done. For it requires, broadly speaking, that prices should rise more rapidly than wages, to ensure which it might be necessary to enact legal prohibitions against higher wages. The social objections to this expedient are obvious. In particular, like a general sales tax it is highly regressive and falls with unbearable weight on the lowest incomes; and it discriminates heavily against fixed money incomes. Moreover, it actually encourages an increase of expenditure by entrepreneurs, the only class whose incomes would be increased more than in proportion to prices. I do not mean to suggest that no aid should be sought from a rise in prices. I rely on some increase in prices relatively to wages in my final budget given below. But this is a remedy which will not be serviceable except in strict moderation.

His third alternative is a scheme of compulsory saving, especially directed at the income group with £3 to £10 a week. I have made proposals along these lines in three articles contributed to *The Times* (14, 15 and 28 November 1939), the outline of which is reproduced in appendix 1 below. The special merits of a scheme on these lines can be summarised as follows:–

(1) Instead of the reward due to the working-class for their war effort being just taken away from them, it is at worst merely deferred. Their sense of security is increased, and, by being given some slight claim on the future resources of the community, they are put in a position a little nearer to that of other classes. This is the only way by which an increased real reward can be given them. It would, indeed, be a betrayal of their interests if their political leaders do not espouse and advocate this solution.

(2) The remaining income, which is left over and above the compulsory saving, will have an increased purchasing power which I have estimated at 8–10 per cent, so that the lower incomes, which are exempted from the savings levy wholly or in part, will actually have a greater consuming power than if inflation is allowed to develop. I calculate that all family men with incomes not exceeding 90s per week will be enabled to consume more and not less. Thus unlike the other remedies, this levy is progressive and not regressive.

(3) Blocked deposits in the Post Office Savings Bank may, when once devised, prove to be a suitable way of making various kinds of payments not here specified in detail.

(4) The power to release a substantial volume of purchas-

59

ing power on the occasion of the first post-war slump, when our productive resources are again in excess of effective demand, may be a valuable temporary expedient to give us time to think out more permanent remedies.

Let us return to the budget of fiscal resources which ultimately emerges from this examination of our income potential. I would remind the reader that I am dealing with an increase of government expenditure of the order of £1,500 to £2,000 million a year, i.e. a total central government expenditure in the neighbourhood of £2,500 to £3,000 million at pre-war prices. An increase beyond the higher of these figures, which would represent more than half the present national income, would require a far more extensive reorganization of our economic life. To fix our ideas let us take a figure half-way between these limits—namely, a government expenditure of £2,750 million a year at pre-war prices. (The Chancellor of the Exchequer has recently estimated the present rate of expenditure at £2,400 million a year.) As before, I am dealing only in the roundest of round figures.

(1) £1,250 million from the yield of the taxes already projected for 1940–41 from the higher national income here presumed and taking no account of time-lags but not including E.P.T.

(2) £550 million (i) from the sale to foreigners of gold and securities,

(ii) from Treasury bills taken up by overseas banks in London out of their increased sterling resources,

(iii) from lending to the Government the proceeds of sinking funds, depreciation reserves and the depletion of stocks of commodities.

(The magnitude of this figure shows

how gross an exaggeration it is to say that practically the whole of the expenditure has to be financed out of current effort and abstention.)

(3) £300 million from normal current savings largely institutional, especially insurance offices and company reserve funds. (On the one hand, I am allowing no increase to correspond to the higher national income and the increased incentives to economy; but, to compensate this, I do not propose to diminish it in respect of the overlap with the compulsory saving proposed below. It includes an amount corresponding to the £50 million lent to the government out of normal savings in the base year.

£2,100 million, that is to say, from existing and normal resources, which falls £650 million short of what we require

£400 million from compulsory savings

£50 million from new taxes including, perhaps a sales tax on non-essentials

£200 million from E.P.T., and from the higher yield of the existing taxes (assisted, if necessary, by increasing E.P.T. to 80 per cent) and the increased voluntary entrepreneur savings indirectly resulting from allowing prices to rise (say) 5 per cent more than wages and salaries.

£2,750 million

It should be noticed that this programme (apart from the rather indeterminate last item) involves voluntary government loans of no more than £850 million in the course of a year, nearly two-thirds of which would come, not from new savings, but in exchange for existing capital assets. Moreover, in so far as proceeds are realised from the sale of gold by the Exchange Fund, this requires no public issue. I am not relying on any increase whatever in the voluntary savings of individuals, in addition to the proposed compulsory savings, apart from increased reserves set aside by entrepreneurs under the last item above. The moderate size of the amount to be borrowed suggests the following conclusions.

(1) The borrowing problem is child's play if the budget problem as a whole is tackled from the right end—that is to say, by controlling consumption. If inflation comes about, it will be on account of an attempt to increase consumption mainly by those with from £3 to £10 a week. A patriotic appeal may have some effect on this. But how can anyone suppose that it can be prevented by issuing government loans at 3 or 3½ per cent instead of at 2½ per cent?

(2) Those are not less misguided who suppose that the consumption of the general public can be prevented from increasing by a policy of borrowing direct from the public without recourse to the banks. The volume of bank credit works through the rate of interest and is only relevant to those factors which are sensitive to moderate changes in interest rates (which a man's desire for a glass of beer is not). The amount which can be prudently borrowed from the banks depends on quite different considerations—namely, on how much of their resources it suits business firms and the public in the altered circumstances of to-day to hold in the form of cash. Certain capital assets will be realised, profits will be saved and held in reserve against contingencies and subsequent tax liabilities; and it is probable that it will suit those concerned to hold a substantial part of the proceeds in liquid bank-cash rather than in investments. In so far as this is the case, these resources do not cease to be genuine savings (past or current). There are the following important reasons why a larger

amount of 'genuine' savings will be kept liquid with the banks:–

> (i) A larger volume of output with higher prices and wages; (ii) money held against heavier taxes to be paid long subsequently; (iii) money which has not yet reached the ultimate holder who is in a position to invest it permanently; (iv) doubt as to the future loan policy of the Chancellor of the Exchequer; (v) a general desire to be rather more liquid than usual at a time when it is difficult to foresee the future and the demands it may make.

The bank deposits of the country are about £2,250 million, of which £1,300 million is on current account, and the active note circulation about £500 million, making a total of £2,750 million. An increase of 15 per cent in output coupled with increases of (say) 10 per cent in wages and 15 per cent in prices, taken in conjunction with the other special circumstances mentioned above, would justify an increase of the order of 20 to 25 per cent of the above total, which means that £550 to £700 million could probably be financed through the banks and the note issue without forcing the pace or raising Stock Exchange prices to an extent which might provoke a speculative boom. In present condition when new investment is strictly controlled, an exaggerated fall in the rate of interest and in risk premiums as measured by Stock Exchange prices is the only indication we need watch that bank credit expansion is becoming excessive. Commodity prices will depend not on this but on the relation of consumption to available output. These figures are not far short of the amount of voluntary loans required in the first year. Thus the indications are that it would be practicable, and probably advisable, to wait for the best part of a year before issuing a loan intended for the public.

But this must not be misunderstood. Borrowing from the banks on this scale is a once-for-all proceeding. It cannot be repeated in the second year. Having increased output 15 per cent in the first year, we could scarcely expect to increase it by a further 15 per cent in the second year; and having allowed an increase in the first year to correspond to an inevitable increase of costs here and abroad, it should be our object so to control consumption as to avoid repeating this movement in the second year. These considerations combine with the factor of time-lags to enforce the conclusion that it is in the *first* year that the bulk of borrowing through the banking system is in order. In the first year the right technique is to borrow mainly through the banking system, and thereafter mainly from the public. The right timing of the loan programme requires no wizardry. The movement of prices in the gilt-edged market will itself indicate the rate at which the legitimate public desire for liquidity becomes satisfied; though, of course, these prices (and also the desire for liquidity) will be profoundly influenced by expectations as to the nature of the Chancellor's loan policy. The market will conform to the best guess it can make of the rate of interest to be carried by prospective loans of different maturities. If the rates are expected to range round 2½ per cent, the market will oblige; and if the Chancellor prefers to borrow at a higher rate they will raise no objection. Meanwhile they wait nervously for him to give a hint.

Appendix 1

Proposals for compulsory savings

[From *The Times*, 15 November 1939 (see above, pp. 47–8)]

Appendix II

Statistical sources for the national income of the U.K. during the financial year 1 April 1938–31 March 1939

		£ million
Gross national income (as defined by C. Clark)	Source: C. Clark, Pritchard Wood, *A Commercial Barometer*, June 1939 (published by Pritchard Wood and partners)	5,800–5,900
Indirect taxation	Source: C. Clark, *National Income and Outlay*, p. 141, brought up to date from data given in the *Economist Budget Supplement*, April 1939, *Financial Statement*, April 1939	670
Transfer incomes	Source: as above, and also *Ministry of Labour Report*, 1938, *Report of U.A.B.*, 1938, *Annual Report of Ministry of Health*, 1938	500
Gross taxable income (as defined above)	= Gross national income as above plus transfer incomes minus indirect taxation	5,630–5,730
Government expenditure	= Government investment plus government consumption plus transfers. Source: Pritchard Wood, June 1939, for government investment and government consumption transfers as above	1,300
Gross private investment (including depreciation)	Source: C. Clark, Pritchard Wood, June 1939	670
Depreciation	Source: C. Clark, *National Income and Outlay*, pp. 86, 185. Estimate for 1938, based on extrapolation	420
Private consumption	= Gross taxable income minus government expenditure minus private investment plus indirect taxation	4,330–4,430
Wages and salaries below £250 per year	Source: Pritchard Wood, June 1939	2,390
Incomes below £250 of independent workers, employees and unoccupied persons	Source: *National Income and Outlay*, p. 250	240
Transfer incomes of income earners below £250 per year minus direct taxes on incomes below £250	Source: *National Income and Outlay*, p. 252, Clark, *Economic Journal*, 1938, p. 446, *Economist Budget Supplements*, *Ministry of Labour Report*, 1938, *Report of U.A.B.*, 1938, *Annual Report of the Ministry of Health*, 1938	230

Appendix II (*cont.*)

		£ million
Total income of income earners below £250 per year		2,860
Assumed savings of income earners below £250 per year	Source: C. Clark, *Economic Journal*, 1938, p. 447	60
Consumption of income earners below £250 per year	Income savings	2,800
Indirect taxes on the working classes	Source: *National Income and Outlay*, pp. 142–6; *Economist Budget Supplements*. Method of calculation similar to *National Income and Outlay*	330
Share of working classes in 'marginal income', 1934–7	C. Clark, *Economic Journal*, Sept. 1938, p. 440	45%

E. ROTHBARTH

Keynes supplemented this article with a shorter note in March 1940.
From The Economic Journal, *March 1940.*

THE CONCEPT OF NATIONAL INCOME: A SUPPLEMENTARY NOTE[12]

The problem of war potential and of maximum national output requires the use of statistics of national income and similar concepts. A number of books and pamphlets, mostly called *How to Pay for the War,* are in circulation in which various figures and estimates are taken as the basis of the realistic argument. The differences between the figures are often due, not to discrepant statistical estimation, but to different ideas of what it is convenient to mean by 'national income'. It is therefore of more practical importance than usual to distinguish the differences of logic and definition,

[12] Supplementary to my article on 'The Income and Fiscal Potential of Great Britain,' which appeared in the *Economic Journal*, December 1939, p. 626.

66

some of which hark back to old-established controversies, from real discrepancies in statistical estimation.

My own opinion is that there are two concepts of fundamental importance and practical utility in the present context, which I will call *national output* and *taxable income*.

I define *national output* as the sum of the following items (for convenience of illustration I give the actual figures for Great Britain in the year ending March 1939 from appendix 1 of my *How to Pay for the War*):–

£ million

3,290   current factor-cost of private consumption, excluding both indirect taxation and the user and supplementary[13] cost of making good current depreciation;

710   current outlay on buildings, plant, transport and stocks, including both new investment and what is required to make good current capital depreciation;

850   current cost of government operations, excluding 'transfer' payments to pensioners, holders of National Debt, etc., expenditure out of which is already included in the previous items.

4,850

Taxable income, on the other hand, is the aggregate of individual income,—of what each of us thinks of as his individual income—including charities, private institutions, and companies (the income of which is reckoned as belonging to the shareholders whether or not it is distributed to them), but not including the non-tax revenue (trading profits) of the Government. Taxable income is larger than national output, since it includes twice over those parts of the incomes of

------

[13] For the precise definition of these terms cf. my *General Theory of Employment*, (*JMK*, vol. VII), pp. 52–6.

individuals (referred to henceforward as 'transfer' incomes), which are transferred to other individuals and reckoned by both sets of individuals as part of their incomes, such as interest on the National Debt, pensions, unemployment relief, etc., but are not in exchange for current services rendered. On the other hand, it is convenient to exclude from the concept of taxable income such part of national output as accrues to the Government as trading profits from services, not provided out of taxation, but sold for cash. Thus if 'transfer' incomes amount to £500 million and government trading profits to £50 million, it follows that taxable income is £5,300 million—namely national output £4,850 million *plus* transfer incomes £500 million *minus* government trading profits £50 million.

These two concepts are reasonably unambiguous. They require, of course, underlying definitions of what we mean by a man's output and what we mean by his income; and it is assumed that these matters have been settled. They are also useful in many contexts, particularly in connection with the problems, which arise in wartime, of the resources of the country, physical and fiscal. It would avoid much confusion if we could restrict ourselves to these two aggregates—national output (£4,850 million) and taxable income (£5,300 million); also taking account in other contexts, of the concept of *gross income*, defined in my *General Theory of Employment*, [*JMK*, vol. VII] p. 53, with the help of the concept of user cost, upon which the amount of effective demand depends.

Mr Colin Clark, whose views must be much respected because we all owe to him an immeasurable debt within this field, has, however, given prominence to a third concept which he calls *gross national income*. He is concerned here, not with individual incomes in the sense of my *taxable income*, so that 'transfer' incomes do not come into the picture, but with *national output* regarded from another point of view; and he might well have called it *gross national output*. It bears a deceptive family resemblance to my *gross income*, but differs from it significantly in that it does not deduct user cost and adds in indirect taxes.

It differs from *national output* as defined above in two respects. In the first place, my *national output* is measured in terms of current cost of output. This is open to the objection that prices as ordinarily understood—the prices, that is to say, which enter into the usual index numbers—are not equal to cost in this sense, but are market prices, and are therefore greater than current cost by (1) an amount equal to the rates and indirect taxes which producers and retailers have to pay out and then recover from their customers in the market prices they charge, and (2) a further amount equal to user cost and any monopoly element due to imperfect competition. Mr Clark seeks to avoid this difficulty by adding in (1) the amount of rates and indirect taxes and (2) an estimated sum to cover current depreciation, before applying the index number of prices. In certain contexts, particularly in temporal comparisons of real output and income, this may be convenient. But in most contexts I believe that the other course is better and (provided that one is careful about the appropriate index number of price) less misleading. Mr Clark's procedure is open to the objection that his *gross national output* can be changed merely as a result of a change in the character of taxation. If, for example, local rates were to be replaced in this country by a local income tax, Mr Clark's estimate of our gross national output would decline by about £200 million. Or again, if the population were to consume more grain in the form of bread, which is now subsidised, and less in the form of beer and whisky, which are taxed, gross national output would decline. Thus there is a misleading suggestion that taxes, provided they are indirect, are part of our national physical resources. Experience shows, I think, that this is at least as serious a trap as the risk of deflating output in terms of money by an inappropriate index number

of price. Moreover, Mr Clark's procedure is not even successful in giving us the market price of output. His addition
of an amount, somewhat arbitrarily determined, to cover
current depreciation is not capable of precise theoretical
determination and is certainly not, in practice, the correct
amount required to convert factor cost to market price.

Let me add, however, that I am on Mr Clark's side in the
controversy about this matter, which he and Professor
Bowley[14] have long pursued off and on. For Professor Bowley,
unless I have misunderstood him, insists on making precisely
the logical mistake from which Mr Clark is endeavouring to
protect us. That is to say, he refuses to add indirect taxes to
the cost of output, and nevertheless deflates money output
to obtain real output by using an index number of prices
which are market prices and therefore implicitly include
indirect taxes.[15]

But there is a second respect in which Mr Clark's *gross
national income* is misleading, if it is meant to indicate (as some
current writers seem to be supposing) the potential amount
of current consumption. For a time at least some resources
which are being devoted to making good wastage, as well as
some stocks, could be applied to other purposes without a
corresponding reduction in current consumption. Mr Clark's
gross national income (and this, I suppose, is why he calls
it *income* rather than *output*) might be supposed to aim at
measuring this maximum potential flow. For he adds to my
national output the whole of the amount of resources devoted
to making good wastage, thus suggesting that these could be
diverted to increase the value of consumption beyond the
value for which I have taken credit. It follows that his *gross*

14 Arthur Lyon Bowley (1869–1957); economist and statistician; Lecturer, London
School of Economics, 1895–1919; Professor of Statistics in the University of
London, 1919–36.
15 At least this is what *Method II* in Professor Bowley's latest discussion of this subject
('The Measurement of Real Income' read before the Manchester Statistical
Society, 8 November 1939) seems to amount to. If not, then there is no real
difference between the contestants.

national income equals the current factor-cost of consumption and net new investment (exclusive of the current cost of making good wastage) plus indirect taxes and rates plus *twice* the current cost of making good wastage (once because the last item is included in the market price of consumption goods and once because it can be diverted to some other purpose). Thus *gross national income* might be, and often is, taken to give us the potential rate of current consumption and investment measured at market prices.

But this is gravely misleading. It gives us the potential rate, not over an annual or any other substantial period, but only over the instantaneous or very brief period in which *no* replacement of wastage is necessary to maintain the current rate of output. When, therefore, Mr Clark proceeds (as he does) to speak of an *annual* gross national income thus defined, he has fallen into the pit he has himself dug and is clearly in error. For the amount of making good wastage which can be avoided without detriment to the rate of output depends on the length of time in view. In the 'long run' it is zero. Even over a period such as a year which Mr Clark specifies, it will fall far short of the *whole* of the wastage normally made good. Nor can one make any precise estimate of the maximum potential rate of current consumption and new investment over a period such as a year, since it depends on technical considerations and the precise character of the plant in use.

Indeed, I see no practical purpose for which Mr Clark's concept can be useful, except for comparisons of real output by means of the usual index numbers over periods between which the fiscal system and the character of consumption are unchanged. For whilst in the above respect it over-estimates the potential rate of consumption and new investment over an annual period, in another respect it under-estimates this rate. For it neglects the fact that there is another way, besides failing to make good wastage, in which we can for a limited period 'live on capital'—namely, by using up stocks of materials and working capital, which is quite a separate thing from failing to keep instrumental capital in good repair. Indeed, not only is Mr Clark's total unreliable over a long period, but over a short period it is much smaller and also harder to come by than the gain from running down stocks of liquid and working capital.

It is quite true that in considering war potential we must make due allowance for the extent to which over a period we can 'live on capital'. But if Mr Clark's *gross national output* pretends to provide a serviceable clue to this, it is an impostor.

One other consideration we must not omit from the discussion. *All* estimates of national resources must be to some extent misleading (and always in the direction of over-statement) when we contemplate diverting them from one use to another, for the reason that their specific character is likely to lead to a loss on such diversion. This point, which deserves the strongest possible emphasis in relation to current discussions of war potential, is true of my *national output* as well as of Mr Clark's *gross national income*. But his concept is, I think, the more misleading of the two in this respect, when we are contemplating a diversion not merely of resources devoted to making good current wastage, but of consumption itself—as is the case in time of war. For if his concept is taken as a measure of divertible resources—i.e. of resources applicable to a different kind of output—he is assuming that there is no loss, on account of the specific character of resources, in the case of durable capital as well as of labour; whereas if my concept is used for a similar purpose, it involves a more limited assumption of the same kind. He even has to assume that rates and indirect taxes are non-specific and apply to all articles equally. For if we economise on a given item of consumption, he assumes that we release resources equal to its *market value* plus the cost of making good current wastage, whilst I only assume that we release resources equal to its factor-cost of output plus the current outlay on making good current wastage—a difference which steadily increases with the length of the period. Loss on diversion through the specific character of labour has, in any case, to be treated on different lines. For if labour is remunerated in its new employment at the same rate as in its old, the loss through its diversion appears on the other side of the balance sheet in the higher cost of the new output. (That is, if we value output on the assumption that the money wage is constant irrespective of loss of efficiency through diversion; for we cannot assume *both* money wages *and* prices as constant if such loss of efficiency occurs. I did this implicitly in my previous article, when I measured the amount of the potential increase in output by the number of additional man-hours which might be worked; and I take this opportunity to make the point clear.)

For these various reasons Mr Clark's *gross national income* seems to me to lead us into water which is unnecessarily deep. At any rate, I was myself misled by it when in the article published in the *Economic Journal*, December 1939 (p. 627) [above, p. 53], I gave a figure of £5,700 million for taxable income, not then realising that Mr. Clark's *gross national income* included the cost of current depreciation, in effect, twice over.[16]

Reaction to Keynes's proposals was immediate and substantial, both in *The Times* and in the rest of the press. The Beaverbrook press, the *Daily Worker*, the *Daily Herald*, and *Tribune* proved hostile, as did Labour and trade union leaders and the Left. However, economists of all persuasions welcomed them, as witnessed by Professor F. A. von Hayek's[17] exposition

---

[16] The full reconciliation between my *Economic Journal* figure of £5,700 million and the figure of £5,300 million given above is as follows: deduct £380 million for depreciation on private investments included twice in Mr Clark's figure (total current depreciation £420 million less £40 million upkeep of roads by the Government not included twice), £50 million for government trading profits previously included in private profits, and £30 million due to a revised estimate of the government deficit.

[17] Friedrich August von Hayek (b. 1899); Director, Austrian Institute for Economic Research, 1927–31; Lecturer in Economics, University of Vienna, 1929–31; Tooke Professor of Economic Science and Statistics, University of London, 1931–50.

of the scheme in the *Spectator* on 24 November. Keynes himself replied to criticisms and comments, both published and private, in *The Times* of 28 November.

From The Times, *28 November 1939*

MR KEYNES AND HIS CRITICS:
A REPLY AND SOME QUESTIONS

The alternative to inflation

The plan for compulsory savings which I put forward in these columns has received widespread comment and criticism throughout the press, some of it helpful and all of it illuminating. If I could keep my feelings wholly on the academic plane (as I am supposed to) I should be well content. Few have questioned the urgency of the problem. None has suggested an alternative solution. There is no complaint that the whole idea is impracticable, though valuable suggestions have been made to improve the plan in detail. But, as a citizen who is practically concerned with the well-being and good government of this country, I am not so comfortable about the character of the general response.

This is not through any conceit of this particular plan. My discomfort comes from the fact, now made obvious, that the general public are not in favour of any plan. That is the real difficulty. The country is not yet taking our financial problem seriously and is still unaware of the sacrifices which present preparations will require when they mature. In one quarter of the press an extravagant frivolity of thought is evident; but doubtless this responds to a readers' demand and is only a *reductio ad absurdum* of an attitude which genuinely prevails. I find myself resting, not for the first time, under a heavy charge of anticipating—of trying, Cassandra once more, to prevent what has not yet happened. It is pointed out with reason that the public cannot be expected to relish the pros-

74

pect of a heavy, calculable burden to avoid an incalculable evil which has not yet arrived; and with, I hope, less reason that no politician can be asked to take the undemocratic course of being ahead of the popular voice.

Yet we should not be surprised. Partly it is a result of the 'queerness' of this war. We have all of us lost our perspective and do not know what to take seriously. I do not take A.R.P. as seriously as the experts tell me I should. If others do not take seriously the budgeting of our physical resources I cannot justly complain. The nation is pledged to everything and ready to endure whatever may be asked. But we have a feeling all the same that, in some way we cannot now foresee, time and chance and the natural retribution which overtakes evil, softly working in the heart of any society of men, will do half our task for us.

But the time-lag of opinion is also to be explained by the failure in organisation which has resulted in our national output being scarcely greater after three months of war than it was before the war began. The need for compulsory saving depends on the assumption that we are straining our resources to the utmost, so that an increase of consumption is not physically possible. With more men out of work than before, this assumption is not yet fulfilled. The rise of prices hitherto has been due chiefly to special causes, and not to a growth of demand beyond the possibilities of supply. Yet there is no doubt about the scale of Government expenditure; and the tardy organization of output only means that the stringency will be increased later on. We have been able so far to combine heavy expenditure with persisting unemployment because we are living on our stocks and have put obstacles in the way of our exports, though of all our economic activities this is nearly the most essential.

Nevertheless it needs no special insight to see that this situation cannot persist. Some comments on my proposal by

Mr Arthur Greenwood[18] are based on the assumption that it is physically possible for the Government programme to be fulfilled and at the same time for the real consumption of the working class to increase more or less in proportion to the increase in their earnings. He believes that the working class have a choice between consuming more or saving more, and that it is not fair, or in their interests, to deprive them of this choice by a compulsory scheme. But I say that they will have no such choice. Goods available for increased consumption will not exist. If they try (as, left to themselves, they will) to exercise their apparent freedom of choice to consume, they will be defeated, if not by taxes, by an inflationary rise of prices, just as they were in the last war. My proposal to credit them with deposits in the Post Office Savings Bank will mean for the workers as a whole an absolute net addition to their wealth, something which otherwise they will just not receive. Taken together, they will consume under my plan just as much as they would otherwise, and they will have these deposits as well wherewith to increase their future security or their future consumption. Indeed this is to understate the advantage to them. For the average worker with less than (say) £4 a week, the scale I have proposed (as I show below) will actually increase the amount of his real consumption in spite of the compulsory saving; for prices are likely to rise, in the absence of the plan, by a higher percentage of his income than that of the compulsory savings. There can be no doubt that the scheme is overwhelmingly in the interests of the working class. Their leaders could only reject it through misapprehending the nature of the alternative or in submission to short-sighted political appearances.

We all know, of course, that the alternative is inflation. And

[18] Arthur Greenwood (1880–1954); Labour M.P. for Nelson and Colne, 1922–31, Wakefield, 1932–54; Parliamentary Secretary to Ministry of Health, 1924; Minister of Health, 1929–31; Deputy Leader of Labour Party, 1935; member of War Cabinet and Minister without Portfolio, 1940–2; Lord Privy Seal, 1945–7, and Paymaster-General, 1946–7.

we also know that the political argument in favour of inflation is almost overwhelming. No one has to take the responsibility for inflation, not even the Chancellor of the Exchequer. The adoption of my plan would require the approval of the Labour Party. But they will never be asked to approve inflation. It will just happen. It is nature's remedy, ebbing up like the tides, silently and imperceptibly and irresistibly. It engages in its support our *laissez-faire* traditions. (I read in relation to my plan that 'the idea of compulsion is anathema to the City', that most naive of all the anonymous entities figuring in the newspapers, which would doubtless prefer that taxes, too, should be voluntary. The German Government, commenting on it in their wireless, and the Communist Party in their press, point out how hateful to any right-thinking person the idea of compulsion must be!) It greatly benefits some important interests. It oils the wheels everywhere, and a régime of rising wages and profits spreads an illusion of prosperity. So if one is to bet on the field, inflation must always be the favourite.

I apologise for the word 'inflation', which may easily convey the wrong meaning. In the early days of the Ministry of Information Lord Macmillan[19] used his brief moment of censorship to ban the word from the popular press. I applaud his design, success in which would have been enough by itself to justify his Ministry's existence, and would have achieved more than his famous Committee on Finance ever did. As I have not been able to live up to it, I should explain that I do not contemplate anything in the least resembling the post-war experience of Germany and other countries. What I should expect to happen to real wages, if we take no steps to the contrary, is much what happened last time, though developing more rapidly. It will be instructive, therefore, to recall the

---

[19] Hugo Pattison Macmillan (1873–1952); Life Peer, 1930; Lord of Appeal in Ordinary, 1930–9, 1941–7; Minister of Information, 1939–40; Lord of Appeal, 1947–52; Chairman, Committee on Finance and Industry, 1929.

movement of prices and wages in the first three years of the last war.

Between 1914 and 1917 (after 1917 the increased resources through the entry of the United States allowed an improvement in real wages) the cost of living rose from 100 to 180, measured by the *Labour Gazette* index (and from 100 to 160 according to a modified index prepared subsequently, which allowed for changes in the character of consumption), and wages from 100 to 135–140. Thus the average rate of real wages fell by 15 to 20 per cent (by appreciably more than this for skilled workers and by less for unskilled). But this did not mean that actual consumption fell to the same extent. It has been calculated that aggregate earnings were sufficiently increased by the greater volume of employment and by longer hours to maintain aggregate working-class consumption at nearly its previous level. That is to say, the working class did their extra work for nothing. My plan is intended to prevent a repetition of this. This time we might hope that both prices and wages would rise much less than the above, since we have adopted price controls at the outset and are more conscious of the problem. In particular we might succeed in keeping a minimum ration of consumption goods at a level price; and having done with this we should also without delay strictly stabilize the general level of wages. But this cannot affect the necessity for retail prices as a whole to rise relatively to wages by (say) 12 to 15 per cent, if total output and earnings rise in this proportion in excess of the output of consumption goods. I reckon that about two-thirds of this fall in real wages could be avoided by my plan of compulsory savings. (The broad statistical assumptions on which I have based these estimates will be published in the December issue of the *Economic Journal*.) If, when the government programme is fully developed, an actual increase in working-class consumption is not physically possible, prices will have to rise in at least the same proportion as aggregate working-class expenditure, in spite of the extra work done. This would precisely repeat the experience of the last war that the workers would be doing their extra work for nothing. How do the critics of my plan propose to prevent this repetition of what happened before?

Criticisms have been made on the actual scale and allowances which I have suggested. I do not doubt that these can be improved and simplified. In any case my original proposal can be set forth in another way which may be clearer. Taking as our standard case the married man with two children, the percentage of weekly income taken as compulsory savings works out as follows:—Exempt up to £3, 6¼ per cent at £4, 8¼ per cent at £4 10s, 10 per cent at £5, almost stationary at 15–16 per cent from £6 to £15 weekly income; on incomes in excess of £15 weekly the percentage begins to fall owing to the much higher proportion taken in income tax, being 12 per cent on £1,000 a year, 11 per cent on £2,000, and 8 per cent on £5,000. It might, therefore, be simpler and more intelligible to leave the element of progression to the income tax, and to make the savings levy a steady 15 per cent (or 3s in the £) on all incomes exceeding £5 a week up to the surtax limit, with substantial concessions for incomes below £5 a week depending on family status, but with all family allowances for incomes in excess of £5 a week given through the income tax.

Above the surtax limit the savings levy could not be maintained at 15 per cent without raising the percentage including tax to an intolerable level (it would become 97½ per cent altogether on the highest incomes); and it might, therefore, be preferable to deal with the surtax class entirely by tax. An interesting alternative might be to maintain the 15 per cent throughout (with abatements, as before, on incomes below £5 weekly) and to give every individual the option of escaping the savings levy provided that he paid 25 per cent of its amount as an outright tax. The fundamental idea is capable of many modifications. But we have started this war with so high a level of direct taxes that some form of combining the savings levy with the income tax will be indispensable sooner or later.

The above way of exhibiting the amount of the levy makes it easy to compare its results with those of inflation. I should expect that a levy on this scale would have the effect of increasing real wages by 8 to 10 per cent above what they would otherwise be. Thus a family with less than 90s a week would actually gain in consuming power (with the gain to the smaller incomes really substantial), the amount left after setting the savings aside being worth more than the whole income would be worth otherwise. In the standard case of 15 per cent savings levy more than half would be recovered in the consuming power of the remaining income; so that the deferred consuming power would be double the immediate consuming power forgone quite apart from the gain in interest. Moreover, the class with fixed incomes of £5 to £15 a week who (to judge from my correspondence) are most alarmed by my proposal, have in fact most to gain from it compared with the alternative of inflation. For in the vain effort to maintain the purchasing power of wages both prices and wages would rise much more than 15 per cent, as happened in 1914–17, before prices could settle down 8 to 10 per cent above wages. I am justified, therefore, in pleading for the support both of trade unionists and of the fixed-income middle class.

Meanwhile let us all wish the best of success to Sir John Simon's appeal to small savers. If concessions are to be made they are best made to this class; though the advisability may perhaps be questioned of offering terms so highly competitive with those of the Post Office Savings Bank and the deposit accounts of the joint stock banks that they are likely to attract normal savings from these repositories. Nothing but good can result from supplying attractive ammunition to the National

Savings Movement. At this stage it is appropriate to ask for a voluntary reduction of consumption in response to a patriotic appeal. Nevertheless this can scarcely be regarded as occupying the same terrain as the present proposal, since the scale of the utmost which can be hoped from it is surely much below what will be required to avoid inflation and the upward spiral of prices and wages when our maximum war effort has developed.

It is no use to say that we got through the last war on a voluntary basis. No doubt we can get through this war in the same way if we are prepared to allow the same degree of inflation. But we do not thereby avoid compulsion. Compulsory savings or compulsory inflation? It is compulsory either way. Inflation takes away compulsorily the purchasing power of the working and middle classes by diverting it into the pockets of the entrepreneur class, whence it is obtained by the Treasury partly through the excess profits and other taxes and partly through the reserves and voluntary savings of the entrepreneurs. I object to being told that I am the enemy of freedom and of the working and middle classes when I try to avoid this.

Keynes soon began to receive suggestions that his *Times* articles appear as a pamphlet. Keynes discouraged simple republication on the grounds that the three articles, plus the contribution to the *Economic Journal*, when combined would be 'rather a mess'. Therefore, he proposed to rewrite the material, as he told Harold Macmillan[20] on 27 November. Macmillan accepted the idea immediately. At that stage, Keynes did not have a title for the book, and his ensuing correspondence with Macmillan contained many suggestions, including an attempt to make use of the words 'economic consequences', before Keynes settled on *How to Pay for the War: A Radical*

[20] Harold Macmillan (b. 1894); then Chairman of Macmillans, Keynes's publishers; Unionist M.P. for Stockton-on-Tees, 1924–9, 1931–45; Parliamentary Secretary, Ministry of Supply, 1940–2; Parliamentary Under-Secretary of State for Colonies, 1942; Minister-Resident, Allied H.Q., N.W. Africa, 1942–5; Secretary of State for Air, 1945; Minister of Housing, 1951–4; Minister of Defence, 1954–5; Foreign Secretary, 1955; Chancellor of the Exchequer, 1955–7; Prime Minister, 1957–63.

Plan for the Chancellor of the Exchequer at the beginning of February 1940. Publication of the pamphlet came on 27 February.[21]

In the interval between his *Times* articles and publication of his pamphlet, Keynes sounded opinion so as to find means of improving his scheme to make it more palatable, in particular to Labour leaders whose initial reaction he had found 'frivolous and unthinking'. On occasion during this period, however, he used the press, replying to *The Times* city editor's questions on repaying compulsory savings as follows.

To the Editor of The Times, *29 November 1939*

Sir,

Your City Editor has raised two questions which I did not deal with in my recent contribution. The first relates to the ultimate repayment of the compulsory savings. I confess that this seemed to me to be the least of the difficulties. In principle these loans would be in exactly the same position as the rest of the short-dated debt which the war will leave behind it. But in practice it will be the most easily dealt with. Repayment can be made by such instalments as it suits the Treasury to fix when the time comes, and when repayment is offered holders are likely to avail themselves of it gradually. Above all, repayment is not to be offered until the first post-war slump, when the demand for capital will be by hypothesis at a low ebb. Purchasing power released at this juncture will serve to sustain employment and relieve the Treasury of having to make new loans which might be necessary otherwise to pay for unemployment or public works. Looking to the future, I regard the repayment provision as the strongest feature of the scheme, worth having for its own sake, and an additional recommendation.

Secondly, he questions my estimate of the quantitative effect of the proposed levy. Here, I admit, we are all guessing on the basis of inadequate data. For we do not know the dispersion of total income between different income groups. I agree with him that pre-war consumption exceeded £4,000 million. (The estimate which I have given in my forthcoming

[21] Reprinted in *JMK*, vol. IX, pp. 367–439.

article in the December *Economic Journal* is £4,350.) But in his subsequent calculation he has not allowed for the yield of the new taxes already announced for 1940–41, which I was treating as a fixed fact in the situation. I have assumed that, apart from changes in prices and wages, the income of 1940–41 will exceed that of 1938–9 by £875 million, from which I have deducted £350 million for the increased accrual of taxation, leaving a 12 per cent rise in spendable incomes of which a levy of £400 million would take away just over nine points. But another way of looking at the matter, which I used as a cross-check, suggests that this may be a little too low. The calculations I have already given suggest that the levy must average more than 12 per cent of taxable incomes between £150 and £5,000, which, allowing for the prospective rise in the lower incomes, should include about two-thirds of total taxable incomes. This means that the levy will exceed 8 per cent of total gross taxable incomes, and is likely, therefore, to be fully 10 per cent of the net incomes available for consumption. This suggests that £400 million is on the conservative side as an estimate of the yield of the levy. On the balance of considerations, I still adhere to 8–10 per cent as the best guess I can make of the effect of the levy on consumption; but that there is a wide margin of error in all these estimates I am only too conscious. If your City Editor prefers the lower of my two limits, which corresponds more closely to the £400 million yield estimate, I shall not quarrel with him.

Yours, etc.,

J. M. KEYNES

A reply to a Rear-Admiral (Retired) who raised the question of the inequities between service men whose peacetime employers made up their service pay to peacetime levels and those who did not saw Keynes adopt the term 'deferred pay'.

To the Editor of The Times, *5 December 1939*

Sir,

I have much sympathy with the letter you publish to-day from 'Rear-Admiral' calling attention to the inequalities of treatment due to the pay of some, but not nearly all, of those serving with the forces being made up by their former employers to their peace-time earnings. In the passage which he quotes from my second article I meant to suggest that these inequalities might be smoothed out by deferred pay to all alike in the shape of blocked deposits in the Post Office Savings Bank.

Would my main proposal be more intelligible and more popular if, instead of speaking of 'compulsory savings', I call it a plan for 'deferred pay'? For that is what it is. May I with your leave substitute this description?

Yours, etc.,

J. M. KEYNES

His remarks on funding in the *Economic Journal* (above p. 64) led to a leader in the *Financial News* of 30 December, which drew two letters from Keynes.

To the Editor of the Financial News, *30 December 1939*

Sir,

I agree with your leader of today that no one can predict accurately at what point the increased demand for liquidity will be satisfied. But, as I pointed out in the article from which you quote, no wizardry is required. When the demand for liquidity at the existing level of gilt-edged prices is satisfied, the fact will become evident in a rise of gilt-edged prices. Why do you consider that this would be so deplorable? To me gilt-edged prices do not appear as yet to have reached the optimum level for the Treasury. When they have, the time for a funding issue will have arrived.

To discover why you think otherwise requires, I suspect, psycho-, rather than economic, analysis. You have to believe that a funding issue will prevent workers and others from spending their increased incomes. This conviction must be a vermiform appendix of the mind, which has survived from the long past days when you genuinely believed in the quantity theory of money. For the rest of your organism reads healthy; and today, I feel sure, you do not really expect the mere fact of a fall in interest by ¼ or ½ per cent to cause earners to spend what they would otherwise save. With new capital construction and the remittance of funds abroad virtually prohibited, the increase of bank money is wholly irrelevant to the inflation of prices, unless it were carried so far as to produce, even in these times, a violent boom on the Stock Exchange which led speculators into extravagant consumption; and this is a danger of which we should receive warning.

Yours, etc.,

J. M. KEYNES

Keynes's first letter led to a note by the editor. As it stimulated a second letter from Keynes we print the note in full.

With Mr Keynes's general approach we are wholeheartedly in agreement; far from being psychological, our differences are purely statistical. They result, as we pointed out in our leader, 'solely from a divergent estimate of the facts'. Our object was to establish the single proposition that to postpone funding for a year and increase bank credits by some £600 million, far from being safe and advisable, as Mr Keynes suggests, would bring about precisely that 'exaggerated' fall in interest rates which Mr Keynes himself regards as the danger signal. We do not believe that a funding issue would prevent workers from spending their increased incomes; but we do believe (and Mr Keynes would surely agree) that any expansion of credit over and above that required to satisfy the increased demand for liquid assets would aggravate an inflation which will be difficult enough to avoid in any case. Just because 'no one can predict accurately at what point the increased demand for liquidity will be satisfied' (nor, therefore, what is a safe rate of interest), we would sooner err, if at all, by funding too early rather than too late.—Ed., F.N.

To the Editor of the Financial News, *3 January 1940*

Sir,

Thank you for your comments on my letter, which seem to confirm my diagnosis. For it appears that the affected part of your mind desires an immediate funding issue in order to prevent any further improvement in the gilt-edged market, which it dreads (heaven knows why!) as being unsafe; whereas there is a passage in your original article which indicates that the healthy part of your organism is ready to welcome that very thing.

If you are not too old, as to which I have no information, I strongly recommend an operation. By modern methods an inflamed quantity theory can be removed with much less danger than formerly!

Yours, etc.,

J. M. KEYNES

He also took part in a 'discussion' with Douglas Jay[22] in the *Manchester Daily Herald*, taking great care to simplify his analysis. However, as Kingsley Martin reported to Keynes on 19 December:

> when it was in type...Lord Southwood[23] protested violently that he could not understand any of it himself and that it must be rewritten in words of one syllable. Strong opposition by his staff finally overcame this objection. It was suggested that it would not be worthwhile offending you by again changing your article. You were financially important, etc. Funny world!'

[22] Douglas Patrick Thomas Jay (b. 1907); Labour M.P. for Battersea North, 1946–74, for Wandsworth, Battersea North since 1974; on the staff of *The Times*, 1929–33, and *The Economist*, 1933–7; City Editor, *Daily Herald*, 1937–41; Assistant Secretary, Ministry of Supply, 1941–3; Principal Assistant Secretary, Board of Trade, 1943–5; Personal Assistant to the Prime Minister, 1945–6; Economic Secretary, 1947–50; Financial Secretary to the Treasury, 1950–1; President, Board of Trade, 1964–7.

[23] Julius Salter Elias Southwood (d. 1946), 1st Baron 1937, Viscount 1946; newspaper publisher and proprietor.

HOW TO PAY FOR THE WAR

From the Manchester Daily Herald, *7 December 1939*

HOW SHOULD WE RAISE THE MONEY?

Mr J. M. Keynes wants to pay for the war by deducting a portion of practically everybody's income as a forced loan during the war years, which would be repaid by the Government when the war was over.

A forced loan would be paid by everybody with incomes over a certain exemption limit. This limit would be something like 35s a week for a single person, and 45s for a married man, with extra allowances for children.

Mr Keynes believes that this is the only way to stop inflation. He argues that if the mass of the people are not forced to reduce their spending by a forced loan, prices during the war will rise rapidly, and although wages will follow they will never catch up.

The majority of the population will thus, he believes, suffer a permanent loss of real income. Under his plan they would be forced to reduce their spending now, but would get their money back after the war.

Since Mr Keynes specially wants the Labour movement to consider his plan, we have invited him to answer certain questions asked by Douglas Jay, our City Editor. Here is what they both have to say.

KEYNES: The fate of my proposals mainly depends on how Labour receives them.

I believe that they are greatly in the interests of the working classes and offer the only way by which the worker will obtain a real reward for his war effort.

But they are novel, complicated and difficult; capable of many variations and amendments and improvements; touching human and social and political, quite as much as economic, problems. Full public discussion both on principle and on details is very advisable before we come to a conclusion.

JAY: *By what argument or calculation exactly do you maintain that forced saving—even by people with incomes below £5 a week—is necessary to pay for the war?*

KEYNES: This calculation is based on the Chancellor's statement that the Government will have to absorb nearly half the total national income and on an estimate of our potential output.

Most authorities consider that I have not gone far enough, and that, so far from aggregate working-class consumption being increased, it will have to be diminished.

It is a matter of opinion whether the exemption limit should be put at £5 a week or lower. My own feeling is that, while incomes of less than £5 should be let off lightly, the limit of total exemption for a man with a family should be nearer £3.

Are you aware that those with less than £5 a week are responsible for nearly two-thirds of the whole consumption of the country? Yet I estimate that less than a quarter of my savings levy would be raised from them.

It would not be fatal to my scheme to take more of the savings from the class above £5 a week. It is for others to say whether it would be fair that the man with nearly £5 a week should maintain or increase his consumption and leave the whole of the war effort to be shouldered by others.

JAY: *Why do you wish to allow the small minority of wealthy (with property of over £10,000), to be paid interest and offered repayment for their savings instead of having them appropriated by a capital levy?*

Do you not agree that a permanent increase in big rentiers' claims on the national income would be far more evil than a temporary inflation?

KEYNES: I was in favour of a capital levy after the last war, and would be in favour of one after this war, if the circumstances prove similar. But it is precisely the temporary inflation which will increase the claims of the rich. The object of my plan is to prevent a repetition of what happened last time.

Much better that the working class should have savings than that they should be deprived of the value of their earnings by inflation, even if the inflation is temporary.

I should not oppose a modification of my scheme to allow no interest on the compulsory savings of the surtax class. But the idea that the war can be financed by those with over

£10,000 a year is a myth. The Chancellor of the Exchequer has pointed out that, if the whole of their incomes were taken away, this would not keep the war going for above a week or ten days out of the year.

JAY: *When you first announced your plan you declared that prices could not be controlled by rationing, which was only a pseudo-remedy. But is it not very necessary that prices of primary necessities should be kept down?*

KEYNES: There is a good case for establishing a standard subsistence ration of primary necessities available at a fixed price, with higher prices for other goods or for larger amounts.

This is rather a different idea from 'rationing' as at present conceived, but I agree that it might be a useful addition to my plan.

Let me emphasise the main object of my plan. It will be physically impossible for the working classes to increase their present consumption. Yet they will be asked to increase their work. It follows that they can only be rewarded for their increased work by being given a title which will allow them increased consumption after the war.

I do not want all the claims to future consumption which will arise out of the increase in the national debt, to belong to the richer classes. The working classes cannot be given increased present consumption, but they can be given a share in wealth, in other words, a claim on future consumption.

The alternatives to my plan all mean that the working classes will get nothing in return for their extra hours and effort.

DOUGLAS JAY sums up: I am glad Mr Keynes is now prepared to wipe out all interest on the compulsory savings of the surtax class. This latter point is surely vital.

If we allow the total debt interest claims of rentiers to rise from £250 million to perhaps £1,000 million there will be very little revenue available for social services for an indefinite period afterwards.

This tragedy can only be avoided if we prevent the claims of the rich rentiers from increasing by imposing an annual capital tax in order to reduce borrowing during the war.

Of course, the incomes of those with fortunes of over £10,000 could not, as Mr Keynes says, pay for the war.

But by an annual capital tax a small slice of their securities could be taken from them (2 per cent would raise £250 million a year), and the government could sell these securities to raise money during the war.

Those with incomes of over £5 a week should be able to buy these securities out of their savings. Their total spendable incomes—after deducting present taxation and saving—are at least £1,500 million a year. I think Mr Keynes's forced loan plan might prove very useful for extracting the necessary savings from the middle incomes.

An official proposal to subsidise the cost of living to prevent wage rises brought the following comment.[24]

To the Editor of The Times, *3 February 1940*

Sir,

The Chancellor of the Exchequer has explained to the House of Commons that he is trying to prevent a rise of wages by subsidising the cost of living.

As an ingredient in a comprehensive plan this would be a wise move. As a stop-gap arrangement to gain time it might be prudent. But taken by itself it is the opposite of a solution. In making money go farther it aggravates the problem of reaching equilibrium between the spending power in people's pockets and what can be released for their consumption. It is like trying to meet the problems of war finance by taking off the duties on tea and sugar. Some hint of an awareness of this would have been reassuring. But I noticed none in his speech.

Yours, etc.,

J. M. KEYNES

[24] This proposal had parallels with ideas put forward by R. H. Brand, Sir Arthur Salter, and Professor and Mrs Hicks. Keynes had shied away from them initially on proper Treasury grounds—expense.

Throughout this period, although receiving support from economists, some M.P.s and some bankers such as Montagu Norman and Reginald McKenna,[25] Keynes continued to have problems with Government, Opposition and trade union opinion, not to mention the leaders of the National Savings Movement. However, he prepared his approaches to these groups carefully, maintaining direct contact with many of the individuals involved and looking for opportunities to discuss matters face to face, while gaining information on attitudes and opinion indirectly so as to prepare the ground.

To take perhaps the best examples, the Labour Party and trade unions, Keynes remained in contact with F. W. Pethick-Lawrence, Sir Walter Citrine and Ernest Bevin, while gaining indirect information from such supporters as Stamp, Professor Harold Laski, G. D. H. Cole and Kingsley Martin.[26]

When, on 24 January, his efforts to make more substantial contact proved successful and he saw members of the Labour Front Bench in the morning and a committee of the General Council of the T.U.C. in the afternoon, his preparations meant that he had a revised set of proposals.[27]

[25] Montagu Collet Norman (1871–1950), 1st Baron 1944; Governor, Bank of England, 1920–44.
Reginald McKenna (1863–1943); Liberal M.P. for N. Monmouthshire, 1895–1918; Financial Secretary to H.M. Treasury, 1905; President, Board of Education, 1907–8; First Lord of the Admiralty, 1908–11; Home Secretary, 1911–15; Chancellor of the Exchequer, 1915–16; Chairman of Midland Bank, 1919–43.

[26] Frederick Wilson Pethick-Lawrence (1871–1961), 1st Baron 1945; Labour M.P. for West Leicester, 1922–31, for East Edinburgh, 1935–45; Financial Secretary, Treasury, 1929–31; Editor, *The Echo*, 1920–5, *Labour Record and Review*, 1905–7; joint editor, *Votes for Women*, 1907–14.
Walter McClennan Citrine (b. 1887), 1st Baron 1946; Secretary, Electrical Trades Union (Mersey), 1914–20; President, Federation of Engineering and Shipbuilding Trades (Mersey), 1917–18; Secretary and Chairman, Wallasey Labour Party, 1918–20; Assistant Secretary, T.U.C., 1924–5, General Secretary, 1926–46; President, International Federation of Trade Unions, 1928–45.
Ernest Bevin (1881–1951); Labour M.P. for Wandsworth, 1940–50, for East Woolwich 1950–51; National Organiser for Dockers' Union, 1910–21; General Secretary of Transport and General Workers, 1921–40; member, Macmillan Committee on Finance and Industry, Economic Advisory Council; Minister of Labour and National Service, 1940–45; Foreign Secretary, 1945–51.
Harold Laski (1893–1950); Professor of Political Science, London School of Economics, 1926–50; member, Labour Party Executive Committee, 1936–49, Chairman, 1945–6.
G. D. H. Cole (1889–1959); Reader in Economics, Oxford, 1925–44, Professor, 1944–57; Sub-warden, Nuffield College, Oxford, 1942–3; Director, Nuffield College Social Reconstruction Survey, 1941–4; Chairman, Fabian Society, 1939–46, 1948–50, President, 1952–9; prolific writer on social, economic, and political questions.

[27] The three major revisions were family allowances, repayment through a post-war capital levy and the option of handing over deferred pay to trade union friendly societies. The family allowances matter had come up in correspondence with Mr

PAYING FOR THE WAR

Summary of Proposals for a Comprehensive Scheme

1. These proposals are based on the assumption of government expenditure at a rate of £2,750 million per annum; or an excess of £1,850 million over the yield of taxation in the financial year 1938–9.

2. I estimate that £550 million can be found towards this out of capital resources—sales of gold and foreign securities, increased Empire balances in London, sinking funds and depreciation allowances which it is not possible to invest in new plant; and £300 million from current savings, *excluding altogether voluntary savings by individuals*, namely £200 million from Building Societies, Life offices, undistributed company reserves and the like, and £100 million accumulating in the hands of the government itself, surplus on the unemployment fund, road fund, pension funds, war risk funds and the like.

(I believe that these last two figures are heavily underestimated, and that they might be £100 to £200 million higher between them. This is my principal margin against mistakes in other directions elsewhere in the scheme.)

3. Thus the gap which remains to be bridged is of the order of £1,000 million; or £1,100 million allowing for the cost of family allowances proposed below. I propose that £500 million of this should be raised from the increased yield of new and old taxes. (For I have not yet taken account of increased yield from the pre-war taxes as a result of the increase in the national income, or from the new taxes imposed by the Chancellor of the Exchequer last autumn).

G. Wandsworth in December. Keynes had followed it up in correspondence and discussions with L. S. Amery (who had raised it in *The Times* of 14 December), Mrs E. M. Hubback (who had written an article in the *Spectator* of 15 December) and Eleanor Rathbone. The capital levy proposal came initially from Professor F. A. von Hayek in his commentary on the proposals in the *Spectator* of 24 November, while the friendly society proposal possibly arose in the course of discussions or came from Keynes.

4. There remains £600 million to be found, which presents the hard core of the financial problem. A third to a half of this might be raised by voluntary methods without any assistance from inflation, provided that the public was allowed to consume the balance. But this is precisely what they cannot be allowed to do. Moreover if other methods are used to secure the balance, this is bound to react unfavourably on the amounts voluntarily saved. Thus in what follows I do not rely on any voluntary saving by individuals over and above the institutional saving for which I have already allowed above.

5. Nevertheless I am not satisfied that the fulfilment of this programme need involve any reduction below the pre-war level in the aggregate consumption of the working class. I am supposing that proper organisation can secure an increase of 15–16 per cent in our output above 1938–9, or (say) £825 million measured in pre-war prices. Thus in order to bridge the gap of £1,000 million, aggregate consumption need not be reduced by more than £175 million. The whole of this amount can be taken without undue sacrifice from the consumption of the highest income group.

6. The scheme which follows aims at maintaining the consumption of the lower income group having £250 or less at its pre-war level, and at reducing the consumption of the higher income group having £250 or more by about a third.

7. But this does not mean that the treatment of working-class incomes presents no problem. I estimate that, as a result of the war, the earnings of the lower income group will be increased by £425 million. Whilst my scheme does not require them to reduce their aggregate consumption below the pre-war level, it is not consistent with their *increasing* their consumption. Thus a sum of about £425 million of the increased earnings of this income group must be withdrawn from current expenditure.

8. Some part of this increase can fairly be taken in taxation,

but the solution is largely found in what follows by deferring until after the war the free expenditure of an appropriate proportion of the increased earnings.

9. If everyone's earnings were increased, as a result of the war, in the same proportion it would be easy to arrive at the right formula. But obviously this will not be the case. Thus our formula taken by itself will be liable to create hardships in particular cases. In order to avoid this two remedies are proposed. The first protects the lowest incomes by a sliding scale which rises steeply. The second protects the family man by an allowance of 5s a week for each child under 15 payable in cash to the mother.

10. As in my original *Times* articles, I propose that a proportion of everyone's earnings in excess of a basic minimum should be taken in direct taxes or deferred for expenditure until after the war and held meanwhile in a blocked deposit (see below). I estimate (subject to a wide margin of error) that the following scale will yield the necessary sum, that is to say about £600 million after deducting income tax and surtax:–

(Standard case—a married man with no young family)

Earnings	Percentage
Up to 45s weekly	Nil
At 50s	3½
55s	6
60s	8¾
80s	15⅓
100s	19¼
£300 annually	21
400	25
500	27
700	29
1,000	35
2,000	37½
5,000	53½
10,000	64
20,000	75
50,000	80
Over £50,000	85

11. The proposed family allowances make the result far more favourable than this for the man with young children in the lower income ranges, as is shown in the following tables:–

	Married man with 2 young children			
Weekly earnings *s*	Deferment of pay *s d*	Existing income tax	Family allowances *s*	Cash remaining for consumption *s d*
35	Nil	Nil	10	45
45	Nil	Nil	10	55
55	3 6	Nil	10	61 6
75	10 6	Nil	10	74 6
80	12 3	Nil	10	77 9
100	19 3	Nil	10	90 9

Thus a married man with two young children would actually have more left in cash for all rates of earnings up to nearly 75*s*; and with three young children up to nearly 95*s*. In addition family men would have substantial deferred pay credited to them for use after the war, as well as their cash for immediate consumption being increased.

12. It will be obvious that the same result could be reached if the whole of the percentage of income shown in § 10 were to be taken in income tax and surtax. If a system of deferred pay is thought to be too new-fangled, this would be the most practicable alternative.

13. Nevertheless there are, I think, important social advantages in accumulating deferred pay to increase working class resources and consumption after the war, thus rewarding present effort when once again we have a surplus capacity. It will have the positive advantage when the time comes of preventing unemployment. Meanwhile it will provide the working classes with better security against misfortunes and

with increased wealth;—for a right to deferred consumption is precisely what wealth is.

14. The amount of the pay deferred should be handed over by the employer to trade union friendly societies and similar approved bodies, or, if the beneficiary prefers, to the Post Office Savings Bank, and retained by them as a blocked deposit subject to withdrawal, pending the ultimate release after the war, only for special purposes. Such deposits should be available at all times to meet commitments to building societies, life insurance and pre-war hire purchase. The friendly society should also be empowered to release them, if it is satisfied that there is need, in the event of illness, unemployment or other family difficulties. No account of these deposits should be taken for means test or other fiscal calculations.

15. The question has been asked from what sources the deferred pay can be met after the war. I do not believe that this presents real difficulties. But to put the matter finally at rest, I now propose that it should be met out of a capital levy (either in a lump sum or in instalments) as soon as possible after the war. A capital levy during the war does not do what we want, which is a reduction of current consumption rather than a transfer of capital assets to the Treasury. But this argument does not apply after the war, and I see no fiscal reason why the consumption deferred during the war should not be met out of a capital levy on wealth after the war.

16. There are many details which I have not attempted to give above, and certain other suggestions of policy which the scheme would make possible but which are in no way necessary to it. The essential substance of the plan is sufficiently indicated in the above.

J. M. KEYNES

22 January 1940

Keynes told many of his correspondents of the results of the meetings. Perhaps the most useful account he gave was to Professor Laski:

To H. J. LASKI, *28 January 1940*

Dear Laski,

To me at any rate—I don't know how they felt—my interview with the Labour Front Bench was much less satisfactory than the one with the T.U.C. The former was satisfactorily non-committal on the whole, but it could scarcely be regarded as a serious discussion of the business.

Of those there Attlee and Lees-Smith[28] ran away after about a quarter of an hour, saying nothing, but I thought Attlee was obviously extremely hostile. Dalton[29] stayed on, friendly and non-committal, saying at the end that he had been against the plan, but was now at least to some extent shaken and prepared to consider it. Wilmot[30], whom I did not know before, was clearly an enthusiastic supporter and said that he was 100 per cent converted. Most of the actual discussion was between myself and Pethick-Lawrence, who was, as usual, candid and delightful, but seemed to want a terrible lot of breaking in if he was to contemplate a new idea. He vehemently advocated voluntary saving on general principles of extreme *laissez-faire*, on the ground that the position of every individual was different from every other, and only the individual himself could possibly say how much he could spare. The whole of his argument would have applied equally to a contention that the system of taxation should be voluntary. I assaulted him vigorously and, though perhaps I flatter myself, I really think he was at the end just beginning to see the point. But I rather felt, as I have felt in the past

[28] Hastings Bertrand Lees-Smith (1878–1941); Labour M.P. for Northampton, 1910–18, for Keighley, 1922–31, 1935–41; Postmaster General, 1929–31; President, Board of Education, 1931.

[29] Hugh Dalton (1887–1962) Baron, 1960; Labour M.P. for Bishop Auckland, 1924–59; Lecturer in economics, 1919–36; Parliamentary Under-Secretary, Foreign Office, 1929–31; Minister of Economic Warfare, 1940–2; President, Board of Trade, 1942–5; Chancellor of the Exchequer, 1945–7.

[30] John Wilmot (1895–1964), 1st Baron Selmeston, 1950; Labour M.P. for East Fulham, 1933–5, for Kennington Division of Lambeth, 1939–45, for Deptford, 1945–50; Parliamentary Private Secretary to Minister of Economic Warfare, 1940–2, to President of Board of Trade, 1942–4; Joint Parliamentary Secretary, Ministry of Supply, 1944–5; Minister of Supply, 1945–7.

arguing with Snowden[31], that I was up against such a terrific degree of nineteenth century *laissez-faire*, that the discussion was more of historical than of current interest. But against this there was, after all, the great advantage of the candour and sincerity and openness of the good old Liberal. I liked him very much.

The T.U.C. was a totally different atmosphere. Bevin remains cagey and has deliberately avoided membership of this committee, so neither he nor Citrine was present. There was a large gathering and, whilst they were extraordinarily careful to commit themselves to nothing, I felt the atmosphere most friendly, and above all most serious and intelligent. They were largely concerned to discover exactly what the scheme would amount to in practice. I went away feeling it rather unlikely that they would feel able to propagate such a proposal themselves, but that, put forward in the right quarters and in the right way without their having to take too much responsibility to their own members, they would pretty readily accept it as a long way better than any possible alternative.

I enclose a copy of the document from which I spoke and which I left with them. You will see that I modified it after our talk on the lines of your criticisms. The position at the end was that they would consider what I had said, perhaps make some comments in writing, and I should hear from them again later on. There was a very good speech summing up from the secretary of the committee, Mr Woodcock. Who is he?[32] It was clear he was in complete and comprehensive understanding of the whole problem.

---

[31] Philip Snowden (1864–1937), 1st Viscount Snowden of Ickornshaw, 1931; entered Civil Service, 1886; retired in 1893 for journalism and lecturing; Chairman, Independent Labour Party, 1903–6, 1917–20; Labour M.P. for Blackburn, 1906–18, for Colne Valley, 1922–31; Chancellor of the Exchequer, 1924, 1929–31; Lord Privy Seal, 1931.

[32] Laski replied on 31 January 1940: 'Woodcock is a young man, I think of great ability and sincerity, who will I hope, one day (maybe soon) be the successor to Citrine at the T.U.C.'

George Woodcock (b. 1904); cotton-weaver, 1916–27; Oxford, Ruskin and New College, 1933; Secretary, Trade Union Congress, Research and Economic Department, 1936–47; Assistant General Secretary, T.U.C., 1947; General Secretary, 1960–9.

Since you have probably picked up some reactions from the other end, the above innocent observations of how I was impressed you may find amusing. If there is anything you can pass on from your impressions, I should be grateful and interested.

Yours sincerely,

[copy initialled] J. M. K.

Most of the remaining exercises in persuasion came in the period surrounding the publication of *How to Pay for the War*. On 20 February, Keynes spoke to a meeting of members of the House of Commons. The next day he spoke to the Fabian Society and on 6 March to the National Trade Union Club. Keynes also successfully encouraged Lord Balfour[33] to institute a debate in the House of Lords on the proposals the day after publication.

Finally, before publication, at the request of Sir John Simon, Keynes provided the Treasury with proofs of his pamphlet and at the same time offered to discuss it with the Chancellor. The Chancellor was unable to arrange a meeting before publication, owing to his wife's illness, but he did see Keynes after publication.

Publication brought with it another spate of comment and controversy. Keynes's speeches represented only one aspect of his activities during this period.

Before publication, Keynes had sent almost one hundred copies of *How to Pay for the War* to friends, colleagues and those he was attempting to persuade. As in the case of the Chancellor, he often accompanied those copies with requests for meetings. As a result, the days after publication were full of correspondence, meetings and visits. Keynes summarised this period in a letter to Geoffrey Dawson.[34]

[33] Lord Balfour of Burleigh (George John Gordon Bruce), (1883–1967); Representative Peer for Scotland, 1923–63; Chairman, Medical Research Council, 1936–48; Member, Central Housing Advisory Committee to 1945; Director, Lloyds Bank, 1945–63 (Chairman, 1946–54).

[34] He wrote in similar terms to J. L. Garvin (Editor of *The Observer*) on 13 March. Garvin, who had written to Keynes on 6 March, was uncertain as to whether Keynes had appropriately apprehended public psychology. Keynes's reply, preceding his report of discussions with leaders of opinion, carried echoes of the first chapter of *A Revision of the Treaty* (*JMK*, vol. III, pp. 1–5). 'If you are thinking of the big public, you may well be right. But surely it is altogether impossible in a war to wait until everything is obvious and more than obvious to the man in the street. If you wait so long as that, forces which one can no longer control will have been set moving. It must be sufficient if representative leaders of opinion in different sections of the community are sufficiently persuaded.'

CANUTE SMUSHES THE WAVES

To G. DAWSON, *11 March 1940*

Dear Dawson,

During the last two or three weeks I have had the opportunity of an unusually wide range of contacts in connection with the deferred pay proposals. It might interest you to know the result broadly speaking. I am marking this letter personal and private because none of those I mention by name authorised me to quote their opinions publicly. (I did not ask them to.) They none of them asked me to treat what they said as a matter of confidence.

Taking first of all the leaders of the Left. I have not seen the Labour Front Bench lately, but did not get much satisfaction out of them when I did. They were clearly waiting to watch developments. Bevin is unapproachable, not only by myself, but by everyone, and his attitude, not only on this matter, is not understood by his T.U.C. colleagues. He has not made any pronouncement whatever against the scheme in public or, so far as I can gather, in private. But he has given no word of encouragement. My impression of the others is that there is widespread sympathy in T.U.C. circles and, whilst they could not conceivably take the initiative or responsibility in such a context, they would do their utmost to bring their followers to accept something on these lines if the Chancellor were to propose it. I only know definitely the opinions of those I have had an opportunity of talking to in private. Citrine; George Hicks,[35] the leader of the builders; Griffiths,[36] the leader of the South Wales miners until he

---

[35] Ernest George Hicks (1879–1954); bricklayer; Labour M.P. for E. Woolwich, 1931–50; National Organiser for Bricklayers' Society, 1912; President, National Federation of Building Trades Operatives, 1919, 1936–7; first General Secretary, Amalgamated Union of Building Trade Workers, 1921–40; Parliamentary Secretary, Minister of Works, 1940–5.

[36] James Griffiths (b. 1890); Labour M.P. for Llanelly, 1936–70; Secretary, Ammanford Trade Council, 1916–19; Labour Party agent, 1922–5; President, South Wales Miners' Federation, 1934–6; Minister for National Insurance, 1945–50; member, Executive Committee, Miners' Federation of Great Britain, 1934–6, National Executive, Labour Party, 1939–59.

became an M.P. instead; have all expressed whole-hearted support, and they are fairly representative.

All the economic advisers of the Labour Party are very strongly in favour,—Cole, Laski, Crossman[37] and Mrs Wootton.[38]

Amongst academic economists there is, I think, almost universal agreement on principle, though some differences on points of detail. This embraces the school of economists from whom I have frequently differed of late; in particular Hayek, who has gone so far as to suggest getting up a circular of support; D. H. Robertson[39] and, I think, Robbins[40].

Amongst economists who are also, and primarily perhaps, administrators, approval has been particularly strong. I have had enthusiastic agreement from Stamp, Henry Clay of the Bank of England, Beveridge, Layton and Salter. Perhaps I might mention R. B. Bennett[41] of Canada, who is a very strong supporter in this group.

Amongst leaders of banking and business I am limited to those whom I happen to have met recently: the Governor of the Bank of England, who says he thinks it is the only solution, and with whom, after long estrangement, this scheme has brought about a personal reconciliation; McGowan; Peacock;

[37] Richard Crossman (1907–1974); Fellow and Tutor, New College, Oxford, 1930–7; Assistant Editor, *New Statesman and Nation*, 1938–40; Psychological Warfare, 1943–5; Labour M.P. for Coventry East, 1945–74; member of Labour Party Executive from 1952.

[38] Barbara Wootton (b. 1897), Baroness 1958; Lecturer in Economics, Girton College, Cambridge, 1920–2; Research Officer, T.U.C. and Labour Party, 1922–6; Principal, Morley College, 1926–7; Director of Studies for tutorial classes, London University, 1927–44.

[39] Dennis Holme Robertson (1890–1963), Kt. 1953; Fellow of Trinity College, Cambridge, 1914–38, 1944–63; Reader in Economics, Cambridge, 1930–38; Professor of Economics, London University, 1939–44; Adviser, Treasury, 1939–44; Professor of Political Economy, Cambridge, 1944–57.

[40] Lionel Charles Robbins (b. 1898), cr. Life Peer, 1959; Lecturer, London School of Economics, 1925–7; Fellow and Lecturer, New College, Oxford, 1927–9; Professor of Economics, University of London, 1929–61; member, Economic Section of Offices of War Cabinet, 1939–41, Director, 1941–5.

[41] Richard Bedford Bennett (1870–1947), 1st Viscount Bennett, 1941; Prime Minister and Minister of External Affairs (Canada), 1930–5; Leader, Conservative Party of Canada, 1927–38.

Catto; D'Arcy Cooper; Samuel Courtauld; R. H. Brand; Horne;[42] McKenna.

I have recently addressed the T.U.C. in private conference, the National Trade Union Club, the Fabian Society, and a large gathering of M.P.s of all parties. It is not too easy to judge the sentiments of a mixed gathering, but I have certainly had in each case a pretty strong impression that at least a majority were persuaded.

If you take a survey of the whole press of the country, you will discover an extraordinary and almost universal support. I think it is fair to say that outspoken opposition (apart from dark questionings by the Labour Front Bench) is limited to Kindersley,[43] Beaverbrook[44], who says frankly that he prefers inflation, and *The Daily Worker*. Camrose[45] has said nothing against the scheme, but is keeping up a semi-boycott in all

[42] Harry Duncan McGowan (1874–1961), 1st Baron 1937; Chairman, Imperial Chemical Industries, 1930–50.
  Sir Edward Robert Peacock (1871–1962); concerned with Dominion Securities Corporation of Canada and London, 1902–15, with Light, Power and Traction Companies in Spain, Brazil and Mexico, 1915–24; Director of Canadian Pacific Railway and of Baring Bros.; Director, Bank of England, 1921–4, 1929–46.
  Thomas Sivewright Catto (1879–1959), 1st Baron 1936; Director of Yule, Catto and Co.; Director, Bank of England, 1940; Financial Adviser, Treasury, 1939–44; Governor, Bank of England, 1944–9.
  Sir Francis D'Arcy Cooper (1882–1941); Vice-Chairman, Lever Bros., 1923, Chairman, 1925; member, Industrial Export Council, Board of Trade, and of Royal Commission on the Distribution of the Industrial Population; Vice-Chairman, Permanent Hops Committee.
  Samuel Courtauld (1876–1947); Chairman, Courtaulds Ltd, 1921–46; Trustee, Tate Gallery, 1927–37, National Gallery, 1931–47.
  Sir Robert Horne (1871–1940), K.C. 1910, 1st Viscount 1937; lawyer, politician, businessman; Unionist M.P. 1918–37; Minister of Labour, 1919–20; President, Board of Trade, 1920–1; Chancellor of Exchequer, 1921–2; Director, Suez Canal Co.; Chairman, Burma Corporation, Great Western Railway.
[43] Robert Molesworth Kindersley (1871–1954), 1st Baron 1941; Chairman, Lazard Bros.; Chairman or Director of other mercantile and investment companies; Director, Bank of England, 1914–46.
[44] William Maxwell Aitken (1879–1964), Kt. 1911, Bt. 1916. 1st Baron Beaverbrook, 1917; Owner of the Daily Express from 1916; Unionist M.P. for Ashton-under-Lyne, 1910–17; Chancellor of the Duchy of Lancaster and Minister of Information, 1918; Minister of Aircraft Production, 1940–1; Minister of State, 1941; Minister of Supply, 1941–2; Lord Privy Seal, 1943–5.
[45] William Ernest Berry Camrose (1879–1954), 1st Viscount 1941; Editor-in-Chief, *Sunday Times*, 1915–36; Principal Adviser, Ministry of Information, 1939; founded *Advertising World*, 1901; principal proprietor of *Daily Telegraph*; Chairman, Amalgamated Press Ltd; member, Reuter Trust.

his papers, which give the whole thing the least possible mention.

I had a very long talk last week with the Chancellor of the Exchequer. It would not be fair to say more than that he is interested. It did not appear to me that any insuperable administrative objections had been raised. The position really is, I think, not that the Government have any alternative, but that they are exceedingly reluctant to adopt any drastic remedy until the necessity of it is obvious, and more than obvious, to the densest member of the public. But, in the light of the above survey of authoritative support from so great a variety of quarters, do you think they need really feel scared about public opinion, if only they will grasp the nettle?

Yours sincerely,

[copy initialled] J. M. K.

Keynes's reference to the Governor of the Bank refers to both Norman's letter upon receipt of the pamphlet and a later meeting. The exchange of letters is of interest.

From M. NORMAN, *28 February 1940*

Dear Mr Keynes,

It would indeed have been disappointing if you had not sent along a copy of your pamphlet and therefore I thank you for having done so. I do not pretend to understand the inwardness of your solution or the technical methods by which it might be carried out. But it has my sympathy and I do not doubt that a drastic solution will be necessary.

I know of no other specific than yours. But what worries me—assuming no drastic solution—is, how along with the savers we here are to raise money from permanent investors at the rate perhaps of £100 million a month for an almost indefinite period. And next time you are in London I should greatly value a talk with you and Clay on this point because I can envisage no such possibility. Yet I must have some sort of ideas for keeping our machine going alongside of Kindersley's.

When you say that you think his methods would be successful if we were spending £500 million less a year, you are allowing, I assume, for raising through the savers and through investors the remaining £700 million, which totals together I reckon may be necessary in the coming year.

I am,

Yours sincerely,

M. NORMAN

To M. NORMAN, *3 March 1940*

Dear Mr Governor,

I should very much like to have a chat with you and Clay. I am coming to town on Tuesday, and it would fit in rather well with my plans to call in at the Bank at about 2.45 that afternoon, if this were to happen to fit in with your plans.

On the question in the second paragraph of your letter, my budget of borrowing, in very broad approximations, is like this:-

	£ million		£ million
Government expenditure	3,000	Savings accruing in Government funds (health insurance,	
Taxation	1,550	unemployment, war risks, etc.)	100
		Sale of gold	150
		Increase of overseas balances in London	100
		Sale of foreign investments	100
		Unspent funds accruing for investment in sinking and depreciation funds	150
		Institutional saving (building societies, insurance offices, and especially undistributed company reserves)	300
		Deferred pay	550
Leaving	1,450		1,450

Some of these estimates are more conservative than others. But on the assumption of deferred pay it brings down the money to be raised by public issues from permanent investors to a manageable figure. The increase of foreign balances in London could presumably be met by Treasury bills and the like, and a large part of undistributed company reserves would probably be kept liquid. Moreover, the capital money becoming available from the sale of foreign investments and in sinking and depreciation funds finds its way into new permanent loans almost automatically; and the same is largely true of those institutional savings which are not naturally kept liquid. Thus, I should say that the new money to be raised from permanent investors is not more than £350 million a year.

This seems to me to be manageable, though you will notice that my total figure is not far short of your figure of £100 million a month. If the deferred pay scheme is not adopted, the £350 million above would become £800 million, or more, and then it seems to me we really are up against it. In reference to your last paragraph, I think that you are assuming a government expenditure of £200 million larger than I am assuming, or else that taxation is £200 million less. On my budget, as given above, if we were spending £500 million less, the balance to be found would be only £500 million, and not nearly all this would have to be raised from permanent investors. So in that case I should expect Kindersley's campaign to be adequate.

Yours sincerely,
[copy initialled] J.M.K.

The weak spot in my calculations is the assumption that the adverse balance of payments will not exceed £350 million p.a. Unless we largely increase our present output and exports, it may exceed this to a very serious extent. But even so it will not aggravate our financial problem of finding money internally, since in effect it will be found externally. The danger will be lest it impairs our powers of endurance.

As he mentioned in his letter to Dawson (above p. 102), Keynes was heartened by the reactions of fellow economists. D. H. Robertson on 6 March called it 'your best work since E.C.P.'.[46] Hayek's reaction, three days earlier had run:

I find myself in practically complete agreement in so far as policy during the war is concerned. It is reassuring to know that we agree so completely on the economics of scarcity, even if we differ on when it applies.

Professor Hayek also offered to sign any circular letter Keynes might want to use in promoting the scheme to highlight the unanimity of professional

[46] *Economic Consequences of the Peace, JMK*, vol. II.

opinion. Keynes thought such a letter would prove useful, but he suggested that it should come without prompting from him. He suggested that Hayek took the idea up with others, although he noted there would be problems as 'so many are now in government departments and therefore silenced'. In the end Professor Robbins attempted to work up such a letter, but he found he agreed so completely that all a letter could do was record the fact, and that, as he told Keynes on 29 March, 'seems to attach importance to one's own utterances which is not warranted by the facts'. Therefore the circular letter was stillborn. However, Robbins concluded his letter to Keynes:

> I would like to add that for me it has been one of the few cheering things about the war that I have found myself in the position of agreement with you. You know that in the past it has always been a matter of intense personal regret that I was not always able to support your plans.

The only economist whom Keynes entered into controversy with over the plan was Professor J. R. Hicks, who reviewed *How to Pay for the War* in the *Manchester Guardian* of 28 February. Keynes was unhappy with the review, which found the proposed family allowances too generous in the light of the iron ration proposal and the proposed taxation of the rich. He therefore replied in the *Manchester Guardian*:

To the Editor of the Manchester Guardian, *28 February 1940*

Sir,

I am sorry that Professor Hicks does not like family allowances, but worse than sorry that he should support this aversion by misleading calculations. If family allowances cost £100 million it is evident that this money must come from somewhere, but Professor Hicks's suggestion that it comes under my revised proposals mainly from the other members of the class below £5 a week, with the effect of largely increasing their contributions, is without foundation.

In the first place, only half the increased sum I now propose to raise can be connected with family allowances, and even this, being presumably permanent, I regard as coming out of taxation and not out of deferred pay. (Professor Hicks's idea that the increase is partly intended to meet the iron ration is not to be found in my pamphlet, where I have not increased my previous estimate of aggregate government expenditure.) The rest of the increase is to cover various concessions in favour of those who are saving in other ways and to meet the task before us more wholeheartedly, with the object of avoiding a further fall in real wages.

In the second place, the scale is so arranged that, whereas the benefit of the family allowances goes almost entirely to the class below £5 a week, the class above £5 a week make a large contribution to them in the shape either of taxes or of deferred pay. The increase in the deferred pay of bachelors below £5 a week is mostly required to prevent a further fall in their real wages and to provide concessions in favour of other forms of saving.

Whilst at one end of the scale Professor Hicks thinks I am unduly tender to poor families, at the other end he argues that I do not 'soak' the rich sufficiently. He would have helped the reader to judge the truth of this if he had mentioned that I defer about 20 per cent of all the higher incomes remaining after taxation; that this is in addition to the increased burden of direct taxes placed on them by last autumn's Budget, which makes no more impression on him than last autumn's leaves; that I assume further taxation of £100 million, not specified in detail but which in aggregate my table on page 37 [*JMK*, vol. IX, p. 398] throws mainly on the higher-income groups; and that the net result is to reduce the consumption of this group by a third, whilst leaving unchanged the aggregate consumption of the group below £5 a week.

The question of the appropriate scale is obviously a matter for legitimate differences of opinion amongst those who approve the principle. We can cut out or reduce the family allowances if we think that they cost the bachelors too much and if we neglect the striking statistics of the high proportion of poverty which is due to the lack of such allowances. But

I could have wished that Professor Hicks had given a more exact account of what my proposals really mean.

Yours, etc.,

J. M. KEYNES

Professor Hicks returned to the charge on 29 February raising two points: Keynes in his aggregation had not taken account of the incidence of taxation and subsidies on different groups of people and had, therefore, overlooked the possible inflationary effects of his revised proposals, and that he had ignored the possibility of dis-saving by the richer classes to maintain consumption. The discussion continued privately.

To J. R. HICKS, *1 March 1940*

Dear Hicks,

I confess that where I was replying to you in regard to the higher incomes I had not the foggiest idea that the point you were raising was that, in their case, compulsory savings would not come out of current consumption. And, looking at your original review again, I am still unable to see how I could have known that this was in your mind. Which is the passage in which you think you mentioned this point?

Also, why would not the same argument apply to taxation in so far as it is a sound one?

I am not intending to return to the charge in the columns of the *Guardian*.

Yours sincerely,
[copy initialled] J.M.K.

From J. R. HICKS, *4 March 1940*

Dear Keynes,

What I meant is this. Suppose a man has a capital of £25,000 in securities, and draws an income of £1,000 a year from it. If you impose a compulsory saving levy of £100 on a man in this situation, the *natural* thing for him to do is to sell securities to the value of £100. For when he has done so, his capital is intact, only slightly less liquid (the fact that £100 out of £25,000 is blocked cannot really make much difference to his liquidity); his disposable income is down by £1, if you are paying 3 per cent on his blocked savings, and by no more than £4, even if you pay no interest at all. There does seem to be a really grave lack of equity between the

109

treatment of this case and that of the man without past savings (or with past savings so small that his liquidity position would be seriously affected if he met the levy out of capital)—the man you are mainly thinking of who would be obliged to contract consumption by an amount similar to that of the levy imposed upon him.

Of course I agree that the capitalist has the option of paying *taxation* out of capital; but there are strong reasons and perhaps stronger prejudices against such 'living on capital'. My point is that he can meet compulsory savings this way without living on capital. I do think this point is really important, and would get your scheme into serious difficulties, if nothing were done to meet it.

What I said in my review was: 'it is not clear that the compulsory investment of so much money in a certain approved direction lays any burden at all on the capitalist, though he may lose a little in interest if a lower rate is paid upon his compulsory savings than he would be able to get elsewhere'. Of course I should have worked it out more fully if I had had more space.

Yours sincerely,

J. R. HICKS

To J. R. HICKS, *13 March 1940*

Dear Hicks,

I doubt if people are often as actuarially minded as your calculation makes them. I fancy that inhibitions against selling out are fairly strong. All the same I do not deny that there may be some leakage in the way you suggest. But that, I feel, is an inevitable consequence of almost any kind of drastic remedy. And the difference in this respect between my proposal and alternatives (if there are any alternatives; I have not heard of them) is of the second order of magnitude.

Moreover, if, as is quite arguable, our existing fiscal system is hard on the man whose income is earned as compared with the man having unearned income, this cannot be put down to my proposal. It is a feature of the whole income and surtax system in its present state of development. If it needs to be remedied, there is no difficulty in imposing a higher rate of tax on unearned income, as was of course the case in former days.

Yours sincerely,

[copy initialled] J. M. K.

To gain a wider audience for his views, Keynes turned to broadcasting, discussing his proposals on 11 March 1940 with Donald Tyerman.[47]

From The Listener, *14 March 1940*

SHOULD SAVING BE COMPULSORY?

Discussion between Donald Tyerman and J. M. Keynes

TYERMAN: *How are we going to pay for the war? That is what we all want to know. It isn't just a matter of money. It is a matter of men and materials. We really pay for the war by producing more things for the Government and consuming less ourselves. We have got to work harder than in peace time. We have got to turn out more goods. That is the first step. And at the same time we have got to use less and spend less than we do in peace time. It is not easy. If we work harder, that is, longer hours with more people at work, women and so on, then between us we earn more than we did before the war—and if we are not careful we shall spend more instead of less. This is where Mr Keynes's plan comes in. He wants to postpone part of our pay so that we can't spend it now. Then, when the war is over, we can have it all back. That is what you are trying to do, Mr Keynes, isn't it, stop us from spending so much now?*

KEYNES: Yes. It is obvious that we must work harder—more men and women in employment and longer overtime. This means that more money will be earned; and by the time we have improved our organisation for war output in the way we must (we are a long way off that yet), the extra money taken home at the end of the week will be very substantial indeed. Bigger output and bigger earnings are just what we want. But they will create a serious problem all the same. The money will have been earned in making stuff for the Government, not in making more for the public to purchase. So it will not increase the amount of goods in the shops available for the public to buy. What follows? More

---

[47] Donald Tyerman (b. 1905); journalist, Assistant, then Deputy Editor, *The Economist*, 1937–44; Deputy Editor, *The Observer*, 1943–4; Assistant Editor, *The Times*, 1944–5; Editor, *The Economist*, 1955–65.

money to spend and less stuff in the shops. There can be only one result if the money is spent. Prices must go up until the goods are so dear that it takes all the increased earnings to buy them. That is what happened in the last war. But what a silly business it was. It meant that those of us who had increased earnings were simply wasting them. And those who had no more money than before were badly hit because at these higher prices their earnings bought so much less.

Yet there is a way out of all this nonsense. During the war the resources do not exist to provide more goods for consumption. But after the war the opposite will be true. We shall be able to produce more than we can easily market. So I propose that everyone should put off spending a proportion of his earnings until that time comes.

TYERMAN: *So your argument is that you have got to force people to save that bit extra. I know a lot of people don't like your scheme because they think it is really an attack on wages. One working man has written me a letter saying: 'Your idea of grabbing some of our small wages compulsorily is a form of Hitlerism.' He goes on to say that the money could be got from more taxes on people who are well off.*

KEYNES: Your friend has a pretty foggy idea of Hitlerism. In Germany the wages are fixed at the lowest possible level and there is very little to buy with them, and there is no proposal to give anything back afterwards. But if he means that we cannot fight Hitlerism, which takes such enormous sacrifices from Germany, without making some sacrifice ourselves, he is quite right. It is not my proposal which will cause the sacrifice. That will be inevitable under any proposal. My object is to divide the sacrifice fairly. And that brings me to his suggestion that the rich can pay for this war. To a large extent they can and should. My plan puts on them by far the greater share of the burden. But the notion that in a war like this the working classes can increase their earnings and then actually take advantage of this to consume more now is surely somewhat unreasonable. Sir John Simon has shown that if you took away the whole of the income of those with £10,000 a year or more, it would only pay for the war for a few days in the year. If you take away the whole of everyone's income in excess of £10 a week, you would only meet about two-thirds of the cost. So it is necessary that those with less than £10 a week must take a share.

TYERMAN: *I can see that. It's a plain matter of fact. But why couldn't you get the same result by voluntary methods, just by simply asking people to save that much more? Won't your scheme damage our fine voluntary effort? I have already heard people saying: 'If I'm going to be forced to save, why should I save of my own accord?'*

KEYNES: I hope everyone will buy all the savings certificates he can and will join one of Sir Robert Kindersley's savings groups. Sir Robert Kindersley and his organisation are doing splendid work. I would not willingly say a word to hinder them. They are working in an extremely practical way to do just what is wanted. Whatever other schemes may be adopted we shall need their efforts and enthusiasm.

And if we were not going to spend more than we spent in the early months of the war, the savings movement might be enough. But this is only a beginning. When the Government is spending half the national income and needs to borrow a hundred million pounds a month, as it soon will be, in addition to the heaviest taxation ever known, and to go on doing this month after month for an indefinite period, we should be deceiving ourselves if we were to believe that we could get on without some further drastic remedy. The voluntary method is vastly preferable. The response is magnificent. If we did not need so much it would provide enough. But to depend on it exclusively when the Government needs half the national income is like trying to raise an army of five million without conscription.

TYERMAN: *Well, what exactly is the way out you want us to take?*

KEYNES: What we need is something like a rule of the road. Remember what the problem is. Consumption will be cut down, anyhow. The stuff will not be there to be consumed. If we try to spend too much of our earnings, all that can happen will be that we shall get in one another's way in spending our money. So let us have a general rule of the road not to get in one another's way. That is what my proposal comes to. All except those who have no margin in their standard of life will be asked to defer spending a part of their earnings which will be put to their credit as their own money to be spent after the war. The trouble is that individual circumstances differ so much. Some people's incomes will have gone up and some will have gone down. Some already have a margin. Others, because their wages are low or because they have young families, have no margin at all. So my proposal needs many safeguards.

TYERMAN: *That seems to me a vastly important point. There are some people who can't really do without anything, people with low earnings or big families as you say. How are you going to look after them?*

KEYNES: To begin with, payments must be steeply graded. I cannot give you all the details here. You will find them in my pamphlet *How to Pay for the War*. A married man with 45*s* a week or less will have nothing deferred. At 50*s*, 1*s* 9*d* will be deferred. That is to say, temporarily withheld until after the war. At 55*s*, 3*s* 6*d* will be deferred; at 75*s*, 10*s* 6*d*, and so on. A man with £20 a week has eight times the income of a man with 50*s*. But the income tax he will pay and his income deferment added together will come not to eight times the 50*s* a week man, but *eighty* times. That is to say, he will pay ten times higher in proportion to his income. If we solve the problem of letting prices rise, as we did in the last war, instead of the £20 a week man paying a much bigger share, it will be the 50*s* a week man who will be the harder hit in proportion to his income. With my scheme, moreover, it would be possible for the Government to keep down the prices of what has been called an iron ration of the chief necessaries of life.

TYERMAN: *Another of my correspondents writes: 'We say rude things about saving and sacrifice—our life is one long sacrifice. Ask Mr Keynes to keep a family on £3 8s 6d a week and see how much he can save.' What would be the position of a man like that?*

KEYNES: I propose a family allowance of 5s a week in cash for every child under 15. This has nothing to do with the employer or with wages, or indeed with the father. It will be payable to the mother in cash at the Post Office and will be her money. Take your friend with 68s 6d a week, he will have 8s 3d of his pay deferred. But if he has two young children, his wife will receive 10s a week towards their cost. So the family will be actually 1s 9d in pocket and will also have 8s 3d a week accumulating to their credit to spend after the war.

TYERMAN: *You say the deferred pay will be accumulating to their credit. They are not losing it for good. But is this really true? Isn't it frankly a sort of hidden tax?*

KEYNES: That is certainly not the intention. The next lot of safeguards are to make it perfectly clear that the deferred earnings really are the property of the man who earned them. In the case of an insured man they would be collected by stamping a deferred earnings card just like an insurance card. The amount of stamps on the card would show how much stood to the man's credit. He would then have to choose in what institution he wanted to keep his deposit—for example, his friendly society, his trade union or the Post Office Savings Bank.

TYERMAN: *Would it carry interest too?*

KEYNES: Yes. At 2½ per cent. And he would be allowed to apply the money to certain other forms of saving if he preferred—for example, to pay his life insurance premiums, to meet instalments to a building society or to pay off any hire purchase agreements he had made before the war. Generally speaking, he must not spend it on new consumption until after the war. But his friendly society or trade union would be allowed to let him draw on it any time if he was able to show good reason on account of illness or unemployment or special family difficulties. And if he died, it would be released for the use of his dependants. After the war, not quite at once but a little later on when there were again surplus resources, the money would be freely his to do what he liked with.

TYERMAN: *What sort of amount would it come to?*

KEYNES: Take a married man with £5 a week. £41 10s a year will be accumulating to his credit. If the war lasts two-and-a-half-years, he will have over £100 in the bank. And if he has two children his wife will also have collected £65 in cash. Now, isn't this much better than to have the purchasing power permanently taken away from you either by taxes or by high prices? For those are the alternatives.

In the last war, most of the rights to extra expenditure after the war belonged to the richer classes. All the rest of the community owed them a huge sum in the shape of the National Debt. If the Government has to borrow, as it certainly will, someone will have the right to extra expenditure after the war. I want this right to be spread through all classes. The wage-earning class will work harder but they cannot consume more now because it is not there to be consume. But that is no reason why they should not have the right to extra consumption later on. Under this proposal they would be accumulating several hundred million pounds to their credit in each year.

TYERMAN: *That sounds all very well. But how is it to be paid back after the war?*

KEYNES: There is no more difficulty than in the case of any other part of the National Debt. And you can be quite sure that any government would regard this part of it as the most sacred. But as an extra safeguard, I would like to see a pledge that it will be met after the war by a capital levy or tax on wealth. In many ways there would be something appropriate in this. And it would have another advantage. We could then afford to do something similar for men at the front. It would be extremely unfair if men who have the opportunity of earning wages at home ended up the war with perhaps £100 to their credit under this proposal; whilst those who had been in the Forces ended up with nothing. If we agreed to pay for the scheme by a capital levy, we could afford to credit the men who had been risking their lives with about the same sum which they would have had to their credit if they had stayed at home. Isn't that a great additional attraction and a very fair thing to do?

The next day, Keynes attempted to put his deferred pay scheme in perspective by relating it to the Treasury's financial requirements. His letter did not appear until 15 March because Keynes thought it should wait until the lists for the first long-term war loan, 3 per cent 1955–9, closed and because *The Times* wanted to make an editorial comment.

To the Editor of The Times, *12 March 1940*

Sir,

In my contribution to your columns last November I put forward a scale for deferred pay of which I estimated the yield at £400 million, and I have subsequently revised this so as to increase the yield to £600 million, or £550 million after allowing something for the cost of certain concessions. In recent discussions I have noticed a tendency to quote the former figure as though it was my estimate of the total annual sum which the Treasury will have to borrow from the public. It may help, therefore, to put the deferred pay proposal in its right perspective to relate its yield to the Treasury's total requirements.

We must, presumably, look forward before long to government expenditure at a rate of £2,750 million a year or more. One thousand three hundred million pounds looks like the utmost expectation from tax receipts within the coming year. This leaves from £1,450 million upwards to be borrowed. After allowing for the proceeds of sales of gold and for money accruing in various government funds, the prospective borrowing programme appears to be of the order of £1,200 millon, or £100 million a month. We have to make ready to stomach this monthly rate of issue for an indefinite period. It does not all represent new savings out of current incomes, since we can live to a limited extent on capital; and a substantial part of it will be properly available for liquid investments such as Treasury bills. Nevertheless this is the figure we must have in mind when we are adding up all the subscriptions to Treasury loans.

It is from the last £500 million of the prospective expenditure that the real pinch comes and the need for a drastic remedy. It has not come yet, because so far the money has not been spent on this scale. In introducing the recent vote of credit Sir John Simon mentioned that expenditure is now at an annual rate of almost £2,400 million, adding, however, that 'the expenses are increasing rapidly'. This is actually less than the rate of expenditure which he gave more than three months ago. Thus the failure of the supply departments to organize output on a larger scale has come to the rescue of the Chancellor and has been, so far, his main bulwark. He can scarcely sit back and rely on this failure as a permanency and a continuing source of comfort. Yet those who put their faith in the adequacy of normal financial methods are assuming this, and their complacency is disturbing. To depend on voluntary methods when the Treasury has to take half the national income is comparable to relying on these methods to raise an army of 5 million men.

The discussion is being carried on as though it was a question of choice between depending on normal methods and the particular drastic remedy of deferred pay. To my mind this misconceives the problem entirely. The Chancellor of the Exchequer has to spend these next weeks in deciding which drastic remedy he prefers—and there is not a wide choice.

Yours, etc.,

J. M. KEYNES

Later he replied to a correspondent in The *New Statesman* who had signed herself White Queen and suggested that Keynes's proposals misunderstood people's psychology, as she would be happier if the authorities told her that the goods would be unavailable rather than that she could not afford them.

To the Editor of the New Statesman, *23 March 1940*

Sir,

I am sorry that I have misinterpreted the psychology of your correspondent 'White Queen', and have underestimated the attractions to a housewife of spending half her time standing in queues.

But I am wondering if you have deciphered her signature correctly. It was the Red Queen who, when inflation set in, found so much satisfaction in running faster and faster:

The most curious part of the thing was, that the trees and the other things round them never changed their places at all: however fast they went, they never seemed to pass anything...

'Well, in *our* country,' said Alice, still panting a little, 'you'd generally get to somewhere else—if you ran very fast for a long time as we've been doing.'

'A slow sort of country!' said the Queen. 'Now, *here*, you see, it takes all the running *you* can do, to keep in the same place. If you want to get somewhere else, you must run at least twice as fast as that!'

J. M. KEYNES

Two weeks later, in the same journal he was replying to Mr H. Barrow who criticised Keynes for being a deflationist and advocated a doubling of the price level to halve the burden of the National Debt.

To the Editor of the New Statesman, *6 April 1940*

Sir,

I welcome Mr Barrow's letter frankly supporting inflation. There is much sentiment of this kind underground too shy to lift its head for execution. For it suits the active capitalists

119

who are owed money by the unhappy rentiers. And there is a flavour of naughtiness about it which some members of the Left find irresistible; there must be something good, they feel, in a proposal so repugnant to all respectable citizens. But before we offer this *bonne bouche* to the rich and the naughty, the following points deserve to be considered.

(1) The reduction in the burden of the National Debt is a subsequent result of reducing the value of money and makes no significant contribution to the current financing of the war. Moreover the justice and expediency of doing this at the sole expense of the holders of government stock and other money obligations and of all small savers to the advantage of the active capitalist is not obvious. It is a last resort rather than a first one, of which the chief recommendation is its facility.

(2) During the war inflation is serviceable only in so far as there is a time-lag between wages and prices. That is how it worked in the last war with prices always about 15 per cent ahead of wage rates, and this figure is about the magnitude of what we should require this time. Inflation pays for the war only if it operates as the equivalent of a flat percentage tax on wages. It is, perhaps, a comfort that it is always there (subject to what follows) to fall back on, if, rejecting juster and wiser alternatives, we let our finances drift. The active capitalist, it will be noticed, wins all along the line, at the expense of wage earners during the transition and at the expense of bond-holders afterwards; though he will presumably have to surrender the major part of his initial gains to the tax-gatherer.

(3) But even in this ointment there is a big fly. In modern conditions will the time-lag be long enough to do the trick? In the last war it was of the order of six months to a year which is long enough to allow us to collect the gains without a galloping inflation (see my *How to Pay for the War*, p. 71 [*JMK*, vol. ix, p. 423], for the details). But can we reckon on this today? I doubt it. Everyone, including the trade unions, has

become index-number conscious. Wages will pursue prices with not so lame a foot. And this new fact means that the old-type *laissez-faire* inflation is no longer to be relied upon.

(4) The only practicable version today is to fix wages by decree as in Russia and Germany and also in France; and then allow prices to rise to the appropriate extent which I estimate at not above 15 per cent in present circumstances. A very gentlemanly programme, take it all in all. Yet perhaps it is my alternative proposal, in spite of its apparent respectability, which deserves the confidence of the wage earner.

J. M. KEYNES

In the next week, in reply to Mr C. A. Rowley, Keynes gave more attention to his capital levy suggestion.

To the Editor of The Times, *18 April 1940*

Sir,

In my pamphlet *How to Pay for the War* I did not attempt to deal with the technique of a capital levy, though I have given some thought to it. Mr Rowley is certainly right that it raises difficult questions, but they are beyond the compass of a letter.

I am myself convinced that either a capital levy or a capital tax would be technically possible on the scale required—which is much smaller than what most people are expecting, being no more than 5 per cent of accumulated wealth if we take Mr Rowley's estimate of the amount of the levy. But I would remind him that I expressed a preference for a capital tax by instalments which technically is the easier alternative. Moreover, I emphasised my own view that it is the redundant savings which will be available in the post-war slump, rather than the capital levy, which will ensure the possibility of releasing the deferred pay. While a capital levy may operate as a popular assurance of repayment, my own reasons for regarding it as a policy complementary to deferred pay are different. A method of financing the war, which avoids both inflation and crushing taxes, necessarily leaves us with an unwieldy burden of war debt, especially if the method of deferred pay enables us to do justice to men serving with the Forces. A capital levy of some 5 per cent of accumulated wealth is the easiest and justest way of avoiding this consequence; while there is also a special suitability in rewarding the risks, the labours, and the abstinences of wartime at the expense of the old wealth which they will have served to safeguard.

He raises, however, another matter of at least equal importance—namely, the rate at which deferred pay could be prudently released after the war. A moderate interim release, almost at once, may be helpful if we are slow at organising the transition from war to peace. But it is an essential part of my proposal that there should be no substantial release in the immediate post-war period; for at first there will be many claims on our productive resources, particularly if the war has lasted for three years. The general release should begin with a first instalment of (say) 10 per cent, when the state of employment shows that effective demand is falling away, with the subsequent rate of release depending on our experience of the scale on which the beneficiaries are spending the money. My own prediction is that a large part would be retained as more or less permanent savings. A rate of release which resulted in an actual expenditure (including the purchase of houses and other durable goods) from £150 million per annum upwards according to the state of employment and other demand, would work wonders in avoiding the post-war depression and would be automatically financed out of current surplus savings which would otherwise be running to waste. This would last long enough to give us a breathing space to work out a more permanent policy for the post-war world. The amount we shall have to spend after the war to prevent unemployment will be exactly the same whether or not we introduce deferred pay. The release of deferred pay will provide us with a useful and justifiable form of expenditure and, by allowing individuals to choose for themselves what they want, will save us from having to devise large-scale government plans of expenditure which may not correspond so closely to personal need.

Thus, quite apart from its primary purpose to finance the war, it would be worth while to introduce deferred pay at a time of scarce resources such as the present, if only with the object of releasing it subsequently at a time of surplus resources and so preventing the shameful malady of unemployment. I think of it as a first instalment of a comprehensive social policy to regulate the general rate of spending so as to avoid the disastrous alternations of boom and slump which otherwise will continue to undermine the foundations of society. War provides an example *par excellence* of a state of boom. It is much better to start our regulation by an artificial restriction of general spending power in time of boom than to begin with an artificial expansion of it in time of slump, which is what, otherwise, will be forced on us.

I am not proposing an expedient, undesirable for its own sake, just for the purpose of financing the war. I am seizing an opportunity, where the need is obvious and overwhelming, to introduce a principle of policy which may come to be thought of as marking the line of division between the totalitarian and the free economy. For if the community's aggregate rate of spending can be regulated, the way in which personal incomes are spent and the means by which demand is satisfied can be safely left free and individual. Just as in the war the regulation of aggregate spending is the only way to avoid the destruction of choice and initiative, whether by consumers or by producers, through the complex tyranny of all-round rationing, so in peace it is only the application of this principle which will provide the environment in which the choice and initiative of the individual can be safely left free. This is the one kind of compulsion of which the effect is to enlarge liberty. Those who, entangled in old unserviceable maxims, fail to see this further-reaching objective have not grasped, to speak American, the big idea.

Yours, etc.,

J. M. KEYNES

By this time, Keynes had prepared for private circulation both inside and outside Whitehall, a Budget of National Resources which attempted to give the ideas of *How to Pay for the War* further significance in the light of the forthcoming budget.

THE BUDGET OF NATIONAL RESOURCES

The object of the first section of this memorandum is to explain the paradox that, so far, a large increase in government expenditure has been accomplished with only a small increase in output and a moderate rise in prices. The object of the second section is to show that a further increase in the rate of government expenditure is likely to produce consequences of a different order.

The figures suggest that a forthcoming budget of £2,200 to £2,350 million at present prices may not create a serious problem, but that any excess beyond this will require special measures of a new kind.

The method of the following analysis is partly logical, partly statistical. I feel more confidence in the logic than in the statistics, much of which is guess-work. Presumably those in government departments will be able to improve on my statistics. (At least I hope they can. They are neglecting their job if they cannot!) But, in doing so, let them remember that this is a balance sheet. If one figure is altered, the logic of the analysis requires that other figures must also be altered so as to balance it. This method of analysis has the advantage, as anyone will find who allows his mind to bite on it, that it forces the statistics within a consistent framework.

31 March 1940   J. M. KEYNES

I

THE PRESENT NATIONAL BALANCE SHEET

(March 1940)

TABLES OF RECONCILIATION

I. Sources of increased consumption in terms of output at current prices. A			
Increased adverse balance of payments	400 B	Increased government consumption	1300 G
Decreased gross private investment	300 C	Increased civilian consumption in terms of money	100 H
Depletion of stocks	200 D		
Increased value of output through rise of prices	400 E		
Ditto, through increased civilian output	100 F		
	1400		1400

A. The figures in the tables represent annual rates in millions of pounds. They do not relate to actual expenditure over any definite period but are intended to give the present annual *rate* (March 1940). Since various figures and estimates in terms of current prices are now becoming available, these tables are in terms of *current money* and not of pre-war prices.

B. This is an estimate of the increase in the adverse balance of *payments*, not merely in the balance of trade. That is to say, it is intended to include on the adverse side of the account government expenditure abroad (including France and the Empire); on the favourable side the increased earnings of our mercantile marine (including those earned in bringing imports to this country), the *gross* receipts of marine insurance on our own ships (since payments for our own ships which are lost are not foreign outgoings), the *net* receipts of marine insurance on neutral vessels; and the net result of changes in other 'invisibles'.

C. This covers output becoming available through diversion of resources previously devoted to private gross investment in durable goods (i.e. both to making good wastage and to providing new capital assets). It is a very rough guess and a reduction on my previous estimate which has been criticised as allowing too little for current gross investment. If gross investment was previously 700 (of which 300 was paid for out of depreciation and sinking funds and 400 out of new saving), this means that we are estimating *current* gross private investment (making good wastage and new private investment, not paid for directly or indirectly out of government funds) at 400.

D. This (a very rough guess) looks a high figure. Certainly it could not be sustained for any length of time. But a reduction of stocks by 100 in the first six months is not unplausible.

E. This assumes an all-over average rise of price of 7½ to 10 per cent—averaged over output of which the price has risen anything from 5 to 50 per cent and many articles of which the price has not risen at all. Perhaps it is on the low side.

F. This means that, in spite of the withdrawal of (say) 1 million men to the forces, new entrants into industry and overtime have been enough to raise output by about 2 per cent. Government departments, which know, presumably, the number of men now employed, will be able to make a much better guess at this. Perhaps this is an over-estimate; if so it may balance an under-estimate in respect of E. If we were to regard the men with the forces as contributing an output measured by their pay and allowances, board and clothing, perhaps 150 should be added to the above, making a total increased output of 250, which would be the figure comparable with my previous estimate of a *potential* increased output of 825.

G. This is intended to correspond to a total central government expenditure of 2350, which is approximately the rate recently mentioned by the Chancellor of the Exchequer.

H. An increase of 100 in money consumption probably

126

means a decrease of 150–200 in real consumption. But this excludes the consumption of men with the forces, and compares the aggregate consumption of the present civilian population with that of the previous civilian population, although the former has fallen by the number of men withdrawn to the forces. Thus it suggests that the real consumption of the civilian population, after allowing for these withdrawals, is not much changed.

II. Sources of increased government expenditure in terms of finance			
Increased yield of taxes	250 I	Increased government	1300
'Living on capital',	900 J	expenditure	
including normal savings			
Increased private saving	150 K		
	1300		

I. This is not the yield in a specific budget year, but an estimate of the current rate of tax accruals neglecting time-lags in collection. For example, it includes accruing E.P.T. which may not be paid over to the Exchequer until one to two years later.

J. This is made up (as shown in Table 1) of 400 adverse balance of payments financed by sales of gold and foreign investments and increased net credits from overseas, 300 from decreased private gross investment and 200 from depletion of stocks and working capital.

K. Since we have already allowed for 400 normal savings in the previous item, this corresponds to an estimate of 550 for current savings in terms of money. The increase represents 30 per cent of increased money incomes (excluding the forces), and must have been materially assisted by the transfer of purchasing power due to the fact that prices have risen by more than wages (cost of living up, say, 12½ per cent, wages up 5 per cent in round numbers). The increase in real savings is, of course, somewhat less than this—say 100 on the assumption of a rise of 7½ to 10 per cent in the price of output as a whole.

III. Disposal of increased civilian incomes			
Increased civilian incomes	400	Increased taxes	250
due to higher prices		Increased money consumption	100
Ditto from larger output	100	Increased money savings	150
	500		500

II

THE PROSPECTS

The above tables suggest that the first 1300 of increased government consumption has been covered with an increase of only 2 per cent in civilian output, and 7½ to 10 per cent in general prices, and without any material reduction in the aggregate real consumption of the remaining civilian population. Thus the paradox of appearances is adequately explained. No less than 1150 out of the 1300 has been obtained from higher tax revenue and 'living on capital', leaving only 150 to be found out of increased current savings.

But obviously this cannot be repeated as a means of covering a further increase in war expenditure. 'Living on capital' is already at a rate which could not be prudently maintained. There is a physical limit to the possible fall in private gross investment. Depletion of stocks, in particular, has been assumed at a rate which cannot be continued. And our holdings of gold, etc. set a limit to the rise in the adverse balance of payments. Let us assume, however, that the export drive is sufficiently successful to give us a net improvement of 150 on the visible balance of trade, so as to reduce the annual rate of living on capital to 750. In this case the future rate of government expenditure which can be covered on the above lines works out at 2200 (2350−150).

This means *first* that, since we must not increase our rate of living on capital, the source of increased government expenditure beyond some such figure as this must come entirely out of increased output. Another 500 to 600 civilian output should not be by any means out of the question with improved organisation, though not capable of achievement at short notice.

But it means *second* that, if the whole of the increased output is required for government consumption or for export so that nothing more is available for increased civilian consumption, the whole of the increased incomes resulting from this increased output must be either taxed or saved, if we are to avoid inflation; since there is no longer any other substantial source on which the Government can draw.

We have assumed, above, a reduction in the adverse balance of trade through expanding exports. In this connection let me emphasise what most people overlook. Assume that we succeed in increasing exports by 150 (net), partly by increasing output and partly by starving home supplies. This will diminish the item 'living on capital' and conserve our resources (as is necessary) with a view to a long war. But for this very reason it will make us more dependent on current savings, since a reduction in item J in Table II must be balanced (other things being equal) by an increase in item K, and, if the savings situation remains the same, it follows that success in our export drive will have a directly *inflationary* effect on home prices, since it will at the same time increase current incomes and diminish domestic supply. Meanwhile the export drive is impeded by the absence of measures to curtail home consumption, since it is difficult in such conditions to withdraw supplies from the domestic market.

It is, in short, the high proportion of our present expenditure met by 'living on capital' which so far has kept inflation at bay. The *less* we live on capital, the *more* we must save out of current incomes.

Let us return to the probable consequences of a further increase of (say) 350 (to 2700) in government expenditure, accompanied by a reduction of 150 (to 750) in the rate of 'living on capital', and an increase in output by (say) 425. The equilibrium of the rest of the above balance sheet can only be preserved if 500 (350+150) is withheld from current consumption either by taxes or increased saving.

Thus in respect of a further increase in expenditure, especially if it is accompanied by a decrease, rather than an increase, in 'living on capital', the fiscal problem takes on an entirely new face.

Let us suppose that a quarter of the increased incomes is recovered in taxation and one-third of what remains is saved, there will still be an increase of 287 (500−213) in domestic civilian demand. This might be expected to increase retail prices (assuming no increased supply) by 12½ per cent, though the particular retail prices which enter into the official cost of living index might be prevented by subsidies from rising so much.

Now these figures are very moderate and do not look alarming. Since the suggested increase in expenditure would take place gradually, no sudden or sensational development is to be expected. At the worst retail prices might rise at the rate of about 2 per cent a month, *pari passu* with the gradual growth of output and government consumption.

Nevertheless the problem of adjustment which these figures would set us is extremely difficult, if we decide to let things drift. The cost of living has already risen by 12½ per cent, and more than 5 per cent relatively to wage-rates. A further rise of 12½ per cent in retail prices would provoke strong forces to break wages loose from their present moorings. If this is allowed, it is hard to see how, in modern conditions, a galloping inflation can be avoided within a year or eighteen months. With each rise in wages, the cost of the budget would increase; and the movement would soon gain an intolerable impetus.

The alternative ways of avoiding this boil down to only two.

To increase normal taxation by the whole amount required is not practicable. No one expects voluntary savings to be adequate on this scale.

The two alternatives are these:

(1) The most 'efficient' method is that which has been adopted in France; namely to fix wages by decree and allow retail prices to rise by the appropriate amount. This would not involve excessive sacrifice. Real wage *rates* would fall by (say) a further 7½ per cent, which would leave them 12½ per cent to 15 per cent below the pre-war level; which happens to be the actual fall in France up to date, apart from their heavy tax on overtime wages, since wage rates are fixed and the cost of living has risen by 14 per cent. Moreover, overtime and better employment might mean that real *earnings* would not decline by more than 5 per cent. They would remain, therefore, higher than at any time until recently—much higher than during the last war, and much higher than in any other belligerent country.

A variant of this method would be a flat 7½ per cent tax on wages accompanied by a stable price level.

(2) Some brand of compulsory savings by which earnings cannot be fully spent. One leading type of this is something on the broad lines of 'deferred pay' proposals. Another leading type is a system of rationing so comprehensive that full expenditure of earnings becomes impracticable or has to be spilt in ways which do not exhaust resources. The latter system would involve so much irritation, waste of time, waste of satisfaction, and complication of the administrative machine that I do not see how anyone in his senses could prefer it to 'deferred pay'.

The choice between wage fixing or wage taxing and deferred pay must depend mainly on social and political considerations. The former is the simpler and very likely the more efficient method. The main objection to it is that it is not graded to different levels of earnings; and unless the result is reached by wage taxing, the profit-earning class will inevitably obtain a rake-off from the higher prices *en route* to the Treasury. The advantage of 'deferred pay' in this and other respects I have argued elsewhere.

If the prospective budget is greater or less than £2,700 million, the above figures can be adjusted and the probable consequences modified accordingly.

It will be observed that the financial problem set by a budget of the above order is, in a sense, extremely mild. (Perhaps not quite so mild as these figures suggest—I have aimed throughout at under-statement.) It is difficult only because it involves putting some restriction on the expenditure of earnings by the group with £10 a week or less. Since this group is responsible for at least three-quarters of present consumption, this is unavoidable. Fortunately the overall reduction required is quite modest and need not threaten the standard of life of those with only a narrow margin above the poverty line, if we choose so to arrange. Severe curtailment of consumption only becomes necessary when the Budget approaches or exceeds £3,000 million.

When the Budget of 23 April 1940 came, introducing purchase tax but little else, Keynes wrote to *The Times*.

To the Editor of The Times, *25 April 1940*

Sir,

The first outstanding feature of the Budget is Sir John Simon's assumption that a failure of the civilian departments to increase our war output will protect him from the full severity of the financial problem, not merely at the present time, but for a whole year to come. Common observation confirms unfortunately the Chancellor's estimate that there will be no great increase over the present rate of expenditure in the near future; but it is disconcerting to be told that at the end of this calendar year the position will not be greatly different. We, by far the richest country per head of the three major belligerents, propose, it seems, to content ourselves, not merely in the preliminary months, with a war effort which falls far short either of our enemy's or of our ally's. I hesitate to quote exact statistics which it is difficult to verify. But it is certainly true that we should have to spend £500 million more than the present estimate before our war effort in relation to our resources would begin to approach the effort either of Germany or of France. Sir John Simon may claim that this is his fortune and not his fault. For the rest of us it is our misfortune and far from our intention. When I read in the press that this Budget is on 'an heroic scale', I marvel how little the country understands (and how shamefully little the Chancellor does to enlighten it) what sacrifices victory will require.

That Sir John Simon has not disclosed any serious attempt to solve even the limited problem which the spending departments have set him is the Budget's other feature. Taking his estimates of prospective revenue and expenditure, and assuming a rate of private saving about the same as that which appears to have prevailed in the last three months, the gap which remains to be filled is of the order of £500 million. Towards this he offers us two contributions, both of them excellent, regarded as secondary and supporting measures. The first is the new purchase tax, for which we are given as yet no details of yield or scale. After deducting the various exempt categories one can, within a margin of error of some 10 per cent, estimate the recent volume of purchases on which the tax would fall at £950 million, reckoned at retail prices or (say) £650 million at wholesale prices; but these figures are on the assumption that saving will not increase and would be much lower (as will be the yield of other indirect taxes) if the Chancellor's ostensible expectations on this head are realised. If he is contemplating a rate of tax averaging 50 per cent of the wholesale price, thus yielding £325 million, he will be tackling his problem seriously. If, on the other hand, something more like 15 per cent is in his mind, yielding about £100 million in a full year and much less in the current year, we are not much further forward. Moreover two-fifths of the taxed expenditure is on boots and clothing, so that we have here just the opposite, so to speak, of family allowances.

The second contribution is the limitation of ordinary dividends. I am grateful to the Chancellor for adopting a part (albeit by much the smaller part) of my proposals for compulsory savings, since it shows that he does not reject the idea wholeheartedly. I suggested to him that company profits in excess of those in the base year not taken in E.P.T. should be retained in a blocked deposit, which is substantially what he proposes. On the other hand, his E.P.T. estimate indicates that the sum involved this year cannot exceed £40 million; and since the whole of this would not have been distributed in any case, we can put the extra contribution at not above £25 million.

Provisionally, therefore, I estimate the contribution from these two sources together (hoping but not expecting to be wrong) at not so much as £100 million in this current year, which leaves £400 million extra to be found from voluntary savings. Six hundred million pounds per annum is an outside estimate for the rate of new voluntary savings from all sources in the first quarter of this year. The Chancellor is therefore choosing to assume that this rate of saving will be raised from now onwards to £1,000 million. More than half of present saving is through institutions, the capacity of which to save is narrowly fixed by various circumstances. Thus the Chancellor pretends to believe that from now onwards voluntary personal savings will be at a rate more than twice what they have been hitherto. He assumes that beginning with next week Sir Robert Kindersley will increase the net sale of savings certificates from £2 million a week to between £4 million and £5 million a week, and that all other sources of individual savings will increase in the same proportion. It seems optimistic.

Sir John Simon's remarks on my proposal for deferred pay need no comment from me at this stage. Sooner or later he has to choose between (1) progressive inflation; (2) the fixing of wages and a limited inflation; (3) shop shortages and comprehensive rationing; (4) a tax on wages; and (5) deferred pay. None of these expedients is free from objection. It is not useful or interesting to defend one of them except against an alternative. The alternative which Sir John Simon prefers he is keeping, for the present, to himself.

I have been reading this week Mr Arthur Hope-Jones's new and fascinating study of Pitt's income tax.[48] In 1799, in the sixteenth of the nineteen Budgets he was destined to introduce, William Pitt came to the conclusion that he needed a new fiscal instrument beyond those already at his disposal if he was to overcome Napoleon; though at the height of that war the Exchequer needed only a quarter of the national income, while we shall need a half of it. In the face of orthodox opinion and of intense unpopularity in the country he brought in the income tax. It was the support of the House of Commons which alone made such a measure possible. 'The comparison of the Roman Senate fighting Hannibal', Professor Trevelyan has written, 'was in the mind of every educated man.' Reorganized in the light of experience in 1803 with its schedules A, B, C, and D as we still know them, and again in 1805 in Pitt's last Budget, yielding nearly a quarter of the revenue at the end of the war, it became the indispensable novelty in the financial system under which on that occasion we rid Europe of tyranny. Let us hope for another, a real, Budget in six months' time in which the Chancellor will prove to us that we still have a Pitt at the Exchequer.

Yours, etc.,

J. M. KEYNES

[48] A. Hope-Jones, *Income Tax in the Napoleonic Wars* (Cambridge, 1939).

After the Budget, Keynes set out the position as he saw it in his preface to a prospective French edition of *How to Pay for the War*. The edition itself was to follow the corrected English edition,[49] except that it would lack the material on the French situation.[50] Owing to the German conquest of France, it was never published.

PREFACE TO THE FRENCH EDITION

The fiscal systems of France and Great Britain have very little in common. The proportion of the national income now taken by the Treasuries of the two countries is, I believe, much the same in the aggregate;—allowing for the war increase of incomes in terms of money due to higher prices and other causes, taxation amounts in each case to between 20 and 25 per cent of the aggregate of personal incomes. But in method and detail the two systems are widely different. In particular, the classes, which escape from the tax-gatherer's net or are, at least, relatively less burdened, are not the same. In France, I suspect, it is the larger agriculturalists who get off lightly, in spite of the heavy handicaps under which they work as the result of mobilisation; for the prices they obtain have risen substantially, whilst so much of their income is of a kind which is not easily reached by direct taxes. In Great Britain, on the other hand, the favoured class is that part of the working and middle classes with incomes from £5 to £12 a week, which includes to-day a considerable number of the most highly paid trade unionists. The class with incomes below £5 are probably paying on the average 13 to 14 per cent of their incomes as a result of the burden of indirect taxes. But the class immediately above these is not paying more than 10 per cent even allowing for the heavier direct taxes imposed on this class in last autumn's first war budget. At the other end of the scale the class of surtax payers (those with more than £2,000 a year) are now so heavily taxed (the percentage of direct taxes to income rising to 80 per cent and over at the higher levels) that, whilst social and political reasons may require still further

<hr>

[49] *JMK*, vol. IX, VI (2).   [50] *Ibid.* pp. 425–8.

burdens, this class is now exhausted as a further source of substantial revenue.

An important, but not the only, object of what follows is, therefore, to devise a means by which the state can secure substantial further resources from the intermediate range of incomes in a manner compatible with social justice and the maintenance of morale and incentive to effort, and avoiding undue sacrifice,—as well as serving certain further-reaching purposes which I shall explain. The proposed system of deferred pay would have somewhat the same effect in preventing inflation by withholding purchasing power from the market which is produced in France by the fixation of wages and the various levies on wages, in particular the levy on overtime earnings. In Great Britain wages have not been fixed and have in fact risen on the average by at least 5 per cent since the outbreak of war; whilst there is no tax on wages or on overtime unless they reach the income tax level. It is evident that my proposal for Great Britain is milder than the system already in force in France if it is measured by the ultimate, as distinguished from the immediate, sacrifice asked from those with modest incomes; it is better calculated to preserve an incentive to maximum effort; and it is more easily combined with provisions to protect the standard of life of the group with the lowest incomes and particularly of families. I shall be interested to learn whether instructed opinion in France considers that there would be advantages in mitigating the existing rigour of the French taxes on *nombreux petits artisans, de modestes employés et de petits fonctionnaires, sur qui les impôts pèsent très lourdement, notamment la 'contribution nationale'*, by substituting something on these lines. The more closely the sacrifices asked of the two countries can be assimilated, the better for the state of opinion in both countries.

I need not repeat in this preface the explanations which are to follow. But perhaps I can usefully distinguish at once the war objects and the post-war objects of my plan. We must be ready for a long war and the greatest possible effort. We shall not solve the financial problem merely with our old tools and without forging a new one. I claim for the following plan that it gives that new tool which we need, that by establishing a basis of social justice it lays a sound foundation for yet further efforts, and that its productivity is capable of being increased if the course of events requires it. After the war the release of the deferred pay will provide us with a useful and justifiable way of increasing demand when we are confronted with the post-war slump; which, by allowing individuals to choose for themselves what they require, will save us from having to devise large-scale government plans of expenditure which may not correspond so closely to personal need. After the last war the productive forces of France received the necessary stimulus by the necessity of restoring the devastated areas. After the present war we are confident that there will be no such necessity. But this will make all the more essential the stimulus for releasing deferred pay by which all sorts of sensible, desirable capital expenditures by individual initiative will be made possible.

Thus, quite apart from its primary purpose to finance the war, it would be worth while to introduce deferred pay at a time of scarce resources such as at the present, if only with the object of releasing it subsequently at a time of surplus resources and so preventing the shameful malady of unemployment. I think of it as a first instalment of a comprehensive social policy to regulate the general rate of spending so as to avoid the disastrous alternations of boom and slump which otherwise will continue to undermine the foundations of society. War provides an example *par excellence* of a state of boom. It is much better to start our regulation by an artificial restriction of general spending power in time of boom than to begin with an artificial expansion of it in time of slump, which is what, otherwise, will be forced on us.

I am not proposing an expedient, undesirable for its own

sake, just for the purpose of financing the war. I am seizing an opportunity, where the need is obvious and overwhelming, to introduce a principle of policy which may come to be thought of as marking the line of division between the totalitarian and the free economy. For if the community's aggregate rate of spending can be regulated, the way in which personal incomes are spent and the means by which demand is satisfied can be safely left free and individual. Just as in the war the regulation of aggregate spending is the only way to avoid the destruction of choice and initiative, whether by consumers or by producers, through the complex tyranny of all-round rationing, so in peace it is only the application of this principle which will provide the environment in which the choice and initiative of the individual can be safely left free. This is the one kind of compulsion of which the effect is to enlarge liberty.

It may interest French readers to have some account of the way in which these proposals have been received by the British public. From the date when the first version of them appeared in *The Times* in November 1939 they have at least received publicity, attention and discussion on an extraordinary scale. No one expects demands on behalf of the Treasury to be received by the general public with enthusiasm or acclamation. Yet they have received strong support in every political and social class from directors of the Bank of England to members of the trade unionist council. They have been widely supported in articles in the left-wing press and the journals of the co-operators, and have been approved in principle by almost every academic economist in the country. The most usual criticism has been on the lines, not that the proposal is wrong in principle, but that it is premature and that the necessity for supplementing in this or any other way the results of normal taxation and voluntary saving is not yet sufficiently obvious to the general public. 'We may come to it later' is a frequent comment.

Outspoken opposition was met with at first in two quarters only. The Communist press, led by the *Daily Worker*, and Sir Robert Kindersley, the chairman of the National Savings Movement, find themselves in an unaccustomed agreement that the proposal is a dangerous interference with the freedom of the individual worker to dispose of his earnings as he chooses. Sir Robert Kindersley believes that voluntary savings will be sufficient and that the discussion of deferred pay interferes with the success of his propaganda in favour of the voluntary method.

Subsequently the opinion of the Labour Front Bench seemed to harden against this or any other proposal for restricting the purchasing power of wage earners. They are demanding larger expenditure and a more intensive effort on the part of the government to increase employment. But they are still at the stage, politically speaking, of demanding that curtailments of purchasing power should fall only on the better-to-do classes.

Finally the Chancellor of the Exchequer in his April Budget rejected the proposal mainly on the ground of its possible effect in discouraging voluntary savings. But he offered no alternative in its place. He outlined a new purchase tax but gave no indication of its scale, its yield or when it would come into operation. No one expects that it will yield above £100 million at the utmost, which will do but little to fill the gap.

The main weight of public criticism, however, has fallen on another aspect of the Budget, namely the inadequacy of the expenditure which it foreshadows during the coming year. Public opinion demands that the war effort of Great Britain should be greatly accelerated beyond the present programme of the Chancellor of the Exchequer.

Nevertheless even on the scale of expenditure contemplated by the Chancellor, voluntary savings would have to rise to about double their present rate if they were to fill the gap.

It is quite clear, on a cool consideration of the figures, that those who believe in the adequacy of the voluntary system unaided by a new and drastic measure are deceiving themselves. And indeed there is hardly any responsible authority in the City or the Civil Service or the financial press who agrees with the Chancellor of the Exchequer that voluntary savings can be adequate.

It is widely held, therefore, that the April Budget must be regarded as an interim measure to be supplemented by much more drastic proposals in the autumn when public sentiment will be more ready for them. So far it has not been too difficult to remain blind to the ultimate necessities of the position because it has in fact been possible to finance the scale of British expenditure up to date largely out of the heavier 'normal' taxation imposed last autumn, a modest rise in prices relatively to wages, and (predominantly) out of various capital resources. I calculate that out of the first £1,300 million additional war expenditure by the British Treasury about £900 million has been found out of various capital resources including normal saving and £250 million out of the increased yield of taxes, leaving only about £150 million to be met out of new efforts and out of the profits resulting from the above rise in prices. These resources, however, have been already exploited to the utmost. Indeed 'living on capital', through the adverse balance of payments, financed by the sale of gold and foreign securities, and through the exhaustion of stocks of commodities and working capital, has been already carried beyond the rate which can be maintained for any length of time. Thus the next £500 million will need a new method if inflation is to be avoided.

I believe that much the same situation exists in France, where the effort up to date has been financed on much too large a scale for indefinite continuation out of the adverse balance of trade met, as in the case of Great Britain, by the disposal of foreign resources.

To meet the fiscal problems which are certain to arise no serious proposal has yet been brought forward officially. Sooner or later the Chancellor of the Exchequer has to choose between (1) progressive inflation; (2) the fixing of wages and a limited inflation; (3) shop shortages and comprehensive rationing; (4) a tax on wages; and (5) deferred pay. None of these expedients is free from objection. It is not easy to defend one of them except against an alternative. That the proposal for deferred pay has important advantages is evident.

Meanwhile let France remain assured that the British public are far from satisfied with the magnitude of the present war effort and that beyond doubt it will be enormously increased. For winning the war this is more important than the precise fiscal measures adopted to finance it. Inadequate preparation is a far more serious danger than unsound finance. Nevertheless our power to persist over an indefinite period ahead will be much enhanced if the Chancellor of the Exchequer will have the courage to lay sound financial foundations.

4 May 1940   J. M. KEYNES

The emphasis on expenditure inadequacy in Keynes's letter of 25 April and in the French preface (above p. 140) reflected a change in tactics, as he told Clement Davies[51] on 3 May.

From a letter to CLEMENT DAVIES, *3 May 1940*

I agree with you that the point should soon come for replacing mere criticism by a constructive programme. My own feeling is that the time is perhaps not just yet.

There is not the slightest hope of getting any useful attention just at this stage. Things have clearly got to stew a bit. Is there not a risk of wasting one's ammunition by discharging it prematurely? I feel one must wait until the progress of events is making some new action obviously necessary.

[51] Clement Davies (1844–1962); barrister; Junior Counsel to Treasury, 1919–25; Liberal M.P. for Montgomeryshire, from 1929; Leader of Parliamentary Liberal Party, 1945–56.

At the present stage I believe there is a good deal to be said for concentrating on the inadequacy of the spending programme rather than on the inadequacy of the fiscal programme. If we can get what is wanted done in the former respect, the inadequacy of the latter will soon be shown up. I should, therefore, press the point as to how far the Treasury are deliberately curtailing home expenditure, as distinct from foreign expenditure which the supply departments are pressing. Take, for example, a case mentioned to me the other day by Oliver Lyttelton[52], though I suppose one should treat it in confidence, since he is the non-ferrous metals controller. He is not allowed to buy all the electrolytic copper he wants in U.S.A. to save dollars, which he agrees is probably quite right. But, when he then applies for cash to set up an electrolytic refinery in this country, months pass before he can get the expenditure through the Treasury. Or again, we are running very short of zinc, but the Treasury obstruct all applications for expenditure in this country to increase our capacity to smelt.

All this, unless my memory is greatly at fault, is quite different from the last war, except possibly in the very early months. After L. G. went to the Ministry of Munitions there was no effective Treasury control whatever of home expenditure, as distinct from foreign expenditure. But this time I suspect that the low figure of prospective outgoings is the deliberate consequence of the Treasury having taken every possible opportunity to obstruct the war effort at home.

I suggest, therefore, that this is the line on which to concentrate the assault at the present moment, leaving constructive fiscal suggestions until a later date. All this, however, is a

[52] Oliver Lyttleton (1893–1972), 1st Viscount Chandos, 1954; Controller of Non-Ferrous Metals, 1939–40; Unionist M.P. for Aldershot, 1940–54; President, Board of Trade, 1940–1; Minister of State in Middle East and Member of War Cabinet, 1941–2; Minister of Production and Member of War Cabinet, 1942–5; President, Board of Trade and Minister of Production, May–July, 1945; Secretary of State for the Colonies, 1951–4.

question of politics on which you are a much better judge than
I am.

Keynes's final discussion of war finance, his last before rejoining the
Treasury,[53] appeared in America on 29 July.

From The New Republic, *29 July 1940*

THE UNITED STATES AND THE KEYNES PLAN

I

In the early days of the war I proposed a financial plan for
Great Britain. It was based on certain premises which should
be obvious and are certainly beyond dispute. War effort on
the scale required in Great Britain must swell the wages bill.
For employment has increased, longer hours are being
worked at high overtime rates and the wage rates themselves
are rising. On the other hand, it is evident that there can be
no similar increase in the amount of goods available for
private consumption, since the whole object of the employment is to produce for war. On the contrary, an adequate war
effort will require some diversion of the production effort
which provided previously for private consumption. Thus
a larger purchasing power will face a smaller volume of
purchasable goods. If nothing is done about it, the sure
consequence must be a rise in prices until the smaller volume
of goods sells for an amount of money equal to the larger
volume of purchasing power. In this way equilibrium is
restored—but at the cost of two serious evils.

For, while aggregate earnings are rising, this does not
mean that the earnings of everyone alike will rise. There will,
therefore, be many individual cases of great hardship. In the
second place, the workers will lose entirely any increased real
reward corresponding to their increased labours. They will
work harder, but they will consume less; and that will be the

---

[53] Keynes had sent the manuscript off on 27 June.

end of the whole matter. The machinery of war finance will have operated by the rise in price diverting real purchasing power away from the consumer to the profit-earning class, who in turn will transfer a large part of these profits to the Treasury and will also save out of them, chiefly perhaps in the shape of undistributed profits. Prices will rise to whatever extent is required to achieve the necessary restriction in real consumption, though the rise will have to be progressive if the war lasts for any length of time. I was able to show that all this is exactly what happened in the last war.

It means, put shortly, that at the end of the war it is the profit-earning class which owns, in the shape of holdings in the national war debt, a claim on future production; while the wage-earning class, in spite of the extra work done, owns nothing, having lost the right to consume now and having gained no rights to consume hereafter. On top of this we have the evil and familiar social consequence of what is usually called inflation.

My prescription to remedy this was simple and straight-forward. In time of war the goods available to consumers are fixed by other considerations than the amount of employment. The size of the cake which can be spared for the civilian population is more or less fixed. Thus, if by some general plan or agreement, consumers spend only a part of their aggregate money incomes, they will be able between them to buy just about as much as if they spent all their incomes, while the unspent balance will still be theirs to spend after the war when productive power can again be released to provide consumers' goods. I described this as a plan to prevent people from getting in one another's way in the shops without affecting how much or what they buy, and I compared it to the rule of the road by which automobiles are prevented from getting in one another's way without reducing the volume of the traffic or changing its destination.

In detail the plan took the form of proposals for deferred

pay on a graduated scale, by which a suitable proportion of everyone's income was withheld by the Treasury either as taxes or as a blocked savings deposit which would not be available, generally speaking (a reasonable number of exceptions were allowed), until after the war. In the case of the richer classes the greater part of their contribution was to be withheld permanently as a tax; in the case of the working classes the greater part or the whole was to be withheld temporarily as compulsory saving and returned to them after the war. There were generous safeguards to protect those with low earnings or with large families. I give a few specimen illustrations in round numbers worked out for married men without taking account of the children's allowance of $65 per child (I have converted sterling at the rate of $5 to £1, which will give a truer comparison to American readers than the wartime rate of $4 to £1):

Total income $	Percentage withheld	Taxes $	Deferred income $
500,000	85	404,000	21,000
50,000	64	26,000	6,000
25,000	54	10,250	3,250
10,000	42½	2,825	1,425
5,000	35	1,100	650
3,000	28	460	380
2,000	25	150	350
1,500	22	75	250
1,000	15	Nil	150
750	8¾	Nil	65
625	3½	Nil	22
Below 625	Nil	Nil	Nil

By this device a number of distinct purposes could be served. A considerable drag would be put on the forces driving up prices and the Treasury would obtain large funds towards the prosecution of the war without the agency of inflation. The workers would receive in due course a real reward appropriate to their war effort. The same plan could be employed to put those engaged on active war service more clearly on an equality with those who had stayed at home in better paid jobs. The biggest step yet would have been taken towards reducing the inequality of incomes. The safeguards attached to the scheme would actually improve, even during the war, the economic status of large families. Moreover, the post-war release of purchasing power might be so timed as to mitigate the evils of the next depression. For the debt thus created would have a signal advantage over past war debts in that the prospective purchasing power which it represents would belong to the general body of consumers and might be expected, therefore, to find its way, when it was released, into consumers' goods, and not so exclusively into producers' goods as if it mainly belonged, as on previous occasions, to the entrepreneurs and profit-earning class. Most economists agreed with me that it was a good plan. But good plans, alas, do not often commend themselves to politicians, who would have succumbed long ago in the bitter struggle for the survival of the unfit—which politics is—if they had ever formed the habit of allowing the merits of what was put before them to obscure their judgment.

II

Now I am asked to say whether any version of this plan would be suitable to the United States in the present circumstances. I reply that the habit and mode of thought which lie behind it are exceedingly relevant to the American problem. My British plan is merely a particular example of a way of thinking about public finance which is of universal application. But I must add that, to the best of my judgment, the United States is still a long way off the special situation for which my British plan was devised.

In past years we, like you, have suffered from chronic underemployment. In those days I argued that the restoration of prosperity required that we should combine inducements to invest in producers' goods with inducements to spend on consumers' goods. More investment *and* more spending. But in conditions of war the facts are precisely reversed, with the result that the same principles of thought led to the opposite practical conclusion. Investment for war has not the remotest connection with private consumption and has no need of the latter to keep it going. On the contrary it was likely in Britain to reduce the supply available for private consumers. In the second place, it was certain that a scale of war investment adequate to our needs, together with the calling up of hundreds of thousands of men to the armed forces, must lead to a state of full employment, after which further war investment can only be made at the expense of normal investment and consumption. One had to expect that the requirements of war investment would be so gigantic compared with our normal scale of investment that we should be faced with the novel consequences of a pressure toward more than full employment. With the approach of such conditions, the practical advice of the economist must suffer a sea-change. More war investment and *less* private spending became the new order of the day.

Why do I say that the United States is a long way from this state of affairs? It is because I am convinced of a fact of overwhelming importance—the most important economic fact to Americans, if I am right that it is a fact, which it is possible to state.

The experiences of Great Britain after nine months of war and of Germany during her years of intense preparation confirm in a high degree the inference which might be drawn with less confidence from the comparative failure of New Deal expenditure out of borrowed funds to produce even an approach to full employment in the United States. I am aware that other explanations of the latter phenomenon are favoured in some quarters; and I should concede that certain of these are not without force as accessory factors working in the wrong direction. But the main explanation of what has happened this year in Great Britain and for several years in the United States is, I am certain, the gigantic powers of production, far exceeding any previous experience, of a modern industrial economy. Coupled with institutional factors which tend to encourage accumulation and retard the growth of consumption when incomes increase, this means that an unprecedented output has to be reached before a state of full employment can be approached. Temporary bottlenecks can be reached and a lack of balance between specialised resources which take a little time and some skill to overcome.

But, subject to the necessary pangs and lags of preparation and reorganisation, I hesitate to estimate the full industrial and agricultural capacity of the United States. It may well exceed 1929 by as much as, or even more than, 1929 exceeded 1914. The wealth-producing capacity which is now going to waste in the United States is so far beyond our powers of measurement that it is useless to hazard a figure for it. The conclusion is that at all recent times investment expenditure has been on a scale which was hopelessly inadequate to the problem, and it is not unlikely that this would have remained true, except temporarily, even if the attendant political considerations had stimulated private-enterprise investment instead of retarding it. Even if a complete harmony between the administration and private enterprise had achieved, momentarily, a satisfactory economic recovery, it would not have endured more than a few months, with institutions and the distribution of spending power what they are today. That full employment would have been reached even so, I do not believe—any more that it was in 1928–29.

It is, it seems, politically impossible for a capitalistic democracy to organize expenditure on the scale necessary to make the grand experiments which would prove my case—except in war conditions. It is thus that, not for the first time in the

SHARE OF BUDGET GOING TO DEFENSE

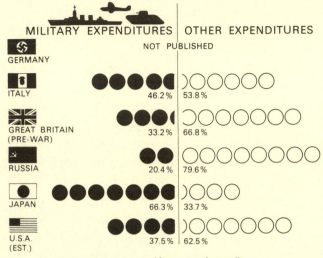

Each symbol represents 10 per cent of expenditures

PICTORIAL STATISTICS, INC

fluctuating fortunes of mankind, good may come out of evil. If the United States takes seriously the material and economic side of the defence of civilisation and steels itself to a vast dissipation of resources in the preparation of arms, it will learn its strength—learn it as it can never learn it otherwise; learn a lesson that can be turned to account afterward to reconstruct a world which will understand the first principles governing the production of wealth and which can endeavour —a harder task—to put it to good use. In the sphere of economics and politics, the mass of men believe nothing which they have not seen, and have no teacher but experience. My own country learns nothing except by dreadful experience. Yours is the same, but is offered an easier path if you will take it.

Let me return to the details of the argument. I said that recent experience in Germany and Great Britain went to prove that we had greatly underestimated the volume of loan expenditure which is required to bring a modern industrial economy to a state of full employment. In the case of Germany the appeal must be to the broad facts rather than to exact statistics. The question is asked everywhere how Germany was able to make so vast a preparation and accumulate great stocks with no outside resources to draw upon and a vast number of men under arms. Even after allowing for the restrictions on current consumption, the enormous potential productive power of modern industry is the only answer. The experience of Great Britain after nine months of war can be stated more precisely. After allowing for the reduction in private investment, for the depletion of stocks, for the drafts on our foreign resources and for the rise in prices, the current rate of aggregate loan expenditure (public and private together) approaches, and perhaps exceeds, three times what it was a year ago; while at the same time between five and ten per cent of the active male population has been withdrawn to the army. Nevertheless, we have not yet (June, 1940) reached full employment, though we may be approaching it, and the utilisation of female labour has scarcely begun.

In the United States a comparable expansion of loan expenditure would be accompanied by a much greater increase in consumption than has been possible in Great Britain in war conditions, a factor which we can offset against our greater withdrawals of men to the army. On the other hand, the potential expansion may well be greater, if we allow for the elapse of a little time, than in Great Britain. In any case there will be many obstacles to a rapid expansion, as we have found to our misfortune. If there is a great increase in war preparations in the United States, the results which I forecast will not occur overnight but will be a steady process over at least a year to come which will give time, and cannot mature until it has been given time, for many readjustments.

I shall not attempt to translate this forecast into statistical terms. No one can say just how much loan expenditure is required to give full employment in the American industrial and institutional environment until we actually try the experiment. It is possible that the time may come when a further expansion in the United States could only be made at the expense of consumption. My plan for Great Britain would then deserve your examination. But I feel sure that this is a long way off. It will not come quickly or suddenly. I should not expect it unless the United States was also supporting a large army in the field, which is a contingency we need not now contemplate. We should not have reached it or approached it in Great Britain even yet, if we had not a great army on a war basis. There is, therefore, no reason why the United States Treasury should be searching out ways to restrict consumption or to stimulate saving by compulsory methods. Normal saving should be adequate without the aid of any greater rise in prices than is inevitable in the event of any large increase in output, however caused. Some increase in prices is inevitable when output increases, as a reflection of the rise in wages and other costs which always accompany such increases. It is not easy to say just when this movement changes its character and takes on the qualities of a progressive inflation, but the distinction is a real one.

Thus the economic consequences of war preparation in the United States, even on a vast scale, are likely to be, for some time at least, essentially different in character from those which confront us in Great Britain. If our war effort is to be adequate, it is necessary that we should curtail our private consumption. You are more fortunate. Your war preparation, so far from requiring a sacrifice, will be the stimulus, which neither the victory nor the defeat of the New Deal could give you, to greater individual consumption and a higher standard of life. You can still invest more *and* spend more. Only in circumstances which no one now contemplates is the reversal, which we in Great Britain are experiencing, likely to come to pass with you; a reversal which is only necessary when you have climbed all the way to the top of the curve of employment.

III

The problems before the United States are of a different kind. I see no major fiscal problem, no need of a special stimulus to saving or of other means to restrict consumption. On the contrary, if the expenditures now contemplated for Great Britain and the far greater expenditures required to put the American War Department in a state of full preparation, are actually fulfilled, it is certain that a great revival of business prosperity and of general consumption must follow.

The difficulties will arise in the initial task of fulfilling the orders with a reasonable rapidity, and not in the subsequent results of their fulfilment. Naval expansion, in particular, is a matter, not of months, but of years; indeed, months are likely to elapse before any large expenditures are practicable. In other directions we can hope for much more rapid results. It may be that the modern American engineer knows how to move quickly. But hitherto all experience goes to show, not least in the United States during the last war, that there are many preliminary troubles to overcome before a new type of mass production can be put into rapid motion. Thus the effective rate of expenditure in the near future may be disappointing.

The best thing that can happen at this stage of expansion is a sufficient confidence that large expenditures on war preparations will mature eventually, to induce American industry to prepare now by a prospective increase of inventories, and by a greater production of durable consumers' goods, such as houses, against the time of a material increase in consumers' purchasing power. But, as recent experience shows, this also has its dangers in the volatile, indeed light-headed, atmosphere of American business. For the preparations run a risk of sudden reversal if they step too far ahead of the more fundamental developments. The American forecaster seems to swing uneasily between trying to peer into the inscrutable distance and refusing to take into account any factor which is more than a week or two off; which is a serious obstacle to stable progress. If I am to risk entering this uneasy business myself, I should advise that the safest course is to be found in a strong and steady optimism which does not expect too much soon but does not doubt the eventual outcome.

And perhaps that is good advice to us all.

IV

A problem of another kind remains for your attention—a task whose significance for America's future comes next in order to the primary duty of throwing the material resources of the United States into the struggle against the powers of evil and destruction.

Let us suppose that the preparations for war now set on foot do indeed restore a measure of prosperity which has not been seen for a decade. You will find yourselves ill prepared for the attendant problems. Almost every contemporary social policy is directed to an environment which will have disappeared overnight. Yet the new and unfamiliar aspects of the social scene will present not less strenuous brain-twisters. Is the war boom to be just like any other boom—like the last war boom in fact—an orgy of profits, gambling, soaring and disproportionate wages and prices? A hectic episode of no lasting significance or value, carrying the seeds of later chaos?

I was nursing higher hopes than that when I said that this emergency might result in your making the grand experiment, which would never be made otherwise, to discover what level of total output accompanied by what level of consumption is needed to bring a free, modern community having the intense development of the United States within sight of the optimum employment of its resources. Is it vain to suppose that a democracy can be wise and sensible? Must the poison of popular politics make impotent every free community? So much hangs on the issue that it is our duty to believe that we can do what we should, until the opposite is proved.

The first condition of a successful outcome is a moderation of mind and speech on both sides. It is only by a gradual evolution of institutions and of business organisation and of the instruments of government that the transition can be made. Recrimination and old hates are out of place. The reformers must believe that it is worth while to concede a great deal to preserve that decentralisation of decisions and of power which is the prime virtue of the old individualism. In a world of destroyers, they must zealously protect the variously woven fabric of society, even when this means that some abuses must be spared. Civilisation is a tradition from the past, a miraculous construction made by our fathers of which they knew the vulnerability better than we do, hard to come by and easily lost. We have to escape from the *invalidism* of the Left which has eaten up the wisdom and inner strength of many good causes.

The old guard of the Right, on their side, must surely recognise, if any reason or any prudence is theirs, that the existing system is palpably disabled, that the idea of its continuing to function unmodified with half the world in dissolution is just sclerotic. Let them learn from the experiences of Great Britain and of Europe that there has been a rottenness at the heart of our society, and do not let them suppose that America is healthy. But I am travelling far from my brief...

Chapter 3

OPERATIONS ON OTHER FRONTS—FEBRUARY TO JUNE 1940

Keynes's preoccupations with *How to Pay for the War* did not prevent him from taking a continuing interest in other aspects of wartime economic policy, in particular exchange control.

At the outbreak of war, the exchange control set up by the British authorities allowed non-residents to dispose of their sterling balances and securities on a separate market not subject to exchange control or official support. It also permitted British exporters to invoice their sales in sterling. As long as this regime continued, non-residents could reduce their sterling assets through free (or black) market sales of foreign exchange to other non-residents who might use the proceeds to purchase British exports. In these circumstances, the exports added nothing to Britain's capacity to purchase goods abroad. Attempts to remove this gap came slowly, but the first, requiring hard currency invoicing of exports of tin, rubber, jute, whisky and furs from the sterling area in March 1940 reduced the usefulness of non-resident sterling and, hence, the demand for it.

Initially, Keynes had unsuccessfully raised the matter of exchange control evasion through transactions in outstanding securities in a letter to Sir Frederick Phillips on 22 February, after a Treasury order requisitioning American securities led to offers of large blocks of BATs (British American Tobacco) shares from America.[1] On 4 March, he promised Phillips a memorandum on the whole problem of exchange control as soon as he was 'less preoccupied in other directions', while the next day he lunched with the Governor of the Bank of England and doubtless discussed the matter. On 12 March he raised another aspect of the problem with D. H. Robertson, then working in the Treasury.

Much consoled to see yesterday's heavy drop in the black sterling rate. The extraordinary policy of the last six months must have cost the country a frightful lot. If, as seems to me certain, we have to put on full restriction sooner or later, it is a pure loss of resources without any compensating gain, to postpone it.

[1] Keynes became aware of this as a result of his activities as an investor, for the requisition order had left him with £1 million to invest in replacement securities.

However, it was Richard Kahn who, working in the Board of Trade, seems to have spurred Keynes to more activity. On 14 March, on the basis of his official experience, he suggested that Keynes try and explode the myth that a discount on black sterling in relation to the official rate of $4.03 was anything but an advantage. To this letter, Keynes replied:

From a letter to R. F. KAHN, *16 March 1940*

The more I think about it and the more extensive the information which reaches me, the more convinced I am that you are quite right about the lunacy of the present exchange control, and particularly about the level of the black rate. Indeed, I wrote to Dennis a few days ago saying how comforted I feel by its decline and pointing out that its previous high rate was symptomatic of the large amount which we must have been losing previously.

All the same, I am much perplexed as to how best to attack it controversially. The matter is frightfully technical,[2] of a kind which you cannot possibly expect the public to understand or form a judgment on. I should think there are hardly more than half a dozen people in the country whose opinion is worth having. Also, in matters of detail, it is extraordinarily difficult to be quite sure of one's facts. And I have learned to be cautious about public controversy unless I feel that I know the other fellow's case beforehand better than he knows it himself. Even if I were not at present using up my publicity powers on another subject, I should rather wonder whether it was the slightest use ventilating this; apart from the fact that public ventilation does no good abroad and calls the attention of foreigners to loopholes of which at present they may be unaware.

I am talking to the currency group at the House of Commons next Wednesday and will take that opportunity to express discontent in general terms. I am, of course, not

---

[2] Keynes had told Henry Clay on 4 March while discussing exchange policy that 'There is nothing else which offers such a combination of difficulty of policy, difficulty of theory, difficulty of fact and difficulty of technique'.

neglecting the Treasury and wrote recently to Phillips. But I feel quite hopeless about making any serious progress there.

On the whole, though you may think that odd, I believe the best chance would be to take it up with the Bank of England through Clay. You may or may not be surprised to hear that, as a result of the deferred pay proposals, I am personally reconciled to the Governor, who is strongly in favour and says that he thinks it the only solution, with the result that, after an interval of some years, I have been again given free entry to the Bank.

As he mentioned to Kahn, Keynes used the opportunity of his talk to the Parliamentary Monetary Committee on 20 March, ostensibly on the rate of interest, to raise the matter of exchange control.

NOTES FOR SPEECH TO THE PARLIAMENTARY MONETARY COMMITTEE ON RATE OF INTEREST

So many reasons for criticising Government on home front that it is a comfort and relief to talk on a matter where great and significant progress has been made.

Before the war almost everyone in financial circles believed that in the event of war a serious depreciation of gilt-edged securities. The experience of the first few weeks seemed to bear this out. I had argued vehemently to the contrary in *The Times* in April and again in July 1939 that an average of 2½ % was possible. This Committee made similar proposals as long ago as Dec. 1938 as Mr Craven-Ellis[3] reminded readers of *The Times* last July.

All that was necessary was to supply the market with all the liquidity it required, to produce the right psychological atmosphere and expectation, and to allow adequate time to elapse.

[3] William Craven-Ellis (d. 1959), National M.P. for Southampton, 1931–45; Chairman, Parliamentary Monetary Committee, House of Commons, 1934–44; company director; published books on rebuilding of Britain and reform of Bank of England.

Today we can, I think, congratulate ourselves that our counsels have prevailed. The policy of this Committee, once regarded as hare-brained, has now become the orthodoxy of the Treasury and the Bank of England. With the new 3 % War Loan,[4] the 2 % Conversion and with Treasury bills only just over 1 %, my ideal of an average borrowing rate of 2½ % is almost fulfilled.

It would be lacking in gratitude—it would be forgetting too soon what might have been—not to recognise the great skill with which the Chancellor of the Exchequer and his advisers have accustomed the public to the new order of ideas and the new programme. I do not think one could reasonably have expected things to move any faster in the right direction than they have done. The new policy, compared with that of the last war, will have saved the Exchequer an enormous sum and have greatly contributed to the future financial stability of this country. Many important financial institutions are still staggered by what has happened and can scarcely believe their eyes when they read the quotations in their morning paper.

My discourse can be, therefore, on quite different lines from that which I might have thought appropriate a year ago. It is no longer necessary to enforce general principles and one can afford to concentrate on some interesting points of detail.

Writing last autumn [above, p. 63] I expressed opinion that the Treasury could go the best part of a year from the beginning of the war, say up to next July, before attempting a funding issue. I still think that this advice was technically correct. I believe that the loan would have been a most outstanding success and could have been floated on slightly more favourable terms if its issue had been further deferred.

All the same I do not feel entitled to press the criticism. The task of issuing war loans is an intensely psychological one. All sorts of things have to be taken into account. The gradual

---

[4] 3 % War Loan 1955–9, for which the lists were open on 12 and 13 March. This issue was a comparative failure [Ed.].

accustoming of the public, not allowing the market to get stale or cold, the future course of the war and the importance of issuing in a comparatively clear sky.

Moreover the terms of the loan are quite suitable as a starting point. It is important that they should leave room for further improvement, so that when the Treasury suggests that future loans will be on less favourable terms they can command credence.

My main reason for doubt is that they will have got the market, for the time being unduly illiquid. There is a risk that markets will not be as good as they ought to be in the near future. But this will cure itself if sufficient time is allowed to elapse. It is most important for future developments that the market should be hungry for stock. But my impression is that, for the moment, they are overfed.

The recent raising of minimum prices seems to me to be a right move with the object of convincing the public that future loans will not be on more favourable terms, though I could have wished that the Chancellor could have been a little more explicit about this.

There is, however, another connected matter, secondary but nevertheless important, about which I am not nearly so happy.

The practicability of maintaining a low rate of interest throughout the war largely depends on our maintaining a closed market so far as the outside world is concerned. To a much greater extent the maintenance of a stable exchange policy and our ability to finance indefinitely an adverse balance of trade depends on this.

Now in an unsatisfactory world there has been, in my judgment, nothing more unsatisfactory than our management of foreign exchange restrictions since the outbreak of war.

This is a highly technical subject which the public cannot be expected to understand. But I wonder how far this Committee, who should certainly be concerned with it, really appreciate what the present situation is.

Almost from the outset necessary and adequate impediments were put in the way of British nationals who might wish to remit money abroad. I have no criticism on that score.

But many people are not aware that there have been no effective restrictions on foreign nationals taking money out of this country. And what is still more surprising and is still less well known there are no obstacles whatever in the way of foreign nationals selling their securities on the London market and to British nationals. Thus, in effect, foreign investment is still continuing and on quite a substantial scale.

Let me take the first point.

A foreigner can sell his sterling on the free exchange. Until recently this was within 1 or 2 per cent of the official rate, so that the sacrifice involved is negligible. The reason for this is that British exports could still be invoiced in sterling, so that there was always a large demand for sterling at the slightly cheaper price represented by the free exchange. In the last week or two this has been stiffened by a new requirement that certain classes of Empire exports may not be paid for over the free exchange—with the result that the free exchange is now 6 or 7 per cent below the official exchange. But meanwhile tens of millions have been lost; and there still remains substantial opportunities for future loss. Loftus and Wilkinson[5].

Let me now give you an illustration of the sale of foreign securities...American requisition...and BAT...But applies equally to the enormous holdings of securities quoted in

---

[5] Pierse Creagh Loftus (1877–1956); National Conservative M.P. for Lowestoft, 1934–45.
Ellen Wilkinson (d. 1947); Labour M.P. for Middlesbrough East, 1924–31, for Jarrow, 1935–47; Parliamentary Secretary, Ministry of Pensions, 1940; Parliamentary Secretary, Ministry of Home Security, 1940–5; Ministry of Education, 1945–7; Organiser, National Movement of Women's Suffrage Societies, 1913–15, National Organiser, National Union of Distributive and Allied Workers, 1915.

London held abroad—which tend to be sold here whenever the London price rises to a satisfactory level.

Yet all this could be remedied by a stroke of the pen—applying to all aliens the provision against enemy aliens.

The only possible motive for the present arrangements is the future post-war prestige of the bill on London and the London market generally.

Yet the future position of London will only gain if we can maintain this laxity throughout the war—which is most unlikely.

It is a major scandal that what easily may be tens of millions of resources which would be available otherwise to finance our adverse balance of trade should be allowed to escape this way.

The balance of trade is our Achilles heel. Yet after six months of extremely adverse experience, we are not taking the most elementary precautions to protect.

I confess that I am utterly perplexed. I am unable to fathom the mentality of the authorities. What do they think they are up to? I can't imagine.

The whole business of exchange control needs re-ordering from top to bottom. I am speaking here privately.

I have felt embarrassed in making these criticisms more publicly. For one does not want to advertise to foreigners all the chinks in Treasury's armour. For though those mainly concerned are probably only too well aware of them, there may be some to whom it has not yet occurred that we could possibly allow what we do allow.

I have said nothing this evening about the adequacy of voluntary saving and the bearing of this on the rate of interest. But I am ready to answer any questions on it.

The main thing I am concerned to urge on members of parliament is that on the economic side it is our unquestionable duty to wage this war with all our might and without reservation; and that in no quarter of the field with which I am acquainted are we in fact doing so.

The House of Commons meeting led to correspondence with Mr P. C. Loftus and Mr R. Boothby.[6] Keynes approved a parliamentary question from Mr Loftus on transactions in outstanding securities for 9 April, which brought an unsatisfactory reply from the Chancellor. He then consulted the two M.P.'s again on the possibilities of further House of Commons pressure.

During this time Keynes had started to develop his views on exchange control in greater detail, promising Sir Frederick Phillips a memorandum after Easter. By 29 April, he had completed a draft memorandum on foreign exchange policy, which he sent to Henry Clay at the Bank. He then discussed this draft with Clay and Mr H. A. Siepmann,[7] who had the day-to-day administration of the control in his charge. In the light of this discussion and further events, such as the prohibition of transactions in outstanding securities on 12 May and the German offensive westwards, Keynes revised his memorandum, forwarding the new version for discussion on 22 May. Further revisions followed criticisms from Clay and Mr G. Bolton,[8] before Keynes sent a final version to Phillips at the Treasury, as well as to Professor F. Lindemann,[9] Stamp, Mr T. Balogh[10], Clay and Bolton, on 24 and 25 May (one small correction followed on 26 May).[11]

EXCHANGE CONTROL AND EXCHANGE POLICY

The following is written on the assumption that the phase of pussy-footing is over and that no legalistic obstacles or considerations of post-war prestige will stand in the way of

[6] Robert John Graham Boothby (b. 1900), Life Peer 1958; Conservative M.P. for East Aberdeenshire, 1924–58; Parliamentary Private Secretary to Chancellor of Exchequer (Winston Churchill), 1926–9; Parliamentary Secretary, Ministry of Food, 1940–1.

[7] Harry Arthur Siepmann (1889–1963); with J.M.K. in Treasury, A Division, during World War I; Adviser to Governors, Bank of England, 1926, Executive Director, 1945–54.

[8] George Lewis French Bolton (b. 1900), K.C.M.G. 1950; Bank of England, to assist in management of Exchange Equalisation Account, 1933; Adviser, Bank of England, 1941–8; Executive Director, 1948–57.

[9] Frederick Alexander Lindemann (d. 1957), 1st Baron Cherwell 1941; Professor of Experimental Philosophy, Oxford, 1919–56; Personal Assistant to Winston Churchill as Prime Minister, 1940–5; Paymaster-General, 1942–5.

[10] Thomas Balogh (b. 1905), Life Peer, 1968; economist in the City, 1931–9; National Institute of Economic and Social Research, 1938–42; Institute of Economics and Statistics, Oxford, 1940–55; Fellow of Balliol College, Oxford, 1945–73; Reader in Economics, Oxford, 1960–73.

[11] Keynes also sent a copy to Richard Kahn, but his criticisms arrived too late for inclusion. He was, however, responsible for the correction sent in on 26 May.

any action which is practicable and useful for the purposes of the war. Future policy will be best conducted in two stages—the first one depending on what can be evolved without undue delay or too much new machinery out of the existing *de facto* situation, the second designed to prepare for the future in such a way that we can go ahead from now on absolutely irrespective of 'financial' considerations. I precede proposals on these lines with a brief outline of the present arrangements and of the main criticisms to which they are open.

I

1. A non-enemy alien is allowed to remit out of this country over the 'free' exchange sterling funds which come into his possession in the following ways:–
 (i) sterling cash balances already in his possession;
 (ii) the proceeds of selling securities and other capital assets to British nationals which are not on the 'Treasury list' (details of what this means are given in an appendix);
 (iii) the profits and reserves of foreign-owned businesses carried on in this country;
 (iv) sums he is able to borrow from any bank outside the U.K. or other lender within the sterling area. There is strict control on loans within the U.K., but the measures to prevent indirect 'bear' transactions, taking the franc and sterling area as a whole, are not watertight.

2. A non-enemy alien wishing to remit sterling out of this country can use it to purchase foreign exchange at a rate which is not prohibitively depreciated because the supply of free exchange is being constantly fed by the demand for free sterling to pay for British exports both visible and invisible which have been invoiced in sterling.

The position is so extraordinary as to be scarcely credible to those who hear it for the first time. The Treasury take on themselves the responsibility to provide foreign exchange at the official rate to any *importer* into this country. But it has not taken steps to collect at the official rate the foreign proceeds of all *exports* from this country. Subject to what follows, the exporter is free to invoice his goods in sterling allowing the purchaser to pay for them over the free exchange, which is greatly to his advantage since at the rates recently prevailing this brings in 20 per cent more sterling than if he handed them over at the official rate. The proceeds thus become available to foreigners wishing to remit funds out of the country.

For the first six months of the war this freedom extended to all exports from this country and from other parts of the Empire. More recently six important commodities, mainly Empire raw materials, were put on a list of exports, the proceeds of which must be handed over to the authorities in foreign currency. I believe that in practice there is also an increasing number of exports which theoretically are on the free list but of which in practice the foreign proceeds are handed over at the official rate. As a result of this depletion of the supply of free exchange, the free rate, which was within one or two per cent of the official rate for many months, fell first to 10 per cent below it and then to 20 per cent. Nevertheless there is still a liberal supply of resources on the free exchange as is clearly shown by its relative firmness during the recent critical period.

3. Any importer of goods into this country is entitled, as stated above, to obtain foreign exchange to pay for them at the official rate.

This implies that there ought to be an ultra-strict control against unnecessary imports. In fact the control on imports is chaotic and has been far from strict during the greater part of the period since the beginning of the war. For several months there was no control worth mentioning on many luxury imports and importers were able to stock up against more stringent times. Opinions differ as to the extent to which

165

things have been stiffened up recently. Some of those concerned maintain that there are no longer any unnecessary imports worth mentioning.

I am not in a position to weigh the evidence. But the principle of control seems to be open to two fundamental objections. Until these objections are met, it would take a great deal to persuade me that the control on imports is as strict as it ought to be. The objections are—

(i) The prohibitions are negative instead of positive. That is to say, any import is permissible unless it is on the prohibited list. The right principle would be that all imports are prohibited unless they are on the free list. The present system runs the risk of allowing a multitude of unnecessary oddments to come in which are individually insignificant but which add up to something which matters. There is also always a chance of an important prohibition being overlooked of an import which would never have been deliberately allowed. I agree, however, that the evils of this wrong principle of control were much more important in the past than they are now.

(ii) The control of imports is divided between the Board of Trade, the Ministry of Supply and the Ministry of Food; and, generally speaking, the actual administration is in the hands of the interested parties, e.g. it is the controller of a particular commodity who gives out the import licences for it. Now it must be obvious to anyone that this must in some cases lead to a certain laxity. A particular controller will be more conscious of the urgency of the demand for his particular commodity than of that for other commodities; and indeed it will be part of his duty to satisfy that demand so far as he reasonably can for purposes that are in themselves unobjectionable. Thus the quantitative control within the permitted list ought to be entrusted to an independent authority with power to override the supply departments though of course depending on their advice. The object would be to allow complete freedom within the limitations of shipping to all war requirements and to criticise narrowly all non-necessary demands for civilians.

4. There is a lack of uniformity in the exchange and import regulations within the sterling and franc area. This gives too many opportunities for clever evasion. Some units within this area are strict on some points, and others on other points. But remittance within this area is so comparatively easy, especially for a foreigner, that the laxest provision existing anywhere tends to be the effective one. This difficulty is particularly present as between this country and France. The gradual introduction of uniformity is important, not only in itself, but as paving the way to a more comprehensive plan.

5. The relation of Canada to the rest of the sterling area, whilst steadily improving, is still anomalous. There are now such stringent exchange (but not import) regulations between Canada and U.S.A. that it would be worth while in present circumstances to approach Canada with a view to her becoming a full member of the sterling area. At present the Canadian banking system is not prepared to retain in sterling (as, e.g., Australia is) the balance of payments in its favour.

6. The Treasury has evolved an awkward system of distinctions between 'sterling', 'hard' and 'soft' currency which depend for their validity, broadly speaking, on the assumption that there are no longer triangular exchange transactions between the three groups. In fact this assumption is very imperfectly fulfilled. It is not clear that it is worth while to make important sacrifices of cash, convenience or enemy warfare in order to observe so rigid a distinction between hard and soft currencies. At any rate, it might be advisable to begin with measures designed to make the Treasury assumption more generally valid and meanwhile to interpret it with more latitude.

II

The amount of resources which we have lost by our failure to enforce drastic restrictions at the outset by the blocking of foreign balances etc. and by strict limitation of imports cannot be accurately guessed. But it can scarcely be less than £50 million on each head (and may be much more), i.e. £50 million from loss of foreign balances, sale of foreign-owned securities in London and withdrawal of profits and reserves from foreign-owned businesses operating in this country, and £50 million from wholly unnecessary imports for civilian consumption. If £100 million is thought of in relation to war preparations and enemy warfare which financial difficulties have impeded in the last nine months, the damage done by the lax policies hitherto pursued is obvious.

The following interim measures are recommended because they represent a natural evolution from the *de facto* position and could be put into force with very little delay and without much new machinery. At the same time they would stop up—though much too late—the most important gaps.

1. No further sales of securities or other capital assets from alien owners to British nationals should be permitted. That is to say the existing provisions to prevent sales from enemy aliens should be extended to all aliens. I am aware that very recently new regulations to prevent sales by enemy aliens make sales by enemy aliens much more difficult than before. But I do not understand what stands in the way of a straightforward and comprehensive prohibition of such transactions.

2. All exporters should be required to sell in terms of foreign currency and hand over to the Bank of England. British recipients of the proceeds of invisible exports should be required to do the same.

3. Banks and other lenders throughout the Empire should be prohibited from making loans, except under licence, to

alien borrowers or to companies under alien control. They should be instructed gradually to call in all existing loans to aliens except where they are licensed to continue them on the grounds of our own business advantage or of undue hardship to the borrower.

4. A new, overriding authority should be set up to control imports with the object of facilitating to the utmost imports for war requirements and cutting all others to the bone.

5. Concerted action should be taken to set up uniform exchange and import controls throughout the British, French, Dutch and Belgian empires.

6. Canada should be expressly invited to impose restrictions on American imports and to become a full member of the sterling area in the sense of being ready to hold banking reserves in sterling.

7. Clearing agreements should be steadily and rapidly extended. They should have a wider scope than current trade transactions and should cover the whole field of financial relations between the Allied area and the country in question. They would give an opportunity for discriminating exchange rates and other special arrangements. They might, therefore, be better described as *bilateral exchange agreements*.

8. An official rate should be established for all countries. This is a corollary of taking over the foreign currency proceeds of all exports. But even apart from this, it is extremely necessary. At present the 'free' dollar rate governs the actual exchange for a group of countries for which no official rate has been established, e.g. Italy. If our policy is to make the free exchange die of inanition, its rate will be highly unstable and possibly depressed, so that it is essential it should not influence the rate of exchange applicable to exports to any part of the world.

The practice of allowing the free rate to govern the effective rate for a number of exports is one of the outstanding futilities of the present system.

It will be observed that I have not included an immediate blocking of all foreign balances as a part of the above recommendations. I am sure that this would have been a right measure to take at the outbreak, and better still before the outbreak, of war. But at the present stage I am not clear that it has sufficiently important advantages over what is proposed above to balance its much greater technical difficulty. It could not be put into force so promptly or so easily as the above. If those who are fully aware of its technical difficulties are ready to face them, well and good. If not, I should proceed without blocking for the time being, though ready to return to this measure if necessary in the light of experience.

III

I conclude with a brief note on the system to which we should ultimately (and as soon as possible) lead up.

1. A comprehensive currency agreement between all the constituent parts of the British, French, Dutch and Belgian empires so that, as long as the war lasts, no 'financial' problem could prevent or impede any transaction useful to the prosecution of the war within this vast area. A uniform, or at least an agreed, system of exchange and import controls by the constituent members of this group is a necessary preliminary to this.

2. Bilateral exchange agreements between this area as a whole and every country outside it, supported by the joint credit of the whole. Neutral countries, which were not prepared to fall in with a reasonable credit arrangement, would be faced with a greater loss of their export trade than they could easily support. We should have machinery for bringing into play the full bargaining power of a market covering half the world. I should be inclined to keep a fair proportion of the gold reserves of the four Empires as a support to their credit and insist wherever possible on covering an adverse

balance by an uncovered credit in the clearing—subject, of course, to all kinds of necessary exceptions and bargains.

On the assumption that the United States is now anxious to find ways and means of affording us financial assistance, I believe that the establishment of a clearing could be so clothed and represented as to be actually palatable and preferable to the American authorities. It has the great advantage from their point of view that the measure of their financial assistance would be closely linked to their own exports. In the last war, the greatest bone of contention arose out of the fact that, in effect through the pegged dollar rate for sterling, we were using our credits from the American Treasury to support the value of sterling throughout the world. Endless difficulties between the Treasuries arose out of this. All that would be avoided by a clearing agreement.

3. A special joint department of the Treasury and the Bank of England should be set up to establish and run this system. It is a matter of great complexity and requires special technical qualifications. It cannot be run as a sideshow by those who have many other important responsibilities.

Keynes met Phillips on 28 May and followed this discussion with a series of memoranda on 30 May, 4 and 11 June. The contents of these reflected the deteriorating course of the war and attempts to buoy up the French and prepare the ground for the approach to the United States, which recent developments had made inevitable. Preparation of the memoranda was interspersed with meetings with the Governor of the Bank, the new Chancellor, Kingsley Wood,[12] J. Monnet,[13] M. Monick,[14] the French

[12] Sir Kingsley Wood (1881–1943); Conservative M.P. for West Woolwich 1918–43; Postmaster-General, 1931–5; Minister of Health, 1935–8; Secretary of State for Air, 1938–40; Lord Privy Seal, 1940; Chancellor of Exchequer, 1940–3.

[13] Jean Monnet (b. 1888); Chairman, Franco-British Economic Co-ordination Committee, 1939; member, British Supply Council, Washington, 1940–3; French National Liberation Committee, Algiers, 1943–4.

[14] Emmanuel Georges Michel Monick (b. 1893); banker, company director; Inspector-General of Finance, 1920–49; financial attaché to French Ambassador in Washington, 1930–4, in London, 1934–40; Secretary-General of Finance, 1944; Governor, Bank of France, 1945–9.

Ambassador,[15] Brendan Bracken,[16] and interested M.P.s. Throughout he appears to have been kept fairly well informed, probably through Bracken, of official proposals made to the French. Some indication of Keynes's activities during this period came from his letter to Brendan Bracken of 12 June 1940 which concludes the series documents.

ALLIED EXCHANGE POLICY

1. I understand that the steps immediately necessary to strengthen the position are likely to be taken, i.e.—

(1) Blocking of foreign sterling balances in U.K.

(2) Prohibition of sales of foreign-owned securities in U.K.

(3) All British (and I hope Empire) exports to be paid for either in foreign currencies (to be handed to the Bank of England) or in official sterling purchased from the Bank of England.

2. This should prevent any important further leakage of resources. But it is merely an interim measure. There is likely to be general agreement that this should be followed up by further measures such as:-

(1) the development and extension of clearing agreements;

(2) the unification and stiffening of controls within the sterling area; and

(3) the mobilisation, in detail, of various untapped sources of foreign assets; to which I should add emphatically

(4) the establishment of a new department solely charged with the detail and technique of these and analogous measures.

3. But there remain some larger matters which have not received much serious discussion.

We can proceed on the above lines by easy stages with

---

[15] André Charles Corbin (1881–1970); Ambassador in London, 1933–40.
[16] Brendan Bracken (1901–58), 1st Viscount 1952; Unionist M.P. for North Paddington, 1929–45, for Bournemouth, 1945–50; Parliamentary Private Secretary to Prime Minister, 1940–1; Minister of Information, 1941–5; First Lord of Admiralty, 1945.

gradually improving technique and more water-tight regulations. Or we can proceed on spectacular lines with the object not merely of the slow conservation and augmentation of our foreign resources but of striking the imagination of the world and of promoting confidence as well as securing resources.

Apart from the larger results which would be secured by spectacular methods if they are successful, they have certain advantages of their own.

(1) A grand policy will rally French opinion, consolidate inter-allied solidarity and increase our public credit throughout the world.

(2) It will facilitate the much-needed unification of the sterling area. If it is part of a grand scheme we can appeal with success to all parts of the Empire, including in particular South Africa and Canada, to come in on a basis which applies to all alike. Without a grand scheme we shall be swamped in details and held up by delays.

(3) It will greatly improve our chances of making satisfactory arrangements with U.S.A. The policy of cautious and timid approaches to U.S.A. is a wrong psychology. They are much more likely to fall for something big and imaginative.

4. The outlines of a grand scheme can be expressed very shortly:–

First stage

(1) A complete pooling of the foreign resources in gold, securities and current trade balances—of the British, French, Dutch and Belgian empires.

(2) The rapid establishment of arrangements for uniform exchange control between this area and the outside world.

Second stage

Clearing agreements or, as a better description, bilateral exchange agreements between the Allied area and each country outside it, based on the adverse balances being cleared in agreed proportions in gold and other assets, with provision for allowing uncleared balances up to a certain amount or for an agreed period. This would bring into play many forms of capital assets which cannot be regarded at present as liquid. Such agreements would automatically have the effect of increasing the volume of imports from those countries with which payment was relatively the easier.

It is not useful to enter into all the details involved at this stage of the discussion.

5. The combined resources of the Allied area are enormous. Their bargaining power as a market unsurpassable. With such a scheme as the above in operation it would be reasonable to assure the war departments that we could finance for three years or longer all imports which it was physically possible for them to acquire.

J. M. KEYNES

30 May 1940

Aide Memoire *sent to the Chancellor of the Exchequer after lunch, 4 June 1940*

THE MOBILISATION OF OUR FOREIGN RESOURCES
AS A WEAPON OF WAR

1. A constructive policy requires the establishment of a new department, combining the work now done by the Treasury and the Bank of England, charged with the sole duty of foreign exchange control, clearing and bilateral exchange agreements, and the mobilisation of our foreign resources. It would be concerned only with collecting and conserving a pool of foreign cash with a view to putting what they require at the disposal of the Treasury and the war departments. It would have nothing to do with expenditure out of the pool.

2. The department would be, constitutionally, a subdepartment of the Treasury in the same position in relation to the Chancellor of the Exchequer as Somerset House. It would be situated at the Bank of England, where numerically

the far greater proportion of those concerned are employed already, and would be a department of the Bank of England for the purposes of staff and of day-to-day management.

3. As regards possible developments of executive action, the objects of the department would be

(1) to establish uniform exchange and banking controls throughout the sterling and franc areas, and also through the Dutch and Belgian empires with a view to the four empires evolving into a single unit for currency purposes, leakage of resources from which into the outside world would no longer be possible;

(2) to negotiate clearing agreements, better described perhaps as bilateral exchange agreements, between ourselves (and ultimately the whole of the Allied area) and each neutral country on terms more comprehensive and much more favourable to ourselves than the existing clearing agreements, which would exploit to the full the bargaining power of the Allied area as the predominant, and in many cases the only large purchaser, of the world's exports;

(3) to use these agreements as the means of obtaining what would be in effect foreign credits (e.g. through using, in effect, the resources of the U.S.A. Exchange Stabilisation Fund);

(4) to use these agreements as the means of making liquid and available the large amount of our foreign assets which we do not at present reckon as liquid (e.g. we should pay for Argentine exports over the clearing by Argentine Government and Railway Bonds taken at par).

All of the above would provide endless opportunity for ingenuity and technical skill in detail.

4. But larger objects of policy would also be in view, in particular—

(1) a genuine pooling of Allied resources in the shape of gold, securities, raw materials and current trade balances (each party taking out at the end of the war a proportion of

what was left equal to the proportion he had put in at the beginning)

(2) and, as a result of such pooling, the abolition of loan transactions between the Allies—the coal, Empire raw materials and munitions with which we furnish France being a free gift.

5. These measures would furnish the Chancellor of the Exchequer with material for a demonstration of financial strength which would impress the world.

The amount of the Allied pool of foreign resources should be of the order of fully £3,000 million, and in conjunction with other measures proposed would assure us of our power to finance any expenditure by the war departments which was physically practicable for a long time to come. We could offer the world a staggering exhibition of strength. By making the pooling of resources with the French a genuine arrangement uncomplicated by loan transactions and by placing the whole of the Allied resources behind the support of the franc, the French people could be reassured at a time when they may greatly need reassurance. The precedents thus created would be of great significance if and when the day comes for American participation, even though their participation is on the principles of limited liability.

J. M. KEYNES

4 June 1940

Handed to the Chancellor of the Exchequer, 11 June 1940

I

The experience of the last war conveys an awful warning against establishing financial relations between the Allied and Associated powers on a pseudo-commercial basis, which apes the conventions of foreign investment.

Instead of this, assistance and cooperation should be determined by what is physically possible, and should be tied up to the least possible extent with formal financial arrangements.

I am sure that we shall be thinking on these lines sooner or later. But two great objects can be served by thinking on them sooner rather than later, and of not once more making the mistake of reaching the inevitable policy after many of the benefits to be obtained from it have finally escaped us.

These two objects are, first of all, the importance of giving the utmost immediate encouragement to the French; and, secondly, now that the United States is on the brink of giving us financial assistance, of creating in good time precedents which would be helpful in moulding the character of such arrangements.

II

So far as concerns France, pending more developed arrangements making a reality of pooling of resources, it would, I feel sure, be of the utmost value to French opinion if the Prime Minister could make some such statement as the following:–

> In this war to save civilisation those who are in the front rank of the fight should know that they are being supported without reserve by all the resources of those who have joined them in this fight. The association of Great Britain and France applies to every sphere, material as well as military. I shall propose to M. Reynaud[17] that all the resources and all the productive power of each country shall be at the disposal of the other during the war to win it and after the war to restore the injuries and damage done. There shall be no question, as there was last time, of one Ally owing large sums to the other. All is freely given for the common cause now and hereafter.

It may be that before the war is over our own damages will be not less than the French. If so, no harm will be done by

---

[17] Paul Reynaud (1878–1966); French politician; Prime Minister, 1940.

the declaration of joint liability. At the present stage, when it is France that is suffering, it would be of real value to know that she has us behind her, not only now, but hereafter. The first sentence might be interpreted as a hint to the United States and is therefore significant.

III

So far as the United States is concerned, the kind of scheme we should be trying to lead up to might be, I suggest, something on the following lines:–

(*a*) All credit transactions should be from the outset between Governments alone (private credit transactions remaining prohibited) and, so far as munitions are concerned, should be expended by a joint purchasing board for the proper regulation of prices and profits.

(*b*) The credits should carry no interest.

(*c*) They should be repayable by annual instalments over a short period of years, but they should not be repayable to the United States. They should constitute a part of the contribution of the United States to the post-war reconstruction of Europe. The instalments of repayment should be allocated to all the countries which have to be reconstituted after the war. That is to say, on the conclusion of the war the U.S. Government would allocate to a Reconstruction Board, which would be concerned with the financial side of the reparation of damage and the rehabilitation of financial credit in all the Allied and Associated countries, the benefit of these instalments (which should be collectable, not in cash, but only in the exports of the countries discharging the debt). Great Britain, on the one hand, would have a claim on the Reconstruction Board, just as France and the other Allies would, in proportion to any devastation she had suffered. On the other hand, the contributions to it of herself and her dominions would not necessarily be limited to the amount of her debt to the United States, but would be related to her capacity and to the need.

(*d*) We might entertain the hope that these instalments would make up a part, but not the whole, of America's contribution to the Reconstruction Fund. It would be in the interest of the United States government, not less than of the world as a whole, if the U.S. were to allocate to the Board in addition a further (say) £5,000 million in gold out of its useless and redundant stock to provide the bank reserves in the countries to be reconstructed. The detailed allocation of these funds between the recipients would be settled by the United States herself.

The proposal under III dovetails into the proposal under II as follows.

All the countries which have suffered damage would have a claim on the Reconstruction Fund under II and the surplus resources of Great Britain under III would be made available for the purposes of this joint Fund until its work was done.

Unless we can at this stage free ourselves from the taint of pseudo-commercial transactions with France, we shall spoil our prospect of the right arrangements with the United States. The existing Anglo-French financial agreement goes a long way in the right direction and provides a firm foundation for such settlements as are suggested above, which, technically speaking, can be made to fit into the existing Anglo-French financial agreement without difficulty.

IV

The immediate matter is the declaration in II for the sake of France. But this should only be the first step to a more general diplomatic manifesto setting forth in a manner which would strike the public opinion of the world and of the United

179

States especially that our cause far transcends financial particularities and that all we have is to be devoted to it in a common pool.

J. M. KEYNES

11 June 1940

To B. BRACKEN, *12 June 1940*

My dear Brendan,

I have just had a message from your secretary asking me to lunch on Saturday. If this is important, I will manage to come. But I have an engagement in Cambridge on Saturday morning which I ought to keep if possible. My present idea is to return to Cambridge tomorrow (Cambridge 54184) and be back in London by next Tuesday.

Sorry to have bothered you on the telephone yesterday. Though we did not succeed in making contact, I managed to do what I wanted. The point was that Monick got me to see him in the morning because he and his Ambassador and Monnet thought it was very urgent and important that the Prime Minister and the Chancellor of the Exchequer should make some financial statement such as would really encourage the French and might also have helpful repercussions in U.S.A. After discussing things with him, I drafted the enclosed[18], the formula in which under II was greeted with enthusiasm by him and the other Frenchmen. I then managed to see the Chancellor of the Exchequer at 5.30, who received the idea most sympathetically, though I suppose what he does will depend on what other people tell him. At any rate, I plugged in the paper, coupled with exhortations by word of mouth, and that was all I could do.

The important immediate points are:-

(1) A public statement something on the lines under II. The French are clear that something of this kind would be of real

[18] The memorandum reprinted above, pp. 176–80. [Ed.]

help to their soldiers in the appalling task of the next days and, one hopes, weeks. Their psychology is such that, if they felt that our guarantee lay behind so that, even if they were killed, there was some assurance to their widows and their houses, they would fight even more desperately. If there is anything whatever in this, surely we owe it them. It did my heart good yesterday to be in contact with the French—their extraordinary courage and determination.

(2) The other point is that they really would very much like a joint Anglo-French temporary committee to look into high policy on the financial side. Monick, Monnet and, perhaps, Corbin would serve on the French side. I believe it would be a good thing if the Chancellor of the Exchequer would himself act as chairman. They feel, I think, that owing to the character of our Treasury they have lost all personal contact and feel that our people would really understand their psychology and point of view a bit better if they were meeting personally a few times engaged in the drafting of a joint document, which would bring out all the nuances to which they attach so much importance and we so little.

I said all this to the Chancellor of the Exchequer in a few words. The exact suggestions I have made about U.S.A. in the enclosed are, of course, in no event urgent and quite possibly not on the best lines, though I fancy they include a rather important fundamental idea. But, whatever the ultimate details of our approach to U.S.A., I am sure that the openness and generosity and lack of reserve in our treatment of the French at this moment will never be to our disadvantage and will always be to our honour.

Yours ever,
[copy initialled] J. M. K.

I had Maisky[19] to lunch today, and, as we were alone, we had a most interesting talk covering the whole field. I

[19] Ivan Mikhailovich Maisky (b. 1884); Counsellor, U.S.S.R. Embassy, London, 1925–7, Tokyo, 1927–9; Minister to Finland, 1929–32; Ambassador, London, 1932–43; People's Commissar for Foreign Affairs, U.S.S.R., 1943–6.

ventured on the prophecy that Hitler would meet his Water-
loo a long way East of Berlin and that we should be there.

During his general discussion of foreign exchange policy, Keynes had
one exchange of letters with Mr Samuel Courtauld, which in the light of
later events[20] is of considerable interest.

To s. COURTAULD, *29 April 1940*

My dear Sam,

I have been thinking rather intensively about foreign exchange policy and about various things which can be done
to preserve and mobilise our foreign assets. During these
reflections, the following idea occurred to me in relation to
the Viscose Corporation, which I should like to put up to you.

Why should not the Viscose Corporation borrow £40
million by raising bonds in U.S.A. and lend the dollars to
Courtaulds? The Treasury would then requisition the whole
of your present sterling preference issue at the present
market price, say, 24s, and would hand these over to you for
discharge in return for the $40 million.

In this way the Treasury would have gained an important
addition to its dollar assets and you would merely have ex-
changed a sterling liability for a dollar liability well covered
by dollar assets.

Yours ever,
[copy initialled] J.M.K.

From s. COURTAULD, *30 April 1940*

Dear Maynard,

Many thanks for your letter of yesterday. We have already thought
about the possibility of utilising our investment in the American Viscose
Corporation for the purpose which you suggest, and of various means of
doing it.

I will talk your scheme over with Hanbury-Williams[21] tomorrow, and
perhaps we could arrange a meeting later. I would only point out at

---

[20] See vol. XXIII.
[21] John Coldbrook Hanbury-Williams (1892–1965), Kt. 1950; Director, Bank of
England, 1936–63; Chairman, Courtaulds Ltd., 1946–62.

present that our preference shares are not redeemable, and that to redeem them compulsorily as you suggest would need a government order, if not an Act of Parliament.

There are also various complications in connection with taxation on both sides of the Atlantic which would affect the financial result of the scheme, and therefore the cost of it.

Yours,
SAM COURTAULD

To S. COURTAULD, *1 May 1940*

My dear Sam,

I was aware that your preference shares were not redeemable. But, to the best of my belief, the Treasury already have power to requisition them at any time. The powers under which they act in regard to American securities are not limited to Americans. There are already in fact some sterling securities in the Treasury list, and, unless I am mistaken, the Treasury is entitled to put any security it likes on this list at any time.

I can see that there will be various complications about taxes. But it seemed to me that these might really be a good deal less than one might have expected at first sight. It would simply mean that the annual dividend that the Viscose Company owe Courtaulds as owners of their common stock will be subject to a counter-claim and corresponding deduction on account of what Courtaulds owe Viscose on account of this transaction, leaving a net sum subject to the complications of taxation. Speaking at random, I should have thought there was about an equal chance of a tax gain or a tax loss, taking everything into account. Perhaps it would make the above sentence clearer if I add that I had been assuming one possibility would be for the Viscose Company to own preference shares in Courtaulds; that is to say, the transaction would consist in the Treasury requisitioning your sterling preference shares, your selling these shares to the Viscose Corporation for $40 million and paying over the $40 million to the Treasury as the dollar equivalent of the sterling sum which the Treasury would be paying out to the existing shareholders from whom the preference shares had been requisitioned.

Yours ever,
[copy initialled] J. M. K.

The transition to total war also raised other questions concerning the mobilisation and allocation of resources. Prompting from Richard Kahn as to official attitudes that had persisted through the change of government and the German successes in the West led Keynes to write to *The Times* on 5 June 1940.

To the Editor of The Times, *5 June 1940*

Sir,

The supply departments have the machinery for absorbing men who are actually thrown on the labour market. But they have no machinery as yet for dragging men out of their present unessential jobs. This should entirely change with the attitude of the Ministry of Labour and the Board of Trade towards the employment problem and the attitude of the private citizen in carrying to the utmost personal economy in normal repairs and improvements as well as in consumption.

If the Ministry of Labour could inform the Ministry of Supply that they had a million able-bodied men immediately available on their books it would be a triumph of good management. From now onwards a high figure of available labour unemployed should be the test of success for the Ministry of Labour and a low figure the test of success for the Ministry of Supply. Let each department try to be ahead of the other in its complementary task.

As the counterpart of this no private person should feel inhibited from making any economy whatever for fear of creating useless unemployment. On the contrary, the release of labour should be his object. We have been so long oppressed by the fear of unemployment, that the public is slow to realise its present duty. Yet the argument in favour of drastic voluntary action on the above lines is very strong. Compulsory measures may be required in due course, but, in the first stage, when we are merely getting rid of superfluities, we can do the sorting out for ourselves more efficiently than it can be done from above, since we know best what we can do without.

Yours, etc.,

J. M. KEYNES

This led to replies from Sir William Beveridge and Mr A. G. McGregor. Beveridge suggested that the problem of unemployment at the time lay in failures of coordination as the structure of the economy shifted to a wartime basis and that, as yet, private retrenchment was unnecessary. Mr McGregor's letter advocated a policy of business as usual until full employment came to pass. To these Keynes replied

To the Editor of The Times, *13 June 1940*

Sir,

The letter which you printed yesterday from Mr A. G. McGregor in favour of 'more of the spirit of business as usual which requires spending as usual' is a *pot-pourri* of dangerous popular fallacies. In the first place, it is difficult to find objects of expenditure which do not use up materials as well as labour. In the second place, an act of expenditure usually sets up a series of subsequent expenditures on the part of those who receive the money, which may lead to a harmful exhaustion of resources even though the first round of spending may look relatively innocent. This is our old friend the 'multiplier' principle over again. I used this principle formerly to show how an initial expenditure sets up a long series of subsequent expenditures which would help to employ labour and materials. In the new circumstances the same argument multiplies the gain to the national resources from almost every form of saving.

I offer this too often forgotten argument as a thought for

185

today in National Savings Week. A few examples of innocent expenditure free from both the above objections can indeed be found. Travelling in trains otherwise empty or attending a cinema where the profits of both the exhibitor and the renter are already above their E.P.T. standard can be recommended. But one soon gets to the end of the list—though some forms of economy obviously remain much more useful and significant than others. Mr McGregor goes on to argue that we must go on spending to keep up the revenue. But there are not many cases where the gain to the revenue will be equal to 100 per cent of the amount which might otherwise be saved, unless the unemployment immediately resulting becomes chronic and prolonged—which ought to be unthinkable from now onwards.

With the greater part of the letter from Sir William Beveridge which you print today I am in hearty agreement. It is an urgent task to organise work of national importance for everyone, particulary the young and adaptable. But when he goes on to argue that we should postpone private retrenchment 'until we have mopped up those (unemployed) we have already' he is relapsing into the mode of thought of a departed world. Those who are at present employed but could be released are likely to be more valuable and more easily absorbed into work of national importance than the hard core of the chronically unemployed. I insist again on the two central points of my previous letter. It would take too long to organise an efficient compulsory system to drag men out of their present employments. Thus voluntary action is necessary; and it is also preferable (just as voluntary saving is) so long as it is sufficient, because 'we ourselves know best what we can do without'.

If Mr Bevin can point to an army of able-bodied unemployed composed of men of high quality who are normally in work, this will offer a challenge to Mr Morrison, which he will surely take up with success. Temporary unemployment is a

186

small price to pay if it hastens even slightly the formidable task of reorganisation.

Yours, etc.,

J. M. KEYNES

This led to a further comment from Sir William Beveridge suggesting that Keynes's 'theoretical' views led him to ignore the nature and institutions of the labour market. Keynes did not carry the correspondence further. However he was to return to the problems of manpower allocation frequently in the period that followed.

On 27 June, Keynes discussed export policy with Professor Lindemann, sending him a note and a letter on the subject the following day. Again Richard Kahn provided much of the information.[22]

To PROFESSOR LINDEMANN, *28 June 1940*

Professor Lindemann,

The discussion in your room yesterday left me with these conclusions:–

(1) The case is made out for an immediate transfer to munitions of all engineers now engaged in export industry —subject to the following conditions.

(2) The transfer is not justified (and would lead to loss without corresponding gain) unless it is accompanied by the immediate maximum application of the existing compulsory powers for dilution so as to make further use of engineers already in munitions; and it should, therefore, be conditional on this.

(3) The case which is made out covers the next six or possibly nine months. It is quite possible that thereafter our fully developed and reorganised capacity will be equal both to adequate munitions and to exports. The export industries should, therefore, be told that they must regard this measure

---

[22] When Kahn went to the Board of Trade, the Treasury, in the shape of the Establishment Department, agreed to his appointment only on the conditon that he had nothing to do with currency questions. On this Keynes remarked to Kahn on 3 July, 'Either all questions are currency questions, or none are. So I suggest you adopt the latter interpretation.'

as temporary and to meet an urgent situation; and they should be instructed to maintain their selling organisation and to continue to accept orders for deferred delivery, at some price concession if necessary.

(4) The loss of foreign exchange resulting from the above is only safe on the assumption of financial support from U.S.A. But this is a good bet; and is unavoidable anyhow. Nevertheless U.S.A. is not likely to finance our purchases from the parts of the world outside U.S.A., so that the earning of foreign resources remains very important. If, therefore, we decide for urgent reasons to cut out certain classes of exports, we must be far more drastic than at present about other methods for conserving foreign exchange—particularly the further restriction of civilian imports, and a much stronger attitude in the negotiation of clearing agreements. Our present policy in these respects is feeble in the extreme. We have already lost by wasteful leakage following on feeble decisions sums much greater than what is at issue in the above. We can still offset by a stronger policy the loss of exchange which it entails.

[copy initialled] J. M. K.

28 June 1940

To PROFESSOR LINDEMANN, *28 June 1940*

Dear Lindemann,

I have been a little bit shaken by a conversation I have had with Layton, who was lunching here today. According to him, the Ministry of Supply are not being held up to any significant extent by a shortage of skilled labour;—and he certainly ought to know. He believed that the same was true of aircraft production, though about that he has not equal knowledge. He says that what stands in the way of a more rapid expansion of output is almost entirely lack of organisation or unsuitable

188

organisation, which can be cured only gradually. Since he has a strong bias in favour of large programmes, I am inclined to believe him.

I do not know that what he says affects the ultimate advisability of curtailing exports, but it does perhaps rather alter the timetable. It makes me feel that the right instruction to the export industries, i.e. in engineering, would be not to cease forthwith, but to warn them that they must be prepared to part with (say) 20 per cent of their present number of operatives in each month from now onwards. In this way the supply of men might be made to synchronise with the demand for them.

There is another factor which perhaps we ought not to forget. Presumably some of our aircraft factories will get bombed sooner or later. This will release men for similar factories. It means that it is unlikely that we shall have to man all the existing factories in being and in erection simultaneously. We need a margin of factories over man power to provide against such losses. It would be a mistake to work out the man power problem without any reference at all to this possibility.

Yours sincerely,
[copy initialled] J. M. K.

At the end of June, Keynes became somewhat more formally involved in matters of high policy. On 28 June, the Chancellor of the new Government, Sir Kingsley Wood, after a talk with Keynes, invited him to join his about-to-be-announced Consultative Council, which was to help and advise the Chancellor on special problems resulting from war conditions.[23] Keynes

[23] The other members of the council were S. R. Beale, C. F. Campbell, Sir Bertram Hornsby, G. Riddle and Lord Riverdale. At the same time Lord Catto became Financial Adviser to the Chancellor.

   Samuel Richard Beale (1881–1964), K.B.E. 1942; Director, Guest, Keen & Nettlefold; President, Association of British Chambers of Commerce, 1934–6.

   Colin Frederick Campbell (1866–1954), 1st Baron Colgrain 1946; President,

told his mother on 28 June that he did not expect that the job would involve much work beyond what he chose to do, but, he continued, 'it will have the great advantage of giving me direct access to the Chancellor of the Exchequer with any bright ideas I may have'. The Council was announced on 1 July and met for the first time on 8 July.

Keynes's efforts at persuasion in the period following the German attack in the West also took place at a more personal level. With the change in the course of the war there was a round-up of enemy aliens who had been previously exempted from all restrictions. The number involved was about 65,000. The authorities proposed to send most of them to the Dominions when shipping space became available. However, 'valuable' aliens would be allowed to remain in Britain with some freedom of movement.

Keynes immediately intervened on behalf of a number of economists, attempting to obtain their release for normal teaching and research duties. Correspondence piled up as he wrote to all possible authorities from the Home Secretary downwards concerning the cases of Piero Sraffa[24], Erwin Rothbarth, H. W. Singer[25] and E. Rosenbaum[26]. Some indication of his feelings on the matter comes from a letter to F. C. Scott, Chairman of the Provincial Insurance Company of which Keynes was a Director.

British Bankers' Association, 1938–46; Chairman, National Provincial Bank, 1933–46.

Sir Bertram Hornsby (d. 1943), Kt. 1926; Governor, National Bank of Egypt, 1922–31; Chairman, Commercial Union Assurance Company.

George Riddle (1875–1944), Kt. 1942; Director of Co-operative Wholesale Society, Manchester, 1923–43.

Arthur Balfour (1873–1957), 1st Baronet, 1929, 1st Baron Riverdale, 1935; Chairman, Advisory Council for Scientific and Industrial Research, 1937–46; company director and chairman; member, Economic Advisory Council, 1930–8.

[24] Piero Sraffa (b. 1898); Professor of Political Economy, Cagliari, 1926– ; Cambridge University Lecturer in Economics, 1927–31; Assistant Director of Research in Economics, University of Cambridge, 1935–63; Fellow of Trinity College, Cambridge, 1939– ; Reader in Economics, Cambridge, 1963–65.

[25] Hans W. Singer (b. 1910); born in the Rhineland of Jewish parents; studied economics at the University of Bonn; came to Cambridge to work for a Ph.D. in 1934 under a scheme to assist graduates whose careers had been cut short by the Nazis; Ph.D. 1936; member of Pilgrim Trust Unemployment Enquiry, 1936–38; University of Manchester, 1938–44; Ministry of Town and Country Planning, 1945; University of Glasgow, 1946–7; Economics Department, United Nations, 1947–69; Fellow, Institute of Development Studies, University of Sussex, 1969– .

[26] Dr Edward Rosenbaum, who in the 1930s had been Director of the famous Commerzbibliothek in Hamburg, had resigned that post owing to the stresses of living under the Nazi regime. He had been in correspondence with Keynes from 1933 about the possibility of finding suitable employment in the United Kingdom and came to the country late in 1934. He was appointed to be an Assistant Librarian at the British Library of Political and Economic Science in the London School of Economics. After release from internment he returned to his work in that library.

To F. C. SCOTT, *23 July 1940*

My dear Francis,

Our behaviour towards refugees is the most disgraceful and humilitating thing which has happened for a long time. Also, rather disconcerting to find that we have such obvious fatheads still in charge. My information is that the War Office is far more responsible than the Home Office, which has been trying to do its best, and the War Office falls back on some panic decision of the War Cabinet which has never been reversed.

The case you quote in your letter sounds peculiarly shameful, stupid and unnecessary. I have been spending a great deal of time behind the scenes about four particular cases in which I am interested. I am glad to be able to report, however, that the general outcry is having some effect and there does seem to be a chance of getting some of the absolutely clear academic cases out of jug.

But, of course, there are thousands of more obscure people who cannot be dealt with in this way. Have you seen Mallan's letter in to-day's *Times*?

I have not met a single soul, inside or outside government departments, who is not furious at what is going on. Yet when one asks for an explanation one is told that the internment has largely been in response to public clamour and to prevent mob violence to the poor things if they were at large! Yet I read in the paper yesterday that there had been an unanimous appeal for his release by all the inhabitants of three streets in some obscure suburb because the Jewish butcher they were accustomed to deal with had been interned.

If there are any Nazi sympathisers at large in this country, look for them in the War Office and our secret service, not in the internment camps.

Yours ever,
[copy initialled] J. M. K.

Eventually, his efforts were successful.

PART II
AT THE TREASURY—
DOMESTIC WAR FINANCE

Chapter 4

THE 1941 BUDGET

Keynes's appointment to the Chancellor's Consultative Council, widely welcomed in the press, only gave Keynes a further entrée into official circles. As his letters to his mother indicate, however, it took him some time to become involved to the extent he desired.

From a letter to F. A. KEYNES, *5 July 1940*

The whole question of war damage is going to be in the first major question I shall be raising on the Consultative Council.[1]

The first meeting of this is on Monday, so our week-end this time will be rather short....I am pretty sure that the work of the Council will be exiguous. But I am hopeful that I may perhaps be able to use the position to establish helpful relations with the permanent Treasury people and persuade them to make some use of me.

From a letter to F. A. KEYNES, *25 July 1940*

I have been extremely busy lately giving the Treasury unsolicited advice. Whether it is possible to produce any effect in this way still remains to be seen. At least it keeps me occupied on matters which interest me anyhow, and are of importance if attended to.

From a letter to F. A. KEYNES, *10 August 1940*

I have now been given more extensive functions at the Treasury, having been put on a small high-up body which is to control generally the major decisions of what was my old dept. in the last war.[2] I am to have a room in the building, and even the sharing of a private secretary! It means more work, but not necessarily a great deal—the work will be very much what I choose to make it. So it suits me very well.

From a letter to F. A. KEYNES, *24 August 1940*

They could not be kinder to me at the Treasury than they are. This week I have been putting in about five hours a day there, and such work as

---

[1] On this matter, see below pp. 432–54.
[2] The body was the Exchange Control Conference. For more discussion of its operation and Keynes's contribution, see vol. XXIII.

there is is interesting and important. But, like Polly Hill[3] I am only just able to occupy my time, and have not *really* enough work to do.

From a letter to F. A. KEYNES, *27 September 1940*

I am now occupied in trying to put across the big guns a comprehensive budget of financial policy. But it is too soon to say whether I shall have the least success. The biggest part of my time, however, is perhaps being taken up by work and conferences on the war damage scheme, which, gradually, but slowly, approaches completion.

However, as the letters suggest, he was slowly becoming involved in so many aspects of official policy that it would be extremely confusing for the reader to ask him to follow all his various activities simultaneously, even though it would take him closer to the realities of Keynes's wartime contributions. For this reason, we shall concentrate separately on Keynes's contributions to various aspects of policy, beginning with the work that led up to the 1941 Budget.

The last pre-war Budget had been presented by Sir John Simon in April 1939. With the outbreak of war, he had presented a supplementary Budget on 27 September. Simon's first full-year wartime Budget came on 23 April 1940, a fortnight after the German invasion of Denmark and Norway but before the collapse of the British effort in Norway brought a change of government and before the German invasion of Belgium and the Netherlands marked the end of the 'phoney war'. Although in retrospect the April 1940 Budget may look timid, in the context of the 'phoney war' it was surprisingly ambitious. However, it was completely overtaken by events. It required some alteration during the passage of the Finance Bill and yet another supplementary Budget from Simon's successor as Chancellor, Sir Kingsley Wood, on 23 July 1940.

Keynes's first attempt to shape budgetary policy from inside the Treasury related to this supplementary Budget. On 11 and 14 July he sent the first of what were to prove a long series of Notes on the Budget to the Chancellor, Sir Richard Hopkins and Lord Catto. This set of notes ignored the issue of deferred pay, as Keynes had already presented the case for that previously.

---

[3] Polly Hill, Keynes's niece (b. 1914); Civil Servant, Treasury and elsewhere, 1940–51; Journalist, West Africa, 1951–4; Senior Research Fellow, University of Ghana, 1954–65; Fellow, Clare Hall, Cambridge, 1965– ; Smuts Reader in Social Anthropology, 1973– .

NOTES ON THE BUDGET   I

The Chancellor of the Exchequer pointed out to us that in the June quarter there had been a deficit of £513 million which had been covered by debt raised in a variety of ways. In order to judge the dimensions of the problem ahead of us, it is important to estimate, not merely the amounts raised in different forms, but where all this money came from. For it makes a great deal of difference to our diagnosis of the position how much came from each of the various sources available. I believe that the information in the possession of the Treasury should make possible a much closer estimate of these important figures that one might have expected. The object of this note is to test out this question, and to estimate the magnitude of the Budget problem in the light of the answer.

I suggest that an attempt be made to fill in the figures in the following table and to continue to do so for each successive month. The majority of the figures are already known to the Treasury and only need to be entered up; so that a moderate amount of guessing might be sufficient to reach interesting results.

The money subscribed in each month to the net additions of government debt must come from one or other of the following sources:-

1. Funds accruing to the government itself from various sources such as the following:-

(a) the Exchange Equalisation Fund (i.e. when the Fund is parting with more gold, foreign balances and requisitioned securities than it is acquiring; when it is acquiring more than it is parting with, this item becomes negative)

(b) war risks insurance funds (ships, commodities, etc.)

(c) social insurance and pension funds, etc.

(d) sundry other sources but *not* including the note issue

and savings banks which are brought in below under a different heading.

All these figures are in possession of the Treasury.

II. The net increase in overseas sterling balances and bills held in London. This figure is known to the Bank of England, which obtains a weekly return.

III. Net resources freshly placed by the public at the disposal of the Government, directly or indirectly, through the following channels:–

(a) Increase in note issue held outside the banks.

(b) Increase in excess of bank deposits (including the Bank of England) over loans and investments and deposits with other banks (including cash with Bank of England but not clearing banks' special deposits under the new scheme).

(c) Increase in Treasury bills held outside the government departments, the discount market and the banks (including overseas banks).

(d) Small savings, i.e. net increase in savings certificates and in savings bank cash deposits (but not investments made through savings banks).

(e) New net government issues (War Loans, 3% Bonds, 2½% N.W.B. etc.) not taken up by the government deposits or funds included under I above.

All these figures are in the possession of the Treasury or are easily obtainable.

I+II+III necessarily adds up to the amount of the current deficit, e.g. £513 million in the June quarter according to the figures given us by the Chancellor of the Exchequer. The total can be analysed in this way by the Treasury, but not by me, without any guesswork at all. In order to illustrate the object of all this, I will make my own guesses without pretending that the round figures given are more than illustrations. In the June quarter I put I at £100 million and II at £50 million; from which it follows that the various items under III must have added up to £363 million.

198

The next stage of the analysis aims at breaking up III into IV, the net proceeds obtained by the public from liquidating other capital assets and V, new savings. Let us begin with IV:–

IV. (*a*) The proceeds of requisitioned securities and sales of foreign securities of which the proceeds have been handed to the Bank of England.

(*b*) Excess of private sinking and depreciation funds against wastage and other capital losses, actual or prospective, over the cost of current replacements and improvements (including under this *all* new private investment).

(*c*) Reduction of privately held stocks of raw materials, goods in process and finished articles. (During the period when stocks previously held privately were being requisitioned by government departments this may have been large. Fluctuations in the aggregate sums insured under the war risks scheme may provide a clue to the amount of this item.)

(*d*) Provision against accruing taxes. At some periods of the year this may be a large sum; e.g. in the June quarter I should estimate this as the largest single item in our analysis, perhaps as much as £130 million (last Budget's estimate of this year's income tax, surtax and E.P.T. £593 million, or say £660 million after allowing for subsequent developments, which is £165 million accruing per quarter less £36 million taxes actually collected in June quarter).

IV (*a*) is known to the Treasury. The other items have to be guessed. For purposes of illustration I put (*a*) at £50 million, (*b*) at £50 million, (*c*) at nil in June quarter, (*d*) at £130 million; making a total of £230 million.

Deducting this from III we have the total of new savings by companies and individuals during the quarter, namely £363 million—£230 million, or (say) £130 million in round figures. This is equivalent to an annual rate of £520 million new savings. But, as I have explained above, a much more accurate estimate than this should be possible for the Treasury.

Now the significance of this method of analysis is the following. Several of the above sources of funds either cannot or should not be drawn on to a greater extent than at present even if total expenditure increases. Up to a certain figure of government expenditure we can depend to a very great extent on resources other than taxation and new savings. Thus, on the basis of the above figures, in order to finance a deficit of £513 million in the June quarter, we only had to depend on new savings to the extent of £130 million—or about a quarter of the total borrowing required. But this means that if the deficit increases by a moderate percentage, our dependence on new savings and new taxes may have to increase by a large percentage.

For example, the Chancellor led us to expect that the quarterly deficit would soon rise to £600 million or more,—say an increase of £100 million. If we have to depend for this entirely on new savings, these must rise from £130 million per quarter to £230 million—almost double. (I must add a *caveat* that these actual figures are not to be relied on pending criticism.)

How much support can be reckoned on from now onwards from sources other than taxation and new savings? The answer to this is very relevant to the magnitude of the Budget problem.

I (a)+IV (a) measures the extent to which we are using up our foreign resources. For a *short* period the possible maximum of this can be put very high. But anything much above £500 million per annum is getting dangerous. I am putting this at £500 million in the year beginning 1 July 1940.

I (b)+(c)+(d) is more or less stable at a figure known to the Treasury. I put down a round figure of £100 million a year pending further information. (*N.B.* This further information, to be serviceable, should not be a 'conservative' figure, i.e. biased in a low direction, but should be as near the truth as possible.)

II I am leaving at £200 million per annum.

IV (b) could be, and should be, increased by further restrictions on private investment (my personal experience in managing a large estate is that there has been *no* significant restriction so far on my spending, if I wish to, a normal amount on repairs and improvements). I put this figure at £250 million per annum from now on.

IV (c) can yield a high figure *temporarily*, but very little permanently. Restrictions on consumption now coming into force might bring a contribution of £50 million from this source in the next year, and perhaps more.

IV (d) only counts seasonally or when prospective taxes are increasing. There is a considerable delay between payment of income tax by companies and their making provision for it, and sometimes a long delay in E.P.T. Perhaps it is better to ignore this in dealing with annual, as distinct from quarterly figures, and to include any allowance for it in our estimate of the yield from taxation.

All this adds up to £500+100+300+250+50 = £1,100 million in the year beginning 1 July 1940. I do not think that this figure is unduly biased on the liberal side. Anyhow, as we *must* take risks, I suggest that this is the right bias with which, if any, to approach the problem. Even if it is pared down somewhat, it undoubtedly remains very large. The Budget problem is often made to appear much worse than it is, because this large contribution from sources other than taxation and new savings is ignored.

Sir John Simon's estimate of revenue in the current year was £1,234 million. This takes no account of the subsequent increase in E.P.T. or of the purchase tax (or some substitute for it). Moreover *if* the Government spends £3,500 million the consequent increase in private incomes will be reflected in a higher yield of taxation. Also this is an estimate of tax collections in the period; tax accruals will be larger. Subject to criticism by those who know more, I put the prospective rate of tax *accruals*, without allowing for the purchase tax, at not less than £1,500 million.

If we add this sum to the £1,100 million from special sources, we have a total of £2,600 million. Thus a total expenditure of £3,500 million would leave a gap of £900 million to be filled by new private savings and new taxes. This compares with my (provisional) estimate of £520 million for the current rate. The higher rate of private incomes corresponding to a government expenditure of £3,500 million will in itself result in some increase in savings; so that the amount of increased taxation required is not excessive. If propaganda, public spirit, severe restrictions on consumption and the high level of national income are capable of raising savings to a rate approaching £700 million a year, as they well may be, we are left with £200 million to find from new taxation including any receipts from the purchase tax.

The summary of the above is as follows for the year 1 July 1940–30 June 1941.

	£ million		£ million
Sales of gold and foreign securities	500	Government expenditure	3,500
Increase of overseas balances in London	200		
Receipts to certain government funds	100		
Depletion of private capital and stocks at home	300		
Accruals of taxation on the existing basis	1,500		
Private savings by individuals and companies	700		
New tax revenue required to balance (including purchase tax)	200		
	£3,500		

What are the weak points in this forecast?

(1) Expenditure in the year beginning 1 July 1940 may exceed £3,500 million.

(2) I am taking a terribly high figure, namely £700 million (£500 million loss of gold, securities and foreign balances +£200 million increased overseas balances in London), for the adverse balance of foreign payments.[4] The Treasury can say whether this is likely to be too big. On the evidence before me I doubt if it can be much less (it includes all kinds of government payments overseas, including Canada and all parts of the Empire, as well as the import–export deficit). Nevertheless the higher (and more dangerous) this figure is, the *easier* is the domestic Budget problem.

11 July 1940   J. M. KEYNES

NOTES ON THE BUDGET   II

In my previous note I suggested that an expenditure of £3,500 million could be covered by £1,100 million from capital sources, £700 million from new savings and £1,700 million from tax accruals. Any one of these figures may be incorrect. Let us suppose that there is in fact a deficiency of (say) £200 million at the present level of prices. What happens?

Private expenditure will in that case be exceeding by £200 million the value of the goods assumed in the above calculation to be available at present prices. Equilibrium will have to be restored in five ways:–

(i) In the first year, and still more in the first six months of such a situation, unsold stocks of consumers' goods would tend to diminish, as a result of the pressure to buy, at a greater rate than we have assumed. For example, the depletion of stocks (including second-hand goods) in the next year, instead of being £50 million as I assumed in my previous note, might be (say) £75 million.

(ii) Shortages in shops would be sure to interfere, in practice, with the full measure of import restriction and export

---

[4] The difference between the present estimates and those I made in *How to Pay for the War* are mainly due (1) to assuming a higher level of prices and national income, (2) a *much* higher adverse foreign balance, namely £700 instead of £350 million, and (3) a considerably higher level of taxation.

encouragement which, otherwise, we should be able to put into force. Theoretically, with perfect controls, this should not happen. But in fact an inadequate Budget is almost certain to lead to some modest increase in the adverse balance of trade. For example, the resources necessary to cover the deficit by the sale abroad of gold and securities might be, as a result, £25 million greater than we have assumed.

(iii) Since controls and organisation are not perfect, the pressure of consumers' buying is quite likely to interfere on a modest scale with the release of labour and materials for the munitions industries. Thus actual government expenditure might fall a little below the programme.

(iv) Some labour, unsuitable for any other employment and otherwise unemployed, might be drawn into, or continue in, the consumption industries under the pressure of strong demand. Also some capacity otherwise incompletely occupied, might attract more purchasing power without really using up any more resources. E.g. cinemas, trains and buses might be fuller.

Let us put the total relief under (i), (ii), (iii) and (iv) at £100 million, which reduces the deficit to £100 million.

(v) This remaining deficit could only be covered by means of a rise in prices, and the rise would have to continue until the increased profits and the higher level of incomes resulting from it were sufficient to raise the yield of taxation and the amount of voluntary savings by the £100 million in question.

The rise in the price level of consumption goods in order to achieve this would not have to be enormous, provided it did not set a wage rise in motion. Assuming stable wages, I should estimate the rise in prices sufficient to bring in £100 million extra in taxes and voluntary savings, at not less than 5 per cent and not more than 10 per cent. If half the goods covered were kept stable in price on the ground of being necessaries by rationing and controls, other articles of consumption would have to rise between 10 and 20 per cent.

I conclude that the Budget problem is not quite as bad as it looks. If we are reasonably strict with ourselves, there is no financial disaster ahead,—no really serious degree of inflation at the present stage.

Nevertheless it is clear from the above analysis that nearly all the consequences of an inadequate Budget are bad. Moreover the maintenance of morale and a high national spirit *requires* a substantial addition to taxes. A substantial addition will be actually favourable to morale. The fact that the financial situation is not yet out of hand and that the Budget problem is still manageable, should act as a further encouragement. I suggest that, if the Chancellor puts on some £200 million new taxes, he should be at pains to explain to the House of Commons that this is not merely a drop in the bucket but does really offer a prospect of something which, for the time being at least, approaches equilibrium. There is a real danger in the uninstructed public becoming too despondent about the apparent financial gap. In a *closed system*, such as we now enjoy, financial problems have a habit of solving themselves provided certain main principles are faithfully observed.

Nevertheless—as is only too obvious—whilst taxes in the abstract and in the aggregate will be greeted favourably, in particular and in detail they all arouse opposition. Furthermore it is a fundamental difficulty in the policy of being dependent on voluntary savings that any severe taxes are liable partly to defeat their object through their repercussion on the level of such savings.

I survey in the next section the opportunities for new taxes which are not highly oppressive in particular cases. I am not including a proposal for deferred pay, since I have already argued this case elsewhere. This would still yield, in my opinion, a larger net sum than the practicable alternatives. But if, psychologically, straight taxes, combined with some rise in prices relative to wages, are preferred by the wage-earning classes, this can be made to yield results sufficiently equivalent for the immediate purpose of financing the war.[5]

14 July 1940   J. M. KEYNES

NOTES ON THE BUDGET   III

The following are suggestions towards the provision of a further yield of £200 million:

(1) My proposal for a tax on immovable property as the price of a guarantee against war damage would bring in upwards of £60 million gross.

(2) It is worth considering whether a very high *ad valorem* import duty, say 100 per cent, on luxury foods and finished goods, not imported under government auspices, is still worth while, as much with a view to discouraging this type of consumption as to raise revenue. It may be that few such imports are now allowed. On the other hand, there may be a fair range of articles, which from one reason or another it is still expedient not to prohibit, which might reasonably be taxed very highly. (This might overlap rather seriously with the purchase tax proposals made below.)

(3) I am not in love with the purchase tax, but there is surely a useful and important field for something of the kind. The worst of it is that the general administrative scheme of the tax, as proposed, is, in my judgment, along the wrong lines. The present proposals suffer, amongst other defects, from being *too good* administratively for a time of war; they put too high the virtue of being completely watertight. We must be content to be more rough and ready. I venture, therefore, even at this late date, to suggest a very drastic modification.

(i) It should be a retail sales tax collected by means of

---

[5] The gap arising through not adopting either deferred pay or equivalent taxes in the spring Budget has been met, partly by the time-lag in the increased expenditure, partly by a further rise in prices, and very largely by using up our foreign reserves at a much greater rate than I then contemplated.

receipt stamps. No doubt there might be evasions, but the risk of this in wartime is less than usual. Beyond some inspectors (a duty which the public themselves could largely carry out) it needs no administration whatever. There should be very heavy penalties for attempted evasion.

(ii) Exemption of necessaries should be effected, largely or mainly, not by a long list of exempt articles, but by allowing every holder of a ration book to buy up to a certain limit of amount free of tax. This would be arranged by adding to each ration book a coupon which the holder could exchange once a month at the Post Office for a book of receipt stamps sufficient to pay the tax on a stipulated expenditure per head per week. By this means the objection that the purchase tax cannot be graded is avoided; and incidentally a small children's allowance is introduced. (No objection to one person selling his receipt stamps to another if he wants to!)

(iii) There is a great deal to be said for dealing with necessaries entirely in this way and having no exempt list whatever.[6] For example retail expenditure up to £1 per week per head might be tax-free. This would have the advantage that the field of the tax would be so wide that it could start at a low rate. At present prices retail sales must be worth £3,200 million. The exempt expenditure would be about £2,200 million, leaving £1,000 million taxable. Thus a tax of 12½ per cent (1½d in the shilling) would bring in £125 million.

If we assume that a man spends two-thirds of his income on retail purchases, a married man would be exempt up to earnings of £3 a week and a married man with two children would be exempt up to earnings of £6 a week. A married man without children earning £5 a week would pay 3s 4d a week or 3·3 per cent of his income; with £10 a week he would pay

---

[6] I should deal with books and entertainments by including them, along with education, religion, medical attendance and medicine etc. as cultural and health expenditure which I should exclude by definition from the category of retail sales for the purpose of taxation.

11s 8d or 5·83 per cent. On the other hand, compared with income tax, he would get off entirely on any part of his income which he saved. Also this method would deal more gently than a direct tax on income with those who had to spend an exceptionally large amount on rent or sent away money to parents etc.

(iv) Alternatively there might be a fairly long list of exempt articles,[7] such as—(a) all rationed articles; (b) a short list of necessary but unrationed articles such as bread and milk; (c) all articles subject to excise; (d) fuel and light. And in this case the exempt expenditure per head per week might be reduced to 10s. If the exempt articles covered one third of total retail sales, and exempt expenditure were thus reduced, the same rate of tax, namely 12½ per cent, would produce about the same yield as the above, namely £125 million.

(v) It will be observed that the method of a certain exempt expenditure per head (including children) gets over all the difficulties about children's clothing etc. It also means that the old-age pensioner and others with small incomes would pay nothing at all. But the first alternative is preferable to the second from this point of view. A newly married couple might be presented by the Registrar with a book of receipts covering an outlay of (say) £25.

(vi) The question of small purchases deserves, perhaps, special mention, since, although it is not important, it is the kind of point which everyone raises. The easiest method would be as follows:–

Total cash expenditure in the shop less than 2½d, nil; 2½d–4½d, ½d tax; 5d–8d, 1d tax; 8½d–1s, 1½d tax; with a request to retailers not to sell unnaturally small units so as to evade tax. The receipt stamps on small cash purchases would be in the nature of a bus ticket. For larger purchases and where an account is rendered, an adhesive receipt stamp would be affixed to the nearest ½d.

---

[7] I am assuming that cultural and health expenditure is excluded from the tax in any case.

(vii) A tax of this kind once established and in running order is capable of extension.

(4) The only worthwhile alternative to some version of the purchase tax is some kind of direct income tax effective on wage earners.

I lay down the following general principles as being essential, or at any rate very desirable, for the practical working of such a tax:–

(i) It must be collected at source—a method of collection now very familiar to wage earners.

(ii) It must not involve the existing machinery of income tax forms and assessments, which are hopelessly unsuitable for a vast number of small incomes.

(iii) It should not take the form of a high standard rate of tax subsequently mitigated by an elaborate system of allowances. It clearly does much harm to talk about a man with £500 a year paying tax at the standard rate of 7s 6d in the £ when in fact he does nothing of the kind. It would be absurd to use this language in the case of a man with £5 a week who is actually being asked to pay 9d to 1s in the £.

If these principles are accepted, it follows that we cannot proceed merely by raising the existing rates of income tax on the lower levels of income. Nevertheless we have to remember that our income tax has evolved by a slow, elaborate evolution into so complete and complex a whole, that it is as dangerous to tamper with it as to operate on a living organism. One day some recasting of the whole system will have to be attempted. But now is scarcely the time for that. So we have to consider what we can do within these limitations.

At present an unmarried man with 55s a week is supposed to pay 1s 3d income tax a week, and a married man without children earning £6 a week is supposed to pay 6s a week income tax. But how many in fact pay it? Is there not a large sum to be obtained merely by making the existing rate of tax more universally effective? The first step, therefore, is to make all Schedule E incomes (wages and salaries) deductible at source, at any rate below a certain income level. The reason why this is not done already is, doubtless, because all deductions at source are made at the standard rate of 7s 6d, which would mean in the case of small salaries a grossly excessive deduction in the first instance. Clearly it is impossible to deduct at the rate of 7s 6d from the £6 a week man when all he owes is 1s. Thus we have to find some escape from initial deduction at the standard rate, which is a difficult technical problem.

Before proceeding to the technical task, let me suggest what we should be aiming at,—namely a national defence contribution of (say) 5 per cent of the excess of each week's income over (say) £3 a week, this to be an addition to the existing income tax. For men earning up to £5 a week this would work out as follows:-

Weekly earnings	Existing income tax	National defence contribution	Total
s	s d	s d	s d
		Unmarried	
45	Nil	Nil	Nil
55	1 3	Nil	1 3
75	4 3	9	5 0
80	5 0	1 0	6 0
100	8 6	2 0	10 6
		Married	
45	Nil	Nil	Nil
55	Nil	Nil	Nil
75	Nil	9	9
80	Nil	1 0	1 0
100	3 4½	2 0	2 0

A married man with one child or more pays no income tax at these levels of income.

The only solution I can see is the following, though probably Inland Revenue can think of something better:-

(i) Each employee to give his employer a signed statement saying whether he is married and how many children he has.

(ii) Inland Revenue to provide each employer with a table

on the above lines, showing the deduction to be made from each week's wages on the basis of that week's pay envelope.

(iii) The employer to buy stamps out of the amount withheld and to stamp cards which remain in the possession of the employee.

(iv) The stipulated deductions from each week's wage to be calculated on the assumption that that rate of earnings continues throughout the year, without allowing for any claims for relief except in respect of wife and children. The cards to be handed in once a year to Inland Revenue together with any other claims for relief, as for example for insurance or for unearned income which has been subject to too heavy a deduction at source, from which the Revenue can calculate the appropriate refund due to the taxpayer, since the card will carry on its face the exact amount of the man's earned income in the course of the year, without his having to make any declarations except such as he may choose to make in order to claim reliefs.

(v) I do not see why the above system should not be applied to all earnings from regular employments. But there is no objection to retaining the present system for earnings in excess of £10 a week if there is a good reason for this which has escaped me.

I should be interested in Inland Revenue's estimate of the tax properly due from weekly wage earners which is *now* (i.e. at present levels of earnings) escaping their net. The prevention of this evasion might by itself be a considerable help to the Budget.

The above tax on earned incomes should be balanced by an additional contribution of 1s in the £ from all other *personal* incomes. But this should take the form of an addition to the standard rate of income tax, e.g. it should not be charged, except in the case of 'one man' companies, on the undistributed income of a company or on income paid by one company to another.

In the main the task of graduation is left to the care of

income tax and surtax which appear to deal with this adequately. If more graduation is required, it should be effected through these instruments. Nevertheless some measure of graduation is implicit in the National Defence Contribution if this is worked out as a percentage of the income remaining after deduction of income tax and surtax. For example, N.D.C. thus calculated for a married man works out at different levels of income approximately as follows: 75s weekly, 1 per cent; 100s, 2 per cent; £6, 3 per cent; £12, 4½ per cent; £20, 5½ per cent; £100, 8 per cent.

J. M. KEYNES

14.7.40

Keynes's approach to Budget accounting was greeted by some rather acid remarks (for instance, by D. H. Robertson) on the usefulness of the calculations for those faced with the need for action. Certainly his advice had little immediate effect.

The second Budget of 1940 had met with considerable criticism as to its adequacy in the face of the problems arising in the summer of 1940, criticism which the official historian of wartime financial problems believes justified.[8] Keynes, on seeing the initial press criticism, wrote to the Chancellor on 24 July.

To the CHANCELLOR OF THE EXCHEQUER, *24 July 1940*

Dear Chancellor of the Exchequer,

There is in to-day's press a fairly widespread criticism of the Budget, that the yield of taxation as proposed is inadequate to the prospective rate of expenditure. It may very possibly be the case that from a strict point of view it may fall short by anything from £100 to £200 million. Nevertheless, I think your critics overlook certain considerations and that there is something of an answer to them along the following lines:

(1) You have made no revised estimate of the yield of revenue from now on on the basis of the increased national income corresponding to the somewhat higher level of prices

---

[8] R. S. Sayers, *Financial Policy 1939–45* (London, 1956), pp. 56–7.

and wages and the considerably increased government outlay. An increase of £500 million in the national income accrues to a very important extent to the Revenue in present circumstances, both on account of the 100 per cent E.P.T. and because the higher earnings lift a great number of people into a higher tax bracket. I do not know if the Treasury prepared for you any such figure. But I should have thought that the tax revenue, excluding your new taxes but including 100 per cent E.P.T., should yield nearer £1,500 million in the year beginning 1 July 1940 than £1,300 million. If this is true, it makes a considerable difference to the picture.

(2) The traditional way of estimating yield of revenue, namely, by reference to the actual tax receipts within the current financial year, is always unflattering to the immediate picture, when an increase in taxation takes place. Indeed, at a time when one's principal object is to restrict private expenditure, it gives quite a false picture of the true immediate situation. What matters in the national balance sheet is the rate of tax *accruals* from now onwards, especially in the case of the profits of joint stock companies. The sums which are now being set aside out of current profits will not reach the Exchequer in many cases before 1942. Yet, for all practical purposes, they are set aside to-day. I believe, therefore, that, if you were to take as your basis the annual rate of *tax accruals* as from 1 July 1940, you could fairly estimate them at not less than £1,700 million. Indeed this figure would be reached by taking the current rate of accruals of the previous taxes at £1,480 million and adding to that the yield of your new taxes in a full year, since, apart from a month or two's time lag in the purchase tax, they will in fact be accruing from now onwards at the full year's rate.

(3) Now a rate of tax accruals of £1,700 million looks a great deal better than £1,300 million, which is your estimate for tax collections in the current financial year.

(4) While you gave full justice in your speech to the sums

accruing from capital sources, you gave no estimate of them. Hopkins tells me that he thinks my figure of £1,100 million a bit on the high side. I hope that my figure for payments abroad may indeed be too high. But, on further reflection and after hearing Hopkins' criticisms, I was not inclined to reduce my aggregate of £1,100 million, since whilst some items may be on the high side, others, I think, are quite conservative.

(5) If £1,100 million be added to £1,700 million, expenditure at the rate of £3,500 million leaves £700 million to be found by new savings. This compares with my estimate of something over £500 million in recent months and is a stiff figure but not necessarily unobtainable.

(6) If, on the other hand, we have to think of expenditure in the ensuing months as being at an annual rate of £3,600 million rather than £3,500 million (which seems to follow, if we take weekly war expenditure as £57 million) then there is a gap of £100 million which becomes £200 million if we reduce the prospective saving to £600 million.

My conclusion is that, if one is thinking of the next six months, which presumably is what you are thinking of, the above final figure states the maximum of your crime, if there is any crime at all. Press comment suggests to me that the public are wrongly estimating the crime at a much larger figure than £100 million to £200 million per annum, and half that sum for six months.

The real criticism of the Budget, to my mind, is not the magnitude of the immediate yield, but the fact that by depending so largely on existing taxes you have shot your last bolt and have done nothing to appeal to the imagination; whereas it would have been possible to lay new foundations which would prepare the way for important further developments if they are required at a later date.

Also, I am perplexed as to how it would be administratively possible to work out a practical scheme of deduction at source in respect of wages without introducing something much more novel than seems to be indicated.

Yours sincerely,

J. M. K.

He also wrote notes to Sir Richard Hopkins on the revenue position as discussed in the Budget statement.

To SIR RICHARD HOPKINS, *25 July 1940*

Dear Hopkins,

I have been looking at the Budget revenue estimates and cannot but believe that the prospective yield of revenue has been ludicrously underestimated, with the result of doing gross dis-service to the Chancellor of the Exchequer's proposals.

It looks to me as though no attention at all has been paid to the new yield from people who have never previously paid income tax, partly as a result of deduction at source (I presume that you are really going to make a good job of this), by the great new class brought within the income-tax range by the new level of earnings, and the increase in rate of 5*s* in the £ on the first £165 of taxable income. Let me give you a little illustration from Coventry, about which accidentally I happen to know something at the moment. As the basis of this I attach two exhibits. The first of these is a letter just received from a stranger, which I should like back when you have read it.[9] The second is the summary of a report of a recent survey on Coventry which I shall be publishing shortly in the *Economic Journal*, The most relevant figures in which are on page 330.[10]

[9] The letter has not survived.
[10] C. Madge, 'War-Time Savings and Spending: a District Survey', *Economic Journal*, June–September 1940. Charles Henry Madge (b. 1912); Reporter on *Daily Mirror*, 1935–6; founded Mass Observation, 1937; directed survey of working class saving and spending for National Institute for Economic and Social Research, 1940–2; member, research staff of Political and Economic Planning, 1943; Professor of Sociology, Birmingham, 1950–70.

Now, unless the information in these documents is grossly erroneous, the whole of the occupied male population of Coventry is now earning £5 a week or more, probably with an average of £7–8. The number of employed males in present circumstances is probably not far short of 100,000. It will not be overstating the case to take an average of £7 since a man with £5 a week and a man with £9 a week pay more tax than two men with £7 a week. Under the new Budget a bachelor with £7 a week pays about £55 in tax, a married man without children about £33, a married man with one child about £20. An average of £35 should certainly not be too high. This means that in Coventry alone the payment of income tax by persons practically none of whom have paid tax previously may well be of the order of £3 million.

For the country as a whole—though now I am guessing wildly—I should have thought that the increased yield might well be £50 million from people who have never paid income tax before and were not allowed for in last April's estimates —and perhaps much more.

Is there even a trace of this apparent in the new revenue estimates? I cannot see it.

I am now inclined to think that my estimate of £1,700 million for the annual rate of tax *accruals* from now onwards may be well under the mark.

I am afraid, however, that the bachelor earning £8 a week will get a bit of a shock when he receives a demand note for £73 income tax!

Yours ever,
J. M. KEYNES

To SIR RICHARD HOPKINS, *31 July 1940*

Dear Hopkins,

May I give you a few further figures in corroboration of my estimate that tax *accruals* are now at the rate of £1,700 million per annum.

Simon's Budget was £1,234 million plus £26 million in a full year. The estimated increase of the new Budget in a full year is about £240 million, making a total estimate from now on of £1,500 million, taking E.P.T. at the modest figure of £100 million.

I do not know what national income the Inland Revenue were calculating on. From some figures supplied to me by Campion[11], I gather that their estimate was well under £5,000 million. My own estimate last February would have been nearer £5,500 million. If, however, we take £5,000 million, the revenue in a full year was estimated at an all-over average of 30 per cent of the national income. Now an increment of income obviously bears tax at more than the average rate. Thus, looked at this way, at least 30 per cent of the increment of national income will accrue to the revenue. Looking at it in another way, I should put the percentage at not less than 35. Those with less than £5 a week probably pay at least 20 per cent of any increment of income on indirect taxes. Those with more than £5 a week pay 20 per cent income tax in most cases on the increment of income, apart from indirect taxes. On the *increment* of income a very large number of incomes are now subject to 3s 6d, and practically all to 5s on the increment of income, and then on profits there is 100 per cent E.P.T.

Now, unless Inland Revenue were reckoning on a much higher income than I think likely, when they made their estimates, and if we really are going to spend at the rate of £3,500 million, it is certain, I think, that money incomes must be at least £600 million more than the Revenue were reckoning on.

The upshot is, therefore, that it is fairly safe to add another £200 million to the yield of existing taxes on the increased

[11] Harry Campion (b. 1905), Kt. 1957; Robert Ottley Reader in statistics, Manchester, 1933–9; Offices of the War Cabinet, 1939; Director, Central Statistical Office, Cabinet Office, 1941–67.

level of money incomes, making £1,700 million the rate of tax accruals from now onwards altogether.

Yours,
J. M. KEYNES

As mentioned above (p. 196), late September saw Keynes begin a major attempt to change the Treasury's approach to war finance in another series of notes on the Budget written between 21 September and 6 October.

NOTES ON THE BUDGET I

The Dimensions of the Budget problem

1. The importance of a war Budget is not because it will 'finance' the war. The goods ordered by the supply departments will be financed anyway. Its importance is *social*: to prevent the social evils of inflation now and later; to do this in a way which satisfies the popular sense of social justice; whilst maintaining adequate incentives to work and economy.

2. The *amount* of the new revenue required is what will meet a given domestic expenditure out of a given national income *without the aid of inflation,* on the assumption that wages and import prices do not rise for other reasons. The ways in which this revenue is raised have to satisfy the other two criteria.

3. A war Budget is concerned with the amount of *domestic* expenditure, not with the total Exchequer outgoings. In war conditions the relevant amount can be arrived at by subtracting the adverse balance of foreign payments on income account from the total Exchequer outgoings. For this adverse balance is necessarily financed either out of capital sources (i.e. selling gold and securities) or by borrowing overseas, and not out of current revenue plus current savings.

4. The size of the adverse foreign balance is increased by

218

the overseas purchases of the war departments and by the liberality of the Board of Trade and Ministry of Food in allowing imports for civilian consumption; and it is decreased by the stimulation of exports. Anything which increases this adverse balance depletes our foreign reserves faster, but it *diminishes* the domestic requirements of the Budget. Given the total Exchequer outgoings, the more successful the Board of Trade is in restricting imports and stimulating exports and the more austere the Ministry of Food in cutting down civilian consumption of imported supplies, the *heavier* are the requirements of the domestic budget and the *greater* the risks of inflation. This should not be a paradox. The faster we draw on our overseas resources, the less onerous are our domestic requirements. If we could borrow all we need in U.S.A. and elsewhere and if we had unlimited shipping to bring in our purchases, the risk of domestic inflation would have disappeared.

5. The volume of domestic expenditure is easier to forecast and is less likely to undergo large changes than the total Exchequer outgoings. In the first year of the war, the adverse foreign balance did not exceed £400 million. It is now running at a rate of from £800 million per annum. If the American programme now under order matures, it is likely to reach a rate of £1,200 million or more some time next year. Thus the prospective increase in total Exchequer issues considerably exceeds the prospective increase in the requirements of the domestic Budget.

6. The following estimates, which I submit subject to the correction of those who know better, will serve to illustrate the position:-

7. I will submit in a separate note a detailed analysis of how 'the balance of £900 million to be met otherwise in the first year of the war' actually was met. The upshot of this analysis is that various government sources furnished £100 million

	(£ millions)		
	First year of war	Current rate	Hypothetical prospective rate
Total expenditure out of the Exchequer	2,600	3,500	4,200
Adverse foreign balance	400	800	1,200
Domestic expenditure	2,200	2,700	3,000
Accruing revenue on past and present basis	1,300*	1,700	1,800
Balance to be met otherwise	900	1,000	1,200

* Actual revenue collections £1,150 million. I am assuming a further £150 million held by taxpayers in reserve against income tax, surtax and E.P.T. accrued but not yet paid over. Perhaps this is an underestimate.

and certain capital sources £150 million to £250 million; so that the voluntary savings of the public (private and institutional) had to provide between £550 and £650 million.

8. The amount of such voluntary savings is necessarily sufficient and *exactly* sufficient (sufficient to the nearest halfpenny) to fill the gap. This is not the test of the existence of budgetary inflation. The test is whether, in order to fill the gap, the yield of taxes and of voluntary savings have had to be stimulated by a diversion of the incomes of the general public into increased profits through a rise in domestic prices relatively to wages. The statistics of prices suggest that the actual budgetary inflation during the first year of the war was negligible, the rise of prices being not significantly greater than could be attributed to the rise in imports and the rise in the cost of living relatively to wages no greater than could be attributed to the worsening of the terms of trade, i.e. the rise in the price of imports relatively to the price of exports. By 'negligible' I mean that the increased yield of taxes and savings attributable to budgetary inflation in the first year of

the war was not greater than £100 million and was probably less than £50 million.

9. This conclusion is not inconsistent with the estimates of paragraph 6. For in the pre-war year the aggregate of personal and institutional incomes after deducting taxes may be put at £4,300 million (£5,300 million−£1,000 million) out of which about £400 million was saved; and in the first war year the former figure was about £4,700 million (£6,000 million−£1,300 million). In peacetime conditions £450 million to £500 million might have been saved out of the latter income, and an increase in this, as a result of more conservative distributions by companies, war economies and war savings propaganda, by £100 million to £150 million, making a savings total of £550 million to £650 million in the first year of war, seems a very reasonable result. I should estimate the current rate of new savings at about £650 million.

10. Let us now consider in the light of this the hypothetical rate of £4,200 million for total Exchequer expenditure. According to paragraph 6 this increases the 'balance to be met otherwise' by £300 million; namely from £900 million to £1,200 million. I see no reason for expecting any material increase in the yield of sources other than saving. It follows that, in this event, to avoid inflation a further £250–350 million more will have to be raised either by taxes and compulsory saving or by additional spontaneous saving.

11. In the hypothetical period, gross incomes may be somewhat higher but net incomes after deduction of taxes at the higher rates now in force are likely to be smaller rather than greater than net incomes in the first war year. Moreover out of total savings of £550–650 million, almost a half were institutional (company reserves, etc.) and contractual (building societies instalments and insurance premiums, etc.) leaving (say) £300 million as the rate of individual spontaneous savings; and there is no room for much increase in institutional and contractual savings. Thus to fill the gap,

there would have to be not far short of *doubling* of the rate
of spontaneous private savings,—i.e. from last year's figure of
£300 million (or perhaps £350 million at the present time) to
the neighbourhood of £600 million. An increase of this magnitude is surely quite beyond the powers of war savings
propaganda.

12. Unfortunately the dimensions of the Budget problem
are somewhat greater than the apparent gap of £300 million.
For an increase of taxation or compulsory savings on this
scale, coming on the top of what is already some reduction
in net incomes, is bound to react adversely on the level of
spontaneous savings. It should not much affect institutional
and contractual saving. But we must be prepared to expect
a reduction of, say, £100 million (or even £150 million) in
private spontaneous savings as a result of collecting a further
£300 million by compulsory methods.

13. I conclude that, subject to the various assumptions
which have been made, the dimension of the prospective
Budget problem is of the order of £400 million.

J. M. KEYNES

21.9.40

NOTES ON THE BUDGET   II

Price and wage policy

1. Note I ended with the conclusion that the dimension of the
Budget problem is of the order of £400 million. This is a
substantial figure, being nearly 25 per cent of the present
revenue. But it is not an impossible amount to raise. For it
is only some 7 per cent of the present aggregate of taxable
incomes (which is probably above, rather than below, £6,000
million). Methods of raising it will be discussed in a subsequent note.

2. It is essential that this budgetary problem *should* be
solved one way or another. For if it is neglected, the infla-

tionary pressure would be very great, probably involving an initial rise of at least 15 per cent in retail prices or, alternatively, acute shop shortages and the evil of queues, which would lead inevitably to all-round rationing on the German model, with obvious reactions on morale. And this is apart from any rise in wage rates which would almost certainly break loose, turning the initial rise into a progressive one, as happened in the last war when the size of the gap was, relatively, much the same. Moreover we should have suffered all this inconvenience and overburdening of the administrative machine and injustice and loss of morale to no purpose. For the reduction in the standard of life through inflation would, of necessity, be *just as great* as through taxation. So it would be a mug's game *not* to solve the Budget problem.

3. Let us, therefore, assume for the moment that this problem *is* solved one way or another. Unfortunately there are other ways in which prices can break loose from their moorings. The above calculations were based on the assumption that prices do not rise for reasons other than budgetary inflation, i.e. we excluded an increase in prices due to a rise in import costs, higher indirect taxation or a rise in wages.

4. It is obvious that wage policy raises far-reaching psychological and political issues. It can only be handled by a simple, *trustful* and imaginative policy which covers a wider field than technical finance. And I would say at once that we must begin, if necessary, with aggravating the Budget problem by our handling of the cost of living problem. Since the stabilisation of the cost of living seems to be an indispensable preliminary to a sound wage policy, I will begin with that.

5. Let us assume, for the moment, that we can hold wages if we can hold the cost of living. In most important respects the problem is easier than it looked like being (or than it was in the last war). In the early months it was impossible to say how high import prices might rise. Today the position is

223

entirely different. World prices of food and raw material are now on the decline (and would fall more if only our buying departments and our enthusiasts for lapping up 'exportable surpluses' would let them). The exchange value of sterling has been stabilised, and we are acting on the (unavoidable) assumption that American assistance will enable us to maintain this position indefinitely and at the same time to import all the goods which our shipping can handle.

6. Unfortunately, there are some developments immediately impending, relatively minor in themselves, which may be sufficient to upset the *status quo* of the prices and wages, unless they are attended to; namely—

(i) The Ministry of Shipping propose to raise freight rates by 30 per cent to meet the losses which they estimate they are now making on account of higher war risk rates and the longer time occupied by voyages. I do not know just how much money is involved, but it is, I suppose, of the order of £50 million. Obviously it will react seriously on the export situation, as soon as the exporters know about it. A large part will be merely transferred from the Ministry of Shipping accounts to the accounts of the supply departments. The cost to the Ministry of Food, which is our immediate concern, is provisionally estimated at £16 million, which might raise the cost of living index 2 or 3 points if it is added to prices. I understand that already, in effect, the above loss by the Ministry of Shipping is being currently borne by the Exchequer; but it is only now that their accountants have disentangled it sufficiently to be in a position to propose its transfer to other shoulders.

(ii) The recent subsidies to British farmers are costing the Ministry of Food some £30 million at present prices. There are also certain other cases, e.g. sugar and tea, where present selling prices will have to be raised if cost is to be covered. If retail food prices were to be raised sufficiently to cover the Ministry of Food's costs (apart from the old-established

Treasury subsidy of £60 million) the cost of living index number would rise some 5 or 6 points. Although no one proposes to throw the whole of the expense of subsidising the farmers on to the cost of living, the Ministry of Food have been considering various compromises. But if for reasons of general policy it is decided to subsidise British farmers, to enable them to raise agricultural wages and their own profits, there is no compelling reason why this should be paid for by what is, in effect, an indirect tax on the particular foods of general consumption through which it is convenient to administer the subsidy.

(iii) Finally, there is the purchase tax. It is said that, when this tax comes into operation, it will raise the cost of living index by another 9 points; though this looks rather a high estimate.

7. Thus it might appear that wholly to offset the effect of all these factors on the cost of living index would cost the Treasury £70 million or more, in addition to the existing food subsidies of £60 million. Fortunately this is an overstatement, since there are various adjustments open to the Ministry of Food, mentioned in more detail below, by way of throwing more of the burden on the prices of semi-luxuries, which do not enter into the cost of living index or have low weights in that index; so that the cost of living *index*, as distinct from food prices generally, could be stabilised for a smaller sum than the above. Moreover by no means the whole of the above is *additional* to the burdens currently carried by the Budget. There is a time-lag between the date at which the burdens actually began and the date at which the accountants of the ministries concerned provide adequate data on which proposals to meet them can be used.

To fix our ideas, let us assume that the stabilisation of the cost of living *index* might cost £50 millon in addition to the existing subsidy of £60 million.

8. The net cost to the Exchequer would, however, be much

less than this. If none of this subsidy is given, the cost of living index might rise 8 per cent (14 points on the index = 8 per cent). In this event it is to be expected that a general wage rise would be set in motion; and upwards of half the wages bill of the country now falls directly or indirectly on the Government. If, in a vain effort to maintain their real value, wages were to rise by just the right *initial* amount, the loss to the Treasury on the wages bill would, of course, be only about half the sum saved by not granting the subsidy. But if there is a compelling reason for rehashing the structure of wages and giving every class of workers a plausible ground for reopening the whole issue, the final result would surely be an average rise in wages much beyond the strictly appropriate figure. Moreover, in any case this is not the end of the story. Even if the initial rise in wages is only in strict proportion to the rise in the cost of living, this sets in motion a progressive increase in prices and, therefore, in wages. If wages rise 8 per cent, the cost of living will also be stepped up; and so on. For the rise in the cost of living must always keep ahead of the rise in wages. In the course of a year or two (just as in the last war) we shall find ourselves with a rise in the cost of living of 50 per cent or more, hotly, but always unsuccessfully, pursued by a rise in [w]ages; until at last the overwhelming pressure of public opinion forces the Treasury to grant the subsidy, after all—at a far higher level of money cost. And this would have happened *even though the strictly Budget problem had been satisfactorily solved.*

9. If international prices were romping upwards or if the sterling exchange was out of hand, the task of stabilising the cost of living might seem hopeless. But in the actual circumstances, I submit that there is a strong case for stabilisation merely on financial grounds. If we add to this the general political considerations, which led to the Cabinet decision on 19 August last 'that the prices of essential foods shall be kept down by subsidy in order to secure cheap food,

to restrain a rise in the cost of living index figure and to prevent prices rising', the case seems overwhelming.

10. Nevertheless, it would, I suggest, be a great mistake for the Chancellor of the Exchequer to agree to the necessary subsidy *as an isolated concession*. It must be part of a comprehensive policy. A subsidy increases effective puchasing power. To grant a subsidy to food without withdrawing the equivalent purchasing power in some other way is merely putting off trouble for a very short time and getting it when it comes in a particularly tiresome form. In the Cabinet papers on this subject which I have seen there was inadequate emphasis on this point. The Minister of Food gave good reasons against either an extension of rationing or a reduction of the existing rations. But was it appreciated that every subsidy to the cost of living necessarily brings these objectionable things nearer? The Food Ministry is already under instructions to assume that there must be a reduction in the coming year in the tonnage of food imports, although it is now hoped that the original allocation of 15 million tons may be increased. If supplies are to be diminished, prices kept down and the wages bill on the increase, there is no possible escape from shop shortages, queues and general rationing, unless the Treasury is taking other offsetting measures. The Minister of Food ought to come to the Board Room on bended knees and implore the Chancellor of the Exchequer the boon of increased direct taxation on wage earners as the only possible means by which the purposes of his Ministry could be achieved as set forth in his memorandum.

11. In short, the corollary to food subsidies, which are the opposite of indirect taxation, is *more direct taxation*. And from every point of view it is desirable that the announcement of direct taxation should be at the same time as the announcement of a stabilisation of the cost of living, and should be *clearly associated with it as the necessary price*.

12. It is, I find, more usual in the memoranda which are

in circulation to argue that the proper price for the stabilisation of the cost of living is an undertaking by the trade unions to stabilise wages. Certainly this would be desirable in itself. But the arguments of those, who think that such a demand would be impolitic, are convincing. Mr Leggett[12] of the Ministry of Labour has put it in conversation that *the possibility* of a rise in wages is an essential safety valve. If the trade union leaders now in authority were to agree to divest themselves of the power to demand higher wages, an agitation would arise to replace them by others not thus restricted. There can be no justification in wartime for a *general* rise in wages, except a rise in the cost of living. But this may not be true of every particular industry. It is difficult to draw the line between wage adjustments and wage increases. Anyway the freedom of the wage bargain is the Ark of the Covenant for the trade union movement, which it is not wise to call in question except for grave and unavoidable cause. My advice to the Chancellor of the Exchequer is, therefore, to stabilise the cost of living without asking for the stabilisation of wages, but to insist that it should be paid for by higher direct taxes.

13. The policy would be, so to speak, to put the trade unions and the Ministry of Labour 'on their honour'. Experience so far does not suggest that this would be imprudent or surely doomed to disappointment. It is sometimes said that the Treasury has not been rewarded for the existing food subsidy. But the claim of the Ministry of Labour to the contrary can be, I think, largely substantiated. I share Sir Horace Wilson's 'impression that, so far, the wage situation is less unfavourable than we at one time feared'. Perhaps a short digression on this will not be a waste of time.

14. It is true that the index of wage rates has risen in almost

---

[12] Frederick William Leggett (b. 1884), Kt. 1941; entered Civil Service, 1904; Private Secretary to Minister of Labour, 1917; Assistant Secretary, Ministry of Labour, 1919; Principal Assistant Secretary, 1930; Under-Secretary, 1939; Chief Industrial Commissioner, 1941–2; Deputy Secretary, Ministry of Labour and National Service, 1942–5.

every month. But so has the cost of living. And the progressiveness of the wage index is chiefly due to the fact that some industries have got their necessary rise later than others. Up to July the wage index had risen 12 per cent; but the cost of living had risen by double this amount, namely 24 per cent. Thus on this basis real wage rates have fallen about 10 per cent. During the period since the beginning of this year wage rates have risen slightly less than the cost of living. Moreover all the experts agree that the true cost of living has risen more than is shown by the index; so that real wage rates have in fact fallen by more than 10 per cent and have continued throughout the war to decline slightly. The exaggerated rise in the earnings of some classes of workers has been due, not to wage rates, but to the excessive influence of overtime rates and the readiness in some directions to pay wages which are in practice out of line with the agreed basic rates.

15. At the same time the machinery for deciding wage rates needs stiffening up. The obvious criticisms to make are (1) that wage applications do not necessarily, or even usually, reach the Wages Tribunal and (2) that the Tribunal is not guided in its decisions by any clear directions. The influence of 100 per cent E.P.T., combined with the increasing competition for labour between different groups of employers as we approach full employment, may lead to voluntary concessions by employers which are dangerously excessive. If the cost of living is stabilised, this is, in fact, the chief outstanding danger.

16. I suggest, therefore, that, if the Chancellor of the Exchequer agrees to stabilise the cost of living, it would be reasonable for him to ask the Minister of Labour—

(i) to provide that wage agreements reached by collective bargaining between trade unions and employers shall require the subsequent approval of the Wages Tribunal; and

(ii) to direct the Wages Tribunal not to approve important changes in basic rates, as distinct from wage adjustments, unless they are justified, in their judgment, either by changes in the cost of living or because wages in the particular industry are below their reasonable parity with other comparable rates.

17. I deal in subsequent notes with the form of the subsidy to the cost of living, and with proposals for higher direct taxation.

J. M. KEYNES

28 September 1940

NOTES ON THE BUDGET   III

Subsidies to the cost of living and indirect taxation

1. A given expenditure on subsidising the cost of living would go much further than at present if the following general principles were approved:–

(i) The existing official cost of living index is sacrosanct for the purpose of many wage bargains, and any proposal to modify it would be open to suspicion. In practice this is rather convenient. For a more up-to-date index, weighted in accordance with the importance of the different articles in wartime consumption, would indicate a somewhat greater rise in the cost of living than the official index. This opens the way to legitimate adjustments by using the subsidy to produce as much effect as possible on the *official index*. No harm is done, since the official index gives the heaviest weights to the articles which are important to the poorer families, with the important and unfortunate exception of milk offset, however, by the existence of the special milk scheme. In short, the object of the subsidy should be to stabilise the *official index*. Indeed we can welcome higher prices in the field of semi-luxuries which mainly fall outside the scope of the official index, as a Cabinet decision has already recognised.

(ii) At present, the different divisions of the Ministry of Food aim at being self-supporting after allowing for specific subsidies allocated to them such as the bread subsidy; and their accountants regard themselves as being 'good boys' from the Treasury point of view in so far as they are successful. But it would be much better if the Ministry of Food were free to apply a lump sum subsidy in whatever directions would produce most effect in reducing the index or in diverting consumption away from articles in short supply and towards articles in surplus. It is for the Ministry of Food to arrange the details. But a conversation which Mr Twentyman[13] and I had with their representatives suggests that as much as £15–20 million might be saved in this way; so that, if the total cost of food rises by £65–70 million, the official index could be stabilised at a cost of £50 million or less. For example, there seemed to be good reasons for increasing the prices of bread and condensed milk and reducing the prices of potatoes, oatmeal and sugar; whilst a new system of meat rationing might bring in more money without raising the price of the cheaper cuts which come into the official index. There may also be worthwhile opportunities for profiteering by the Ministry in non-staple and semi-luxury foods which fall outside the index.

(iii) It is safer to reduce the prices of rationed, than of non-rationed, articles, since there is a safeguard against the lower price leading to a higher consumption of the particular article.

2. Subsidies on food are the opposite of indirect taxes on food. It is rather odd to subsidise one half of the breakfast table and then tax the other half for historical and administrative reasons which are irrelevant to the present situation. I suggest, therefore, that the major part of the relief to the cost of living should be given by abolishing the duties on domestic, but not on manufactured,[14] sugar and on tea. I have

---

[13] Edward Twentyman (d. 1945); Treasury, 1920–40; Head of Division concerned with food policy if war broke out, 1937–40; transferred to Ministry of Food, 1940; Second Secretary, 1941; Chief Representative, Ministry of Food, Washington, 1943–5.

[14] This would revive the practice followed by the Sugar Commission in 1920, in order to confine the subsidy then paid to sugar sold for domestic use' (Memorandum of Inter-Departmental Committee on Food Prices).

not the data for calculating the exact cost of this, but it would be, I think, about £30 million. There are the following strong reasons for adopting this course:—

(i) It happens that £1 million spent in reducing the price of sugar has more effect in reducing the cost of living index than £1 million spent in any other direction, and nearly twice as much effect as £1 million spent on the average of other foodstuffs generally, whilst the effect of £1 million spent in reducing the price of tea also has an effect on the index above the average. Indeed the effect on the cost of living index of abolishing these duties would be so great that if the consequences of the purchase tax could be offset in some other way, the Ministry of Food might be able, or almost able, by using all the expedients mentoned above to keep the food index stable without any further assistance; so that the estimated cost of £50 million would be reduced to nearer £30 million.

(ii) Both these articles are rationed, with the rations already drawn on up to the hilt, so that there is no danger of a reduction in price leading to an inconvenient increase in consumption. This is not affected by the fact that the Minister of Food already intends in any case to increase the rations of both these articles.

(iii) Both articles are the particular object of expenditure by the poorest classes and old age pensioners.

(iv) The psychological effect of abolishing these duties in producing an atmosphere, in which higher direct taxation becomes more acceptable, would be incomparably greater than that of frittering away the money in other less obvious directions. If the Chancellor of the Exchequer announces that the Ministry of Shipping has to increase freights but that he hopes to offset this so far as food is concerned, or that the new prices to farmers will require yet another increase in agricultural subsidies, it will cut no ice at all. But if he announces that, to hold back the rising tendency of the cost of living, he proposes to abolish the duties on tea and sugar, the new policy comes out with a flourish of trumpets; particularly if he can persuade the Minister of Food to withhold until the same date his announcement that the rations of both tea and sugar are to be increased.

3. There remains the effect of the purchase tax on the price of clothing which enters into the cost of living index. This is particularly unfortunate because the clothing ingredient in the index has already risen by nearly 50 per cent, which is far greater than the rise in any other group. The matter deserves more attention than it seems to be receiving; though perhaps something is going on of which I am unaware. Could not some standard line of cloth be put on the market at a cheap price which would hold the cost of living index without breaking unduly into the yield of the new tax as a whole? I do not know enough to make any specific suggestion.

4. It is suggested in some quarters that a very gradual rise in the cost of living index would be comparatively harmless in its effect on wages. I distrust this view. A gradually rising tendency will create the wrong atmosphere. And no one can predict at what point a general movement to raise wages will break loose. I believe it would be better to adopt the contrary policy, fully offsetting rises in some directions by declines in others, even to the point of a slight reduction in the cost of living index when the new policy is introduced. The importance of creating a psychological atmosphere, in which heavy direct taxation can be accepted, is paramount. This does not mean that there should not be minor *seasonal* fluctuations in the index.

5. How far do these proposals raise the gap in the Budget to be filled by direct taxation above the figure assumed in my first note? They must have some tendency in that direction. But my figures had so little reasoned estimate behind it, that I cannot say by how much it should be increased. I merely took the present apparent rate of expenditure and assumed an increase of £300 million in domestic outgoings. A fairly

important part of the losses of the Ministry of Shipping and of the higher subsidies to farmers are already included, presumably, in the present rate of expenditure; but I do not know how much. I propose, therefore, to retain my previous figure for the gap until it is replaced by closer estimating. For I do not believe that the proposed stabilisation of the cost of living will cost so much as to affect the order of magnitude of the gap. At the same time I am fully conscious that closer estimating may disclose a wider gap.

J. M. KEYNES

29 September 1940

NOTES ON THE BUDGET   IV

Direct taxation

1. All the arguments converge to the conclusion that the budgetary gap must be closed by increased *direct* taxation. Most of them are so obvious that I need not waste time by recapitulation. But one of them deserves emphasis. Until recently it was taken for granted that indirect taxes are politically easier to impose; and, indeed, that they are virtually the only means of securing a significant contribution from the wage-earning class. There are now strong indications that public opinion, especially in labour circles, is opposed to further indirect taxation and *prefers* direct taxes. With this change of mood the public are favouring what is, on general principles, unquestionably the better alternative.

2. Further direct taxes on the relatively rich (meaning by this the new surtax class having £1,500 a year or more) are also, by general admission, incapable of raising an adequate, or even an important, revenue. (The total confiscation of the excess of all incomes over £1,500 a year would yield not much more than £100 million gross above the existing taxes.)[15] Higher direct taxes imposed on this class will be for reasons

[15] The net benefit to the revenue would be appreciably less than this.

234

of social justice to match heavier taxes on the lower range of incomes, more than for the revenue they bring in. Indeed we can go further than this. Three-quarters of the aggregate income of the country belongs to the below-£500 class.

3. Higher direct taxes on the below-£500 class must be collected at source if they are to work; and the new Budget has provided the administrative machinery for this.

4. If we agree that the yield necessary to fill the gap must be found from some kind of direct impost on the below-£500 class, the field of discussion is greatly simplified. We can tackle, first of all, this essence of the problem; and then consider what further trimmings are necessary to preserve equality of treatment and to make the main proposition psychologically and politically acceptable.

5. The method of raising the standard rate of income tax and reducing personal allowances must surely be rejected. The claims of administrative convenience have been allowed to prevail already beyond what is psychologically prudent if the public is to understand and tolerate the system. An increase in the standard rate of tax has the effect, so far as appearances go, of greatly overstating the burden on the lower income ranges and greatly understating the burden on the higher income ranges. A flat all-round increase of 1s in the basic rate, unaccompanied by any changes in allowances or in surtax, does not appear to discriminate against the higher ranges. Yet measured as a percentage of the net income which remains to be taxed after deduction of the existing taxes, which is the fair method of reckoning, it works out in practice as a graduated scale beginning at 5 per cent of the lowest net incomes steadily rising to 25 per cent of the highest. The war Budgets up to date have left so little margin of taxable capacity at the higher ranges, that the Chancellor cannot afford to express his new scheme of taxation in terms which are likely to mislead the public as to the relative further burden he is putting on this class. If the Chancellor were to

announce an increase of 1s in the basic rate unaccompanied by greater personal allowances or by any change in surtax rates, it will be no more obvious than it has been hitherto that he is in fact taxing the highest ranges five times heavier than the lowest.

6. I attach therefore, great importance to *expressing* the new impost as a percentage of the *net* income which remans after deduction of existing taxes and not as a percentage of gross income. This would be easier administratively than to attempt a complete re-hash of the existing system by doing away with the basic rate and substituting a graduated rate which would be the alternative.

7. My proposal is, therefore, for a graduated war surcharge, superimposed on the existing income tax and surtax, and falling on the *net* income remaining after deduction on these taxes, the *whole* of what is required, say £400 million to £450 million, to be raised in this way. A surcharge ranging from 20 per cent on the excess of net incomes over £100 should bring in enough, conservatively estimated. I have not the data to calculate precisely the appropriate graduation. But I offer the following scheme, which might bring in as much as £600 million, by way of illustration:-

The first £100 of net income	Nil
The next £400 of net income	25 per cent
The next £2,000 of net income	30 per cent
The next £2,500 of net income	35 per cent
The next £5,000 of net income	40 per cent
The excess over £10,000 net income	50 per cent

Different levels of *gross* income (taking the case of a married man without children) would pay under this scale as follows:-

Unless it is intended to make the war an opportunity for what could legitimately be regarded as confiscatory treatment of the higher incomes, a steeper graduation than this is scarcely justified. But it is, of course, perfectly easy to steepen the graduation to any extent without detriment to the main principle if it is desired to do so for political or other reasons.

Gross income	Existing tax	Proposed surcharge
£	£	£
150	Nil	12·10
200	Nil	25
300	20	45
500	76	81
1,000	253	174
2,000	643	357
5,000	2,399	735
10,000	6,049	1,208
20,000	14,611	1,751
50,000	41,611	2,931

8. No special allowances are proposed for dependants. It seems more convenient to deal with all such allowances through the existing income tax, increasing them if in the new circumstances they seem to be inadequate. I believe that there is a good case for increasing the existing personal allowances in respect of children. If, however, it is desired to introduce such allowances into the surcharge scheme, it could be done by exempting the first £40 of income for each dependent member of the household in place of the first £100 irrespective of the number of dependants.

9. The scale proposed for the surcharge works out not very differently from the scale which I proposed previously for deferred pay. So far what I have proposed is an outright tax. But it is open to us to consider whether any part of it should be turned into deferred pay. In my previous proposal the *whole* of the surcharge was to be ultimately repayable irrespective of its amount. Some at least of the objections raised to this proposal might, however, be met by providing that only the first £50 (or, if you like, the first £100) of the surcharge should take the form of deferred pay, the balance being retained as an outright tax. That is to say, no one could accumulate more than £50 (or £100) a year of deferred pay, however great his income. Thus the opportunity for the

237

rich to evade the purpose of the surcharge by selling capital assets against their prospective deferred income would be negligible. Moreover the ultimate cost to the Treasury (particularly if only £50 could be deferred) would be much less, so that the advisability of coupling with it a post-war capital levy would not be so clear. At the same time the whole of the surcharge would take the form of deferred pay on gross income up to about £300 if £50 could be deferred; and up to about £650 if £100 could be deferred.

10. The political advantage of this approach is that deferred pay is clearly seen as an alternative to a tax of the same amount. No one, and certainly not the Chancellor of the Exchequer, would wish to force this concession on anyone. Perhaps the conversion of part of the tax into deferred pay might be made voluntary if anyone feels it as a restriction on his liberty! If the Labour leaders were to hold that the concession is objectionable, by all means away with it. If, on the other hand, when offered a maximum of £50 deferment, they were to ask for £100, there might be no harm in meeting them. It is for them to *ask* for deferment as a mitigation of the ultimate real burden of the surcharge on the lower ranges of income, not for the Chancellor to force it on *a priori* grounds. Nevertheless I remain of the opinion that there are immense social advantages in accumulating upwards of £50 (or ?£100) a year for post-war purposes to the credit of every wage and salary earner.

11. In the case of personal earnings the surcharge could, presumably, be collected at source along with income tax. In the case of surtax payers it could be collected on the basis of the *previous* year, subject perhaps to subsequent adjustment, i.e. the surcharge for 1940–41 would be collected on the income in respect of which surtax is due on 1 January next. In the same way, in order to avoid time-lag, the first surcharge to be collected might be on the income for which the first instalment of income tax falls due on 1 January next. There

remains the difficulty of the unearned income of taxpayers below the surtax limit, from which income tax is deducted at source. My suggestion for dealing with this is a uniform surcharge of 15 per cent on gross unearned income deductible at source; which in the case of taxpayers below the surtax limit would be in final discharge (subject, however, to appropriate right of recovery where their earned income is less than £100 and to a deferred income certificate where the surcharge on their earned income is less than £50 on the application of the taxpayer for such relief) the rate of surcharge on their earned incomes ignoring their unearned incomes, and in the case of surtaxpayers would be credited towards the surcharge eventually due from them on their total incomes. I shall sympathise with Inland Revenue if they declare that inflation is inevitable and must be swallowed because they have not enough staff to collect any more revenue; but I hope, all the same, that they *will* feel able to shoulder the gigantic task of seeing our finances through this war by the instrument of direct taxation. Would it help to make the Revenue a reserved occupation at all ages and to recover immediately all those members of the staff who have been called up? So far as work is concerned, the Revenue is surely in the front line and should rank with skilled munition work. I have done my best in framing this proposal to provide that the Revenue shall not have to collect any more information than they collect already, though the job of filling up demand notes will be more complicated.

12. I take this opportunity to repeat a proposal which is not logically linked with the above but is, nevertheless, a valuable ingredient in a comprehensive financial policy. If deferred pay certificates are introduced, I suggest that these should be the instrumentality for somewhat closing the gap between the pay of those serving in the forces and the earnings of those who are allowed to remain in civil life. Deferred pay certificates might be allotted in addition to existing rates of pay at

a uniform rate from private to field marshal at the rate of £50 per annum for time spent serving in this country and at the rate of £100 per annum for time spent serving abroad, at sea or in the air.

13. I propose to submit some supplementary notes on special questions, in particular (1) an analysis of how the first year of the war was paid for, (2) the prospective rate of expenditure and the timing of the Budget, (3) E.P.T., and (4) loan policy. But the broad outlines of the suggested policy are now blocked out.

J. M. KEYNES

6 October 1940

In the course of September, Keynes, with the approval of the Treasury, broadcast on the B.B.C. on the financial problems of the first year of the war. The broadcast exists in five versions: Home Service, Empire, American and Latin American (Spanish and Portuguese). Here we print the Home Service version, broadcast on 24 September.

BRITISH FINANCES AFTER A YEAR OF WAR

In general conversation I find people far too depressed about our finances. The usual opinion seems to be that the war will leave this country seriously impoverished, and that we are heading straight for inflation. After looking closely into the real position, I feel much more buoyant than that. I will tell you my conclusions. And I shall be careful to say only what I am sure I could substantiate.

Take the national wealth. The wastage of national resources, which we have suffered so far, is easily exaggerated. What, as a nation, have we lost in the first year of the war? We have parted with some of our more liquid assets in the shape of gold, etc. mainly to the United States. A million and a half tons of shipping has been sunk by enemy action. Buildings have been destroyed from the air, but only in the last month of the year on an important scale. We have not made good all the current wear and tear of buildings and plant in use. On the other hand, allowing for the big reserves of the main foods and raw materials which the Ministries of Food and Supply have built up, our stocks of commodities, so far from being diminished, are probably increased. After taking all these things into account, our total loss of wealth is certainly not greater than the amount by which we had increased it in the two or three years before the war; which means that after a year of war Great Britain remains richer in national wealth than she was at the beginning of 1937.

Does that surprise you? If so, be of good cheer, and stop thinking that after the war we shall have to lower our standards of life. I see no likelihood of that. On the contrary, I hope that we shall have learnt some things about the conduct of currency and foreign trade, about central controls, and about the capacity of the country to produce which will prevent us from ever relapsing into our pre-war economic morass. There is no reason why most people should not look forward to higher standards of life after the war than they have ever enjoyed yet.

Popular exaggeration is just as great when we come to details. Take ships. Our loss of a million and a half tons of shipping is far from negligible. Yet this loss of ships in the course of a year is no greater than our normal capacity to build new ones in a single year.

In losses by bombing from the air the case is not yet worse. Up to the end of July, before the *blitzkrieg* from the air began, the total damage to property in the previous eleven months could have been made good in a couple of days by the country's peacetime building capacity. In August damage was much more considerable. But even during that month it was certainly far short of what our normal building capacity could have made good within the month. There is not yet an accurate estimate of the heavy destruction in London in the last three weeks. It might be rash of me to say that the damage done since the beginning of August up to date has not been much greater than the normal capacity of our building trade to reinstate within the same period; but I believe that I should not prove far wrong. London is a big place. There can be a mighty power of destruction before the building properties of the country as a whole are seriously touched. A million pounds' worth of destruction is a frightful sight to see. But if we were to suffer a million pounds' worth of damage every night for a year, we should not have lost more than 4 per cent of our buildings and their contents, or more than we could restore in a couple of years. And we have the capacity to replace what is lost by something much better. Some of the major glories of London date from the Great Fire. London will, I should hope, rise from the present mess handsomer and healthier than before.

Fortunately or unfortunately, it is not physically possible to meet more than a small proportion of the costs of war out of our accumulated wealth. We cannot turn council houses into aeroplanes or arterial roads into tanks. The main expense of the war has to be met either by drawing resources from overseas or with what we produce at home here and now. It can be met in no other way. And this has an important moral. Since we must mainly depend, not on our accumulated wealth, but on our daily production, output for war purposes can only be released by our economising in our daily consumption and by our saving all we can from our current incomes. And that brings me to the budget problem. Are we saving and taxing on a scale heavy enough to prevent the social evils of inflation?

We have not adopted the German method of limiting expenditure by strictly rationing a wide range of articles of general consumption. As a method of organising acute scarcity, nothing can be more efficient than this. We admire the skill with which it has been carried out. The elaboration of a system for preventing individuals from doing or getting what they want appears to be a task peculiarly suited to the Prussian genius. Our object in rationing a limited range of articles is a different one, namely, to divert consumption away from certain goods which happen to be for special reasons in short supply. Taking the country as a whole, there has been no significant reduction, apart from voluntary savings, in the scale of peacetime consumption—an average reduction of 5 per cent at the outside. Our problem is a different one, namely, to prevent the better conditions of employment, the overtime earnings and the higher wages, which now prevail, from resulting in a pressure to buy *more* than in peacetime. For we cannot afford that in time of war. If more money is being earned and can be freely spent, a rise of prices can only be prevented if a sufficient proportion of these earnings is recovered by the Government in the shape either of taxes or of saving.

I return, therefore, to my question. Is the Government getting back in taxes and are we saving enough income to prevent an inflationary rise in prices? I shall not be suspected of a tendency to undue optimism in answering this question. I spent all my energies during the early months of the war in calling attention to this danger. I advocated a remedy, namely a system of deferred pay, without the adoption of which I doubted if inflation could be avoided. The Government have not yet adopted this remedy. I am still of the opinion that, sooner or later, some more drastic methods than those yet adopted will be necessary and that no better remedy than my own has been proposed by anyone else. Moreover the opinion is widely spread throughhout the financial press that we are already heading for inflation, precisely because the Government have failed to adopt either my remedy or any alternative for it.

Clearly my natural bias would be to agree with this view. Nevertheless I am unable to do so. I am no less convinced than before that new and drastic financial methods will be required when our rate of expenditure is at full flood. But my investigations lead me to the conclusion that there has been no significant degree of budgetary inflation up to date. The British public, rather surprisingly, have underestimated the weight of Sir Kingsley Wood's July Budget. If we calculate on the basis of taxes which are now accruing for subsequent payment, the tax revenue provides for appreciably more than half of that part of our total budget expenditure which we have to finance at home. A considerable further contribution comes from various capital resources. The savings movement has been more successful, in my opinion, than its leaders seem to think. In the early months of the war the published statistics were misleading, since they included a large proportion of money which was not newly saved but merely transferred. Today they include very little which is not new money. At any rate these various sources between them have been very nearly adequate up to date.

After all, the real test of inflation is the actual movement of prices. At the beginning of the war and for some months after there was a considerable rise in the price of imports due to freights, insurance, exchange and a sharp rise of prices abroad. Domestic prices did not rise, and have not risen, by more than half the rise in import prices. Moreover international prices are now falling, whilst the exchange value of sterling is now stable for all purposes. The result is that the domestic price level is not now rising. There is none of the evidence of domestic inflation, which, if it exists, must show itself beyond all concealment, as it showed itself during the last war, in steeply rising prices, shop-shortages, queues and an exhaustion of retailers' stocks. No such symptoms are apparent.

The financial position is, therefore, still under control. All the more reason for keeping it so. Much greater economic sacrifices are in prospect for us. We are so little touched at present because we are only beginning to put forth our economic strength. It has not been necessary in the first year of war to ask of us any serious economic restrictions. This second year is, in truth, the first year of the real war for Britain. We have the freshness of a fighter in the first round of the combat; whereas Germany has already suffered the nervous tension and muscular exhaustion of five years of prodigious effort. But we must not be deceived about what will be required from us when we are fighting and producing up to our full capacity. My point is that in the financial field nothing has happened up to date to give us excessive anxiety. So it is well worth while to have a policy, however drastic, about taxes and savings, wages and prices, which will keep the position as sound and good as it is now.

On 21 October, Keynes turned his attention to the Excess Profits Tax, introduced at the beginning of the war and raised to 100 per cent in the May 1940 Budget. His memorandum, as well as circulating with the Budget papers for 1941, was the subject of discussion at the Consultative Council on 4 November, along with a memorandum on the subject by Lord Stamp.

EXCESS PROFITS TAX

I

I know no responsible person who does not think that the present version of 100 per cent E.P.T. is an injudicious, an inefficient and a seriously unjust measure, leading to a wasteful use of resources in circumstances where we can least afford it, which hampers our war effort and will hamper it increasingly as time goes on. When the Chancellor of the Exchequer originally agreed to 100 per cent, it was understood that this tax was to be a part of a complete system of controls in other directions, which, in fact, has not even begun to come into operation.

Nevertheless a very potent argument in favour of the

principle holds good. A levy of 100 per cent has a strong popular appeal because it appears 'to take the profit out of war'. Any abatement of the principle of 100 per cent would be widely regarded as 'a step backwards'. One is forced to doubt whether any of the technical justifications of such a change, which could be brought forward, would be successful in reaching the popular mind or in allaying the suspicions which such a move would arouse. At the same time, it is not right to acquiesce in the tax without explaining in the clearest manner to those, who have the responsibility of guiding public opinion, the evils inherent in it. As Lord Stamp expresses it, the raising of E.P.T. to 100 per cent is a revolutionary measure, the full implications of which are not appreciated by public opinion at large. It is not a trifle where it might be wise to accept a popular sentiment however misguided. It is a matter of the first importance to our economic effort and organisation, which may be playing an important part already in slowing up what ought to be a much more rapid expansion of output. If the war continues two or three years more, its results can be disastrous. There is no fiscal question on which there is such complete unanimity amongst expert and independent authorities, and it would be a pity to accept the view that under a democratic system of government uninstructed opinion must necessarily prevail, not merely on the principle but even to the point of preventing advisable amendments in detail.

The objection is not against E.P.T. as such. A tax of this kind is in time of war indispensable on grounds both of social justice and of yield to the revenue. The point is that, like other taxes, it loses its virtue and acquires vices, new in kind and not merely in degree, when it is pushed beyond a certain point and, above all, when it reaches the limit of 100 per cent.

The several distinct grounds of objection to which the tax of 100 per cent is open have been fully explained by Lord Stamp in a memorandum dated 30 July 1940. I have little to add to his analysis, to which reference should be made for many important points of detail justifying what follows.

(1) The 100 per cent tax is extremely unjust as between different firms, since there is no formula which can provide for the many anomalies involved in taking a pre-war year as the basis. In particular, it operates as an endowment of elderly firms, of firms which have ceased to expand, which are no longer increasing their efficiency or are decreasing it, which have lost their enterprise and do not venture a risk,—in short, of the obsolescent. It stops dead the process of survival of the fit which is the main justification of private enterprise, and replaces this process by nothing whatever. It is reasonable that firms, however young and enterprising, should forego a large part of the exceptional profit for which conditions of war offer an opportunity. But it is undesirable that their energy and enterprise and skill and extra work should be deprived of all reward whatever. Indeed young firms without established credit are deprived thereby of their normal means of expansion, namely by ploughing back their profits into the business.

(2) Not merely does it take away all the profits due to energy, expansion and risk-taking. It means in many cases that indulgence in energy, expansion and risk-taking may result in actual loss. In time of war we need the greatest possible incentives to an intensity of output, even though it leads to abnormal depreciation, to an expansion of plant for temporary employment which is not justified on long-term commercial principles, to the over-rapid exhaustion of wasting assets, to a risky change-over from normal types of peace-time output in favour of war products, to enterprise in seizing foreign markets which are far from safe and, in general, to boldness and activity. It is not the best way for securing these things to provide that any profit resulting from exceptional activity shall belong to the Government and that any loss from them shall fall on the entrepreneur. It may be argued that

247

a business man should invite loss and even insolvency in the public interest at least as readily as a soldier in the firing line should invite wounds and even death (though experience goes to show that in fact many people are readier to risk their lives than their money). But, questions of pluck apart, this is asking him to calculate his course of action on principles to which he is unaccustomed and which have not been explained to him. And it is going a long way further than merely 'taking the profit out of war'.

'It is not likely', Lord Stamp points out, 'that this conflict of interests, however acute, will lead to many gross and glaring cases of a refusal to undertake work of national importance that is clearly within a manufacturer's capacity. The danger is more subtle; it is likely to take such forms as a gradual decline of zeal and energy and enterprise, a growing bias against the adoption of new methods the expediency of which is open to reasonable doubt, and perhaps a disposition to insist, with inevitable consequence of delay, that this or that financial risk must be shouldered by the state before certain work wanted by the state is undertaken.'

(3) In time of war it is more important than usual to avoid extravagance and waste and to insist on all possible economy. It is asking too much of human nature to suppose that the best way of securing this is to deprive those who are responsible of all the usual incentives towards care and economy. As soon as a company's profits have reached its E.P.T. basis, it becomes an unremunerated and unsupervised agent for the Government. It is not safe to assume that all those concerned will treat the interests of the Exchequer in exactly the same way as they would treat their own, especially if the tax which they are involuntarily administering on the Government's behalf is one which has given them a sense of personal injustice.

(4) For similar reasons the tax increases the risk of inflation. Inflation can set in on the demand side because the Exchequer

is failing to withdraw sufficient purchasing power from consumers in the shape of taxes and savings. But it can also set in on the supply side owing to a rise in costs. If entrepreneurs are deprived of the usual motives for keeping down costs, the risk of this second type of inflation is obviously increased. Moreover this result can follow from excessive zeal to increase output just as easily as from slackness and inattention. A manufacturer impressed with the national importance of increasing his own output may be tempted, if he is not a man of comprehensive wisdom, to be a little reckless, when it costs him nothing, in oiling the wheels of his own concern by outbidding other manufacturers in the price he is prepared to pay for scarce resources whether of material or of skilled labour.

(5) A tax is demoralising which opens the way to so many devices for tax-saving and tax-dodging and at the same time goes much beyond what the individual tax-payer feels to be fair and reasonable in his own particular case.

All this can be summed up in a sentence. One hundred per cent E.P.T. deprives private enterprise of its normal incentives to enterprise, of its checks on inefficiency and extravagance, and of its means to expansion, without substituting anything in their place. There are arguments in favour of 'war socialism', which already covers a considerable field; and we ought to move much further in this direction as time goes by. But we are not moving rapidly towards a general socialisation of all munition industries, largely for the reason that to organise this efficiently seems to be beyond our powers of immediate improvisation. Meanwhile with the height of unwisdom we are providing ourselves with the worst of both worlds.

II

Nevertheless the popular appeal of a tax which appears to 'take the profit out of war' is very great.

The force and justice of this appeal need, therefore, to be examined carefully. Even though a tax is socially just, one has to hesitate in time of war if it is of a character to hamper the war effort. But is it socially just?

In the last war inflation and war-time scarcities flung vast profits into the laps of many firms who had done nothing whatever to earn them,—profits which were not required in order to influence their action in the right direction. Shipowners were an outstanding example. On that occasion E.P.D. became the main, though a very partial, mitigation of this evil. This time there was a universal determination not to allow a repetition of such a state of affairs. For this purpose a great variety of measures were adopted at an early stage of the war, and very successfully. Take shipowners again as an example. The anti-profiteering measures, requisitioning, strict costings by the war departments, the control of raw materials, the avoidance of significant domestic inflation, 60 per cent E.P.T., the extreme severity of income and surtax, and the limitation of interest on war loans, all these measures adopted from the very outset, were quite sufficient, between them, to prevent significant abuses. Even without 100 per cent E.P.T. no one worth mentioning has been in a position to 'profiteer', i.e. to make profits which have not been genuinely earned by exceptional enterprise, efficiency or risk-taking; and a good many of the exceptions to this are, as it happens, untouched by E.P.T. Thus this measure was not necessary for the purpose of 'taking the profit out of war'.

The intensification of E.P.T. to 100 per cent can only be justified as the result of a serious confusion of thought; namely by confusing the prevention of profiteering with the doctrine that in time of war no one shall be rewarded for energy, extra work, exceptional efficiency or courageous risk-taking. If this was an incidental aspect of a sort of war communism, well and good. But in the actual circumstances of the case it seems pure nonsense. For the pre-war level of profits, whatever it may happen to be, is to remain secured. The system is one of *discrimination* against extra energy and enterprise called forth in time of war. Moreover there is no suggestion that the same system should be applied to wage earners. If we are to 'take the profit out of war' in the above extended and as I think perverted sense, money wages should be fixed at the pre-war level; overtime, so far from being remunerated at a higher rate, should not be remunerated at all; and a man who was unemployed in 1937 should not be allowed a wage in excess of the dole, if he obtains employment today. No one is so foolish as to suggest such a thing. Yet that is what we are doing to industrialists.

I have heard it argued that, if in time of war an industrialist is capable of being influenced in the slightest degree by pecuniary motives, this is convincing evidence that he is a person of low morals and unpatriotic propensities to whom it would be a sin to make concessions. Yet, apparently, the same thing is not true of wage earners in whose case a demand for an overtime bonus is consistent with a good character. Moreover if human nature is occasionally, if only in a minority of cases of such a disposition that pecuniary motives are not wholly suspended in time of war, some regard must be paid to this fact if we are to wage a war with maximum efficiency, just as we do well to remember that not everyone is equally healthy or equally brave.

III

If the case for making a change is conceded, a choice of method is open to us. Should we, out of regard for popular sentiment, retain the principle of a 100 per cent E.P.T. and secure at least part of our object by re-defining the meaning of 'excess' so as to avoid some of the grossest existing inequities and inexpediencies? Or should we frankly reduce the rate of tax below 100 per cent?

A great deal can be done by re-shaping the details of the tax to mitigate some of the grosser anomalies. Since most of these modifications are desirable in any case, we may begin by outlining them:–

(1) Some part, possibly an important part, of the profits made during the war from abnormal activities will be offset by losses during the transitional period back to normal after the war, which losses will not be recoverable because they are incurred after E.P.T. has come to an end or because they are technically *capital* losses so that the Revenue will not allow their deduction in computation of profits.

At present E.P.T. is recoverable if profits fall below the basic figure in a subsequent E.P.T. year, but it is indefinite how long this right will continue. The incentive to the earning of E.P.T. would be considerably increased if it were laid down that E.P.T. will be recoverable in the event of profits falling below the basis in any year during the war or for two years afterwards. This would meet the first point above. In particular it would give reason for confidence that profits made during the war as the result of price rises can be offset against losses which may be made during the transition after the war as the result of price falls.

The second point could be met by a provision treating capital losses more liberally for purposes of E.P.T. than for income tax. A firm might be given the right up to two years after the war to re-value any capital expenditure incurred during the war and to deduct for the purposes of E.P.T. any book loss resulting from this re-valuation, including loss incurred from war damage in excess of compensation received. This should remove inhibitions on war-time expansion which is not justified by peace-time prospects.

Both these changes are essentially fair. Nor do they go too

252

far, since recoverable E.P.T. will, in so far as it is brought back into revenue, become subject, presumably, to income tax (which will not be the case when it is offset, as proposed above, against capital losses not allowed for purposes of income tax). They are substantially the same as proposals made by Lord Stamp.

(2) In another respect it is reasonable that capital losses should be treated more liberally for E.P.T. than at present, namely in cases of wasting assets such as mines. At present, for example, it is in the private interest of the Rhodesian copper mines or the Malayan tin mines to restrict output as much as they decently can, since maximum output involves them in actual loss.

(3) The rate of interest allowed on new capital should fluctuate according to the character and risk of the business (as was provided, I think, in the last war) and should be higher for a new business, instead of at a flat rate.

(4) This rate should be allowed on the employment of new capital in the business irrespective of how it is raised; whether by loan or overdraft, or by a reduction in liquid resources held outside the business, or by increased share capital. For the risk of expansion falls on the share capital in any case.

(5) The provisions for raising by adjudication the basis of young firms should be made more liberal, and might allow any firm founded since 1935 to claim such an adjudication.

(6) It would be fairer to small firms, which usually depend more on enterprise and risk than on volume of capital, to raise the minimum basis from £1,000 to £2,000, and correspondingly for each working partner; the extra allowance thereby becoming, of course, liable to income tax.

(7) Firms might be given the right to borrow from the Revenue sums due by them for E.P.T. at 2½ per cent up to two years after the war, provided the money is actually employed in the business as additional capital and its employment is certified by a government department to be in the

national interest. (Lord Stamp has proposed a variant of this substantially similar in effect.)

(8) Lord Stamp favours, in principle, an allowance for increased output, but he admits that the administrative difficulties are formidable. It might, however, be possible to make an extra depreciation allowance in respect of abnormal wear and tear.

None of these proposals strike at the principle of a hundred per cent levy. But they would, between them, meet a considerable part of the practical objections, even though the rate of the tax remains at 100 per cent.

It may be thought wiser to stop at these amendments in detail rather than attempt to reduce the rate of the tax down to (say) 75 per cent. It is for the experts in such matters to measure the effective weight of popular sentiment. But is there any reason to expect serious or weighty objection to the above amendments, which, without departing from the general principle, are of the first importance for determining what the war profits of a business really are over the war period as a whole? Indeed public opinion and its essential reasonableness deserve more respect than would be shown by a tacit acquiescence on the part of the administration in the present state of affairs, whilst actually convinced that it does serious mischief.

J. M. KEYNES

21 October 1940

Keynes's second set of Notes on the Budget had their intended effect on Treasury opinion. On 21 October Keynes joined Lord Catto, Sir Horace Wilson, Sir Richard Hopkins and Sir Frederick Phillips for a meeting with the Chancellor on Budget strategy. At that meeting Keynes explained how he arrived at his estimate of a budgetary gap of £400/450 million, how he proposed to meet the problem and the evidence being obtained in the surveys of wartime patterns of saving and spending carried out under the auspices of the National Institute of Economic and Social Research. Lord

Catto, who agreed with Keynes's estimate of the size of the Budget problem, also presented his proposal for solving the problem.

The Chancellor then asked for a rapid, but complete examination of the main alternatives likely to produce substantial sums of money, paying particular attention to:

(1) Keynes's proposal for a graduated surcharge on net incomes, possibly coupled with deferred pay.

(2) Lord Catto's proposal for a flat-rate war tax on gross income.

(3) Lord Stamp's proposal for an income tax equivalent to E.P.T.

(4) Alterations in existing income tax schedules and rates.

He also asked to be kept informed of the progress of the National Institute surveys, which Keynes was to discuss further within the Treasury.

The Stamp proposal disappeared fairly early in the subsequent discussions, owing to the administrative burdens involved in handling such matters as exemptions and pre-war standard income. Keynes's and Catto's surcharge proposals fell later to administrative problems and the belief that they looked 'too much like a rehash of income tax'. However, the idea of forced saving through the tax system proved hardier and managed to survive the administrative hurdles in a modified and less ambitious form as post-war credits. Thus by February 1941 the Chancellor had decided that changes in the existing income tax schedules and rates, with post-war credits grafted onto them, would form the centrepiece of the new Budget proposals, and from that point onwards Budget planning proceeded to fashion the details.

Throughout this period, Keynes kept up a stream of memoranda to the Chancellor and his advisers, meeting objections, altering proposals and providing new information, often from the Madge surveys. The following memoranda give some idea of Keynes at work during the period of intense discussion between late October and early February.

A SUPPLEMENTARY NOTE ON THE DIMENSIONS OF THE BUDGET PROBLEM

In a note on this subject which I wrote three months ago (21 September 1940) I argued that the degree of budgetary inflation in the first war year had been insignificant, but that drastic steps would be required to avoid it in the second; and I estimated the dimensions of the prospective Budget problem at £300–400 million. In the intervening period much has happened. The elements of the current situation are the following:–

(1) There is, so far, no indication of domestic expenditure exceeding the annual rate of £3,000 million which I assumed in my previous note. (I hope to prepare next month an analysis of the first quarter of the second year, and am expecting to find domestic expenditure in the near neighbourhood of the above figure—a little below more likely than a little above.)

(2) If, however, the munitions and recruiting programme of the War Cabinet and the manpower requirements committee is to be taken seriously, a material increase in domestic expenditure should occur before June 1941,—by (say) £300 million. Nevertheless, since the War Cabinet are taking no sufficient steps to cause this programme to materialise, perhaps we can safely write the prospective increase by next June down to (say) £100 million.

(3) Even if the programme matures more fully than this, we need not expect much increase (assuming wage rates unchanged) in the total wages bill of the country. The equivalent average earnings of a man who is drafted into the army are probably £1 to £2 a week less than in civil life. The earnings of a man brought into employment from unemployment or of a woman brought into employment from outside the ranks of industry are increased by about £2 a week. It is proposed to draft 1,741,000 men into the army between September 1940 and the end of 1941, and 800,000 workers into the munition industries by August 1941 to be replaced or supplied by (say) 1 million persons (mainly women) not now gainfully employed and the balance of 1,500,000 from those now producing for civilian expenditure. Even if this programme were to be carried out in full (of which there is not much sign), it is possible (assuming wage rates unchanged) that the total wages bill would not be increased, the diminished earnings of the recruits more than offsetting the

increased earnings of the additional persons gainfully employed. Since it is easier to draft men into the army than to bring new trainees into industry, a partial fulfilment, following the line of least resistance, might actually reduce the total wages bill.

(4) This means that the nature of our problem is significantly changed. In the first year of the war the danger lay in a greatly increased wages bill over against a quantity of goods available for consumption which was not much changed. In the second year of the war we have to expect a wages bill not much changed (I am dealing separately, below, with the question of a rise in wage rates) over against a quantity of goods available for consumption which is greatly diminished. It is much easier in time of war to persuade the public by voluntary methods not to increase their standard of life than it is to persuade them to diminish it, when they have the money in their pockets with which to *attempt* to maintain it.

(5) The effect of the diminution in the supply of goods and services for civilian consumption, due to the reduction in the number of workers in these industries, is greatly aggravated by the simultaneous diminution in the supply due to shipping difficulties. The Ministry of Food estimate the prospective reduction of the food available to civilians at £150 million a year in terms of retail prices, as a result of the recent curtailment in the tonnage at their disposal. The restriction of civilian (non-food) supplies by the recent restriction orders of the Board of Trade may be provisionally estimated at £175 million in terms of retail prices. (I hope to have a more exact estimate shortly.) Both these measures will come into force gradually and their full effect is being retarded by the exhaustion of stocks, so that six months may elapse before they are fully felt. It should be noted that these measures, in distinction from the manpower requirements, are actually in process of operation.

Personal expenditure at retail prices at mid-1940 is estimated at £1,400 million on foodstuffs and groceries and £825 million on household goods, apparel and other merchandise. Thus the above restrictions are of the order of 10 per cent of food expenditure and 20 per cent of other retail expenditure respectively.

The restriction of imported food supplies should release some labour previously employed in distribution, and the Board of Trade restrictions are directly intended to release labour. Indeed when in full operation these measures between them should release upwards of 500,000 persons. If we suppose that the army and munitions programme comes into operation in the course of next year to the extent of 50 per cent, these and other occupations for civilian consumption will have to release at least another 250,000 persons, of which (say) 100,000 are likely to be taken sooner or later (though this is not, at present, the intention) from the export industries.

Altogether, therefore, we must expect a gradual diminution ultimately approaching £400 million p.a. in the value (at present market prices) of what will be available for the public to buy. This is some 10 per cent of present expenditure by the public on all purposes, including rent and rates, public utilities, and drink and tobacco, but it is 18 per cent of all retail purchases (excluding drink and tobacco, economy on which will help us, on balance, very little).

(6) The effective magnitude of our eventual problem is appreciably greater than £400 million p.a. for the following reasons:–

(a) We were not in equilibrium in the late autumn of 1940, as was shown by the evident pressure on prices and stocks;

(b) Whatever method is adopted, whether by design or by drift, is likely to react on the willingness to make voluntary savings, because of the effort which some people will make to maintain their standard of life;

(c) On the assumption that there is no material increase in wage rates or in national money income, which, if it occurs, will aggravate our difficulties on balance, the revenue will suffer directly and indirectly. If £400 million were to be withdrawn from expenditure either by direct taxation or by voluntary saving, excise and customs would suffer and so would the income tax on the profits and earnings no longer made. (We shall see below that this might be made good by a rise in prices not followed by a rise in wages.)

(7) The restriction on total consumption, indicated above as necessary, is about the same as in 1917; and since it is a restriction of a much higher standard, it is much less burdensome. Even after this cut our standards would remain as high, or higher, than they were in peacetime before 1914; and as high or higher than in Germany or in most European countries before 1939. Humanly speaking, the cut is supportable and not too much to ask. The difficulty lies in the choice of mechanism by which it is to be brought about.

(8) It is unlikely that the solution can be found by means of taxation alone. But we must probably depend on taxation for a large proportion, because the instrument on which we largely depended in 1914–18 is no longer available, except on a condition to be stated below.

In 1914–18 there was a time-lag between rising prices and rising wages of nearly a year. This meant that a progressive inflation was an effective instrument for cutting real consumption, since prices could be continuously kept about 15 per cent above wages at the cost of a serious but not astronomical deterioration in the value of money. In *How to Pay for the War* (p. 72) [*JMK*, vol. IX, pp. 422–3] I have shown by mere arithmetic that 'if prices have to keep 15 per cent above wages and if wages rise half this amount in the first year and then follow prices with a time-lag of a year, we can get through four years of war by a little less than a doubling of prices'; and then by actual statistics that this is just about what happened. This was far from an ideal method and left evil consequences behind it; but at least it was effective.

Fortunately or unfortunately, a repetition of this technique is not open to us. So large a body of wage contracts is now automatically tied to the cost of living and the influence of wage rises in this group on others is so strong that there is no sufficient time-lag. The combined method of moderately high taxation, rationing in particular directions and a not too rapid progressive inflation for the rest, which served us last time, is no longer practicable. So we must think again.

Since, in any case, we shall have to make *some* use of the expedients other than taxation I will begin with these.

(9) There is a great deal to be said for a controlled rise of prices if this can be prevented from reacting on wage rates. I would urge that the Chancellor of the Exchequer should put this expedient fairly and squarely before his Labour colleagues both because there is something to be said for it on merits if it is accepted, and because, if it is rejected the case is strengthened for not shirking an alternative remedy.

Would his colleagues agree to a general standstill of money incomes during the war on the following broad lines (I forbear, at this stage, to fill in any details)?—

(i) A general prohibition against any further increase during the war in wage rates, scales of salary or dividends above those ruling at the end of 1940. (This would not prevent individuals from getting an increase of income as a result of promotion, seniority or harder work.)

(ii) A gradual rise in the cost of living to a figure not more than 5 per cent above the level at the end of 1940, together with a controlled rise in other prices on a carefully chosen variable scale, which might eventually reach an average of 20 to 25 per cent according to the rate of progress of mobilisation and the scale of direct taxation.

(iii) A control of raw materials, consumed by civilians, sufficiently comprehensive (which would need no great change in present arrangements) to provide that the whole of the permitted price rise can be directly absorbed by the supply departments in the higher charges made by them for such materials, so that no increased private profit would ensue.

It will be observed that this, in effect, is a solution by means of a system of indirect taxes administered through the control of raw materials and foodstuffs.

The standstill of wage rates, etc. could be accompanied by other measures aimed at making the programme as a whole socially just and politically acceptable. The choice of such measures is mainly a psychological and political problem, but the following list is given as an indication of the sort of thing I have in mind:-

(*a*) An increase of 10–15 per cent in old age pensions and unemployment benefits;

(*b*) More liberal provisions for feeding school children and the thin end of the wedge of children's allowances by a grant of 5*s* a week for each child in excess of two;

(*c*) A minimum wage of (say) 1*s* per hour for all adult male workers;

(*d*) Some moderate extension of rationing where required to ensure fairness of distribution;

(*e*) A considerable reduction in the rate of interest on new government loans;

(*f*) An increase in the standard rate of income tax to 10*s* without any reduction in allowances or any increase in the 5*s* rate on the first £165 of taxable income.

If, on the other hand, the organised standstill of wage rates etc. is totally rejected, the difficulty of finding *any* solution is intensely aggravated. Members of this Committee will be well aware by now how hard it would be to solve the *whole* problem by taxation without any recourse to higher prices. After a lull during the summer both prices and wages are now on the move again. In the *eight* months from 1 December 1939 to 1 August 1940 the cost of living index rose 12 points; and in the *four* months from 1 August to 1 December 1940 it rose

10 points. The prices of goods not covered by the cost of living index have risen much more than this, and there is strong evidence that severe shop-shortages are impending in several directions. The policy of drift has gone on too long already.

Thus the standstill is necessary even if it is thought wise (as I think it is) to use the instrument of direct taxation more and the instrument of controlled price rises less than is suggested above.

Three months ago I was of the opinion that it was unwise to ask for this and that we had better rely on the commonsense of the trade unions. We have, indeed, no cause for complaint about the policy of the latter in the intervening period. But I did not then appreciate how significantly our problem would be changed by its becoming a question of a deficiency of goods rather than of an excess of incomes.

If the advisability of a standstill is accepted by the Chancellor on its merits, the Labour Ministers are entitled to have the facts and arguments placed before them before it is rejected.

(10) The method just discussed is, in substance, a method of indirect taxation. The method employed in 1917–18 was, in substance, a method of indirect taxation through inflation *plus* excess profits tax. The next method to be mentioned is, in substance, the method of forced voluntary saving by a system of general rationing so drastic that the average man is unable, even though he wishes, to spend the whole of his income. This method has its advocates, but the more I look at it the more hopelessly impracticable does it appear. It is for those who believe in it more than I do to work out the details; for it is on the details that such a scheme breaks down. If Sir Gerald Canny[16] by being shy in his own field forces an attempt along these lines, the administrative difficulties for someone will be fifty times what he is escaping.

[16] Sir Gerald Bain Canny (1881–1954), K.C.B. 1939, K.B.E. 1937; entered Civil Service, 1904; Chairman, Board of Inland Revenue, 1938–42.

Rationing is essentially a means for securing a fair distribution of *particular* articles of necessity. We shall probably have to carry this kind of rationing further than we do at present, just as in 1918. But as a means of securing a *general* restriction of expenditure, it is surely far the worst and far the most difficult of the expedients open to us. The Germans, I believe, have been driven on administrative grounds to reject entirely the method of rationing by restricting the amount of money to be spent in favour of restricting the quantity of each type of goods to be bought. Yet a gradual extension of rationing by quantity of particular goods merely drives the consumer from pillar to post and makes no allowance for variety of tastes. We are finding this already with price controls unaccompanied by formal rationing by which a shortage in one direction becomes the means of creating shortages in half a dozen others.

Another kind of policy is becoming urgent because we are steadily drifting in this direction. General shop shortages and queues will very soon become the order of the day. We only have to await the end of the time-lag, provided by the exhaustion of stocks, on the full operation of the measures *already taken* by the Ministry of Food and the Board of Trade.

(11) There is great risk that inaction will impede the prosecution of the war, besides upsetting civilian morale. If we do nothing, the acute demand from the army and munitions for men to be taken from civilian production will mature at a time when to fulfil them will provoke an acute crisis in civilian supplies. The situation will, of course, develop gradually. But even half of the War Cabinet programme cannot be fulfilled unless we prepare for it by adopting one or other of the means of adjusting civilian demand to supply *deliberately*.

We can be legitimately sceptical about the complete fulfilment of the War Cabinet programme by the dates proposed. But it would not be proper for the Treasury to proceed on the assumption that this programme is 75 per cent poppycock. So far the Board of Trade appears to be the only department which is taking the War Cabinet seriously.

(12) There is a point which deserves the very careful attention of the apostles of inaction. There are *two* obstacles to our getting through somehow on the lines of 1914–18. One of these I have already emphasised, namely the absence today of a sufficient time-lag between wages and prices to make inflation an effective instrument. But there is another obstacle, namely the comparative efficiency of our price controls. In 1918 prices rose sufficiently for the existing supply of goods to absorb the available purchasing power; and that was an essential condition for the success of the policy adopted. The rationing system (of foodstuffs in particular) became more extensive. But the general rise of prices was sufficient to prevent general shop shortages.

It is precisely our comparative success in restraining price increases and the force of public opinion in favour of this, which will create, if we do nothing else, a problem of shop shortages on a scale not previously experienced. Each maximum price imposed by the Ministry of Food releases purchasing power to create shortages elsewhere.

(13) I come finally to the third and last method, namely direct taxation including in this a 'withholding tax', a convenient name lately adopted in Canada for deferred pay or compulsory saving. On the details of this I am preparing a separate paper in the light of Sir Gerald Canny's latest memorandum. Meanwhile it will serve to complete the argument of this paper if I indicate what seems to be the best policy open to us.

I believe that we can raise a further £300 million by direct taxation including a withholding tax and that it is imperative for us to attempt this as a minimum. This will not be sufficient by itself and will not make us independent of the method of indirect taxation exercised partly along the lines which Sir

W. Eady[17] advises as practicable and partly by means of controlled price rises, as proposed above, the proceeds of which would accrue to the Exchequer. But it would probably be sufficient, at any rate for some time, to enable us to stabilise the cost of living as measured by the index.

Even so an agreed standstill of incomes would be highly advisable. But if we put on enough direct taxation to allow for a stabilisation of the cost of living and a more sparing use of controlled price rises in other directions, it is no longer essential. At any rate the standstill agreement could be on the basis of *no* increase in the cost of living index, instead of a 5 per cent increase.

(14) (i) Controlled price rises accompanied by a standstill of incomes;

(ii) Forced voluntary saving by general rationing, or, failing that, by the chaos of queues and general shop shortages;

(iii) A withholding (or equivalent direct) tax on incomes; being distinct from income tax, it lends itself to conversion into a withholding tax;

(iv) The abandonment of 75 per cent of the War Cabinet's programme for the increase of the armed forces and output of munitions;

Is there any fifth alternative?

Personal savings are now running at an average of about 12 per cent of personal incomes. They would have to rise to 20 per cent to fill the bill, at a time when this involved a reduction of 10 per cent in total real consumption or 18 per cent in the total of retail purchases. Thus the task is beyond the powers of voluntary methods.

J. M. KEYNES

26.12.40

[17] Sir Wilfrid Griffin Eady (1880–1962), K.C.B. 1942, K.B.E. 1939; entered Civil Service, 1913; Ministry of Labour, 1917–38; Deputy Under-Secretary, Home Office, 1938–40; Deputy Chairman, 1940–1, and Chairman, 1941–2, Board of Customs and Excise; Joint Second Secretary, Treasury, 1942–52.

APPENDIX I.   REVISED PROPOSAL FOR A WAR SURCHARGE

1. *Objects.* The objects of this revision are (*a*) to provide a higher exemption limit and increased progressiveness; (*b*) to meet Sir G. Canny's administrative criticisms; (*c*) to effect these objects without loss of yield.

2. *Income tax.* My previous proposal embodied, in addition to the war surcharge, a change in the existing income tax in the shape of a reduction of all personal allowances from £100 to £80 for single and from £170 to £140 for married men. My present proposal substitutes for this a total abolition of the earned income allowance, and an *increase* of personal allowances in the case of earned income from £100 to £110 for single and from £170 to £180 for married men. This provides an exemption limit of 42s 3d a week for single men, 65s 6d a week for married men without children and 107s 9d a week for families with two children. It does not bring in (I think) much more than 500,000 new taxpayers and thus meets one of Sir G. Canny's major objections. Nevertheless it provides a substantially greater yield from income tax proper than the previous proposal.

To balance the abolition of earned income allowance, personal allowances in respect of unearned income to be reduced to £90 for single and £160 for married men. (Where income is partly earned and partly unearned, the allowance would be £90 or £160 plus two-elevenths of the earned income subject to a maximum of £20.)

3. *War surcharge on earned incomes.* As before, the surcharge is on net assessable incomes, i.e. on incomes remaining after deduction of tax and personal allowances. The increased yield now asked from income tax proper makes possible the following revised, and much more progressive, scale of surcharge:–
Income equal to personal allowance *plus* income tax and surtax

£	Percentage
[First 100]	Nil
Next 500	15
Next 500	20
Next 500	25
Next 500	30
Next 500	35
Next 1,000	40
Next 1,500	45
Balance	50

This works out in particular cases as follows:–

Gross earned income (£)	Single person			Married, no children			Married, two children		
	A	B	C	A	B	C	A	B	C
110	Nil	Nil	Nil	Nil	Nil	Nil	Nil	Nil	Nil
120	Nil	2·5	1·12	Nil	Nil	Nil	Nil	Nil	Nil
150	6	4	4·5	Nil	Nil	Nil	Nil	Nil	Nil
200	17	5	10	Nil	5	2	Nil	Nil	Nil
300	37	15	21	20	10	13·5	Nil	5	2
500	106	31	38	76	31	32	37	28	23
1,000	283	66	83	253	66	75	211	66	66
2,000	672	101	179	643	101	194	600	102	182
5,000	2,429	101	576						
10,000	6,079	101	1,119						

A = existing tax; B = increase in income tax; C = war surcharge.

4. *War surcharge on unearned incomes.* 15 per cent paid at source on all company profits whether distributed or not and other unearned income.[18] This is equivalent to an increase up to 11s 6d in income tax on unearned income. Recovery, in case of small incomes, would be the same as in the case of income tax; namely in full on the first £90 (or £160) of income and 3s 6d on the next £165. This works out very well in relation to the increased tax and surcharge on earned incomes at almost all levels of income, as is shown below, where the figures relate to the total of increased income tax plus surcharge.

[18] But see below for a special provision relating to Schedule A.

Gross income (£)	Single person		Married, no children		Married, two children	
	Earned	Unearned	Earned	Unearned	Earned	Unearned
	110	Nil	6	Nil	Nil	Nil
120	3·6	7	Nil	Nil	Nil	Nil
150	8·5	11	Nil	Nil	Nil	Nil
200	15	19	7	8	Nil	Nil
300	36	34	23	23	7	8
500	69	66	63	55	51	38
1,000	149	141	141	130	132	113
2,000	289	291	295	280	285	263
5,000	677	741				
10,000	1,228	1,491				

5. *Adjustment for surtax.* To prevent total tax from rising above 19s 6d in the £, surtax on all excess of income above £20,000 would be fixed at 8s, in place of 8s 6d rising to 9s 6d as at present.

6. *Yield in a full year.* It is rash for me to attempt an estimate; but on the basis of Sir G. Canny's figures my guess is in the near neighbourhood of £300 million.

7. *Comparison with procedure by income tax changes.* Much the same yield and incidence could, I expect, be produced by a straight increase of 3s in the standard rate of income tax in combination with certain adjustments of personal allowances. But this would conceal the genuine progressiveness of the tax. There are also advantages, as I have claimed before, in the new levy being ostensibly distinct from income tax. I claim below that the distinction is a help in avoiding the usual time-lag in collection. In particular, it lends itself more appropriately to conversion into a withholding tax, as proposed below.

But not the least important reason for the new formula is the fact that, if it works well, it is capable of further expansion. If an equal sum is raised by an increase in the standard rate of income tax to 10s and a very drastic reduction in allowances, we have so obviously shot our very last bolt.

8. *Administrative difficulties.* I hope to have learnt enough

from Sir G. Canny's criticisms to have devised a scheme which presents him with no greater difficulties than any other scheme capable of yielding an equal sum. I ask him to look friendly-wise on the following features:–

(*a*) The number of new taxpayers brought in is kept at a minimum. The old income tax cannot yield as much without bringing in at least as many and perhaps more.

(*b*) For earned incomes, each assessment of income tax has an amount of war surcharge uniquely associated with it. A table can be prepared which shows the war levy appropriate to each case alongside its income tax. No new information or calculation is required. The Revenue clerk merely writes down two figures instead of one in writing to the taxpayer and adds them together in writing to the employer. The abolition of earned income allowance will save more trouble than the war levy will add; so that on balance Sir G. Canny will gain.

(*c*) The treatment of unearned income does not differ in any respect from the income tax procedure, though the war levy should be shown as a separate item by companies etc. on their dividend vouchers.

9. *Time-lag in collection.* I do not clearly understand why Sir G. Canny thinks that so long a time-lag is inevitable or why the new assessments should not apply forthwith in respect of the income of 1940–41. In respect of unearned income the sums deducted at source would all be due on 1 January 1942, or earlier, by a back assessment where necessary on all profits belonging to a year part of which fell after 1 April 1940, exactly like an increase of income tax levied in an interim Budget. In the case of earned income the levy would be deducted currently from all income earned after 1 April 1941, on the basis of the assessment for 1940–41 with the usual reliefs where there has been a great change in income; so that, generally speaking, three-quarters of the total sum due would be collected in the next financial year.

Since, however, I am sure to be told that all this is quite wrong, we must be prepared, if necessary, to accept the time-lag in collection, which is not a peculiar feature of this particular proposal, but applies generally.

10. *Cost of living.* If a further £300 million is raised by new direct taxation, it would be safe, and highly expedient on other grounds, for the Chancellor to undertake to stabilise the cost of living index number. Politically I should make this a prominent feature of the next Budget. And I should do so irrespective of whether Labour formally agrees to a standstill of wage rates. It is not merely that this will soften the blow humanly speaking. There is a close logical connection between the two. A rise in the cost of living and more direct taxation are genuine alternatives. If the public accept the war levy, they will have literally earned the reward of a stable cost of living.

11. *A withholding tax.* I have kept this until last, because, as Sir R. Hopkins has pointed out, it is a conception which is applicable to any new scheme of direct (and even, as Sir H. J. Wilson has shown, of indirect) taxation. But the war surcharge as proposed above is, I think, particularly adapted for conversion into a withholding tax, and I have had that in mind throughout when preparing the details of it.

I propose that the war surcharge, as distinct from the increased tax, should be a withholding tax in the sense that it will be ultimately repayable to the taxpayer. The general idea can be worked out in a variety of forms. I have tried my hand at several in the past year. The following scheme has been drawn up in the interests of administrative simplicity:–

(i) The Revenue need do no more than give a separate receipt for the amount of the surcharge deducted from earned incomes. In the case of unearned income the company's voucher will give a certificate of deduction of surcharge on the dividend warrant paper, separated from it by an additional perforation, just like the present certificate of deduction of income tax. At his leisure a taxpayer would be entitled to set up a blocked account at any Trustee or Post Office savings bank, to which he would pay in his receipts or his vouchers for the sums to be credited in his name.

(ii) These deposits at Trustee and Post Office savings banks will be unblocked and freely disposable not later than two years after the end of the war, or immediately (to the extent of the sum standing to a taxpayer's credit at the time) on the occurrence of any of the following events:–

(a) his death;

(b) his marriage;

(c) the birth of a child;

(d) his drawing of sickness benefit or unemployment relief for more than six weeks consecutively;

(e) his joining up, provided that he assigns it to a wife or dependant;

(f) his evacuation from his house compulsorily or because it is rendered unfit by war damage;

(g) to meet a Schedule A contribution to war damage (i.e. the 3s surcharge under Schedule A would not be on top of the 2s contribution to war damage, but part of the former would immediately be applied to discharge the latter, leaving 1s net as a withholding tax);

(h) in the case of the surcharge on a company's undistributed profits, if the appropriate government department certifies that the money is required for expenditure in the national interest.

(i) These deposits will be ignored by all means tests.

An undue extension of this list (though suitable additions to it will doubtless occur to others) should be resisted. It would be better not to include contractual savings such as life insurance and building society repayments, though it may be difficult to resist them.[19]

---

[19] I included these in my 1939 proposals. But the present proposals are considerably lighter up to £500, especially for married men. though about 5 per cent heavier

(iii) There would be great social advantages in converting the income tax of small taxpayers up to a limited amount into a withholding tax; and this might considerably mitigate the hardship of the present high level of this tax.

For example, the first £25 per annum of income tax and war surcharge might be converted into a withholding tax. The effect of this can be seen in the table given above, e.g. a single man with £200 would pay £7 (instead of £22) in income tax and £25 in withholding tax, and a married man without children with an income of £300 would pay £185 (instead of £30) in income tax and £25 in withholding tax. This concession would only affect incomes below (approx.) £350 for single men, £450 for married men without children, and £550 for married men with two children. This concession should apply only to the tax on earned incomes, both on merits and for administrative reasons. It would be necessary that the part of the income tax converted into a withholding tax should be credited to the taxpayer after the end of the year.

(12) *The political aspects.* I find it impossible to believe that the withholding tax would not be more popular than a straight tax and would materially mitigate the severity of the blow. If, however, the Labour Part[y] prefer a straight tax *of the same amount* and feel that the withholding principle would demoralise the working classes,[20] there is no more to be said.

In considering the reactions on voluntary saving, one must compare the withholding tax with a straight tax of equal amount. It is evident that any severe Budget must have some unfavourable reactions on voluntary saving; and the same is true of a high cost of living and high prices generally. It will in any case be difficult to maintain working class savings when

for the higher incomes. Owing to income tax increases meantime, the withholding portion of the present proposals is a much smaller proportion of the whole than I proposed in 1939.

[20] When I was very young I examined in the Cambridge Locals and asked 'What is Socialism?' A small girl replied: 'The Socialists think it would do the poor good to make them just like the rich. It would not. It would spoil their characters.' I am hoping that the Labour Party is still socialist in this sense!

saving has to be at the expense of current standards and not merely of a postponement in improving them. Moreover non-contractual working class savings, i.e. excluding insurance, clubs, building societies and the like, is playing a very small part in war finance; whilst in the case of larger incomes those who will save anything material after meeting the proposed level of taxes and the high level of prices[21] must be so thrifty either by disposition or on account of public spirit that they will save anyhow. And is not the element of public spirit and patriotism underestimated by those who think that voluntary saving will dry up under a withholding tax but not under a straight tax of equal amount?

A tinkering with the existing income tax, however drastic, will have no popular or political appeal. When such great burdens are being imposed, the form of presentation is enormously important. It is not necessary or advisable that the form of presentation should seek to disguise the magnitude of the burden. What the public require is a sense that imagination has been used, that a novel fiscal instrument has been forged, that social justice has been preserved, and that a basis for further social improvement has been laid.

If the Chancellor can announce that he is stabilising the cost of living and is making provision by which most working men are either exempted from direct taxation or are accumulating a reserve for the future up to a rate of 10s a week, the Budget will evoke greater applause and be more generally popular, than if he acknowledges defeat and just puts another 1s 6d on the old income tax.

J. M. KEYNES

5.1.41

---

[21] E.g. a man with £1,000 a year after paying £430 in taxes or a man with £5,000 a year after paying £3,124, with prices 20 to 30 per cent higher than before.

To H. WILSON SMITH[22], *10 January 1941*

MR MADGE'S LATEST REPORT ON SAVINGS IN FOUR
YORKSHIRE WOOL TOWNS

I have just received one copy of this which I am putting into circulation. It is probably longer than most people will want to read. But for those who have time there is much in it worth a glance, since Madge manages to convey so much atmosphere. Meanwhile I summarise one or two outstanding points.

His results for different towns are on the whole remarkably uniform and suggest a fair degree of reliability in spite of the smallness of the samples in some cases.

1. The poorer families save a much larger proportion of their income than those with better earnings. The reason for this appears to be that the former have generally known hard times recently and have a strong motive to provide against their occurrence.

2. With the exception of Halifax, where the population are optimistic about its prospects after the war on account of its diversity of trades, the pessimists outnumber the optimists by about 4 to 1. The great majority are convinced that there will be terrible times facing them after the war. This appears to be the *main* motive towards saving. There is an interesting table in which it is shown on what a much larger scale the pessimists are saving than the optimists. It seems that it is not out of their surplus that the wage earning class save but out of their fears.

3. The average weekly savings in all forms per family seem to range between 4s and 5s. The major part of this is directed towards various forms of insurance and is, therefore, semi-contractual. The amount saved through savings certificates,

---

22 Henry Wilson Smith (b. 1904), K.C.B., 1949, K.B.E., 1945; Assistant Private Secretary to Chancellor of the Exchequer, 1932; Principal Private Secretary, 1940–2; Under-Secretary, Treasury, 1942–6; Permanent Secretary, Ministry of Defence, 1947–8; Additional Second Secretary, Treasury, 1948–51.

savings groups, defence bonds, Post Office and trustee savings banks, co-operative savings banks, building society deposit accounts and joint stock bank deposit accounts does not, all told, average as much as 1s per family per week. The following analysis of the average amount saved in pence per week in the two categories of saving is very striking. It would seem that the National Savings Movement savings, to the detriment of which a withholding tax might operate, are so trifling as scarcely to affect the picture.

Average amounts saved in two categories of saving

	Bradford	Huddersfield	Halifax	Dewsbury	Bristol
Average amount saved per family in national savings or banks (*pence*)	15	10	8	10	10
Average amount saved per family in other ways (*pence*)	46	51	40	44	41

4. On this occasion Madge has used a questionnaire relating to preferences for deferred pay as against other alternatives. He proposes to make a short subsidiary report on this which has not yet reached me. In the present report he gives a statistical summary. It will be seen that when he was at Bradford he was asking for a comparison between deferred pay and rationing. After a discussion which we held at the Budget Committee some little time ago I asked him to discover the preferences as between deferred pay, higher taxes and higher prices. The first question was too unfavourable to deferred pay, since it was not giving the real alternative. On the other hand, the later form of question may have been too favourable in the way in which it was put. Nevertheless, the very high preponderance of those with a definite preference who expressed a preference for deferred pay is very striking, namely, four out of five. It would be hard to maintain that this expedient is positively unpopular.

Answers to question: 'To help pay for the war, would you rather (a) have everything rationed (b) have higher prices (c) have part of your wages saved for you till after the war?'

	Per cent of those with a preference who preferred			Per cent without a preference
	Rationing	Higher prices	Deferred pay	
Bradford families	68	2	30	51

NOTE. Cf. Bristol table XVIII. This question was asked of the first 191 families in the Bradford sample. The results are directly comparable with those in the Bristol table, and they are very similar. The rest of the Bradford sample, and the sample in the other three towns, was asked a slightly different question, which is given below, with analysis of the answers.

Question: 'To help pay for the war, would you rather have (a) increased taxation (b) higher prices (c) part of your wages saved for you till after the war?'

	Per cent of those with a preference who preferred			Per cent of all asked who		
	Higher taxes	Higher prices	Deferred pay	Opposed all three	Had their own plan	Didn't know
Bradford	11	10	79	17	3	40
Huddersfield	26	3	71	3	3	67
Halifax	16	5	79	7	2	61
Dewsbury	7	11	82	3	2	68
Four wool towns						
Middle class	22	11	67	11	3	36
Trader class	12	0	88	9	5	48
Working class A	17	9	74	6	2	57
Working class B	11	7	82	12	2	58
No earners	0	11	89	2	2	78
All families	15	8	77	8	2	57

NOTE. The number of those who 'didn't know' was formidable in answers to this question, but there was an undoubted general preference for deferred pay. I hope to make a short subsidiary report on the terms in which this preference was expressed.

The large number who, not surprisingly, expressed no definite opinion, doubtless had no very clear picture in their minds of exactly what the alternatives were.

J. M. KEYNES

10.1.41

To SIR RICHARD HOPKINS, *19 January 1941*

INCOME TAX

Obeying your behests as usual, I have tried to obtain an income tax formula which would have an incidence closely similar to my proposed surcharge, and find that you were right (as usual) in believing that this could be done, namely as follows:–

(1) earned income allowance reduced to 1/10 with other allowances unchanged;

(2) standard rate raised to 11s 6d with reduction to 8s 6d on first £200 of taxed income;

(3) as before, this would involve, presumably, a fixing of surtax on all excess of income above £20,000 at 8s, in place of 8s 6d rising to 9s 6d as at present.

Withholding tax

Canny's suggestion that this should be applied to the part of the tax collected at a reduced rate seems a good one. To make the whole of the reduced tax on the first £200 of taxable income a withholding tax would include some part of the pre-war tax and might, therefore, lead to difficulties when

	Single man	
£	Increased total tax under above proposal compared with last year's Budget	Amount of withholding tax at *one half*
120	4	2
150	6	7·5
200	20	18·5
250	26	26·5
300	35	36
400	49	42·5
500	65	42·5
700	98	42·5
1,000	147	42·5
1,500	229	42·5
2,000	275	42·5

we return to normal peacetime taxation. The choice lies, therefore, between making either *half* or *three-quarters* of the tax at the reduced rate a withholding tax. A *half* would mean that at the lower levels of income the withholding tax would almost exactly correspond to the increase of tax now proposed, as shown.

But the withholding tax could be raised to *three-quarters* of the tax at the reduced rate without getting us into difficulties with peacetime rates. This has the advantage of actually improving the lowest income grades compared with the present situation:–

	Single man		Married man without children	
£	Increased total tax proposed compared with pre-war Budget	Amount of withholding tax at ¾	Increased total tax proposed compared with pre-war Budget	Amount of withholding tax at ¾
120	4	3	Nil	Nil
150	13	11	Nil	Nil
200	32	27	4	3
250	45	40	25	20
300	59	54	37	32
400	85	63	68	61
500	114	63	95	63
700	174	63		
1,000	263	63		
1,500	412	63		
2,000	533	63		

This means that up to about £300 (or £400 for married men and £500 where there are two children) nearly the whole of the wartime increase is in the form of a withholding tax, whilst at £2,000 nearly 90 per cent of the increase is an outright tax. I prefer the *three-quarters* proposal which means that a single man with £4 a week will have 10s a week accruing to his credit, or with £6 a week a little more than £1 a week so accruing; and that a married man with £5 a week (or £7 a week if he has two children) will have 8s a week accruing. This would fit in well with deferred pay at 10s a week for men called up to the forces.

Either of the above proposals would make the burden of subsequent repayment much smaller than that of earlier proposals; and should be acceptable politically. Indeed it is difficult to see how anyone could wish to accept the tax proposals and reject the withholding portion of them.

Yield

I am disappointed that the yield of this proposal is put so low as £225 million. Nevertheless if the suggested indirect taxes are also adopted, the total yield of the Budget (in a full year) should not fall far short of £2,000 million, which would be a considerable achievement approaching two-thirds (certainly 60 per cent) of domestic expenditure. This might be just not enough to keep free purchasing power within manageable limits, and allow the Chancellor to promise a stabilisation of the cost of living index number, which should be, I feel sure, an essential feature of his proposals as a whole.

Taking everything into account, is not the above about the best we can do?

19.1.41

After the February decisions on the detailed shape of the Budget, Keynes's efforts turned more towards the exposition of the Budget's strategy to others, including the Chancellor. The first two memoranda printed below show Keynes at his best here. The final, longer document is Keynes's late March draft Budget statement for the Chancellor, only small segments of which survived to the day when Keynes listened to the speech from the gallery.

To H. WILSON SMITH, *17 February 1941*

About a fortnight ago the Chancellor asked me to prepare the draft of a memorandum which would enable him to consult his colleagues on certain general issues associated with Budget policy. I have prepared this draft on the assumption that it is to the Lord President's Committee that it would go forward.

It avoids any detailed information about Budget proposals,

and is not intended to lead up to any discussion of such details. It seems to me that the Chancellor could take the line that he needs advice on the more general issues raised in this paper before he can usefully proceed to any final decisions on Budget proposals and that he is not yet in a position to discuss the letter.

I am sending copies of this to Sir H. J. Wilson, Sir R. Hopkins, Sir A. Barlow[23] and Lord Catto.

J.M.K.

17.2.41

THE POLICY OF THE BUDGET

1. In the first year of the war, no significant curtailment of civilian consumption was necessary. Our task was (1) to prevent a pressure of purchasing power due to high earnings and high profits from forcing up the price of supplies, the quantity of which could not be increased, to a level unjustified by higher costs; and (2) to prevent wage *rates* (as distinct from total earnings) from fully reflecting the rise in prices which the higher cost of imports made inevitable.

By a variety of means—the Prices of Goods Act, E.P.T. and drastic general taxation, rationing of certain foodstuffs, considerable subsidies to the cost of living, the success of the savings campaign and, not least, the loyal policy of the trade unions—we solved the problem, not perfectly, but with a considerable measure of success. Indeed this problem was not unduly difficult.

2. In the current year the problem is changing not merely in degree but in kind. As the Prime Minister has pointed out, the war industrial machine only gets into its stride in the second year of war; and its full demands on manpower

[23] James Alan Noel Barlow (1881–1968), K.C.B., 1942, G.C.B., 1947; Clerk, House of Commons, 1906; Board of Education, 1907–16; Ministry of Munitions, 1916; Principal Assistant Secretary, Ministry of Labour; Principal Private Secretary to the Prime Minister, 1933–4; Under-Secretary, Treasury, 1934; Joint Second Secretary, 1938–48.

mature at the same time as those of the forces. Thus it is now necessary to curtail domestic production available for civilian consumption; whilst, unfortunately, supplies for the same purpose from overseas are sharply reduced by our shipping difficulties.

Spread over the whole of consumption expenditure, excluding rent and rates, the necessary curtailment looks to be, on present indications, somewhere in the neighbourhood of 10 per cent (say £360 million a year). Certainly, it should not reach 15 per cent. This is far from insupportable. It will leave the standard of life higher than it was in peacetime until recently, higher than it was in Germany *before* the war. No one can complain of that, when we are desperately at war.

Nevertheless it is enough to create social confusion and impede the war effort if it is neglected. For an unsatisfied shortage of supply in one direction slops over into another, until there is trouble and acute dissatisfaction everywhere at once. The inconvenience and unfairness of distribution would be acute; and the withdrawal of labour from civilian production might become impracticable on the scale at present contemplated.

3. In 1917 we allowed a rise of prices sufficiently steep to absorb the excess purchasing power in spite of the reduction in the quantity of supplies on the market. China is adopting this method today. This expedient is undesirable because it throws an intolerable share of the burden on the classes in the community whose money incomes are not easily increased. But, apart from this objection, we can dismiss it without further discussion, because with the existing system of wage contracts it is *impossible* to effect a rise which is sufficiently steep to restore equilibrium. In 1917 wage rates as a whole lagged six months to a year behind prices. Today about half of total wages are tied to the cost of living by a formula and rise automatically after the briefest interval. Thus this traditional outlet is denied to us. Probably a good

thing that it is denied to us. But the technical difficulty of solving our problem is thereby greatly increased.

4. We are left with two other weapons—rationing and taxation. I suggest that we shall do better by using both of them than by depending on one of them exclusively.

Comprehensive rationing is being advocated in some quarters; for example, a limitation on retail purchases as a whole to a maximum of (say) £1 per head per week. War-communism on these lines has its attractive side. I reject it on the grounds (i) that it concentrates the expenditure of all classes on the cheapest article to the disadvantage of the poorer groups and at the cost of wasting some useful sources of supply, (ii) that it ignores the variety of individual circumstances and needs and breaks down on details, (iii) that it would take many months and use up much manpower to create a machinery capable of administering it, and (iv) that it goes beyond the necessities of the case and also beyond what public opinion is prepared for. There is no good reason to behave as though we were much worse off than we are.

On the other hand, *selective* rationing is open to the objection that it merely drives the consumer from pillar to post and creates difficulties in new directions by diverting consumption to the articles which are still unrationed. Demands for standstill price orders spring up all over the place, until there is a shortage of everything. Quite a small average deficiency of supply is capable, if accompanied by price fixing, of producing a universal shortage and thus creating in the minds of the public an impression of a very great general deficiency. Each unfulfilled demand becomes multiplied a hundredfold in every housewife's experience.

5. Selective rationing on a fairly extensive scale is, I fear, inevitable in the ensuing months. The obstacles thus placed in the way of expenditure will assist my task as a collector of taxes and savings from the public. But unless I deliberately withdraw by fresh taxation a considerable part of the redun-

dant purchasing power, I may be setting the Minister of Food
and the President of the Board of Trade an impossible task,
and drive them stage by stage to fresh complications and fresh
difficulties. Rationing and taxing should be regarded as
complementary policies, each assisting the other. Neither of
them increases the burden on the public or requires any fresh
sacrifice beyond what the basic facts of the situation—shortages
of manpower and shipping—have made inevitable. In any
case the public will consume all the supplies which it is
physically possible to make available, and no more. Both
methods are, therefore, to be judged by their success in
securing a fair, efficient and acceptable system of distributing
what supplies there are without putting an excessive burden
on the administrative machine or on the patience and adapt-
ability of the public. I would add that the scale of war effort
which we are contemplating will not prove practicable
otherwise. An inadequate Budget and a faulty system of
rationing will mean that the manpower required by the
munition programme and by the forces will not be, in fact,
forthcoming. It is ridiculous in present circumstances to speak
of new taxation as involving 'too heavy a sacrifice' from the
public. It involves no sacrifice whatever and merely distributes
an already existing burden. Nevertheless, I do not think it
either necessary or desirable to cover the whole of the so-called
'gap' by new revenue. Pushed to this limit, taxation would
have to be high enough to absorb the leakages due to the
pressure to live on capital or on what would otherwise be
saved and to other forms of evasion; which would mean a
level at which the task of collection would break down the
administrative machine. The best result will be obtained by
advancing on all fronts at once—an increase of selective
rationing, a considerable increase of taxation, and an intensification of the savings campaign.

6. I suggest to my colleagues that we shall have the best
chance of carrying public opinion with us if we represent the

severe measures of rationing and taxation which will become necessary this spring for what they are, namely as connected parts of a coherent economic policy; and I particularly invite the collaboration of the Minister of Food and the President of the Board of Trade to this end.

7. There is, however, a further problem to tackle before we can offer a coherent economic policy, namely price policy and its relation to wages. Here it is the Minister of Labour who can help me most. May I set out the general lines along which our discussions in the Treasury have been moving and be given the benefit of the advice of the Lord President's Committee?

8. I should like to make the *stability of prices* the keynote of the forthcoming budget. This is the practical test of our success in the avoidance of inflation. Moreover with the level of direct taxation which I have in view, the public will have *earned* the benefit of stable prices; and it will make the new taxes more acceptable if this beneficial consequence can be made clear and definite. But I must explain what I mean by 'stability of prices'. And it is here that I need to be advised just how much it is safe to say.

9. We are already spending some £110 million a year in stabilising the food items in the cost of living index number; and whilst no promises have been made, it is our *de facto* policy to prevent any significant further increase in the food factor of the cost of living index, apart from seasonal movements. I am not satisfied that we are getting the full credit for this from public opinion. The other items in the index have not, so far, received any direct subsidies. The cost of living index number has, for one reason or another, been rising steadily; and, for all they know, the public have no sufficient reason to expect this to stop. The movement of the various groups up to date has been as follows:– [see below]

10. Since the purchase tax had not produced its full effect by 1 January, it would be safer to assume that the index as

	1 September 1939	1 January 1941
Food	100	125
Rent and rates	100	101
Clothing	100	160
Fuel and light	100	118
Other items	100	124
Index as a whole	100	126

a whole will have reached 130 by 1 March next. Can we expect to hold it at that figure thereafter? To answer this, we must examine the causes of the increases so far:–

(i) Higher prices abroad, coupled with the fall in the dollar value of sterling. This was the main influence in the early months of the war. The value of sterling is now fixed and prices abroad have ceased to rise. Thus the influence of this factor is probably exhausted. Indeed, if our purchasing departments were less ready to repeat first-year-of-war prices in the second year, we might succeed in reducing somewhat the average f.o.b. cost of our civilian imports. A definite instruction to aim at a reduction of (say) 10 per cent wherever we are buying articles in surplus supply internationally might be wholesome and beneficial.

(ii) The general Treasury policy hitherto has been to expect departments to load on to current prices substantially *all* the current costs which they are incurring, thus maintaining a fully commercial price policy. This has meant in practice that current prices include a provision for what, from another point of view, it might have been reasonable to charge to the general costs of the war. For example, the prices which the public are now paying for consumption goods include a provision for the following costs (substantially offset by subsidies in the case of the food items)—

(*a*) the eventual cost of replacing our mercantile marine sunk by enemy action;

(*b*) the current cost of the supplies destroyed by enemy

action at sea or on land as well as the cost of those supplies which are reaching the consumer;

(*c*) the cost of writing-off reserve or shadow factories, erected as an insurance against enemy action, or other new construction probably surplus to post-war needs;

(*d*) the cost of writing down the price of stocks acquired at a higher price than we can reckon on realising when they are ultimately disposed of at the end of the war.

In effect this amounts to meeting part of the cost of the war by indirect taxes on the commodities particularly affected. There are three good arguments for this policy. Strict accounting, by which those responsible for a particular article have to aim at being self-supporting, is favourable to efficiency and economy. The higher price tends to divert consumption away from vulnerable, and therefore exceptionally expensive, articles. And the yield to the Exchequer is very substantial;— the gross receipts from war risk premiums in respect of hulls, cargoes and commodities amounted to £87 million in the first year of war and to an annual rate of yield of £160 million in the three months ending 31 December last (though upwards of half of this may, in fact, have been met by the Exchequer itself in respect of government purchases). On the other hand, the effect of these charges on our export prices may be undesirable.

Nevertheless, the line of division is somewhat arbitrary;— we do not charge up the cost of a convoy or of anti-aircraft guns.

Absurd results might follow from pushing this policy to its logical conclusion. My advisers are of the opinion that we have now carried it fully as far as is advisable, and that no further price increase should be required for any of the above reasons. That is to say, the rates of premium for war risks on hulls, cargoes and commodities should not be increased further, even if losses increase; and similarly with the other minor items of cost mentioned above.

(iii) Up to 1 January 1941, additional taxes on sugar, tobacco and matches were responsible for an increase of 1¾ per cent in the cost of living index number; and the purchase tax for an increase of 1½ per cent. When the purchase tax is fully reflected in current prices, the increase due to additional indirect taxation imposed by the Budget may amount altogether to about 5 per cent.

I incline to the view that this is enough and that there should be no increased indirect taxation in the forthcoming Budget whether affecting the cost of living index or articles outside it.

(iv) Under the Prices of Goods Act higher overhead and distribution costs due to a reduction in turnover can be legitimately added to prices. The further restriction of supplies now in prospect, and particularly the Board of Trade restriction orders when they have produced their full effect, are likely to justify some further increase under this head; —to which must be added the possibility of compensation costs, incurred to facilitate the concentration of output. I should be glad to have an estimate of the possible amount of this, which, I hope, is not large, and to be told whether its average influence on the index number could be conveniently offset by a reduction in certain war-risk premiums under the commodity scheme or in some other way.

(v) The prevention of higher costs under the above headings as a reason for higher prices apart from inflationary pressure of demand on supply, seems to be within our own control. But there remains the factor of wage rates.

If I were to undertake to stabilise the cost of living index number at the level ruling on 1 March next, would it be reasonable to expect that there would be no further significant increases in wage rates beyond those ruling at that date and those called for under cost-of-living sliding scales?

This question is to be interpreted in the light of two explanations. In the first place, it is not intended to stabilise *all* prices. We must not cut ourselves off from every opportunity of absorbing excess purchasing power in higher prices. I hope that the Minister of Food will find semi-luxuries where he can innocently and successfully profiteer. I should make it clear to the public that I was contemplating classification of articles of consumption under three heads,—the cost of living index number, where we should aim at preventing any further increase whatever; articles of common consumption outside the index where further increases, if not avoided altogether, would be kept within a narrow range; articles of non-necessity or semi-luxury where no special steps would be taken to hold down prices apart from the Prices of Goods Act.

In the second place, I am not proposing that the trade unions should be asked to give any definite undertaking. I regard the freedom of the wage contract as a valuable safeguard with which we should not lightly interfere. But like other freedoms in time of war it must be exercised with moderation and public spirit. We have reached a stage in the war when the general standard of living must inevitably suffer some reduction; and any sectional gain must be at the expense of the rest of the community. Even where in ordinary circumstances there would be a strong case for a relative rise, we have now reached a stage where it is reasonable to ask that the remedy even of such strong cases should be deferred until a time when we can afford them better. If the cost of living index is now stabilised, would there be any likelihood of a significant further rise in wage rates, subject always to the necessary occasional exceptions to which any such rule is properly subject?

I believe that by administrative action we can, if we choose, control all likely causes of an inflationary rise of prices apart from a rise in wage rates. But if by gradual stages and slow degrees there is such a rise, we can scarcely hope to prevent its reflection in prices; and the spiral would have to move steadily, and before long rapidly, upwards. Thus my undertaking would have to be in the form that, apart from minor seasonal changes, we should take steps to prevent any further upward movement of the cost of living index number and any substantial increase in the prices of articles in common use outside the index number, provided always that there is no significant further rise in wage rates.

My question is, therefore—would this be a sensible and prudent undertaking to give? Judging from the loyal and reasonable policy of the trade unions up to date, I hope I may say Yes.

11. If so, we have the elements of a coherent economic policy likely to be intelligible and acceptable to public opinion which is not asking for soft and easy ways (quite the contrary):–

(i) a gradual extension of rationing, by direct and indirect methods, in accordance with the necessities of the case and in step with the evolution and improvement of our administrative machine;

(ii) no further indirect taxes in the Budget but an increase in direct taxes sufficient to raise the yield of the revenue (in a full year) to 60 per cent of our domestic expenditure and 30 per cent of the national income, a standard higher in proportion than the present tax revenue of Germany—higher, indeed, than any nation at war has achieved hitherto;

(iii) A final stabilisation of the cost of living index number at about 30 per cent above pre-war, subject only to the above qualification, together with a check on other price rises by the adoption of the various administrative measures recommended above.

17.2.41

THE THEORY OF THE 'GAP'

1. At any given time there must of necessity be momentary equilibrium and no 'gap'. For the income of the public must always be exactly equal to the sum of (1) what they pay in taxes

THE GAP
Cartoon by David Low from *The Evening Standard* of 7 April 1941
by arrangement with the Trustees and *The Evening Standard*.

plus (2) what they spend on consumption *plus* (3) what they save.

Looking at the same thing from the government angle, total government expenditure is always exactly equal to (1) their receipts from overseas resources and the liquidation of domestic capital plus (2) what the public pay in taxes plus (3) what the public save. The idea that the government can borrow funds 'created by inflation' which have not been saved by the public is a delusion. If additional sums are borrowed from the banks or through the note issue, the bank deposits of the public and their holdings of notes are correspondingly increased; and these bank balances and notes represent additional savings which, for the time being at least, the public are not spending. The only peculiarity of saving in this form is that it is a little easier for the public to change their mind later on than if, for example, they have bought savings certificates. But what matters at all times is the firmness of the public decision to save instead of spending and not the particular form in which they choose to hold their savings.

2. But this equilibrium has to be maintained partly by appropriate changes in prices, and partly by changes in saving habits through obstacles in the way of consumption or otherwise.

Starting out from the position of momentary equilibrium which actually exists let us suppose that the government takes no steps to increase its revenue but increases its net domestic expenditure[24] by £500 million;—partly by employing persons and plant previously without occupation at a cost of £200 million, partly by diverting to munitions persons previously occupied in producing for civilian consumption or for export at a cost of £150 million, and partly by reducing by £150 million the excess of the value of imports available for civilian consumption over the exports they are producing. This means that the incomes of the public are increased by £200 million and the value of newly produced goods available for them to buy is reduced by £300 million valued at the old prices. That is to say, there is a 'gap' of £500 million between the disposable purchasing power and the value (at the old prices) of the good available in the market.

The 'gap' can be measured either by the increase in government net domestic expenditure uncovered by new revenue, i.e. £500 million; or by the increase in the total incomes of the public (£200 million) *plus* the reduction in what they earn from producing for civilian consumption or export (£150

---

[24] By net domestic expenditure I mean the expenditure requiring domestic finance, i.e. the total government expenditure *minus* the adverse balance of overseas payments which is being paid for out of overseas resources.

million) *plus* the reduction in the excess of imports over exports available for them to buy (£150 million). And the two methods of measurement must necessarily lead to the same result.

In such circumstances how can equilibrium be reached between the total incomes of the public and the sum of what they pay in taxes, spend on consumption and save?

3. There are only three ways,—apart from higher taxes and an increased willingness to save.

The most effective and the most usual way is a rise in the prices of consumption goods, so that at the higher price level the increased purchasing power is fully absorbed by the reduced quantity of goods. Let us suppose that an average rise of 10 per cent is sufficient for this purpose on the first round. That, however, is not the end of the story. For the rise in prices will increase the incomes of the lucky vendors of the goods. Some part of this increase they will pay away in increased taxes especially E.P.T., some part they may save, but some part they may spend in an endeavour to maintain an increase in their own personal consumption; with the result of a further rise in prices at the second round. Moreover the initial rise in prices may cause higher wages and therefore higher incomes to wage earners, also with the result of a further rise in prices. Thus an initial 'gap' of no more than 10 per cent may lead, sooner or later, to an unlimited rise in prices. That is the stupidity of this method of meeting the problem.

At any rate prices will have to rise until a level is reached at which, for the time being at least and before the time-lags have worked themselves out, someone or other is paying enough increased taxes or has decided in the new situation to increase his personal savings up to a total sufficient to provide the government with an amount of money equal to the 'gap'. The greater the time-lags between the increase in someone's money income and the ultimate repercussions of this, the smaller will the initial price rise have to be in order to produce momentary equilibrium. But this does not mean that a greater rise will not be required later on merely to maintain equilibrium even apart from the necessity to offset a brand-new 'gap'. (That is the ever-increasing danger of the present situation—lest past events still have to produce their full effect. I do not now put very high the future effect of past events, but it is here that I may be too optimistic.)

The second way is to prohibit price rises and to put such obstacles in the way of consumption by rationing and shop-shortages that people are physically unable to spend what they want to spend and are compelled to save more than they intended. This can be brought about only on a small scale by *selective* rationing on the present model. For people divert most of what they cannot spend on meat or bacon to buying some unrationed article. Since there is an aggregate shortage this means that the last customers cannot be satisfied—there is nothing left in the shops—with general discontent and waste of time. Thus *comprehensive*, or at any rate very wide-spread rationing, is necessary sooner or later for this method to be workable.

The third way, but obviously no more than a temporary expedient, is to live on stocks, i.e. to allow the shops to sell more than is being currently produced or imported, or to use up some other form of domestic capital.

At the present time each of these methods is producing some effect,—enough in the aggregate exactly to fill the gap which increased government outlay would otherwise cause. I expect that at the moment we are depending to a very dangerous extent on the third way, namely the exhaustion of stocks.

4. For the coming financial year I have estimated that the increased gap to be filled in one or another of these ways is of the order of £500 million. But if upwards of £300 million of this is met by increased taxes, perhaps it is reasonable to

hope that the balance can be covered one way or another without precipitating any uncontrollable movement. The sources to fill this balance are

(1) living on stocks to a further, moderate extent;[25]

(2) higher prices in certain, relatively innocent, directions;

(3) some stimulus to increased saving, partly as a result of higher incomes, partly as a result of propaganda, and partly as a result of obstacles in the way of expenditure through an extension of rationing and the lack of attractive goods in the shop windows;

(4) time-lags generally.

If we were to depend on these sources for the whole amount we should be likely to let loose forces which could not be left uncontrolled and would require remedies far more difficult administratively and objectionable politically than £300 million higher taxes. We must remember that these sundry sources have to look after the delayed effects on private spending of government expenditure in the recent past as well as the current effect of present government expenditure uncovered by new taxes.

If there is an error in these calculations it undoubtedly lies in putting the minimum new taxation required so low as £300.

3.3.41   J. M. KEYNES

NOTES FOR THE BUDGET STATEMENT 1941[26]

I

In time of peace it is for the Budget proposals to determine the amount of resources which shall be taken from the public and placed at the disposal of the departments of state. But

---

[25] This only helps in so far as we can afford to live on stocks at a *higher* rate than hitherto. A continuance of living on stocks at the *present* rate is required to bridge what would otherwise be an existing gap.

[26] Where there are gaps concerning numbers these are in the original [Ed.].

in time of war this is reversed. The war departments take, and ought to take, all they require that can be made available. The task of the Budget is, not to determine the weight of the burden, but to distribute it with justice and efficiency, and by doing so to make sure that the maximum resources can be released. A weak Budget will not lighten the burdens on the public. On the contrary it would increase them. The reduction of consumption through our shipping difficulties and through the withdrawal of workers into the forces and into munitions would be the same. If the resulting shortage of goods meets an unrestricted surplus of purchasing power, the burden is distributed by the cruel and random inflictions of high prices and shop shortages, with much injury to order and organisation and to equal treatment between one man and another. My Budget today may seem heavy to some, but in truth it will not increase what we have to carry. Its object is to distribute with forethought and fairness of purpose a burden which we cannot avoid; and in doing so to make it more tolerable.

(This section is rather perfunctory and might be omitted.)

II

The Budget must be regarded as a part, and only a part, of a comprehensive economic policy. The contributions of my colleagues to the subsequent debate will bring this out more fully than is possible in my Budget statement taken in isolation. We have calculated the man-power and the shipping requirements of the forces and the munitions industries. This requires a drastic limitation of supplies to the civilian population, which cannot be enforced efficiently without organised concentration of production and an individual combing out of inessential workers in place of reservation by classes. The further curtailment of civilian consumption thus made necessary is substantial but far from intolerable. To the best of my belief it should not exceed 10 per cent as an overall average and will still leave the standard of life at a higher level than was enjoyed until recent years. But it will affect different articles of consumption very unequally. Thus order and equitable distribution will continue to require an increase of price controls and of rationing. The President of the Board of Trade and the Minister of Food would, however, be set an impossible task unless their problem is eased by my with-holding a substantial part of the surplus purchasing power through the instrument of taxation. For the purchasing power, which cannot find an outlet in one direction, will force an outlet in another direction; and each problem that is solved would thus create a new problem somewhere else.

III

After outlining the outcome of revenue and expenditure in the last year, the Chancellor continues:–

These figures by themselves do not in present circum-stances tell us a great deal about the inner financial history of the past year. To understand this it is necessary to know many figures which it has not been our practice to publish. Since it is impossible for Parliament to exercise an instructed judg-ment on financial policy without this further information, I have decided to circulate[27] along with the usual White Paper certain tables which disclose all the most essential facts which are available to myself;—the exact amount of the internal resources available to the Exchequer, the strain on our gold and other overseas assets, the amount and the uses of the national income, and much else. I am hopeful that the House will appreciate this unconventional course, even though such a full analysis involves elements of conjecture and approxi-mate estimation. Members will, no doubt, take anything told them by statisticians, as I do myself, with a grain of salt. It

[27] Note A [p. 320].

may seem strange that we should publish in time of war fuller information than in time of peace. But for one thing our tasks require a more comprehensive knowledge. And in the second place we do in fact know more, because a much larger part of the national economic life falls within the purview of government departments. I would point out to the House that the tables of national income and expenditure are the very valuable first-fruits of our new Central Statistical Office set up by the Prime Minister's instructions. This office now assembles for the information of the War Cabinet and government departments regular series of statistics much more comprehensive than we have possessed hitherto.

Let me analyse the sources of our finance up to date in the light of these figures. During the first eighteen months of the war we have drawn on our overseas resources on a scale which would have been imprudent if we had not felt a confidence, which has proved magnificently justified, in the prospect of financial help from the United States when we should most need it. Altogether we have met an adverse balance of overseas payments in excess of £1,000 million mainly out of the gold which we had accumulated in the Exchange Equalisation Fund, the cash and securities which private citizens have handed over to the Exchequer, and the substantial sums which the Dominions have been able to accumulate in London out of the purchases we have made from them. During this period we not only paid in hard cash for everything we obtained from the United States but made in addition heavy advance payments in respect of future deliveries.

During this phase it has been a major task of the Treasury and the Bank of England to mobilise the foreign cash and securities which were privately owned, to prevent the movement of capital outside the sterling area and to establish a comprehensive exchange control through the negotiation of payments agreements with nearly every neutral country in the world. The loyalty and uncomplaining spirit in which private citizens have surrendered their possessions to the needs of the state deserves at least a passing mention. In the organisation of the sterling area we have created a powerful instrument for international exchange which has enabled us to solve successfully most of our financial problems outside North America. By these means we have been able to meet net expenditures abroad not covered by our exports and other sources of current income which, as I have mentioned, exceed £1,000 million. From now on this problem is transformed in character and greatly diminished in size by the Lend and Lease Bill of the United States Administration.

After deducting from our total expenditure the sums raised in this way we are left with the amounts which I have had to meet out of tax revenue and strictly domestic loans. In the first year of the war such net expenditure came to £2,055 million, and in the first half of the second year, which roughly corresponds to the period since my emergency Budget, it rose to an annual rate of £3,176 million. The corresponding figure for the coming year, to which I shall return later, will give us the measure of our financial task at home.

Part of this domestic expenditure we have met by borrowing the sums normally set aside out of the sale proceeds of current output to make good depreciation, repairs and renewals of buildings and plant, the execution of which has to be postponed until after the war, and from capital released by the diminution in the value of stocks privately owned. A large sum has become available in this way. But I must point out emphatically that this is not, in present circumstances, a true indication of the reduction in the national wealth. Whilst stocks privately owned are much reduced in amount and new private investment has fallen far short of the wear and tear of buildings and plant, the stocks owned by the Government at home and abroad are greatly increased[28] and the new capital investment we have financed is on a large scale.[29] The

[28] Note B [p. 321].   [29] Note C [p. 321].

increased value of government-owned stocks of commodities and investment in new factories and plant, all paid for out of the Exchequer, considerably exceed the estimated reduction in the value of privately owned stocks, plant and buildings. You will be gratified, and perhaps surprised, when I tell you that the stocks of raw materials and foodstuffs warehoused in this country on the 1st January last were materially greater in volume than on the 1st January 1940,[30] a year previously. Compare this with the position in Germany where the official statistics admit that stocks were reduced by 5 milliard marks (which is more than £300 million) in the first year of the war and are likely by now to have fallen by a much greater amount than this. In our case we need have no anxiety in having drawn on this source of funds to meet a part of our current expenditure, since it represents no more than a transfer from private to public financing; though a time may be expected to come sooner or later, when the strain of war increases, when receipts from these sources will genuinely represent a reduction of national capital.

We have also had the benefit of substantial current receipts of certain extra-budgetary funds, mainly the accumulations of the unemployment fund and of the government insurance schemes.

The balance of the Exchequer expenditure in the first eighteen months of war has been met out of revenue amounting to some £2,000 million and out of new savings which, it is estimated, have exceeded £1,000 million. The proportion of about two-thirds raised in revenue proper is surely a matter for some satisfaction. The growth of private savings, through the stimulus provided by the National Savings Movement under the leadership of Lord Kindersley, has been truly remarkable. It is estimated that new private savings are now accumulating at a rate nearly double the rate in the first year of the war, which was itself an enormous increase on

[30] Note D [p. 321].

peacetime standards. Nevertheless we shall need yet further efforts. Domestic expenditure in the next *twelve* months is likely to exceed the total of such expenditure in the first *eighteen* months of the war. Whilst new personal savings, leaving out companies and institutions, is now running at an estimated rate which approaches £700 million a year, I expect to need from this source in the coming year a sum of at least £1,000 million.

Let me add that it is not easy to disentangle the amount of new personal savings from the weekly statistics which include companies and institutions and also the reinvestment of old savings. Moreover it makes all the difference whether the money is saved by the man who earns it or whether the money circulates through *his* spending it and perhaps the next recipient spending it too, before it finally reaches safe hands. For if the money is allowed to circulate, the strain on our resources is not avoided and the harm is done, even though the money is saved in the end and thus gets into the statistics—as indeed it must, if we are to reach equilibrium at all. Lord Kindersley's task is to persuade the public to save the money at the source, what I shall call *primary saving*, and not allow it to circulate by spending.[31] A man who unnecessarily puts money into circulation does harm even though the purchase which he himself makes may seem to him exceptionally innocent.

The £1,000 million which I need in the current year from primary savings withheld from circulation by those who earn the money is a fine target for Lord Kindersley and his men. For it is not beyond attainment. What does it mean in terms of individual incomes? It is about one-fifth of our net personal incomes after deducting what we pay in direct taxes. The statisticians tell me that in 1940 the public probably saved about one-eighth of their net incomes. We are already doing better than that—saving today perhaps one-seventh. But

[31] Note E [p. 322].

from now on anyone who saves less than a fifth will be doing less than his share. Since there are many individuals who may not attain this proportion because their incomes are small in relation to their family and other responsibilities, it means that anyone who has no special excuse is not doing his duty unless he saves a quarter of his net income, though, of course, it is not as high a proportion as this in terms of his gross income before paying taxes. Let me put it concretely for those without young families. A man earning £6 a week should save £1 a week; with £500 a year he should save £80, with £700 he should save £110 and with £1,000 he should save £150. Clearly it is easier for those above £6 a week to beat these figures, and they should try to do so. Let every member of the public work out for himself whether he is doing what he should on this standard. Nothing impossible in all this. It is no more than what the prudent and thrifty did in peacetime. I may be told that the greatly increased burden of taxes makes all the difference. Of course it makes a difference. But there is a big factor on the other side. My Right Honourable friends at the Ministry of Food and the Board of Trade are proposing to remove temptation from the way of shoppers. They will do all they know to keep the housewife on the straight and narrow path. That should help a lot. It will seldom have been so easy to save as in the coming months —such good earnings, so few unnecessary things to spend them on.

IV

This fine and exhilarating theme has diverted me a little from my course. Before I turn to the future let me review for a moment the results of my emergency Budget last summer. It had two main features—the purchase tax and the combination of a heavy increase of income tax with collection at source from salaries and wages.

The yield of the purchase tax up to date, namely £25

million, has been disappointing for reasons which are easily explained. Administrative problems led to a long delay in bringing it into operation, during which there was an opportunity for a large amount of stocking up. Subsequently the restriction orders have considerably curtailed its field of operation. Nevertheless it is now working most successfully and with the minimum of friction. The Englishman has a genius for co-operating with the tax collector. The assistance which the Customs have received from traders and the promptness of payment have been beyond praise. There are about 40,000 registered traders and it may interest you to know that nearly half the tax is paid by about 100 firms.[32]

The ease and lack of complaint with which so heavy an income tax has been collected at source has been truly remarkable. At many income levels I raised the effective burden of tax to twice and even three times what it had been a year previously. The deduction of these substantial sums at source has been faced throughout the country with scarcely a complaint. In recent weeks an enquiry under the auspices of the National Council [sic] of Economic and Social Research has been conducted in an industrial town near London [to find out] how wage earners were feeling about it. The result is most interesting and does very great credit to those affected. Of those paying tax who expressed a definite opinion (a great majority of those asked) four-fifths favoured the tax in varying degrees. I should like to quote some of the actual comments, some from the men, some from their wives:–

'Well, you're sort of paying for the war as you go.'

'He doesn't mind. The war's got to be paid for. It's stopped out of his wages. It's better that way.'

'A very good idea. What you don't have you don't miss.'

'He's a proper Englishman and doesn't mind if it's for a good cause.'

'We paid £35 last year. We're lucky to earn money—he doesn't mind if it's helping to win the war.'

[32] Note F [p. 323].

302

'It's not what you feel but what you've got to do. He doesn't mind.'

'He did mind at first, but he's got used to it.'

He doesn't mind. Or, if he did, he has got used to it. That is how the Englishman takes what he knows to be necessary.

I fancy that a first-class revolution in our fiscal system has happened, almost silently, in the last year. The country has been finally converted to the great superiority of direct taxation at all levels of income. With that conversion we have reached, so to speak, a higher standard of fiscal civilisation. We have made up our minds that for all of us, the wage earners not least, direct taxes are better than higher prices.

v

Another revolution in our financial practice has followed from our great success in borrowing for the war at a low rate of interest. In 1916 we were paying 5 per cent as a general minimum and by July of that year even Treasury bills were yielding 6 per cent. Compare that with the position today. Who would have believed that in the second year of the war I should be able, in seeking borrowing powers, to accept an amendment fixing 3 per cent as the maximum rate to be paid? Since our short-term borrowing is costing 1⅛ per cent or less, the average rate payable is much below 3 per cent. Indeed, up to March 25th last, we had borrowed under all heads a net sum of £   million at an additional cost in interest of £   million. This means that the future gross cost to the taxpayer of borrowing a given sum is less than a third of what it was in the last war; and the high standard rate of income tax means that the net current cost is smaller still. We shall certainly not borrow on worse terms in the future, and it may yet be possible to work them a little lower.

It is evident that the aggravation of our post-war financial problem by the burden of the war debt will be correspondingly less. Moreover we shall avoid the evils which we incurred after 1918 from starting the period of post-war expansion and recovery with a rate of interest which proved in the long run embarrassing and even crushing to the borrower. Half the trouble of our housing problem after the last war was due to the burdensome costs of interest when even local authorities had to pay 6 per cent. Indeed it is only now that they are escaping from it, and it is a remarkable thing that I should be able in time of war to give them the opportunity to refund at less than two-thirds the previous cost. It gave me exceptional pleasure to be able to announce a short time ago that we are now able to afford them this relief. In rebuilding our cities after the war the maintenance of a low rate of interest will halve the financial problem.

VI

Am I, in the light of subsequent events, open to the criticism that I should have done more last summer to avoid inflation? That is a hard question to answer for certain. I believe that I did the utmost which was advisable, having regard to the strain on our administrative machine and the wisdom of not moving too suddenly all at once—of 'allowing him to get used to it, so that he doesn't mind', of securing the consciousness of consent, which is no mean part of the art of government in a democracy.

But was it enough to avoid inflation? No two men agree just what they mean by that question. That prices have continued to move upwards is beyond dispute. Is it inflation when prices rise as a direct or indirect result of a higher cost of imports? If so, it could only be avoided by an actual reduction of wages. For no amount of taxation will cause goods to be produced and sold below cost price. If, as I think we should, we exclude that sort of price rise from the symptoms of inflation, it is clear that what remains is small and that the situation is still well in hand. The tables which I am circulating show that in 1940 the money value of the national output at the current price was about 32 per cent greater than in 1938. I am told that this was probably the joint result of about 14 per cent greater volume, due to better employment, an increased number of workers and more overtime, and 15 per cent higher unit costs. This higher cost was mainly due to higher wages which were largely a repercussion of the higher cost of living which resulted from the higher cost of imports, for the cost of imports is now 50 per cent higher than before the war. It is beyond my powers to estimate precisely how much of the higher prices of domestic output can be ascribed to inflationary expenditure, uncovered by taxes and primary saving. But no one can say that it has been large or out of hand. There is another satisfactory feature. The quarterly estimates of domestic output at current prices give no indication of any progressive inflation in the last half of 1940 since my emergency Budget. For the increase in the total value of domestic output in the third and fourth quarters of 1940 seems no more than can be accounted for by increased volume.

VII

It is now time for me to turn to the future. It is neither useful nor possible for me to give an estimate of the coming year's total expenditure such as is usual in peace time. The accounting procedure for what we receive under the Lend and Lease Bill will be abnormal. It is impossible to say, so soon after the new system has come into operation, at what rate deliveries will mature. Fortunately it is not necessary to estimate total expenditure for the purposes of a wartime Budget. What I have to forecast is the net government expenditure which has to be met out of tax revenue and domestic loans, apart from those taken up by the reinvestment of the sterling proceeds of the sale of overseas assets,—what, for short, I will call our domestic expenditure.

The rate at which this expenditure will increase must depend on the success of our handling of the manpower problem and the rate at which we can draft additional hands into the munitions industries and the armed forces of the Crown. Some time must elapse before this mobilisation reaches its maximum. The actual rate which will be attained cannot be forecast accurately many months ahead. We aim at reaching a domestic expenditure at least double the figure in the first year of the war. But this rate of expenditure cannot be attained quickly and it will certainly not be reached on the average of this financial year. I put the figure of our domestic expenditure, for which it is prudent that I should make provision now, at about £3,700 million.[33] No one will be more pleased than I, if the progress of industrial and military mobilisation shows signs that this figure will be exceeded. In that case I shall reconsider the position in the light, not only of the increased rate of expenditure, but also of the progress of tax collections and primary saving. I should add that this estimate is made on the assumption that there will be no further increase in domestic costs. The justification for that assumption I will give you later.

Though it is not necessary for my purpose that I should give an estimate of our total expenditure during the year, it may interest the House and meet any possible criticism that we are falling short in our war effort if I add that the above figure for our domestic expenditure averaged over the financial year as a whole is compatible with government spending under all heads having reached an annual rate of more than £6,000 million by the first quarter of next year. Since this approaches the total net national income of Germany for all purposes, it must considerably exceed the maximum war effort of which she is capable. Indeed I anticipate that our total war expenditure will overtake and exceed hers within the next six months.

[33] Note G [p. 323].

VIII

How is this sum of £3,700 million to be raised from domestic sources? I propose to provide a half of it, namely £1,850 million[34] out of taxation, including in this about £   million which will have accrued but will not have been paid into the Exchequer before the end of the financial year. It is impossible to estimate with any precision the demand which the balance required will make on new primary saving. There are several miscellaneous sources of funds apart from personal savings. The receipts of extra-budgetary funds will be increased by premiums received under the War Damage Act, whilst most of the claims which are paid under the various insurance schemes will remain available, since, in general, they cannot be employed during the war in actual replacement. The restriction orders, with the resulting fall in the scale of consumption of certain articles, are likely to lead to some further reduction in privately owned stocks, which will also fall as a result of the ever-widening scope of government ownership of stocks. Depreciation charges, renewal funds and sinking funds are believed to exceed £400 million a year in gross amount, of which in present circumstances only a portion can be employed in repairs and replacements and new private investment, the balance being available for the purposes of national finance. There are also the savings of local authorities and institutions and the undistributed profits of companies, an item, however, which is not likely to increase in face of E.P.T. In the first half of the second year of the war these miscellaneous items were running, according to my statistical advisers, at a rate of more than £900 million a year. Perhaps I may reasonably expect to borrow at least £850 million[35] from these sources in the coming year.

If so, there remains about £1,000 million to be obtained from primary savings.[36] I have already explained what this

---

[34] Note H [p. 323].   [35] Note K [p. 323].   [36] Note K' [p. 324].

means in terms of personal incomes. The figure will be reached if individuals have the wisdom and public spirit to save what they have been spending hitherto on those unessential articles which will be no longer obtainable. But if they compete against one another to buy more out of an unchanged supply of other articles, there will be an inflationary pressure tending to raise prices wherever they are uncontrolled, to create unfairness in distribution wherever this is not closely regulated, and to bring about a dangerous depletion of stocks. If primary saving is deficient, the money will only reach my hands after having produced these injurious results *en route*. But, as I am not asking more than is reasonable, I do not expect to be disappointed.

IX

Before I turn to new sources of revenue, let me consider the prospective yield of the existing taxes.

(Here follow the estimates of next year's yields)

The increase in the yield of income tax is chiefly due to our having the benefit of a full year at the new rates. For an increased yield from profits is not to be expected in face of 100 per cent E.P.T. It is from E.P.T. itself, which is also assisted by the prospect of a full year at the higher level, that the main improvement, namely from £90 million to £200 million, is derived.

It is evident that 100 per cent E.P.T. is a fruitful tax-gatherer which we can ill do without, either on the score of revenue or of social justice and propriety. The general principle of the tax commends itself to all sections of opinion. Nevertheless its actual operation at the 100 per cent level has been the subject of scarcely less universal criticism. I have, therefore, given very careful examination to the question how it could be amended and improved. I have reached the conclusion that important modifications ought to be made. I believe that these will commend themselves to the good judgment of the House and its sense of fairness.

I have, first of all, a group of amendments the object of which is to ensure with more accuracy than at present that the income which we are taxing really is an excess profit. It is one thing to 'take profit out of the war'; quite another to tax a business in such a way as to leave it worse off at the end of the war than it was at the beginning. Certain provisions which did rough justice when the tax was at 60 per cent are not so easily defensible at the 100 per cent level. The House must remember that the tax was not recast when, somewhat hastily, the change from 60 per cent to 100 per cent was introduced. The amendments in detail which I now propose are the result of a very careful examination of the tax by the Board of Inland Revenue in the light of their actual experience.

My first modification will be of great importance and real value to every business subject to the tax. There is at present a right to recover E.P.T. previously paid if in a subsequent period during which the tax is in force profits fall below the standard. But there is no undertaking how long this right of recovery is to hold good. I am proposing that traders shall be given a right to claim relief for deficiencies of profits below the standard for a period up to two years after the war. The relief, which will be given by way of repayment out of E.P.T. already paid, will be calculated at a percentage rate, not exceeding 80 per cent of the deficiency. This means that an opportunity will be allowed to offset any losses which may be made during the adjustments of the post-war period against profits made during the war, so that no business will pay any substantial sum in E.P.T. unless it has enjoyed an excess profit over the war and the immediate post-war period taken as a whole. Since few businesses can be certain how they will fare over a period so long and so perilous, there will be a strong incentive to everyone to earn excess profits, so that the tax paid against them may constitute a reserve on which the business can draw if necessary when circumstances change. This only repeats what was done after the last war. But a prior undertaking that the concession then made will be repeated on this occasion will be found, I feel sure, of great comfort by those concerned when its full implications are realised.

In view of the manifold risks attendant on new investment in present times, I am satisfied that there is a good case in computing the standard profit for raising the rate allowed (*a*) on the capital of new businesses and (*b*) on the increased capital of old businesses from 8 to 10 per cent (with a corresponding increase where 10 per cent is allowed now). This increased rate will be restricted to trades and businesses. It will not apply to banks, assurance business, investment business and building societies.

My third concession will provide that *borrowed money* shall be included in computing the capital of new businesses and the increase in the capital of old businesses. The percentage rate allowed will be the same as for capital in general, subject to the limitation that it shall not exceed the rate of interest payable on the borrowed money by more than 5 per cent. The present provision, or lack of provision, has been the subject of general and well-founded criticism. With the new issue market closed a business which is expanding at a greater rate than can be financed out of its own profits has no alternative except to borrow, which means that at present it is not allowed to earn any margin whatever against the risks and contingencies of expansion. It is a great mistake actually to penalise boldness, enterprise and a spirit of expansion, which is what we are doing now—especially when all the expanding businesses are of necessity engaged on work of national importance.

Businesses which were running at a loss or low profit in the standard period can fairly claim that they should be treated a little more liberally in computing their substituted standard.

I have already agreed that trading losses incurred since 1 January 1929 shall not be debited in computing the capital employed. I now propose to take borrowed money into account, in respect of which an addition of 2 per cent to the existing standard will be allowed.[37]

Finally there is the problem of allowing appropriate relief to concerns engaged in the working of wasting assets and to concerns undertaking the management of government factories.

(Here follows the approved solution).

It is intended that all these modifications in computing the standard profits shall apply to accounting periods or parts of accounting periods for which the 100 per cent rate is in force. Certain other matters of less importance will be dealt with in the Finance Bill. In particular, provision will be made to prevent the avoidance of E.P.T. by the amalgamation by sale or otherwise of two businesses one of which is making excess profits and the other is making a deficiency. I estimate that these various changes in the aggregate will reduce the prospective yield of the tax in the current year by £   million.

These provisions will go a long way to mitigate some of the more obvious anomalies and to provide a more adequate incentive to risk-taking. But it remains in the very nature of an excess profits tax that it should fall hardly on businesses which were depressed in the base year or are exceptionally active and valuable at the present time. This arises out of the principle of the tax and is not open to criticism so long as it is not carried to extremes. When, however, the tax is raised to 100 per cent and takes everything, what is intended as a measure of justice and equality is liable to work out unjustly and unequally. No one suggests that a worker, who was on the dole in the base year, becomes a war profiteer if he now earns full wages; or that men working overtime should receive no additional pay, on the ground that no one should be better

[37] (I do not clearly understand this. J. M. K.)

off as a result of the war and that loyal citizens do not require a money reward to do their best for the state.

Moreover the comparison between the circumstances of this war and those of the last war must not be pressed too far. We have taken steps on this occasion to prevent the earning of large profits as a mere windfall from the rise in prices or in freights, which was a potent source of excess profits in 1914 to 1918. Today the major part of excess profits arises not as a windfall but as the result of intense activity of output by firms which have prepared or adapted themselves to serve the most vital purposes of the country at war.

I have examined proposals for something in the nature of an output allowance as a means of remedying this. But we have not discovered a formula which is administratively practicable or serves the purpose well. Indeed an allowance of this kind is too much contrary to the principle of the tax to be grafted on to it with any success. My need of revenue is too great to allow me to lose the fruits of the 100 per cent level so long as the war lasts. I am, therefore, falling back upon a compromise which does something at least to meet the difficulties without loss of current revenue and without a serious departure from the general principle of the 100 per cent levy.

I propose that 20 per cent of the net E.P.T. paid by firms during the period for which the 100 per cent rate is in force shall be refunded to them at a date not later than two years after the end of the war. This refund will be added to the firm's current profits for the purpose of computing liability to income tax at the date when it is received; so that the net effect of this concession is less than may appear at first sight. It is, I feel, just sufficient and no more than sufficient to provide that modicum of reward which the most severe critic of the profit system would perhaps allow in his more genial moments as a not improper reward to energy, industry and success.

I do not propose, at this stage, any statutory provision as to the manner in which this refund shall be employed. But I must make it clear that it is not intended to facilitate the declaration of higher dividends either now when it is in prospect or later when it is received. The object is to furnish to British industry liquid resources with which to meet post-war developments and expansion, to provide for the expenses of the transitional period, to pay off indebtedness, to meet extra depreciation and obsolescence, and, generally speaking, to improve productive capacity and to strengthen capital structure. I may recommend some statutory provision at a later date if on further reflection and with more experience it seems to be necessary. But we are dealing with businesses of which the special and legitimate requirements vary widely from case to case. I would much prefer to leave the disposal of the money to the judgment and discretion of each firm on the understanding that they will employ it in loyal conformity to its intended purpose.

X

I estimate the yield of existing taxation, thus revised, at £1,595 million.[38] I propose to raise the further £255 million which is required entirely by direct taxation. For I believe that all classes of the community are now converted to the view that, if the money has to be raised, direct taxation at source is the fairest and least burdensome way of raising it.

I have considered carefully some excellent arguments for recasting the existing income tax or for superimposing on it some new tax calculated along more novel lines, including a tax on excess earnings. But the importance of quick and certain results and the growing shortage of bureaucratic manpower stand in the way of attempting drastic changes of method at the present time. The framework of the British income tax is a marvellous thing, built up of law and custom

[38] Note L [p. 324].

and practice and great experience; an intimate part of our lives, one might almost say; perhaps the most efficient and best contrived instrument of high taxation ever created. One tampers with it at one's peril—especially in difficult times. I shall, therefore, raise the whole amount required (£255 million) by a revision of the existing tax.

The standard rate of income tax will be raised to 10s in the £, an increase which will bring in £90 million in a full year and £   million in the current year. This brings the taxation of the wealthier classes to an extraordinary figure. In order to enjoy a tax-free income of £5,000 a year, it will be necessary to have a gross income of £77,000 a year. If such an individual seeks to increase his future net income by earning an additional sum and investing in War Loan the whole of what is left after paying the tax on it, each £1,000, which he thus earns and saves from, will increase his future income by 1s 6d a year. For all practical purposes the tax collector will have put a ceiling on net incomes at a figure which a few years ago was reckoned a very moderate level of individual wealth. Under our war finance, £5,000 a year is the net income of a multi-millionaire; for the ownership of £2,500,000 in government stock will not yield as much as this. £2,000–£3,000 a year is now the wartime limit for the vast majority of the wealthy class. I should not be surprised to hear that the differences between rich and poor are now greater in the Soviet Republics of Russia than they are in this country.

At the same time the existing system of personal allowances provides a taxable margin at the lower levels of income which I can no longer afford to leave untouched. It is here that the main part of the untaxed residue of income is to be found. Moreover there are at present no more than 5½ million taxpayers who are subject to income tax. If, as I am proposing, I keep my hand off all further indirect taxation, it is inevitable that the net of direct taxation should be cast more widely.

I propose, therefore, the following reductions in the existing personal allowances. The reduced rate of tax, which applies to the first £165 of taxable income, will be raised from 5s to 7s 6d. The earned income relief will be reduced from one-sixth to one-tenth of the earned income, the maximum relief remaining, however, at £200. Personal allowances will be reduced from £100 to £80 for single persons and from £170 to £140 for the married. Only the children's allowances will be left undisturbed.

I estimate that these reductions will bring in a revenue of £165 million in a full year and £   million in the present financial year, and will increase the number of income tax payers by 3,250,000. The approximate levels of earned income at which income tax begins to be paid will be £90 for a single man, £156 for a married man without children, £121 for a married man with one child, and £267 for a married man with two children.

These abatements of personal allowances are necessary and advisable at a time when some reduction in the standard of life is inevitable for those with incomes in excess of the tax-free standards indicated above. But I am persuaded that there will be great social benefits and a better distribution hereafter of the spending power of the community if these sacrifices required by war conditions are made temporary and not permanent. I am, therefore, proposing that the portion of the tax which results from the reduction of personal allowances shall be treated as a withholding tax. That is to say, the sums which are withheld as a result of the reduction in the personal allowances will be credited to an account in the name of the taxpayer and and refunded to him not later than two years after the end of the war.[39]

The way in which this works out in detail is shown in the White Paper. It means that the whole of the tax due from the three million and a quarter new taxpayers will be eventually repaid them. It is estimated that of the total amount

[39] Note M [p. 324].

of £129 million increased tax to be paid by some eight million taxpayers having incomes of less than £500 a year, £123 million will be provided by the withholding tax and subsequently repaid, and only £6 million by the increase in the standard rate. Of the balance of £84 million provided by the increase in the standard rate and not repaid, £10 million will come from 500,000 taxpayers with incomes between £500 and £1,000 a year, and £74 million from 300,000 taxpayers with more than £1,000 a year and from companies' reserves. Of the total new tax taken from persons with less than £1,000 a year, 90 per cent will come from the withholding tax, so that only 10 per cent will be permanently retained by the Exchequer.

It follows from the operation of this formula that the total amount returnable to an individual taxpayer, however wealthy, is strictly limited. For taxpayers with incomes between £500 and £1,000 the amount of the withholding tax ranges from £47 to £69. It never rises above £86 and for the higher income levels the maximum is in the neighbourhood of £60. In two years' time any taxpayer who is liable to a total annual income tax of £20 or more will have from £30 to £120 standing to his credit.

The House will appreciate that I have done my best to soften the blow to those, a permanent reduction in whose purchasing power and standards of life we should most regret. I cannot believe that this concession will do the smallest injury to the voluntary savings movement as compared with an outright tax of the same amount. Indeed by providing the small saver with an initial nest-egg we increase, rather than diminish, his motive for adding to it until he has a sum sufficient to enable him to face with a brave heart the uncertainties of the post-war world.

The amount of increase in the liabilities of the state arising from my proposed treatment of E.P.T. and the withholding tax taken together will be about £200 million a year, or less than one-tenth of the liabilities we shall be incurring in other ways. I do not feel that this additional burden outweighs the advantages of providing the average industrialist with the means of restoring his plant and working capital after the war, and of providing the average consumer with the means of improving his house and wardrobe on the scale to which the work he has done entitles him but which it was physically impossible to provide during the war itself.

Since we must time this release of purchasing power to coincide with our ability to provide the additional goods, I am taking discretion to postpone it up to two years after the war. We shall release it sooner if plain indications such as the state of employment and a potential surplus of output recommend it. But we must exercise a proper self-restraint and not allow pressure of any kind to cause hasty action and thus lose the advantage of so novel a social experiment.

XI

I have a further statement of far-reaching importance to make to you. To avoid a further cause of higher prices I have refrained from indirect taxation. In my estimates of expenditure I have assumed that there will be no further increase in domestic costs. By submitting to so substantial an increase of taxation at source, and still more if he does what I hope and expect he will in increased saving, the average consumer will have earned the right to a stable purchasing power for what is left to him to spend. If this Budget is to be a coherent whole, the stabilisation of costs and therefore of prices near their present level must be its keynote.

I have, therefore, included in my estimate of expenditure a sum which is believed to be sufficient to offset by one means or another the main causes of increasing costs other than a further rise in wages. In particular I propose to provide means to stabilise the cost of living as measured by the

Ministry of Labour's index number at approximately its present figure, that is to say, not above 30 per cent in excess of the pre-war level apart from small seasonal fluctuations, by offsetting the average effect of all factors other than a further rise in wage rates. Between 1914 and 1918 the cost of living rose by more than 100 per cent and continued to rise after the armistice. Many difficulties and many evils followed from this. If on this occasion we can be successful in limiting the rise to 30 per cent, the cost of doing so will be repaid to us many times over in direct and indirect benefits.

It would be unwise to enter into a more absolute undertaking than this, since we do not intend to interfere with the present freedom of the wage contract. If in fact, for reasons beyond our control, wage rates were to rise to any significant extent, it would be futile and dangerous to peg the cost of living. For this would facilitate an increase of consumption at a time when an increase cannot be permitted. But whilst I must attach this condition in point of form, I have no reason to suppose that it will be practically operative. If we stabilise the cost of living, we can safely trust the rest to the common-sense and the loyalty of the trade unions. For we shall be accepting their own advice and doing what they themselves have long pressed on us. At no time during the war has the index of wage rates risen so much as the index of the cost of living; and in recent months there has been a marked tendency towards stability in spite of some exceptions. The most glaring disparities between different industries which existed before the war have now been remedied. Nevertheless, a further upward trend in the cost of living would undoubtedly lead to difficulties sooner or later and to unrest in the industrial world. But with the stabilisation of the cost of living the only legitimate ground for particular wage increases, in circumstances where general consumption must suffer some inevitable curtailment, will have disappeared.

Even so, the stabilisation of prices is a serious undertaking involving a heavy cost, which I estimate at an amount well in excess of £200 million a year including the costs we are already incurring for this purpose. For in time of war there are many factors which increase costs apart from higher wages. The most important of these are shipping and transport costs including insurance. But scarcely a day passes when the Treasury is not asked to choose for every variety of good reason between allowing a higher price or granting relief by subsidy or otherwise. The upward pressure is continuous and cumulative. It is in any case difficult to draw the line between the general costs of war and costs which it is proper to load on to particular commodities or services. At present we do not charge up to the freight the cost of the convoy which prevents it from being sunk but we do charge up the cost of replacing both the cargo and the vessel which carries it if it is sunk. I have come to doubt the wisdom of recovering some part of the cost of the consequences of war by a sort of indirect taxation which loads this cost on the price of the articles more particularly affected.

Let me leave no room for misunderstanding about what I have in mind. My absolute undertaking relates to the Ministry of Labour's index of the cost of living. This is open to the criticism that it is out of date since it relates to the habits of consumption which prevailed before the last war. But I am satisfied that there is, rather surprisingly, nothing in this point. The Ministry of Labour have collected up-to-date family budgets appropriate to 1938. If these are substituted, it makes a difference of less than 1 per cent to the resulting rise in cost in January 1941 compared with September 1939, and the old index shows a slightly greater rise than the revised index.[40] Since the old index is incorporated in many wage settlements, there is a good reason not to depart from it unnecessarily.

Outside the articles which enter into the cost of living index

[40] Note N [p. 324].

there are many other goods of general consumption; and in wartime conditions there has been some substitution in favour of these away from the staple articles. It would not be practicable or prudent to adopt a rigid policy in regard to all these. But in the case of foodstuffs it is the policy of the Minister of Food to allow no further increases of a more than moderate amount, except in the case of luxuries and specialities. I shall facilitate the maintenance of this policy.

There are other commodities and services which are in the nature of luxuries or are not of common consumption or from which it is especially necessary to divert consumption. In these cases a rise of price corresponding to increased cost or increased scarcity is sometimes desirable. The Minister of Food may himself find opportunities to make a profit in one direction by which he can pay for cheapness in another direction. All this will be advantageous if our main purpose is secured of stabilising costs in the neighbourhood of their present level.

On a short-sighted view I may seem to increase my financial problems by adopting this policy, and to cut us off from the natural remedy against scarcity. But in these days of total war where the state has to take hold of every activity of the community, such ideas have ceased to hold good. If we allow costs to rise we shall throw our public finances into chaos and assuredly involve ourselves in a cost in terms of money many times what we may have saved in the first instance.

That I am ready to undertake this pledge can at least be taken as sufficient proof that my advisers and myself have confidence in our hold over the financial situation and in our ability to keep the body politic free from the poison of inflation.

Note A

This assumes that the new White Paper will be circulated on Budget day. An alternative, and perhaps preferable, course will be to make it available on Saturday morning, 5 April, for Sunday's and Monday's newspapers, so as to give members of the House and the Press a little more time to digest it before the Budget, and to relieve the pressure on newspaper space on Tuesday morning, after the Budget, when it will be very great.

Note B

At the date of the last return for the Ministry of Food, October 1940, they owned stocks worth £ million. Stocks purchased overseas which we cannot ship are valued at £ million. I have no estimate of the value of the stocks of raw materials owned by the Ministry of Supply, but it must be very great. Some, though not all, of the stocks in transit, which amount perhaps to three months' supply, are already paid for. Altogether there can be no doubt as to the accuracy of the statement in the text.

Note C

As an illustration of the large amount of new investment now made on Government account, Dr Coates[41] told me that in 1940 I.C.I. invested £43 million in new factories and plant, of which £40 million was paid for by the Exchequer. Much of this would be of peacetime utility. I have heard it said, I do not know with what accuracy, that government departments are now erecting new buildings at a cost of some £250 million per annum. Not all of these can be entirely useless for post-war purposes!

Note D

The attached statement of stocks in January 1941, compared with January 1940, justifies the statement in the text.

[41] William Henry Coates (1882–1963), Kt. 1947; entered Civil Service, 1900; War Office, 1901–4; H.M. Inspector of Taxes, 1904–19; Director of Statistics and Intelligence, Inland Revenue, 1919–25; Secretary, Nobel Industries Ltd., 1925–6; Treasurer, Imperial Chemical Industries Ltd., 1927–9; subsequently a Director of I.C.I.

Stocks		Jan. 1940	Jan. 1941
Iron ore	000 tons	2,562	3,043
Pig and scrap iron	000 tons	1,118	1,453
Steel (finished and semi-finished)	000 tons	772	875
Tungsten	tons	1,655	2,967
Molybdenum	tons	1,944	1,102
Ferro-chrome	tons	10,890	10,638
Copper	000 tons	46	138
Zinc	000 tons	66	78
Lead	000 tons	85	166
Tin	000 tons	18	17
Nickel	000 tons	7	7
Bauxite	000 tons	284	189
Alumina	000 tons	16	43
Chrome ore	000 tons	24	50
Magnesite	000 tons	37	74
Pyrites	000 tons	306	337
Phosphate rock	000 tons	155	78
Coal	000 tons	13,800	19,714
Molasses	000 tons	374	333
Industrial alcohol	million gallons	2	3
Raw cotton	000 bales	1,276	946
Cotton yarn	million pounds	35	35
Wool	million pounds	233	366
Jute	000 bales	328	335
Flax	000 tons	23	20
Hemp	000 tons	33	57
Raw hides	000	1,384	1,366
Imperial softwoods	000 standards	478	729
Imperial hardwoods	000 standards	22	24
Pitwood	000 standards	498	725
Wood pulp and esparto	000 tons	402	150
Newsprint and paper	000 tons	676	538

Note E

The above explanation about *primary saving* may look rather academic and complicated. But it is the essence of the argument. The term 'primary saving' is a new one (on the analogy of the term 'primary investment' used in connection with public schemes to cure unemployment). The point is that primary saving and secondary saving taken together are necessarily exactly equal to the amount of the Budget deficit to the nearest ½*d*. Whether or not we avoid inflation depends on there being adequate primary saving.

Note F

I have received an interesting letter about the working of the purchase tax from Sir W. Eady, which is available if required. I believe, however, that he has sent a similar note to Mr Wilson Smith, so I am not appending it to these papers.

Note G

The figure of £3,700 million is provisional and subject to adjustment. I am collecting material which may enable a closer estimate to be made. I should be happier if this figure could be raised to £3,750 or £3,800 million.

Note H

The figure of £1,850 million is subject to amendment when more exact particulars are available.

Note K

The figure of £850 million is highly conjectural, but is probably on the safe side. I should like to have the opportunity of adjusting all the items of this balance sheet when fuller particulars are available. It runs at present—

	£ million		£ million
Domestic expenses	3,700+100	Revenue	1,850
		Sundry capital sources	850+100
		Personal savings	1,000
	3,700+100		3,700+100

Note K'

Reconciliation with estimates of the 'gap' (£ million)

Annual rate	6 months to February 1941	Currently	Next financial year
Revenue	1,600	1,600	1,850
Miscellaneous sources	900	900	850–950
Personal savings	600	700	1,000
Domestic expenditure	3,100	3,200	3,700–3,800

Note L

This figure is a guess to be corrected later. I have not the exact figures of prospective yield nor the cost of the proposed amendments to E.P.T.

Note M

I am not aware what decisions have been reached as to the precise machinery for crediting the withholding tax. Since this is likely to be the subject of questioning, it will be necessary for such a decision to be reached. Perhaps the best plan would be for the Revenue to set up at their leisure a blocked account at the Post Office Savings Bank in favour of the taxpayer.

Note N

Between September 1939 and January 1941 the old index rose from 155 to 196, whilst the revised index adjusted to 1938 budgets rose during the same period from 155 to 195. Since the weights attached to the different groups are enormously changed, the small effect on the final result is rather a miracle, though one has seen cases of it before where the number of separate items was considerable.

324

September 1939	Weights under the old index	Weights under the revised index
Food	53·4	39·4
Rent	16·8	12·5
Clothing	15·9	10·8
Fuel and light	9·4	7·4
Other items	4·6	29·6
Total	100	100

The 1941 Budget, as well as being notable for its use of a national accounting analytical framework, also saw the publication with the Budget of a White Paper providing the relevant figures for a pre-war year and the previous year.[42]

The origins of the White Paper lay largely in the official response to *How to Pay for the War* and Keynes's other private attempts to measure the implications of the war for the British economy. Austin Robinson[43], who had heard the original Marshall Society talk that eventually became the pamphlet, succeeded in persuading Francis Hemming,[44] and with his assistance Sir Edward Bridges,[45] that authoritative national income estimates were essential for the economic planning of the war and the formulation of fiscal policy. During the spring of 1940 James Meade,[46] then working for the League of Nations in Geneva, was invited to take charge

[42] *An Analysis of the Sources of War Finance and an Estimate of the National Income and Expenditure in 1938 and 1940*, Cmd. 6261.

[43] Edward Austin Gossage Robinson (b. 1897); University Lecturer in Economics, Cambridge, 1929–49; Assistant Editor, *Economic Journal*, 1934, Joint Editor, 1944–70; member, Economic Section, War Cabinet Office, 1939–42; Economic Adviser, Head of Programmes Division, Ministry of Production, 1942–5; member, British Reparations Commission, Moscow and Berlin, 1945; Economic Adviser to Board of Trade, 1946; Professor of Economics, Cambridge, 1950–65, Emeritus Professor since 1966.

[44] Francis Hemming (1893–1964); Secretary, Economic Advisory Council, 1930–9; Principal Assistant Secretary, War Cabinet Offices, 1939–41; Administrative Head, Central Economic Information Service, 1940, and Central Statistical Office, 1941.

[45] Sir Edward Bridges (1892–1969); Treasury, 1919–38; Secretary to the Cabinet, 1938–46; Permanent Secretary to the Treasury, 1945–56.

[46] James Edward Meade (b. 1907); Fellow and Lecturer in Economics, Hertford College, Oxford, 1930–7; member, Economic Section, League of Nations, Geneva, 1938–40; Economic Assistant, 1940–5, and Director, 1946–7, Economic Section of Cabinet Office; Professor of Commerce, London School of Economics, 1947–57; Professor of Political Economy, Cambridge, 1957–68.

of this work. He returned to England and began work in June 1940 in the Central Economic Information Service of the Offices of the War Cabinet.[47] In the course of June and July he evolved a framework for the proposed national accounts. At the end of August 1940 he was joined by Richard Stone,[48] who became responsible for organising and perfecting the statistical data.

Thus when Keynes joined the Treasury in July 1940 at the invitation of Sir Kingsley Wood there was the nucleus of a system for preparing more authoritative and well-founded estimates of the national income.

There may, as the following comments by Lionel Robbins and Richard Kahn indicate, have still been obstacles and departmental jealousies to overcome. But with Keynes in the Treasury these difficulties, now long forgotten by those concerned, were quickly removed and Sir Richard Hopkins became a friendly supporter of the work.

From L. C. ROBBINS [*October or November 1940*]

Dear Keynes,

The main facts of the episode about which I spoke to you yesterday are as follows.

(1) After much coming & going, the nature of which you can guess, our Minister prepared for submission to the Economic Policy Committee a proposal for a thorough investigation of the present position as regards financial potential, the budgetary gap & various methods of restricting consumption. Before circulating this, however, he decided to show it to the Chancellor.

(2) After a short interval, the Chancellor rejoined with a very stiff letter, obviously drafted by officials. The gist of this was that he deprecated the whole proposal, did not mind the Minister's economists messing about on their own but insisted that (*a*) as regards facts, most of the knowledge & all the prescriptive rights lay already at the Treasury and (*b*) as regards policy, the right place for discussion was the cabinet.

(3) To this, the Minister returned the soft answer—said that he had no desire to invade the Treasury preserves, maintained, however, that the business of economic coordination must involve regard to finance & suggested that while the preparation of memoranda regarding policy was a

---

[47] In January 1941 this service was subdivided into the Economic Section of the Offices of the War Cabinet and the Central Statistical Office.

[48] John Richard Nicholas Stone (b. 1913); with C. E. Heath & Co., Lloyd's Brokers, 1936–9; Ministry of Economic Warfare, 1939–40; Central Economic Information Service, 1940; Central Statistical Office, 1940–5; Director, Department of Applied Economics, Cambridge, 1945–55; P. D. Leake Professor of Finance and Accounting, Cambridge, since 1955.

matter for discussion, it was essential that the survey of financial potential & national income should be made.

(4) To this, in turn, the Chancellor replied that he must have misunderstood the Minister's initial proposal & suggested a meeting between Hemming & Hopkins.

(5) This meeting took the form of a lunch discussion. Hopkins seems to have been very friendly but he took the amazing line that while he didn't mind our preparing memoranda on policy he had strong objections to any investigation of the size of the national income.

(6) Confronted with this, Hemming attempted a compromise and suggested that at least we might collaborate in an investigation of the national income of 1938 and decide later on whether the national income of 1940 was wholly sacrosanct.

(7) To this Hopkins replied that he must seek further instructions from the Chancellor. He promised however to submit to the Chancellor the various arguments which Hemming had put forward in favour of the whole inquiry.

I ought perhaps to add that, some time before all this started, Hopkins had already expressed concern to Hemming at the report that Meade was looking into national income problems. At that time Hemming met his strictures by suggesting that he should speak to you. Quite obviously this was never done.

My belief is that the optimal solution of all this is the setting up of a joint group to report on financial potential & the implications thereof for policy. Is it even now too late for you to assume the chairmanship of an informal committee which should prepare a report to be submitted to Greenwood & the Chancellor? Of course there are plenty of other ways in which the thing could be done. But I see very great value in a paper which is prepared at the suggestion of Labour Ministers &, as I said to you yesterday, it was solely with this in mind that we ventured into this dangerous territory.

Yours,
L. C. R.

From R. F. KAHN, *4 November 1940*

My dear Maynard,

Quite clearly your proper course is to see Meade, letting him know that I have dropped you a hint and that he should be perfectly open with you. I can only pass on what he has told me, although Hemming, I believe, can supply authoritative confirmation. There has been correspondence on the subject between the Chancellor and Mr Greenwood. The only actual instance of positive obstructionism which I can call to mind takes the form of an instruction (subsequently, I believe, withdrawn as a result of protests) by the Treasury to the Registrar-General to withhold certain information. What is more serious is that rightly or wrongly (I believe rightly but that is neither here nor there) Meade believes that his activities enjoy Treasury opposition. For example his work on investment, if it is to be properly done, involves obtaining certain information from the finance officers of some of the departments. Meade does not feel that, as things are, he can approach the finance officers.

Yours,

R. F. K.

By December 1941, the first results of Meade's and Stone's work had become available. Soon after the New Year, Keynes circulated their paper 'National Income, Saving and Consumption', dated 6 January 1941, to the Treasury Budget Committee. He also suggested to Francis Hemming that the results of their work appear as a technical article in *The Economic Journal* for March 1941. The reorganisation of the Central Economic Information Service prevented a quick decision on the suggestion.

The question of the publication of Meade's and Stone's work arose again when *The Economist* for 1 February carried an article entitled 'The Future of Spending'. On reading it, Keynes minuted.

To SIR RICHARD HOPKINS *and* SIR HORACE WILSON, *7 February 1941*

You may have seen the article in last week's *Economist* on 'The Future of Spending', which included a number of fabulous figures, in particular an estimate of £8,120 million for national income at the present time and 'at least £9,000 million for the national income, on the average, of the next financial year'.[49] In yesterday's Vote of Credit debate Pethick-Lawrence quoted £8,000 million as an authentic estimate of national income today, doubtless drawn from the *Economist* article. Lord Balfour told me that, if the debate in the House of Lords had taken place on Wednesday, he had originally intended to base his speech on these *Economist* figures.

[49] The estimates for 1940, 1941 and 1942 eventually indicated that the approximately accurate figures were £7,990 million and £8,780 million respectively [Ed.].

328

I have already circulated some reliable estimates, made by Messrs Meade and Stone of the new Central Statistical Department, showing that in mid-1940 the best estimate of the national income was £5,900 million. I believe that they are now bringing this up to date, and a preliminary guess at their results suggests that national income is now about £6,100 million.

Thus the *Economist* estimate is about £2,000 million wrong. I suggest that it is inconvenient and even dangerous for outside commentators to be so far off the rails. I wrote to Hemming some little time ago suggesting that the results of Meade and Stone, which are so far as I can see in no way confidential, should be published as a private article by them over their signatures in the next *Economic Journal*. I have not yet got a reply from him owing to the uncertain state of his department in the intervening period. But I gather that he is hesitating. These estimates are much more suitable published, I think, as personal rather than as official estimates. But I do think that some opportunity should be taken to have them published one way or another. What do you think?

In this connection I append a note I have just prepared on the relation between the English and the German figures. Here again very erroneous comparisons are prevalent.[50]

I am sure it is most dangerous for too wide a gap to develop between inside and outside statistical information. There was hardly a figure in the *Economist* article which was not more than £1,000 million wrong. Yet everyone regards this as highly authoritative, and it is quoted as almost semi-official in foreign countries.

J. M. K.

7.2.41

Five days later, he added a further minute.

[50] Not printed. [Ed.]

To SIR RICHARD HOPKINS, *12 February 1941*

PUBLICATION OF FINANCIAL AND ECONOMIC
FIGURES

I have given some further thought to this question and agree with you that it is most important to get the public somewhat better instructed well in advance of the Budget. Lord Catto is strongly of the same opinion. He says that he has been attacked in all quarters on the basis of the *Economist* article, which everyone outside takes quite seriously.

Two questions arise: the form of publication; the matter of publication.

As regards form of publication, the following seem to me to be the alternatives.

1. It is much too long a story to be given in an answer to a question in the House and too long also for a written answer. It might well take the form, however, of a Treasury memorandum which the Chancellor would undertake to circulate to members in answer to a question asking for further information. This seems to me much the best alternative. Its adoption depends, however, on your willingness to break the usual rule of only publishing in an official form figures which have been definitely ascertained. In this case it would be absolutely essential to include some more or less conjectural figures. My idea is that the Chancellor would say in his answer that no definitely ascertained figures were to be had, but that he thought it important that members should be in possession of the same information that he had himself, that is to say, the best estimates which can be made in the circumstances by those who have access to all the information there is. Properly safeguarded, there seems to me no objection to this. Certainly it is impracticable to do what is wanted solely on the basis of definitely ascertained figures.

Another argument in favour of this mode of publication is that it would be a good opportunity for bringing into the public light the new Central Statistical Department. My suggestion is that a considerable part of the figures, namely, all those relating to national income and consumption, should be published on their authority. If this department is to be any good, it will have to get into the habit of making itself responsible for 'best guesses'. In fact the work which its staff has been doing in this connection is, in my judgment, of the highest quality and will redound considerably to the public credit of this new organ of government. I am sure it will create a very good impression if we are a little less strait-laced in the matter of imparting information which we are ourselves using for purposes of guidance in matters of policy, even though it is not 100 per cent accurate, when it can scarcely be of any material value to the enemy.

2. An unsigned article or series of two or three articles contributed to *The Times*.

3. Two or three signed articles, not necessarily all over the same signature, contributed to *The Times*, if early publication is desired, or to the *Economic Journal* if we can wait (which we cannot).

My suggestion as to matter to be included is the following:–

(1) An estimate and analysis of national income, national consumption and national savings on the lines of the paper by Messrs Meade and Stone, which I have already circulated. The figures which I circulated were up to mid-1940. They tell me that they might be able to bring this up to the end of 1940 by some time next week, provided they can get hold in time of a crucial figure for which they are waiting from the Ministry of Health.

(2) A financial analysis of how the war has been financed up to date, on the lines of the paper which I circulated some little time ago. I have just finished bringing this up to date to the end of the first quarter of the second year of the war and will be circulating my revision shortly. I have now agreed all my figures for the first year of the war with the Bank of

England and with Debenham,[51] with the result that we are in substantial agreement as to the magnitude of the adverse balance of trade.

(3) Such figures as we have of German government expenditure for purposes of comparison.

Of course, care would have to be taken to make sure that nothing of value to the enemy was included. This would mean that none of the above tables could be quite as full as those which have been circulated for office purposes. (Even the full version could scarcely be of material help. But we had better be on the safe side.) This can easily be done by combining certain figures into a global total without giving the complete analysis. There will be other cases in which this was advisable not for the above reason but in order to avoid in certain cases highly conjectural analyses which are not necessary for the main purpose.

As soon as the decision is come to, the material could be prepared very rapidly, since most of it already exists in draft form, provided you will be prepared to trust Professor Jewkes'[52] department, the new statistical department and myself without wanting to submit every figure to the criticism of every department which might be concerned in it. If it is to serve our purpose, I suggest that the material should be marked for press not later than the end of next week.

J. M. K.

12.2.41

On receiving this second minute, Hopkins wrote to Sir Horace Wilson recommending action on the proposal, for, as he put it, 'Unusual circumstances call for unusual remedies'. Wilson raised the matter with the Chancellor on 14 February. The Chancellor agreed that it was necessary to

---

[51] Piers Kenrick Debenham (1904–64); Staff, Economic Advisory Council, 1930–9; Assistant Secretary, Cabinet Office, 1934–41.

[52] John Jewkes (b. 1902); Professor of Social Economics, Manchester, 1936–46; Director, Economic Section, War Cabinet Office, 1941; Director-General of Statistics and Programmes, Ministry of Aircraft Production, 1943; Principal Assistant Secretary, Office of Minister of Reconstruction, 1944; Stanley Jevons Professor of Political Economy, Manchester, 1946–8; Professor of Economic Organisation, Oxford, 1948.

counteract the impression *The Economist* article had given and suggested that the Treasury see what Keynes's proposed *Times* article would look like and then consider a Budget day White Paper. A week later, Keynes had prepared a draft of *The Times* article and suggested figures for inclusion in the White Paper. The projected White Paper then received official approval in principle. Ideas as to other methods of publication were then dropped.

On hearing of the proposal, Henry Clay wrote to Keynes on 5 March: 'The proposed White Paper is a bit of a revolution. I welcome it; the public are much more likely to be co-operative if they are allowed to know what is required of them.'

Keynes's reference to his analyses of the sources of war finance (above, p. 331) picks up a development in the Treasury contemporaneous with the Meade–Stone national income estimates. For following on his earlier work in *How to Pay for the War*, his March 1940 Budget of National Resources and his various memoranda for the Treasury, Keynes, using inside information, circulated in the Treasury on 2 December 1940 a paper entitled 'An Analysis of the First Year's War Finance'. He also sent copies to the Cabinet Office and the Governor of the Bank.[53]

[53] On sending the copy to the Governor, Keynes drew the following implication from the figures on 5 December:

'There are two outstanding points emerging from my analysis which it might be worth calling your attention to.

In the first place, this analysis fully confirms the view you expressed that all the available money was being drawn by Kindersley through various schemes and different issues. Indeed, I am convinced, in my own mind, that the amount newly available for private investment fell short of the sums raised and that private bank deposits must have been drawn on. The second point is that the resources upon which we had been depending, other than new savings, whilst very large, are more or less stationary in amount and cannot be increased when expenditure increases. According to my calculation, out of a total sum of £1,169 million borrowed from outside sources, personal savings contributed only £385 million. But the sources, other than private savings, cannot easily be increased and are not likely to be materially greater in the second year of the war than they were in the first. Thus, if the total amount we borrow from outside sources increased by the somewhat moderate amount of £770 million, the amount to be obtained from personal savings might have to be trebled. I estimate that the current rate of personal savings is probably 50 per cent greater than it was in the first year of the war, having increased from £385 million to an annual rate of £562 million. But I do not see how we can expect a continual progressive increase at this sort of rate.

I wonder whether, in the long run, the war weapons weeks and all the ballyhoo and faking of statistics may not do more harm than good. At present I gather, to give one example out of many, that the local branches of banks celebrate war weapons week in a particular town by turning some of their Treasury deposit receipts into war bonds subscribed locally, thus swelling the statistics and having no other results except that the money costs the Treasury twice as much as before. With the propaganda campaign carried on as at present,

AN ANALYSIS OF THE FIRST YEAR'S WAR FINANCE

Table I shows that the net amount borrowed by the Exchequer from outside sources was £1,169,145 million.

Table II analyses the *forms* of these borrowings.

So far we are dealing with ascertainable figures. The next step is to attempt an analysis of the *sources* of these borrowings. Table III gives a fairly accurate estimate (not subject to an error of more than £100 million) of the amount obtained by the liquidation of privately owned capital assets, namely £723 million. If this is added to the utilisation of the pre-war assets of the E.E. Account, the total exhaustion of capital assets in the first year of the war is approximately £900 million, of which £575 million is gold and overseas assets and £325 million assets at home. All the items out of which this total is built up are based on actual returns except those to which an explanatory footnote has been appended in Table III. The doubtful estimates are, however, not only reasonable in themselves on the basis of the direct information available, but are also confirmed as a result of estimates of the national income and of the adverse balance of trade approached on completely independent lines. Nevertheless, in order to be on the safe side, this has been written down by £100 million (the other possible errors are likely to work the other way) in the subsequent analysis.

This leaves a total of £546 million at the utmost (£1,169 million−£723 million) net out of current savings. Total new savings must have exceeded this by the amount necessary to pay for death duties and the expenses of capital transactions normally charged to capital, estimated at £122 million, giving

the alleged weekly returns have practically no relation at all to the actual progress of savings.

All this does not mean that the savings campaign has been disappointing—quite the contrary. If I am right, personal savings have been increased from £385 million in the first year of the war to something like £562 million currently. That is an enormous achievement. I only doubt whether organised efforts to fog the public mind as to the true position are really serviceable.'

a total of £668 million. The following is a very rough analysis of the sources of this:–

	£ million
Undistributed profits of companies	173
Miscellaneous institutions	38
Savings of local authorities	72
Personal savings	385*
	668

Of the personal savings, 'small' savings may have reached, but are unlikely to have exceeded, £150 million. The incomes out of which this sum was saved were of the order of £2,000–2,500 million. According to Mr Madge's enquiries it is unusual for small savers to save as much as 10 per cent of their incomes and it is unlikely that the average exceeds 5 or 6 per cent. This would leave £235 million for 'other' personal savings, which leaves about £100 million net after paying for death duties etc. How small a part personal savings played in the national finances during the first year of war is some-what striking, even after assuming, as above, the maximum statistical error in their favour.

If we assume that the proceeds of privately owned capital assets which are liquidated are re-invested in the same sort of way, we find no indication of any unexplained increase in the floating debt. Market bills and deposit receipts increased by £488 million of which £269 million can be regarded as in replacement of British short-term assets abroad taken over, leaving only £219 million, which is less than the increase in the portfolios of the clearing banks and the Bank of England. Longer-term issues yielded £261 million, of which £128 million can be regarded as in replacement of long-term overseas assets taken over, leaving £133 million.

The increase in bank deposits (£236 million) seems

* Savings made through life insurance are reckoned here as personal.

insufficient to provide for increased company balances on account of heavier turnover, provision against taxes and uninvested depreciation. Thus private purchases of savings certificates and defence bonds may have been paid for on an important scale out of pre-war privately owned bank deposits. But an attempt to push the analysis any further would take us into very doubtful country.

J.M.K.

2.12.40

Table I. *1 September 1939–31 August 1940*

	£ 000
Total Exchequer expenditure	2,623,755
less Increase in Departmental and Exchequer balances	36,292
True expenditure	2,587,463
less Revenue	1,147,978
Deficit	1,439,485
less Net receipts of National Debt Commissioners and war risk schemes excluding savings banks	87,555
	1,351,930
less Utilisation of pre-war assets of E.E. Account	191,785
	1,160,145
plus Telegraph advances	9,000
Net amount borrowed from outside sources	1,169,145

Table II. *Analysis of form of borrowings from outside sources*

	£ 000
Post Office and Trustee Savings Banks	81,583
National Savings Certificates (net)	124,550
Defence bonds	146,477
Longer term issues (net)	261,060
Fiduciary issue	67,000
Market bills	458,475
Bankers' deposit receipts	30,000
	1,169,145

Table III. *Privately owned capital assets liquidated during the first year of war*

	£m	
1. Short-term overseas assets		
Privately owned gold and foreign balances requisitioned	177	
Decrease in balances held abroad (70 in foreign countries less 7 increase in Empire)	63	
	240	
less Foreign sterling balances in London repaid	76	
	164	
Increase in Empire sterling balances in London	105	
		269
2. Long-term overseas assets		
Overseas securities vested as repatriated	170	
British Government securities purchased by Empire countries	31	
	201	
less British Government securities repurchased from non-Empire countries ... 23		
Other sterling securities repatriated ... 50†		
	73	
		128
3. Disinvestment at home		
Depreciation of fixed plant not made good and depletion of privately owned stocks		326‡
		723

* The gross reduction recorded is £88 million, but it is estimated that some £25 million of this probably overlaps with the total of balances requisitioned already entered above.
† This is a guess. The true figure might be as much as £25 million greater.
‡ Based on an estimate (not covering quite the same period) of Mr Greenwood's staff—subject to a substantial error either way. The depletion of privately owned stocks is greater than the depletion of total stocks, since many types of stocks are now held by the government. In order to be on the safe side, the argument in the text writes this total down by £100 million.

In the course of January 1941, Keynes revised his analysis of the sources of war finance and added figures for the next quarter. He circulated these for comment on 12 February.

With the decision in principle to attempt to produce a White Paper came a period of re-drafting and statistical revision before, on 1 March, the first of many proofs was ready for circulation. With this proof and each of its successors came a round of discussions, improving the estimates, clarifying the presentation and meeting objections. Some of the most interesting of these came after the fourth proof of 19 March, for it began a discussion among Keynes, D. H. Robertson and H. D. Henderson, some of it conducted through Sir Richard Hopkins.

Robertson favoured publication, but he remained cautious and bristled with fine points of criticism and imaginary examples. Henderson, on the other hand, with his strong doubts about quantitative economics in general and the White Paper's method of obtaining individual figures by difference in particular, was much less happy with the exercise. The following series of exchanges between Robertson and Keynes gives some indication of the spirit of the discussions.

From D. H. ROBERTSON, *23 April 1941*

NOTE ON 'AN ANALYSIS OF THE SOURCES OF WAR FINANCE, ETC.'

1. The question arises, does not the paper fall between two stools? It departs from official precedent in presenting estimates of quantities (such as 'net disinvestment') which are both difficult to define and difficult to evaluate. But it does not, as an article in a learned journal would be expected to do, either examine the conceptual difficulties involved or disclose in any detail the basis of the estimates adopted. Still less does it discuss the economic implications of the statistical results which it purports to establish.

2. To take this last point first. The crucial proposition of the paper is that the annual rate of 'voluntary' personal savings has risen from £150 million in 1938 to £400 million in the first year of war and £700 million in recent months. This *might* mean either that the official economy campaign has been overwhelmingly successful or that our feet are firmly planted on the high road to inflation. Which *does* it mean? The paper is silent.

The answer to this criticism is, I imagine, that the paper does not stand on its own legs but is a statistical supplement to a Budget speech which will be available to the reader and in which this crucial issue will be discussed. But we cannot be sure that the two documents will always circulate hand in hand; and I should feel much more comfortable if the paper itself contained a few sentences drawing attention to the nature of the conundrum which the figures pose, even though refraining from offering a solution.

3. The question remains whether, if it is to carry weight with serious students of the course of events, the paper should not be more explicit as to the grounds for some of its estimations. The figure which hits the eye is that for 'net disinvestment' at home, which is put at £70 million in the first year of war and £220 million in the first half of the second year,—a sixfold increase in annual rate. Even those who do not happen to know that Mr Keynes was recently estimating the first year figure at £200 million or possibly £300 million are bound to be greedy for more enlightenment. It is hinted that the low figure for year 1 is partly due to the presence of a counter-element in the shape of an appreciation of stocks. A retailer who receives a refund of money capital through the requisition of half his stocks by the Government will nevertheless find the money value of his stock in trade unimpaired if the remainder of that stock has doubled in price; if therefore he re-invests in War Loan the money he has received from the Government, he is regarded as performing an act *not* of re-investment but of new savings. The attentive reader will certainly wish to know how far the lowness of the figure of £70 million is estimated to be due to saving of this peculiar kind. Another figure which cries out for annotation is that for tax accruals,—is the drop to zero in the last six months conceived of as purely seasonal or partly as a reversal of trend?

Once the paper is published, it will, I imagine, be impossible for 'the Treasury' to enter into controversy or even into explanations. That is all the more reason for being generous of explanations in the first instance; and I feel that (unlike 99 out of 100 documents) this paper could be enormously improved for its purpose by expansion.

4. At two critical points the support of the second paper is claimed for the conclusions of the first. It is not easy for the reader to satisfy himself as to whether this claim is justified, since the first paper is in terms of war years and the second in terms of calendar years. (My first impression was that the second paper pointed to a considerably higher rate of 'voluntary savings' during the war than the first; but this may not really be the case.) This difficulty unfortunately cannot now be entirely removed; but it could be very much diminished if the quarterly figures from tables B and C in the second paper, which contain the vital item of 'voluntary' personal savings, were printed as well as those for table A. It would be for consideration whether they should be presented with or without seasonal correction or both. The difficulty could be further lessened if the material at the disposal of the authors of the second paper permits of any estimate, even in verbal and imprecise terms, of the behaviour of their key items in the 'missing' quarters of 1939 and 1941.

5. If the paper can be strengthened in these ways, I think the balance of argument is strongly in favour of its publication. It would still be open,

of course, to critics to dispute those of its calculations which are not based on definite official information, and to criticise policy so far as it is based on these calculations. But they would be given an assurance which they sometimes profess to lack that policy is being framed in the light of *some* interpretation of the contemporary facts: nor would they be able to complain (as I think they might if the paper were published exactly as it now stands) that they are being presented with crossword puzzles of which the Treasury and the Central Statistical Office possess, but have majestically withheld, the solution.

D. H. R.

23.3.41

Appendix

I append some minor suggestions for consideration by Mr Keynes.

P. 5   line 5 of text: read 'which they have sold themselves or which the Treasury has acquired from them and sold'.

line 8: read '...withdrawn; the total of these two items is estimated at £358 million...'

Line 7 from end: read '...government, less any increase in value, through rising prices, of stocks not so disposed of'. (But I hope the whole matter will be set out much more fully.)

P. 6   For clarity, deduct savings of L.A.'s and companies from total net savings *before* scaling up net savings by death duties etc. to get gross savings.

P. 8   Last sentence.[54] Stated thus categorically, I believe this to be a fallacy. It depends on *why* an adverse balance has developed in the private sector. If, e.g., it is due to a maintenance of consumption in face of a reduced capacity to export, the proceeds of the foreign securities sold are required to finance this extravagance in the private sector, and are not available for lending to the government.

The treatment of positive acts of investment (e.g. in factories or houses) is to me confusing. By wrapping them up as a negative item

[54] The paragraph containing the sentence ran as follows:
The net Government expenditure requiring domestic finance is the amount which has to be met out of tax revenue and domestic loans (apart from those taken up out of the sterling proceeds of the sale of overseas assets); but it is not the same thing as total domestic expenditure by the Government. If imports for private consumption exceed exports, the cost of this excess (in addition to the cost of imports for Government consumption) has to be paid for out of overseas resources, the proceeds of which thus become available to finance an equivalent amount of domestic expenditure.

340

in 'net disinvestment' it is made to appear as though all net personal savings are available for government use, whereas in fact this is not so,—some of them are directly absorbed in, and tied up with, these acts of positive investment.

D. H. R.

From D. H. ROBERTSON, *26 March 1941*

Mr Keynes

1. A nation consists of 9 coalminers and 1 Prime Minister, each earning £100 a year and paying 10 per cent of his income in tax.

The coalminers produce entirely for export, and with the foreign currency received buy wheat, which they sell to each other and to the Prime Minister. Nobody consumes anything except wheat and Prime Ministerial services, or saves anything. The Prime Minister is paid out of taxes.

	£
National income	1,000
Exports	900
Imports	900
Adverse balance	—
'Government expenditure requiring domestic finance'	100

2. One of the coal mines is flooded; but the owner sells £100 foreign securities and continues to import and to sell £100 of wheat, to buy £90 of wheat and to pay £10 taxes.

	£
National Income	900
Exports	800
Imports	900
Adverse balance	100
'Government expenditure requiring domestic finance'	100

(as before)

3. We can complicate the story (a) by adding internal recipients and disbursers of income (b) by making the person who sells foreign securities different from the person whose exporting capacity is impaired. But the fact remains that with an adverse balance arising from this kind of cause, the proceeds of the liquidation of foreign assets are *not* available to the government, and the 'government expenditure requiring domestic finance' is exactly what it was before.

D. H. R.

27.3.41

To D. H. ROBERTSON, *27 March 1941*

Professor Robertson,

You do not hold that the proceeds of requisitioning securities make *no* difference to the amount which has to be raised by taxes and savings. So you do not think your own conundrum correct as stated.

Won't you, therefore, try to solve it yourself, or get it in a modified form you do think correct before trying it on me?

If after a week you are defeated, I'll give you a *hint!*

J. M. K.

To D. H. ROBERTSON, *28 March 1941*

Professor Robertson

I think you will find the answer to the conundrum more convincing if you reach it yourself! But perhaps I ought to add this. The example you sent me in writing about the coalminers and the Prime Minister raises, I think, a different point from what was in your mind when we talked in the morning, and one which is easier to answer. At any rate I think that the assumption which my statement strictly requires is unquestionably fulfilled in the case of that one of your points, but not so unquestionably in the case of the other. I attach what I think is the solution in a sealed packet!

J. M. K.

This was Keynes's 'solution'.

Strictly speaking, in place of 'requiring domestic finance', the passage should read 'requiring to be financed out of taxation and primary saving, if inflation is to be avoided, on the assumption of no change in the propensity to spend.'

J. M. K.

The coalmine example assumes in effect that a vesting order affects the propensity to spend of him who is vested against —this is scarcely reasonable.

Your other point was, I thought, that if imports are maintained the propensity to spend will be higher than if they are not—which is at least partly true.

From D. H. ROBERTSON, *31 March 1941*

Mr Keynes

I

A = total government expenditure

B = government expenditure abroad[55]

C = adverse balance of payments—assumed to be greater than B.

D = government expenditure requiring to be financed out of taxation and primary savings if inflation is to be avoided.

ϕ = propensity to spend (a function of income).

Your proposition is that in any period $D = A - C$, assuming there is no change in ϕ.

This as it stands, makes no sense. Change from what or since when?

To make sense the proposition must be restated as '$\Delta D = \Delta A - \Delta C$, unless there has been a change in ϕ'.

II

The story of the miners, as you rightly suspect, raises a new point. But you have not seen what that point is. The story is concerned with the effect of changes, not in the propensity to spend, but in the capacity to export.

(i) The story quite obviously does not assume that 'a vesting order affects the propensity to spend', since it does not mention vesting at all.

(The White Paper figure of reduction of foreign assets in the first year of war includes some £60 million for unvested and £10 million for vested securities.)

(ii) But let us, if you like, introduce the complication of vesting. My unlucky miner, instead of selling his securities direct to a foreign buyer, sells them to the Prime Minister, who sells them to a foreign buyer and with the proceeds buys wheat abroad which he sells to the unlucky miner, who pays for it with the domestic money which he received from the sale

---

[55] I define this to include not only finished munitions etc. imported on government acount but raw materials, e.g. copper & aluminium, imported by private firms and sold to the government in the form of finished goods: and to exclude goods (e.g. wheat, bacon) bought by the government and sold to the public. This total is not at all easy to evaluate in practice. Is your definition the same or different?

343

of his securities. The fundamentals of the story are unaltered. It is *not* being assumed that vesting has any effect on the propensity to spend. And *D* is *not* diminished by the fact that *C* has increased from zero to a positive quantity.

(iii) In point of fact, it is not being assumed that ϕ alters at all. It is merely being assumed that ϕ is of such a kind that if a man's income is reduced he reduces his spending by an amount smaller than the reduction in his income,—which I thought was common ground in all discussions of this sort. The precise case illustrated in the story was (intentionally) an extreme one,—the man represented as losing *all* his income and making a *zero* cut in his consumption. But only the milder general assumption enunciated above is necessary to the establishment of the proposition which the story was meant to suggest to you, viz. that an adverse balance which emerges as a result of a reduction in exporting power has no effect in reducing *D*.

You ought to hold—I don't know if you do—that every enemy bomb and every administrative muddle which damages our exporting power eases the problem of domestic public finance.

III

Contrived changes in the propensity to spend and undesigned changes in the capacity to export are, in my view, important sorts of change under war conditions. By and large, I should be inclined to guess that, in any recent period, $D = A - B$ is a nearer approximation to the truth than $D = A - C$. Certainly the latter is not a self-evident truism, and should not be put forward as such.

D. H. R.

31.3.41

To D. H. ROBERTSON, *1 April 1941*

1. The last sentence of your 1 is what I mean. I am comparing the change as against some base period.

2. My argument does require that the changes in the adverse balance are not correlated with changes in domestic employment as well as being not correlated with changes in the propensity to spend. You get your result because there is a change in domestic employment and income between the two periods. I can be taken to assume either that there is full

employment or that changes in the adverse balance do not affect employment.

3. Unquestionably a diversion from exporting to production for home consumption does ease the problem of domestic public finance and *vice versa.*

4. Surely what I am saying is a self-evident truism *in present conditions.* If we persuade Canada to supply us with more cheese, the proceeds of selling that cheese in this country diminish by that amount what we have to raise in tax and primary saving. Imported cheese paid for by borrowing, and savings certificates printed at negligible expense, are interchangeable for the purpose of public finance. The more we sell of the one, the less we have to sell of the other. The more cheese we can provide in that way, the less primary saving there has to be in order to avoid inflation. Why do you disagree with that? It is all I am saying.

J. M. K.

1.4.41

From D. H. ROBERTSON, *2 April 1941*

1. There is no indication of this in the White Paper.

2. I must press for one further concession,—you are assuming that an increase in the adverse balance is not associated with any decline in the *efficiency of effort* devoted to export, due to port and traffic delays, the creaking of the machinery of Customs pre-entry and export licensing, etc. etc. This *does* seem to me a big assumption under war conditions.

3. I have not denied this.

4. I find the example rather confusing,—cheese is (on my definition) a private import in connection with which the government appears as a mere middleman, and should be left out of the story. But I think it is only the old point again—you are assuming that whatever our import policy, the total propensity to consume is unchanged.

D. H. R.

2.4.41

345

To D. H. ROBERTSON,[56] *2 April 1941*

1. E.E.A. and Bank of England buy the sterling[a] proceeds of all exports paying out $£E$ to exporters, and sell all[b] imports for sterling receiving $£I$ from importers.

The Exchequer spends $£X$ in this country.

2. I am saying no more than $£(I-E)$ is available to pay for part of $£X$, leaving $£(X-I+E)$ to be met out of taxes and domestic loans. This is an exact paraphrase of the last para. on p. 8 of the White Paper. To which part of this statement do you object?

I do not follow how your (2) is relevant to this.

I do not think that (1) arises on the actual form of statement in the White Paper.

You must be thinking of something much more complicated than I have mentioned or have in mind[c], namely the consequences of changes in the size of I and E on other parts of the economy. I don't think my statement involves me in taking up any particular line on this.[d]

J.M.K.

From D. H. ROBERTSON, *2 April 1941*

Sir R. Hopkins

1. The new edition amply fulfils my two main requests, viz.

    (i)   for full discussion of the figures of 're-investment of domestic capital assets' and 'tax accruals'.

   (ii) for clarification of the relation between the two halves of the paper.

---

[56] Lower case letters indicate the points where Robertson made manuscript comments on Keynes's note. The comments were as follows:

[a] 'sterling' was crossed out and the words 'foreign currency' inserted.

[b] After the word 'all ' the words 'the foreign currency required purchasing' were inserted.

[c] Robertson put an asterisk at this point and commented at the foot of the letter 'But not, as I should say, of something more complicated than you might have had in mind before doing your subtraction sum.'

[d] Also at the foot of the letter were written the following words: 'I do not see how 2 follows from 1. You leave out half the story. How is it that EEA is willing to sell more foreign currency than it buys? By (inter alia) obtaining foreign currency from the sale abroad of vested private assets, for which it pays $£Y$. Assuming (for simplicity) that this is the only kind of 'foreign resource', we get $Y = I-E$. I.e. you are maintaining as self-evident that the whole of Y is lent back to the Government, which I say is *not* self-evident.'

2. In spite of the explanations given, the 8-fold increase in the annual rate of the former figure remains astonishing to me, and I should not be surprised to find it successfully challenged by someone who has made a serious independent study of its components, which I have not.

3. I retain my theoretical objection to the procedure of Table V, where the *nation*'s adverse balance of payments is deducted from the *Government*'s expenditure to yield a residual called 'Net (Government) expenditure requiring domestic finance'. I think Mr Keynes would now agree that the theoretically correct statement of the case would be as follows:–

'As between any two periods, the increase in government expenditure requiring, if inflation is to be avoided, to be financed out of taxes or primary savings, will be equal to the difference between the increase in total government expenditure and the increase in the adverse balance of payments, provided the increase in the adverse balance of payments is not associated either with an increased disposition on the part of the public to spend money, or with an impairment of the efficiency of effort devoted to export.'

I am not prepared to press my objection to the point of saying that Table V gives a seriously misleading quantitative picture of the 'relief' afforded to the problem of domestic public finance by the adverse balance. But since it is obviously impossible for the whole matter to be set out fully in the White Paper, I should feel happier if it were thought possible to omit altogether the whole paragraph which follows the table. I think they will give many people an uneasy sense of paradox for which there is considerable intellectual justification, even though it might be possible to satisfy them, in the course of extended argument, that quantitatively there is not much amiss.

D. H. R.

2.4.41

The situation as far as Henderson was concerned is best summed up in a letter from Keynes to James Meade.

From a letter to J. E. MEADE, *28 March 1941*

The critics are now all content except Hubert. He still maintains that the very different rates of domestic disinvestment in the first period and the second period are not plausible. He holds this view for no reason that he is able to give but merely because he has a bluff businessman's hunch to that effect. I believe he intends to come round shortly to cross-examine you and Stone about it.

The principal explanations I gave him were the following:–

(1) The rise in prices, chiefly relating to the first year of the war.

(2) Replacements and renewals and private investment were on a much more normal scale in the early months of the war.

(3) Much more both of fixed and working capital for increased munitions output had to be privately financed in the first period. This was the case even when it had been agreed in principle that the Exchequer should pay. For there were delays in settling the matter so that capital expenditure was incurred in the first period and privately financed at that date which was subsequently taken over by the Exchequer. I mentioned Imperial Chemicals as an example of this. The time-lag in paying armaments firms for munitions once established has not increased so that the brunt of the private financing required by this was borne in the first period.

As against this, stocks taken over by the Government from private hands were probably greater in the first period, as was also the reduction of stocks by depletion apart from this. I might have mentioned to him that in the last two months of the first period, immediately after the collapse of France, when output was at a particularly low ebb, it is possible that there was a serious draft on stocks.

I shall be interested to hear if you can produce figures which will convince him. He has not been convinced, as I think he ought to have been, by a note which I sent, dated 27 March, of which I enclose a copy. This seems to me to produce overwhelming indirect evidence that domestic dis-investment must have been much larger in the second period than in the first.

The minute to Henderson forwarded to Meade ran as follows:

To H. D. HENDERSON, *27 March 1941*

The following are the results of following up your supposition that the estimate of savings is of the right order of magnitude but that there is nevertheless a large error in the estimate of disinvestment. I am here taking the total disinvestment at home and abroad.

1. The conclusion requires that there should not only be an error in the estimates of net national income and of personal expenditure but that these errors should be of the *same* magnitude and in the same direction. Since the estimates in question are entirely independent, one of them being based on Inland Revenue figures and the other on consumption figures, this is not very likely.

2. What you find unplausible is the high rate of disinvestment in the second period compared with the rate in the first period. But these can only be brought nearer together by assuming that the mistakes in the estimates of national income and of personal expenditure are in *opposite* directions in the two periods. In other words, you have to suppose that the statisticians got these two independent calculations too high by the same amount in the first period and too low by the same amount in the second period.

3. I am not clear from what was said this morning that you appreciated that any plausible mistakes in national income and personal consumption would have the effect either of increasing the figure of disinvestment in both periods or of reducing it in both periods. They can only be brought nearer together by making corresponding changes in the estimates of personal savings. But these, on the other hand, would have to be in the *opposite* direction in the two periods; that is to say, if liquidation was larger than estimated in the first period and smaller in the second, personal savings have to be smaller in the first period and larger in the second. For instance, if disinvestment in the first period ought to be increased by 150 and disinvestment in the second period reduced by 50

349

(corresponding to annual rates of 210 and 390) net personal savings would fall to 172 in the first period and rise to 367, i.e. an annual rate of 674, in the second period; that is to say, the rate of savings would have jumped to four times, which is wholly inconsistent with the savings figures.

4. I repeat, therefore, that a superficial study of these tables does not show the extent of their interlocking character and the difficulty of making a large change in any one of them without producing absurd results in some other. It is, I believe, certain that domestic disinvestment was much larger in the second period than in the first period.

5. I have redrafted my text as below in an effort to make all this clearer.

J.M.K.

27.3.41

WHITE PAPER

I. *The Comments of H.D.H.*

Para. 3. We asked the compilers of these indices whether they allowed any inference to be drawn about the relationship of stocks at the end of February 1941 compared with August 1940. They told us that the method of compilation of these statistics, which is rather peculiar, being based I believe on comparative percentages without absolute figures, made any such inference impossible. That is why they are always published in the peculiar form they are without any reference to absolute amount.

Para 4. Nevertheless I am not inclined to quarrel much with the conclusion that the reduction in the value of retailers' stocks has not been a major factor in the first half of the second year. The Limitation of Supplies Orders had not had an important effect until towards the end of the period. On the other hand, the purchase tax operated in a double manner so as to diminish stocks in the hands of wholesalers and manufacturers rather than retailers. In the first place consumers anticipated purchases from the retailers; in the second place retailers filled up their stocks all they could from the wholesalers, since the tax did not apply to goods taken over by retailers before it came into operation. Thus the brunt of the reduction was higher up the list of suppliers. Moreover, retailers' stocks are not the major item in total stocks. There was probably a seasonal reduction after Christmas of at least £35 million. But I should not have supposed that the total reduction of retailers' stocks in six months was more than £25–50 million, and may easily have been less than £50 million. Indeed I should not be greatly surprised if the net reduction was quite a minor factor.

Para. 5. I should say that much the most important element was in the amount of working capital privately financed. In the early part of the war, to take an example, motor-car manufacturers, in spite of disposing of practically all their working capital invested in the production of motor-cars, were needing more money rather than less in connection with the change over to aeroplanes, partly for materials and partly to finance new factories. The financial arrangements with the government were such that the major part of these expenses were to be taken over by the Exchequer in due course. The time-lag in settling these matters meant that up to August last a great deal was being privately financed which was not strictly meant to be so financed. Coates gave me some very striking figures on this relating to I.C.I. In the last six months, on the other hand, the accounting arrangements have got into better order and munition and aeroplane firms have probably got much more liquidity.

Para. 6. I should certainly expect that this was a very large factor indeed in the last half year, though not so in the first year of the war. The companies' accounts which have been the subject of remarks by chairmen up to date mainly relate, of course, to a period earlier than 1 September last.

I have been considering whether there is any other sidelight on this issue. Do you or H.D.H. attach any importance to the following figures:–

In present circumstances firms are not very willing to invest in a permanent form sums realised through a diminution in their stocks or working capital, or sums which would normally be used for repairs and renewals, expenses which are deferred for the time being but not it is hoped, for any prolonged date. Thus the effect of physical disinvestment is likely to be largely reflected in increased financial liquidity by businesses. Do the banking statistics throw light on this? In the first year of the war current accounts increased by £214 million and advances fell by £92 million, giving a total of £306 million. We have to take off this tax accruals accounted for under a different head, estimated at £140 million. This indicates an increased liquidity of £166 million for the first year of the war. Now this covers the period in which cash balances abroad were requisitioned to the extent of over £100 million. Firms which were not allowed to keep cash in one form are likely to have replaced it by cash in another form. Also in the first year of the war private individuals were probably aiming at holding larger bank balances than usual. In the early months the war savings campaign had not got going, and in the last 10 weeks of the year there was the collapse of France and the fear of invasion. Increases of balances by Dominions etc. were largely held in Treasury bills and the like, and so far as cash is concerned are not likely to have much more than balanced the withdrawal of foreign balances. Thus the increased bank liquidity of businesses was probably less rather than more than £166 million.

Compare this with the last six months. Current accounts have increased by £210 million and advances have fallen by a further £19 million; although this covers the income tax paying period when the movement is seasonally the other way. To this total of £230 million we have to add £20 million reduction in tax accruals. Thus liquidity increased by £250 million in six months, or at the rate of £500 million per annum. With war weapons weeks etc. in full flood, it is unlikely that private current accounts increased much during this period. And it is also more likely that under the stimulus of war weapons weeks, some businesses subscribed to government issues sums which they would have preferred to keep liquid left to themselves. There was probably some increase in overseas balances held with the clearing banks, an amount which could be ascertained through the Bank of England given time. There are also doubtless many other adjustments to be made. Nevertheless, such indications as the above figures supply suggest a change in the rate at which businesses were getting more liquid, very similar, indeed almost indecently similar, to the rates indicated in the White Paper.

The end came with the circulation of the White Paper after the Budget speech of 7 April. As J. R. N. Stone recalled, 'It was a great day. We drank champagne that night and we felt we had accomplished something.'[57]
After the Budget Keynes summed up his reactions as follows.

From a letter to F. A. KEYNES, *14 April 1941*

I don't expect to be quite so busy now that the Budget is out of the way, for I've been writing endless memoranda on that subject.

I am as well satisfied with the Budget as I could reasonably expect; and indeed got my way on a number of points as much as is good for me. The limited acceptance of deferred pay is most associated with me publicly. But the two points I attached most importance to and where I played a part were the stabilisation of prices, for which I have been fighting very hard, and the logical structure, and method of a wartime

[57] J. R. N. Stone, 'The Use and Development of National Income and Expenditure Estimates', in D. N. Chester, ed., *Lessons of the British War Economy* (Cambridge, 1951), p. 85. Professor Stone's paper has proved most useful in organising the papers in this section.

Budget which, together with the new White Paper, is really a revolution in public finance. The chief officials Sir Richard Hopkins and Sir Horace Wilson, as well as the Chancellor, have been extraordinarily good to me and open-minded and ready to be persuaded; and Lord Catto has been a great help all through. Indeed we were a wonderfully united team. The opposition which has given me trouble and worn out my nerves was mainly from Hubert Henderson.

Chapter 5

THE LATER BUDGETS

For the rest of the war, budgetary policy operated within the principles established in April 1941, both in form and substance, doing little more than consolidate the ground and polish the rough edges. In the process of consolidation and smoothing Keynes took a relatively less active part than previously in areas beyond his continuous brief concerning the national income and expenditure estimates and their implications. Given his other preoccupations, this is understandable. Nevertheless, on occasion his contributions were important.

Keynes's opening proposals for the 1942 Budget represented his last large-scale attempt to shape the overall structure of a budget.[1]

NOTES ON THE BUDGET

I

1. The features of the last Budget were (*a*) a great increase of revenue; (*b*) a concentration on direct taxation; (*c*) the stabilisation of prices. It might be described as a *financial policy Budget.*

I suggest that the next Budget should be of a different character, fit to be described as a *social policy Budget,* and should primarily aim at adjusting various social anomalies which have developed out of the war situation and also out of the previous Budget itself.

2. It is too early to give a reliable estimate of expenditure. But two forecasts can be made with some confidence:–

(i) The yield of taxation on the basis of existing taxation will considerably exceed the estimates of this year's revenue,

---

[1] The idea of a services tax had been suggested to Keynes by Austin Robinson in March 1941. As the Chancellor's Budget speech indicated, at the time it had proved an unsuccessful candidate for inclusion because it would not meet the needs of that Budget (H.C. Deb. 55, volume 369, columns 1328–9).

—partly because we shall have the benefit of a full year of the new taxes, partly because the buoyancy of the revenue is much above expectations. It is probable that, without any additional measures, next year's revenue will reach or exceed £2,000 million, which compares with this year's estimated revenue of £1,786 million.

(ii) This revenue will be collected out of a national income which is not materially increased. The effect of some slight further reduction in unemployment, of a considerable increase in the employment of women, and of wage increases lately granted or in prospect will be largely offset by the diminished earnings of men taken for the forces. Moreover further enquiry indicates that the White Paper estimate of national income was a little too high. Thus the proportion of next year's revenue to next year's national income according to the new estimates is likely to work out higher than this year's revenue to this year's income according to last Budget's estimates.

It follows that if national expenditure is much increased, more of it than in previous years will come from diversion of existing output and less from increased output.

3. 2(ii) above has a significant bearing on the question whether direct taxes should be further increased. In view of this and of the very recent date at which last Budget's direct taxes will have taken effect, it may be agreed that there is a sufficient case for *not* raising the average level of income tax any further in the coming year. This does not mean that there is no room for equitable and socially desirable adjustments between one class of taxpayer and another (as will be seen below).

4. If the various adjustments to be suggested below were to have the effect of increasing the net yield of the revenue by some £50–100 million or more, that would be all to the good. But this is not their only purpose, and they must not be judged merely by the revenue they may raise. They are

proposed in the interests of a sounder social policy to meet the revolutionary change of conditions.

5. With this preamble I venture to throw out a number of half-thought-out suggestions as a basis of discussion, in the value of which I have varying degrees of confidence.

I have arranged these under two main headings. The first aims at accentuating the difference of treatment between luxuries and necessaries; the second at making adjustments of direct taxation in favour of children and women in employment. A third possible heading, relating to provisions for post-war employment, I reserve for discussion in a subsequent paper.

II

The last Budget aimed at stabilising the cost of living index number and at limiting the price increases of semi-necessaries. In this it has succeeded at a smaller cost than was expected at the time. This policy has, indeed, proved the sheet anchor of our whole economic price–wage structure.

At the same time, it has been the declared policy of the Treasury in interdepartmental discussions to allow luxuries to fetch their full price. In practice this has not been completely realised, partly because, even in conditions of 100 per cent E.P.T., there is a reluctance to allow excessive profits to reach private hands, because there is a public opinion against *any* profiteering, and because it is undesirable to stimulate the transfer of resources to luxury output. These objections would not apply to the taxation of luxuries, since this would divert into the Exchequer the higher prices which the weaker savers amongst the public are now prepared to pay.

2. It is suggested, therefore, that the next Budget should emphasise the difference of treatment to be accorded henceforward to luxuries. Such a policy would deliberately aim at taxing incomes which are employed neither in saving nor in essential or semi-essential consumption, nor in meeting old

357

unavoidable commitments. This would have the advantage of satisfying a larger amount of peccant purchasing power with a smaller volume of output, and would stimulate voluntary savings as well as increase revenue. It is an appropriate complement and aid to the rationing policy for necessaries, to the manpower policy for output, and to the national campaign for savings. I append a list of measures designed to this end which *prima facie* deserve examination, without at this stage entering into any details or attempting to meet possible criticisms.

(i) The purchase tax on the group of articles now charged at the full rate to be increased in general to 50 per cent with some suitable exceptions.

(ii) A substantial increase in the duty on wines and spirits (leaving beer and cider alone) coupled with some increase in imported supplies (e.g. from Spain and Portugal).

(iii) 10 per cent increase in the tobacco duty. (This differs in intention from the other taxes in this list, since I suggest that it should not be passed on to the public but should be absorbed by reduced expenditure on advertising and packing.)

(iv) Increased entertainments tax on admissions costing more than 1s 6d and limited to cinemas.

(v) A tax, deducted at source by the exhibitor, of 33⅓ per cent on royalties payable on imported films.

(vi) A tax, payable by the employer, of 5s a week on female and £1 a week on male domestics and attendants, including those employed in gardens, restaurants, hotels, places of entertainment etc., but with necessary exceptions for (e.g.) canteens, British restaurants, hospitals, educational establishments etc. A paper recommending proposals on these lines, sent me by Mr Meade, is appended.

(vii) A similar tax on all employees in non-essential industries, should Mr Bevin carry through his proposal to schedule this distinction.

(viii) 20 per cent tax on restaurant bills exceeding 3s 6d per head per meal, and on hotel bills exceeding 10s per head per day.

(ix) 20 per cent turnover tax on auctions of second-hand goods on all lots fetching more than £1.

(x) 50 per cent increase of first-class railway fares.

(xi) 100 per cent increase of cost of licence, collected by the petrol rationing officer, on cars, not qualified to receive a supplementary ration (which may be assessed at nil).

(xii) 100 per cent increase of taxi-fares collected by a licence charge proportioned to their petrol ration.

(xiii) 33⅓ per cent ad valorem tax on paper in all its uses, balanced by the exemption of books from the purchase tax.

(xiv) 33⅓ per cent ad valorem tax on advertisements in daily and weekly newspapers.

3. On the other hand, the purchase tax on articles now charged at the reduced rate and the duty on sugar (except for use in chocolate and confectionery)[2] should be abolished in the interests of the cost of living index number.

But it is not intended that the consumer should obtain the full benefit of this. The object is to rationalise the absurd system into which we have drifted of taxing some articles entering into the cost of living index and of simultaneously subsidising other (and sometimes the same) articles.

Moreover, it is much better to reduce the price of an article such as sugar which is rationed, so that cheapness cannot lead to extravagance, than an article such as bread which is not rationed, so that dearness may lead to a desirable economy and avoidance of waste.

The proposal is, therefore, to offset the above reductions in taxation by getting rid (subject to any obviously advisable exceptions) of all direct subsidies to the cost of living (i.e. apart from subsidies to shipping services, milk schemes and

---

[2] This is administratively easy, as there is already a difference in price, though an increased difference in price rather than the maintenance of the duty might be the best way of doing it.

agriculture) with the exception of the subsidy on bread which would be much reduced,[3] leaving the consumer, nevertheless, with some modest advantage on balance and the Treasury with a margin against contingencies, which is badly needed, for stabilising the index in future.

This would have the incidental advantage of bringing the index cost of food and clothing nearer together. At present clothing has increased in price nearly 50 per cent more than food; yet we tax the former and subsidise the latter.

Thus the proposal taken as a whole would introduce more common sense and correspondence to the underlying facts of actual cost in our price system for necessaries.

(I consider that there is a clear case for the abolition of the purchase tax on clothing, but not so clear a case for the abolition of the sugar duty balanced by a reduced subsidy on bread. In the latter case the advantages, definite though they are, may not be enough to balance the disadvantages of upsetting an established and accepted situation.)

III

1. In the field of direct taxation I do not suggest any increase in the average rates of contribution. But certain adjustments in the weight of the burden are called for by reasons of equity and social policy.

2. At a time when we wish to encourage the employment of married women the traditional inequitable treatment of their earnings becomes doubly inadvisable. I suggest that a married woman, whose earned income is high enough to attract income tax, should be entitled to a personal allowance of £80, a relief of one-tenth of her earned income (with a maximum allowance of £150) and the reduced rate of tax on the first £140 of taxable income. In this case her husband's

---

[3] It is very desirable to increase the price of bread relatively to potatoes, the price of which should be maintained or even reduced.

personal allowance would be reduced to £80. Her unearned income would continue to be aggregated with her husband's for the purpose of the tax. To pay for this concession (I cannot calculate whether this proposal is more or less than enough) the reduced rate of tax might be applicable only to the first £140 of each individual's taxable income, instead of £165 as at present. Thus the position of a married woman's earned income would be completely assimilated to that of a man's or of a single woman's.

The strength of the case for this concession is illustrated by the calculation that if the wife of a man earning £6 10s a week (or £7 10s a week if they have one child) enters employment, she pays the full rate of 10s tax on all her earnings in excess of the existing maximum exemption of £45 a year, i.e. if she earns even as little as 40s a week she pays no less than 12s out of this in tax, and out of 60s a week she pays 22s in tax. How personal allowances are divided at present between man and wife for the purpose of deductions of tax at source I do not know.

3. The strengthening of the economic position of the family unit should be a main purpose of social policy now and after the war. I cannot understand how any person concerned in social well-being or human happiness can doubt this, though the scale and method of the first initial move in this direction are not easily decided.

At present we pay family allowances through the income tax to all parents except those who need it most. A man begins to qualify for a family allowance when his earnings rise to 68s 6d a week. A woman who enters employment earns a family allowance towards the child she is no longer able to look after so well, provided her husband earns at least 68s 6d a week. If he earns less, there is no family allowance. The family allowance gradually rises with the size of income, reaching a total of 5s a week *irrespective of the number of children* for a man earning 90s a week and reaching (e.g.) 30s a week for a man with three children provided his earnings are not less than £10 3s a week. I have no quarrel with the principle of larger deductions for families with higher incomes and therefore (presumably) higher standards of life. But I can see no justification for making *no* allowances for families below the income tax limit.

As an initial step, the obvious thing to do is to raise the allowance to a minimum of 5s per week for all children in the case of widows and for all children after the first where the father is alive. This would cost something under £50 million net. No man would benefit from it unless he had at least two children and earnings of less than 110s a week.

The technical method of carrying this out would be to allow parents the option of the present income tax allowance *or* a cash payment of 5s per week for children in excess of one, the Revenue working out for them the most advantageous alternative.

Much also to be said for an increased allowance to the middle classes, where educational expenses are greater, i.e. to the class with more than £500 a year. This might take the form of allowing them to pay tax at half-rate in addition to the existing allowances, in respect of any sums paid by them, not exceeding £50 a child, to a recognised educational estab-lishment. This, at its maximum, is approximately another 5s a week per child if used for education. It could be worked on the analogy of the reduced rate for insurance premiums, and would automatically become less expensive when income tax falls.

4. As a means of paying for the above, and also on its own merits, a drastic extension of compulsory savings to juveniles is properly called for.

Half of the earned income, after taxation, in excess of £100 a year of a worker under 21 and in excess of £80 a year of a worker under 19 should be deferred on the lines of the existing scheme.

5. The increased tax due to reducing the income paying half rate from £165 to £140 should also be credited as deferred savings.

6. Lord Catto has proposed a withholding tax on foreign income arising in this country, similar to the taxes imposed in U.S.A. and in some of the Dominions and in India, to offset the fact that the recipients are not liable to surtax. It is suggested that 15 per cent of the gross income might be a suitable proportion. I am strongly in favour of this proposal, which will save a significant amount of dollar remittances as well as yield revenue.

7. I am not able to calculate how far (1) the reduction of the half-rate allowance from £165 to £140, (2) compulsory savings from juveniles and (3) the withholding tax would go towards meeting the cost of relief to the earned incomes of married women and of the proposed children's allowance. If these adjustments fell materially short, the question whether further adjustments should be made to provide the difference might depend on the extent to which the suggestions under II above may be adopted. If action under this heading is drastic, this source might be regarded as bridging the gap.

3 November 1941

J. M. KEYNES

Appendix by Mr J. E. Meade

I am asked to put down on paper my ideas about a tax on domestic servants. The main arguments, as it appears to me, in favour of such a tax are as follows:–

(1) At the present stage of the war it is very important to get women into war work, and domestic service is one of the largest groups of women from which we may hope to draw. A tax on such employment might greatly ease this transfer, as it would work with, and not against, attempts to mobilise such labour by direct means.

(2) As a general principle, it would seem wise at this stage of the war to tax inessential consumption goods and services heavily and to keep down

the price of essentials. Essentials can then be distributed fairly by rationing, etc., and inessentials can be left to market forces to be distributed by higher prices. This has the double advantage of preventing shop shortages and such like difficulties in the distribution of inessentials; and at the same time it maintains some of the incentives for earning more, since those who do earn more can hope to buy a little more of something. A tax on domestic servants would fit in well with this general principle.

(3) A tax on domestic servants, as on other forms of inessential goods and services, will help to raise revenue and to fill any budgetary 'gap' which may develop. Our information about the number of domestic servants is unfortunately scanty. But it has been assumed in recent manpower discussions that there are about 1 million female indoor domestic servants and that in mid-1939 there were some 108,000 indoor male domestic servants. A tax of 5s a week on 1 million female domestic servants and of 10s a week on 50,000 indoor male domestic servants would yield £14,300,000 a year.

It is, no doubt, important not to penalise too heavily expenditure on domestic service which enables housewives to undertake war work themselves. Perhaps this point would be met in part by confining the tax to full-time domestic servants living in the employer's home (so that charwomen would be exempt) and in part by making more generous allowances under the income tax for the earnings of married women.

I do not know that I have any very useful observations to make on the administrative problems which would be involved in levying such a tax. Clearly the problem would be much simplified if domestic servants were compelled in some way or another to register their names. Such a registration should be most useful both in aiding the administration of the tax and in enabling the Ministry of Labour to 'call up' such workers for war work. Might it not be worth while considering a registration of such workers for the joint purposes of the Treasury and the Ministry of Labour? The actual payment of the tax might possibly be organised through the affixing each week by the employer of a stamp to a card on the lines of the National Health Insurance cards. Possibly here it might be possible to arrange with the Ministry of Health that special cards were issued for domestic servants to which both the National Health Insurance and the 'domestic service tax' stamps were affixed. (Any such arrangement would have the incidental advantage of enabling Stone to calculate much more accurately the wages of domestic servants!)

J. E. MEADE

Offices of the War Cabinet
29 October 1941

Although H. D. Henderson put forward similar proposals, especially in the area of family allowances, the Inland Revenue proved a strong opponent of the direct taxation proposals, arguing that 'the purpose of the income tax is not the redistribution of income'. With this opposition, the Chancellor fought shy of the more dramatic proposals, although subsequent Chancellors framed their proposals with social policy considerations in mind and family allowances reached the statute book before the end of the war with Japan.

At the end of 1941 Keynes made a brief BBC broadcast that looked both backwards at past achievements and forwards to future preoccupations.

Tax on Lower Incomes Broadcast 22 December 1941

Last Friday, the Chancellor of the Exchequer explained to you the importance of paying readily the income tax which most weekly wage earners will find deducted from their pay beginning next month.

I have a point about this which is both interesting and important. I can make it clear in a few sentences.

The goods which can be supplied to the public are limited in amount. There is not enough manpower to make more for you. There are not enough ships to bring more into the country.

Thus, unless prices go up, the total amount which can be bought in the shops and spent on rent, light, fuel, travelling, entertainment, and all else you can spend your money on, is a fixed amount. It can't be increased. We can actually calculate it, because we know with some accuracy, both quantities and values. It comes to about £12 millon a day, at the prices you are now paying. But your personal wages and other incomes, before you have paid your income tax, are more like £16 million a day. All these are figures of personal incomes. Mr and Mrs John Citizen and all the other Mr and Mrs Citizens are, between them, getting incomes of £16 million a day. All the things on which you and the others can spend this money are worth only £12 million a day. That means there is a balance of £4 million a day, which it is useless for you to try to spend. For if you do try to spend it, there can only be muddle and waste and nuisance. Either prices are forced up, so that you pay more money for the same things, or the money just cannot be spent, for there is nothing to spend it on. But the effort to spend it, besides raising prices, will mean more black markets, longer queues, more waiting, more disappointment; and no one will be better off except at his neighbour's expense. The best system of rationing we can organise will not prevent all this.

Therefore, I say, there is an excess of £4 million a day which must not be spent. Personal savings are now, I suppose, in the neighbourhood of £2 million a day, —not bad, very good comparatively, but it covers only half the gap. So that a balance of another £2 million a day still remains. I'm giving you round figures.

A tax on earnings is much the fairest way to meet this. For such a tax can take proper account of the size of people's incomes, and their family responsibilities, which is not possible with any other kind of tax.

If you agree with me that the money must not be spent, and if you agree with me that people left to themselves will not save the whole amount required,—and even if they did, the war has to be paid for—is not a tax on income the right policy?

Besides, there is a concession which you must not forget. A large part of what those with small earnings have to pay in income tax is only taken from them temporarily, and they will be given a post-war credit, to be paid back when the war is over. Take the married man who earns £4 a week. If he has a child, he pays nothing. If he has no children, he pays nearly 6s a week in income tax,—practically the whole of which will be returned to him after the war. How can he complain! A bachelor pays a bit more, and so he should.

I emphasise the fairness of the system, because for many

taxpayers it is new—by next year there will be more than three million income tax payers who have never paid income tax before—because it looks worse than it is, and chiefly because people will pay cheerfully if they can see that it is fair. Besides which, the fact remains that even if the tax were not charged, you could buy no more goods than you are buying now.

The 1942 Budget also provided several good examples of Keynes's use of the national accounting framework in the light of the regular statistics becoming available.[4] Of these, two are printed below.

THE WHITE PAPER FIGURES FOR 1941

These are now available together with revised figures for 1940. The latter have been considerably amended in detail as the result of further work, but the more important aggregates of national income etc. are not much changed on balance. The salient results emerging from the 1941 figures are summarised below. The detailed tables, prepared by Mr Stone, from which this summary has been compiled are appended (B.17).[5] For the purposes of the White Paper these tables would be considerably abridged but their substance will be the same. Proposals as to the manner of their abridgment will be made shortly.

I. The 'gap'

If taxation, in conjunction with the propensity to save (as influenced by habits, rationing, propaganda and patriotism), is inadequate, this will show itself partly by a rise of prices relatively to wages and partly by excessive drafts on stocks. Since the last Budget the rise of prices relatively to wages is insignificant when averaged over the whole field of

---

4   Keynes was responsible for the 'literary sections' of the 1942 national income White Paper.
5   Not printed [Ed.].

consumption.[6] The following table throws light on the draft on privately owned stocks and on the accuracy of the Budget forecast.

	Budget forecast financial year 1941–2	Actual calendar year 1941	Actual calendar year 1940
	(£ million)		
Government expenditure[7]	4,507	4,653	3,334
Revenue	1,786	1,866	1,254
Deficit	2,721	2,787	2,080
Extra-budgetary funds and savings of local authorities			
Public authority deficit	2,521	2,567	1,904
Foreign disinvestment	800	741	738
Requiring domestic private finance	1,721	1,826	1,166
Net personal savings (including increased accruals of taxation)	1,000	889	607
	721	937	559
Undistributed profits including increased accruals of taxation	200	189	267
	521	748	292
Depreciation and sinking funds	450	450	450
	71	298	−158
Compensation paid to public under War Damage schemes[8]	—	249	36
Residue	71	49	−194

The reduction in stocks held under private finance is considerably greater than the above 'residue'. We have already taken credit for the *whole* of the depreciation and sinking

[6] Wage rates rose from 100 in 1940 to 109 in 1941; the cost of living from 100 in 1940 to 107·5 in 1941. Thus, allowing for a greater rise in non-cost-of-living items, the statement in the text remains true. It would be still safer if reckoned from the date of the last Budget to the date of the next Budget.

[7] Excluding lend/lease and after deducting proceeds of lend/lease supplies sold for cash and other appropriations-in-aid.

[8] In so far as these totals include items paid out to non-residents they are, to that extent, overstated.

funds (namely £450 million) and the *whole* of the compensation paid out under war damage schemes (namely £249 million), and we have made no allowance either for the finance of new *net* investment privately financed or for replacements paid for out of depreciation funds and war damage compensation. Thus the reduction in stocks must have been sufficient to provide not only for the above 'residue' but also for gross private investment including replacements of war damage losses as well as to make good normal depreciation. On the other hand there is a small credit against this in respect of payments out of the Exchequer to the public for the acquisition of already existing domestic capital assets (e.g. land, buildings or stocks of commodities). We have no direct estimate of any of these items. In 1940 there must have been a considerable amount of gross investment privately financed (especially as there was a greater volume of government production privately financed in that year, on account of time-lags in payment, which has to be included in this figure). But it is not likely to have exceeded £100–150 million in 1941.[9] If this is correct, the reduction in privately owned stocks was of the order of £150 million, or perhaps £200 million. This is not unsatisfactory, if we consider that it is reasonable and proper in time of war to run down stocks of non-necessaries; and that stocks of food and raw materials, almost wholly government-owned, were considerably increased in 1941, the increment in these during the year being valued (very approximately) at £90 million. (The stocks of food and raw materials reported monthly by the C.S.O. to the Lord President's Committee and almost wholly owned by the Govern-

---

[9] The large payments out under war damage schemes will have been partly offset by larger replacements, but this would only affect the 1941 figures in so far as replacements took place *in 1941*, whereas some part of such replacements as was possible, e.g. blitz first-aid and replacement of raw stocks destroyed in the 1940 blitzes, took place earlier. New ships purchased by private owners only count (net) towards gross private investment in so far as their cost exceeded sums for total losses paid out to British shipowners by marine insurance companies, together with sums reserved by the companies against deferred claims for loss and damage, in respect of non-war loss and damage.

ment have a value at current market prices of the order of £500 million.)

The Budget forecast relates to the financial year 1941-2. The White Paper statistics for this period will not be available until some time after the forthcoming Budget statement. If they were available, they would probably indicate that the Budget forecast was too low all along the line. As the only figures available in time will be those given above, I suggest that the Chancellor, after admitting that he was too low for the financial year, should make his comparisons with the White Paper figures for the calendar year 1941, which will show that he was not far wrong in respect of the period which it was rather easier to foresee accurately at the date of the Budget.

The chief point overlooked in the Budget forecast was the greatly increased amount which would be paid out under war damage schemes, a considerable part of which could not be spent on replacements and would, therefore, be available to be lent back to the Government. The excessive estimate of foreign disinvestment was due to a misunderstanding. The round figure of £1,000 million forecast for personal savings was, I think, for gross savings,[10] whereas logically it should have been for net savings. The increase in personal savings in 1941 over 1940, namely £282 million,[11] has more than reached the £250 million increase for which the Chancellor asked. In general it can be claimed that the Budget forecast has been remarkably close to the facts,—as close as one can hope to get in time of war.

II. *Personal incomes, consumption and saving*

The last line [in the following table] assumes (very approximately) a rise in values of about 15 per cent on the average of the year 1940 compared with 1938, and a further rise of

[10] Gross personal savings in 1941 were in fact £983 million, which is very near the forecast of £1,000 million.

[11] This includes, however, a larger reserve for taxation, accrued but not paid, than in the previous year.

	1941	1940	1938
	(£ million)		
Personal incomes	6,185	5,598	4,637
Taxation, direct and indirect, falling on personal incomes (excluding death duties)	1,764	1,310	967
Available personal incomes	4,421	4,288	3,670
Gross personal savings (including provision for death duties and accrued taxation)	983	692	226
Personal consumption at factor cost	3,438	3,596	3,444
Reduced to 1938 values	2,865	3,118	3,444

about 5 per cent over 1938 on the average of the year 1941. If this is correct, real consumption in 1941 was about 8 per cent less than in 1940 and 17 per cent less than in 1938. In terms *of money* personal consumption at factor cost (i.e. excluding indirect taxes) has been almost constant throughout, the increase of £1,600 million in personal incomes in 1941 over 1938 have been, almost exactly, either paid in taxes or saved.

In terms of 1940 values personal consumption in 1941 was £3,295 million or about £300 million less than in 1941. A year ago we forecast that new supplies for civilian consumption in 1941 would be about £400 million less than in 1940. This estimate of consumption, therefore, agrees pretty well with the estimate, obtained along quite a different route, that civilian stocks (which probably declined in 1940, if correction is made for price changes, by upwards of £50–100 million) declined in 1941 by something between £150 and £200 million, i.e. the deterioration in the privately owned stock position was £100 million greater in 1941 than in 1940.

Savings

The above estimates of net personal savings, namely £607 million for 1940 and £889 million for 1941, have been obtained

371

indirectly by deducting estimates of personal consumption and direct tax payments from estimates of personal incomes. An attempt has been made to check this by comparing these figures with direct evidence of the volume of personal savings.

We have, first of all, the types of new issue, etc. which are likely *prima facie* to be taken up out of personal savings, as follows:–

	£ million	
	1940	1941
Government stock on Post Office register	158	181
National Savings certificates	166	215
Post Office Savings Banks	101	174
Trustee Savings Banks	29	51
Building societies	31	(14)
Life assurance: ordinary	32	(32)
industrial	54	(53)
Trade unions and friendly societies	7	(7)
	578	727

(The figures in parentheses are provisional estimates where exact returns are not yet available.)

It is unlikely that any significant portion of these sums can come otherwise than from personal incomes. It is not equally clear that they must represent *new* savings. In 1940 an appreciable amount may have represented transfers from other investments, etc.; but in 1941 this is much less likely. However that may be, the amount still to be accounted for, if our estimate of total personal savings is correct, is as follows:–

	1940	1941
Estimated total of personal savings	607	889
Sources in above table	578	727
	29	162

Since we have still to take account of personal savings in the following forms:–

(*a*) increased bank deposits;

(*b*) increased currency holdings;

(*c*) hire purchase repayments in excess of new transactions;

(*d*) repayments of debts (net) to businesses;

(*e*) direct purchases (net) of investment goods (e.g. houses);

(*f*) farmers' increase in deposits, repayment of overdrafts and purchase of farm equipment, since they are not included in 'undistributed profits of businesses';

(*g*) subscriptions out of *new* personal savings to 'large' government issues not included in Post Office register; our estimate of total savings looks too small rather than too big. The evidence as to the amount of personal savings in these forms in 1941 is as follows:–

(*a*) It has been ascertained from the clearing banks that their personal, as distinct from their business, deposits increased by £43 million in the year ending 30 June 1941. Let us take £45 million as the estimated increase of personal deposits in all banks in the calendar year 1941.

(*b*) The total currency in circulation increased in 1941 by £137 million. We might, arbitrarily, attribute one third of this, or (say) £45 million, to personal, as distinct from business, holdings.

(*c*), (*d*), and (*e*) are not likely to have been large in 1941, say £20 million.

(*f*) is estimated at about £30 million in 1941. (This would leave for net new personal savings in all government stock apart from stock on the Post Office register only £22 million *plus* any portion of subscriptions to 'small' savings issues which represent transfers or business investments (e.g. proceeds of liquidation of stocks by small shopkeepers) and not new savings. This seems a modest enough figure and suggests that personal savings have not been overestimated.)

373

Forecast

In December last Mr Brittain[12] estimated total government expenditure (*net*, i.e. after deducting lend/lease relief including proceeds of sales) in 1942–3 at £4,675 million. He has since raised this to £4,880 million. Taking the *calendar* year 1942, to which the following forecast relates, £4,800 million should be a fairly liberal estimate compared with £4,650 million in 1941. Since foreign disinvestment is likely to be a good deal less in 1942 than in 1941, this represents an increase of £350 million, or 9 per cent, in domestic expenditure. But personal incomes in 1942 should be at least £200 million greater than in 1941. This leads up to a provisional balance sheet as follows.

Since personal incomes in 1942 should be at least £200 million greater than in 1941, taxation plus saving sufficient to close the gap entirely assumes a reduction of about £400 million in 1942 consumption compared with 1941. This is about 12 per cent and is probably more than is reasonably possible. If, however, personal incomes (at 1941 values) increase by more than £200 million, or if private stocks are further reduced, or if gross private investment can be kept below £100 million, the curtailment in consumption can be that much less. Thus, one way or another, Mr Brittain's estimate of government expenditure should be physically feasible even if calculated at 1941 values, whereas he has, I believe, included a margin for a further rise in wages and prices.

The Chancellor's forecast of revenue and expenditure must necessarily relate, in accordance with tradition, to the coming financial year. But it is suggested that his forecast of the 'gap' should relate to the *calendar* year 1942, even at the expense of the illogicality of the estimated gap for the

---

[12] Herbert Brittain (1894–1961), K.B.E. 1944, K.C.B. 1955; entered Treasury, 1919; Third Secretary, 1942–53; Second Secretary, 1953–7.

	(£ million) Calendar year	
	1942	1941
Government expenditure	4,800	4,650
Foreign disinvestment	550[13]	750
	4,250	3,900
Extra-budgetary funds, savings of local authorities, war damage compensation paid out	450	450
	3,800	3,450
Total savings, personal and institutional	1,100[14]	1,100
	2,700	2,350
Depreciation and sinking funds (gross)	450	450
	2,250	1,900
Net requirements of private gross investment (say)	100	100
Taxation required	2,350	2,000
Taxation obtained		1,850
'Gap'		150

calendar year leading up to his requirements of new taxation for the financial year. This would have two advantages:—first, that it is not quite so hopeless a task to make a forecast for nine months, as for twelve months, ahead; and second, that this would make possible in the subsequent Budget statement a comparison between the estimated and the realised results.

[13] This figure has been increased in the light of recent experience and in view of the forecasts of Indian expenditure. But it includes Canadian expenditure met out of the Canadian grant and American expenditure which U.S. have not yet agreed to take off our hands. If additional take-outs are arranged in U.S. or if a revised settlement is made with India or if the Canadian grant is treated as an appropriation-in-aid, the initial estimates of government expenditure and the amount of foreign disinvestment will each be reduced by the same amount, leaving the amount requiring domestic finance unchanged.

[14] The figure for savings next year is left unchanged because the figure of £1,100 million in 1941 includes a much larger increase in reserves against unpaid taxation than will be required in 1942 and because of the greater effective weight of taxation. If taxation yields less than £2,350 million in 1942, some part of the deficiency may be saved and not all of it used to increase prices or deplete stocks. The question how much more saving the public must be asked for in 1942 can only be determined *after* the amount of additional taxes has been settled.

The White Paper tables will always relate to the calendar year, and the full statistics for the financial year will never be available at the date of the Budget statement.

In Paper B.4[15] the proceeds of sales of lend/lease goods were brought in separately from other lend/lease assistance. On second thoughts this seems undesirable, though for internal purposes in calculating the requirements of the vote of credit the best available estimate of the cash proceeds will be necessary.

I suggest that the total amount of lend/lease assistance, if given by the Chancellor, should be based entirely on the American figures of transfers and other expenditure actually incurred, which is, in fact, the most accurate measure of the expenditure which the lend/lease system has excused us. At present we are supplied with these figures for the British Empire as a whole, without a separate total for lend/lease assistance to the Empire outside U.K. But no doubt the separation can easily be made (I suggest a telegram to Mr Allen[16] asking for a separate U.K. figure both up to 31 December 1941 and 31 March 1942—the latter figure should be available in time for the Budget statement). Assistance to the British Empire as a whole up to 31 December 1941 was approximately £400 million, of which (up to that date) nearly the whole was for U.K. Lend/lease assistance [which] is now running at about £2·5 million a day, or (say) £1,000 million a year. Since it will increase rapidly from now on, £1,500 million should be reached or exceeded in the calendar year 1942, and perhaps £2,000 million in the financial year 1942–3. This leads to the following:–

[15] Not printed [Ed.]
[16] Roy George Douglas Allen (b. 1906), Kt. 1966; Assistant Lecturer and later Lecturer in Statistics, London School of Economics, 1928–39; Reader, 1939–44; Professor, 1944–73; Statistican, Treasury, 1939–41; Director of Records and Statistics, British Supply Council in North America, 1941–2; British Director of Research and Statistics, Combined Production and Resources Board, 1942–5.

	(£ million) Calendar year		
	1940	1941	1942
Total expenditure	3,350	5,050	6,300
less Lend lease	—	400	1,500
	3,350	4,650	4,800
less Foreign disinvestment	750	750	550
Domestic expenditure	2,600	3,900	4,250
Provided from current output	2,300	3,350	(3,700)
Domestic disinvestment (exclusive of war damage) not made good	300	550	(550)

I do not know if credit for profits under the railway agreement has been taken in the forecast of expenditure. May I put in a plea that these profits should be brought in as miscellaneous revenue and not as an appropriation-in-aid to the Ministry of War Transport vote of credit, since the latter course will make confusion in the White Paper figures? Why should not the Chancellor make public in his Budget statement the excellence of the bargain made for the taxpayer (estimated profits of £34 million in the current financial year and perhaps even more next year), including this in his estimate of miscellaneous revenue (which will be quite a help) for next year?

The burden of the National Debt

The cost of the National Debt was £216 million in 1938 and £257 million in 1941, an increase of £41 million. The cost of unemployment relief was £110 million in 1938 and £28 million in 1941, a decrease of £82 million. Thus, up to date, good employment is saving the Exchequer more than the war debt is costing it; and there may be enough margin here to carry us nearly to the end of the war.

But the prospective post-war budgetary situation, if we can

377

keep good employment, is (apart from war pensions) even better than this. For the war debt adds considerably to taxable capacity, whereas unemployment relief does not. Up to date, about half of the war debt, namely £2,500 million out of £5,000 million, replaces disinvestment at home and abroad. If the capital now lost yielded twice the income from the war debt, taxable capacity (apart from death duties where it is increased) remains, for the time being, about the same. But disinvestment (so far), which measures the real loss from the pre-war position, could be made good by four years' post-war savings, by which time increased taxable capacity (assuming good employment) should go far towards meeting the increased cost of war pensions.

Each subsequent year of the war after 1941 will cause a real capital loss which it will take rather more than a year's post-war savings to make good. War damage, up to date, will not require much more than four months' post-war savings to make it good.

There is no reason why, with good employment, our current real output should not be at least 10 per cent greater after the war than in 1938. After allowing for all losses up to date and for another two years to come, this would permit a full return to pre-war standards, apart from the difficulties of the transition and of foreign markets. And any further secular improvement, say 3 per cent per annum cumulative, should put us that much to the good. So, financially at least (leaving out the balance of payments problem, which is another story and the clue to recovery) *sursum corda*!

J. M. KEYNES

23 February 1942

REVISED NOTES ON THE BUDGET

1. The amount to be raised cannot be determined closely until up-to-date estimates of expenditure and of revenue on the existing basis are available. B.16, assuming £4,800 million

for expenditure, arrived at revenue requirements of £2,350 million as a counsel of perfection for the calendar year 1942. But the figure for foreign disinvestment may be £50 million too low (a more exact estimate is being compiled), and some credit can be taken for profits from the railways. On the other hand, as the Budget is concerned with the financial year 1942–3, its requirements are likely to exceed those of the calendar year 1942. What follows is based on the provisional assumption that a net yield of £100–150 million from changes in the basis of taxation is the least which would be satisfactory.

2. Earlier discussions at the Committee suggest the provisional conclusion that no further increases in direct taxation are advisable and that concessions to married women may be called for which may cost as much as £20 million.

3. Since a further curtailment of real consumption is inevitable and since this must not be allowed to interfere with the stabilisation of the cost of living, it follows that the general character of the Budget must be in the nature of an attack, by means of increased indirect taxation, against expenditure on non-essentials. This has the double merit of acting either as a deterrent to such expenditure, or, if this fails, of absorbing more purchasing power in respect of the same real consumption and, moreover, of diverting this excess expenditure direct into the Exchequer.

4. The revenue backbone of such increased taxes must be the duties on tobacco and alcoholic drinks. But a Budget limited to such changes, apart from the fact that such taxes by themselves would not yield enough, would have a drab and timid and unimaginative aspect, and would not make the proper impact on the public mind or convey adequately the importance of *all-round* restriction of real consumption on non-essentials. A scheme of taxation in time of war must be intelligible and convincing to the public as well as adequate to the Exchequer. Thus an advance on a broad front is called for.

379

5. Sir Wilfrid Eady has provisionally estimated that the practicable increases on tobacco and alcoholic drinks might yield as follows:–

	£ million
Tobacco	45
Beer	40
Spirits	15
Wine	3
	103

6. Where else can we look? Apart from 'fancy' taxes which might have social value and psychological appeal such as taxes on expensive restaurant meals and personal services, the main proposals deserving attention seem to be the following:–

(*a*) Cinemas—increase of entertainment tax and, perhaps, a tax on royalties—(say) £18 million. This would require 3*d* extra per admission above 6*d*, and 1*d* extra below 6*d*.

(*b*) A tax on railway passenger fares, excluding workmen's tickets, season tickets and travelling on government warrants. It is important that there should be a deterrent on unnecessary travelling (the railways had a revenue from full fares in the second half of 1941 which was 50 per cent higher than in the first half of the year). A tax of 25 per cent might yield upwards of £10 million.

(*c*) 4*d* on petrol for private uses and an increased licence fee on taxis etc., balanced by an increase of 50 per cent in fares, yielding £12 million.

(*d*) A tax on newspaper advertisements might bring in £10 million.

(*e*) There remains perhaps the most advisable of all, namely an increase of the purchase tax to 50 per cent on all articles now paying at the 33⅓ per cent rate (leaving unchanged those categories now paying 16⅔ per cent). When the purchase tax was first introduced, care was taken to put all those categories, within which any important classes of necessaries fell, at the lower rate. A reduction in the actual supply of most goods in the 33⅓ per cent classes is both inevitable and desirable. Price control for such articles is difficult or impossible. Thus the case for advancing the tax is very strong. The yield is estimated at £20 million.

7. This would provide a yield of £70 million altogether, or (say) £170 million including tobacco and alcoholic drinks. This might be sufficient to allow an important concession in another direction which is recommended for quite different reasons, namely a substantial reduction in the duties on sugar, tea, cocoa and coffee, costing £30 million.

8. Since sugar and tea (cocoa and coffee are of no importance) are rationed, this concession cannot lead to any undesirable increase in consumption. But the reason for making the concession is a different one. This concession would result in a reduction of 4 full points on the cost of living and is the cheapest, practicable means of effecting such a reduction. The policy of stabilising the cost of living is in prospective difficulties because most other expedients for holding or reducing prices have already been applied to the full extent that is convenient. By April something further will be urgently required, and as the year goes by there are sure to be inevitable increases in other directions which will have to be offset. By taking off these duties, it may be possible to keep other prices nearer their 'natural' level and thus avoid a spate of small and arbitrary subsidies. In the long run this concession will cost the Exchequer little or nothing, because it will make it possible to avoid subsidies in other directions which the stabilisation policy would otherwise require. To make the concession in a single act before it is required will give the public more sense of relief than a series of small, concealed subsidies over a period. Politically it can be regarded as a concession which justifies the increase in the purchase tax. Socially the removal of these duties, which bear with particular severity on the poorest classes and on young

families, at the cost of severer taxes on unrationed and largely uncontrolled non-necessaries, will surely meet with general approval.

9. We are left with a net gain of £120 million after giving £20 million relief to married women and £30 million relief to the cost of necessary, rationed consumption.

10. A budget on these lines, together with a finance act embodying changes in E.P.T. and income tax on wage earners which are being separately discussed, will make very good sense. It will be generally intelligible. The public will perceive what the Chancellor is driving at, and will like what they perceive.

J. M. KEYNES

2 March 1942

The remaining wartime budgets saw Keynes even less involved, beyond his annual White Paper statistics, occasional advice and budget speech drafting. This last activity drew the following comments in 1943.

From a letter to F. A. KEYNES, *28 March 1943*

The last two days I have been writing a big wad of the Budget speech —rather a heart-breaking job—for I know well by experience that the better I make it the less likely it is to be used!

From a letter to F. A. KEYNES, *10 April 1943*

One more issue, with improvements, of the statistical Budget White Paper is finished. One more Budget speech will be delivered on Monday. Assisting at the latter is a heart-breaking procedure! Every phrase, every fact in what one provides which could conceivably attract attention is erased. For anything which is capable of attracting attention might also attract criticism! It is indeed the dregs of human dignity and morale. Or as Hoppy more politely expresses it, 'The Chancellor proceeds *from* the pedestrian'.

Although the Pay-As-You-Earn arrangements for income tax were not introduced as part of a wartime budget, they are best dealt with here. Before 1940 the problem of collecting income tax from weekly wage earners had not proved serious, as few were subject to tax and the sums involved were relatively small. As a result, there was no arrangement for collection at source beyond a limited voluntary system whereby employers deducted sums at source in anticipation of half yearly or yearly payments made on the basis of earlier income levels. However, rising taxes and rising incomes brought more wage earners within the scope of the tax system and led to the compulsory extension of the pre-war voluntary arrangements to all employers. When this scheme came into operation in January 1942, it was the object of considerable criticism owing to the problem of seasonal fluctuations in earnings. Within the Treasury, the reaction was to stonewall, although Keynes, worried about the problems that lagged collections on higher wartime incomes might cause in a post-war slump, suggested that 'stonewalling against so varied an attack will score no runs and be bowled out in the end'. Nevertheless the Treasury and the Inland Revenue stone-walled with a White Paper defending the existing arrangements.

In the course of 1943, the trade unions and other officials also realised that the 1942 White Paper attitude would not do in the face of a post-war decline in income, and in his Budget statement for 1943 Sir Kingsley Wood said that his officials were examining the situation. This brought renewed pressure for speedy action.

When the Inland Revenue in June 1943 came up with the solution eventually adopted, Keynes provided one memorandum the first part of which dealt with the problem of 'forgiveness' or the cancellation of overlapping liability.[17]

From a memorandum to T. PADMORE,[18] *12 July 1943*

INCOME TAX 'PAY AS YOU GO' PROPOSALS

The Chancellor asked me to let him have my comments on the proposals of the Revenue.

This strikes me as a very ingenious plan, which, so far as I can see, ought to work and does not involve any obvious consequential difficulties.

The only important comment which I have to make is on

---

[17] The rest of the memorandum dealt with administrative matters. He also provided a suggestion for a one-week lag in deduction to ease firms' accounting problems, but this met with Inalnd Revenue objections and failed.

[18] Thomas Padmore (b. 1909), K.C.B. 1953; Secretaries' Office, Board of Inland Revenue, 1931–4; transferred to Treasury, 1934; Principal Private Secretary to Chancellor of Exchequer, 1943–5; Second Secretary, 1952–62.

the forgiveness problem. There are three ways in which the subsequent yield of taxation may be affected.

(1) Through a subsequent reduction in the rate of tax or increase in the scale of allowances.

(2) A subsequent reduction in the incomes on which tax is paid compared with the income of the year which would be forgiven.

(3) A long deferred loss at the extreme other end, largely made up, as the Revenue point out, by new entrants coming under taxation at an earlier date.

The Revenue rightly brush the third on one side as not very large in amount and long delayed. Their argument seems to be entirely devoted to prospective loss on the first heading. But I should have thought that most people were thinking much more of the prospective loss under the second head. It is precisely because people's incomes are expected to drop after the war that this scheme is thought to be essential. In effect the income of a post-war year would be substituted for the income of the year 1943/44. It is because incomes are expected to be at a lower level in that year that the burden of taxing them on the higher income of an earlier year looks like being so heavy in the period of transition. Is not the major loss to the Revenue the substitution of a year in which incomes may be anything up to £800 million less than in the year which is being forgiven?

This prospective source of loss seems to me more important than the loss through an increase of allowances or a reduction in the standard rate. For the latter loss can be offset, and no doubt will be, by reducing rates and increasing allowances a little later on or a little less liberally than would otherwise be the case. The Chancellor, when he comes to reduce taxation, will not get the advantage he otherwise would in the yield of the tax through the time-lag in its taking effect. The Chancellor will find himself with a certain amount of revenue in hand, which he feels he can safely remit. I should have thought that the introduction of the proposed system would not cause a loss to the Revenue but an increased burden on other tax-payers. For example, part of the loss would be paid by income tax payers under Schedule D, who do not benefit from this particular relief, but nevertheless get a reduction of the standard rate a little later than they otherwise would owing to the cost of the concession to the Schedule E taxpayers.

Indeed, I am not sure that this does not really apply almost equally to the other source of loss, namely, the reduction of incomes. This also means that in the first post-war year the prospective yield of a given rate of income tax will be less than it otherwise would be, with the result of a more delayed remission of tax and, therefore, a heavier burden on other taxpayers.

I do not regard this as an argument against the scheme. I only want to point out that the effect of forgiveness is better regarded as an additional burden on other taxpayers than as as a loss to the Revenue. The Chancellor has to raise a given amount of taxes.

Perhaps, however, this is an extra reason for spreading the benefit of the change of system as widely as possible. I am sure that the answer to the question raised in paragraph 18 of M.716 is that all schedule E incomes should be treated alike, whether they are large or small. I suggest that the remission to Schedule E taxpayers may also be an argument for increasing simultaneously the depreciation etc. reliefs to Schedule D taxpayers. If the further report which the Revenue is to make leads the Chancellor to propose some concessions to business, the fact that he is simultaneously making this other concession to wage and salary earners may help him to explain that his proposals are fair, taken as a whole.

In the 1944 Budget papers, there are almost no written contributions by Keynes beyond the usual commentary on national income estimates.

However, it is clear from the papers that Keynes's growing concern with the post-war position of industry left its mark on the discussions of the Budget Committee, for he provided the inspiration for a Budget concentrating on industrial problems rather than a mark-time Budget, although he was unsuccessful in pushing the changes as far as he had hoped. The following summary memorandum by Sir Richard Hopkins with a brief commentary by Keynes, clearly set out the position and the nature of Keynes's concerns for the remaining budgets of the war.

Chancellor of the Exchequer

As I have already made known to you the Budget Committee have had considerable discussions on the possibility of introducing in the next Budget important reliefs and reforms in favour of industry.

2. The discussion arose out of a suggestion of Lord Keynes that it would be a good thing if this Budget could be regarded as a Budget of reforms in the industrial sphere rather than as a mark-time Budget.

3. On the matters dealt with in this note it is clear that Sir C. J. Gregg must be your principal adviser for he alone has all the material at command and it is not possible for me to do more than record general impressions derived from our discussions.

4. As a result of the enquiry into the incidence of the income tax on industrial profits it is clear that the Board of Inland Revenue at an early date will have an important body of suggestions ready for your consideration regarding the changes to be made in the income tax as part of the post-war reconstruction policy. These changes would operate only after the cessation of hostilities. With the possible exception of research expenditure, they are not likely to be sufficiently advanced and elaborated to be ready for inclusion in the forthcoming Finance Bill and it is felt that they should be announced in broad outline as the post-war policy of the Government in the Budget speech leaving the detailed legislative provisions to a later Bill. Lord Keynes suggests the desirability of such a Bill being passed in the autumn so that business people may know the precise details of what is afforded them.

5. Our discussions were chiefly concerned with the possibility of announcing important reliefs in the Excess Profits Tax at the same time, and indeed implementing them in the next Finance Bill.

6. The first question here is that of the rate and the post-war credit. Since 1940 the rate has been 100 per cent and since 1941 it has been provided that one-fifth of this tax shall be not an absolute and final payment but a post-war credit. Originally it was laid down that this credit was only to be granted upon 'such conditions as Parliament may hereafter determine' the

intention being that the money was invested in the business in a manner approved by government. But as very few business people persuaded themselves on this basis that they could really rely upon the receipt of this money, a further announcement was made in 1942 and put upon the statute book, to the effect that the post-war credit will be ascertained after the termination of hostilities and paid at such a date as Parliament may determine, with the one condition that the money shall not be distributed— whether in the form of dividends or otherwise. The reason for the condition (both in the original and the later form) was political, your Labour colleagues taking the view that there should be no absolute and unqualified right.

7. On the one hand it has seemed to all of us to be pretty clear that the condition is unworkable in practice. On the other hand it is still insufficient to prevent scepticism on the part of business people about the payment, and it never appears as a contingent asset in balance sheets. From the point of view of industry there is everything to be said for getting rid of the condition and saying, for example, that the post-war credit shall be repaid unconditionally after the end of the war either subject to a time limit of say not later than three years after the end of hostilities or without alteration of the existing statutory phrase.[19] This would largely get rid of the need to give any present consideration to the question of a reduction of the 100 per cent rate; it might, however, possibly have inconvenient reactions still to be looked into in regard to the income tax post-war credits, which are to be paid on a date (to be fixed by the Treasury) as soon as may be after the termination of hostilities.

8. We discussed also the question of the profit standard. At present businesses may take the year 1935 or 1936, or the average of either of those years with 1937, and every year that passes the standard gets more and more out of date. The history, I understand, is as follows. In April 1939 (before the war) there was introduced the armaments profits tax, an E.P.T. limited to munition firms. 1938 was ruled out and 1937 partially ruled out because in these years these firms were deriving benefit from the rearmament programme. When the E.P.T. was introduced at the outbreak of war it was felt necessary (largely no doubt on political grounds) to follow the same lines. It has been urged by some that after this lapse of time it might be possible to bring 1937 and 1938 fully into the standard (not retrospectively) without a political upset. It would benefit all firms who had good years in 1937 and 1938 and would do a good deal, I should say, to mitigate the extreme severity of the E.P.T. in a great many cases, though it would not,

---

[19] Sir Hubert Henderson has suggested the possibility of adding interest at a low rate for the period till the credit becomes payable.

of course, help new firms or the firms that were struggling in all the pre-war years.

9. We also had some rather inconclusive discussion on the question of increasing the percentage rate on capital (say from 6 to 8 per cent in the case of companies and from 8 to 10 per cent in the case of firms) to provide some mitigation in the last-named type of case.

10. In regard to all these leading matters my own feeling, which was shared by several of my colleagues, is that the next Budget, coming presumably at a time when the Second Front is either in being or widely expected, is not a natural time for dealing with any of them and that they would more appropriately wait for the end of hostilities with Germany, assuming that it is not greatly delayed. But Lord Catto, Lord Keynes and Sir Wilfrid Eady all suggest that it would be wise to get rid of the condition attaching to the post-war credit at once. I append Lord Keynes's note on this subject.

11. We discussed also a question which seems to present much less difficulty and could well be the subject of legislation now, namely the standard provided for small businesses with working proprietors. At present as an alternative to the ordinary profits standard or a percentage on capital employed, a minimum standard is available of £1,500 per working proprietor (with a limited right of increase in certain cases). It seemed to us that it would be both practicable and desirable to add to the £1,500 per working proprietor 8 per cent on all capital employed over £5,000 and that this might mitigate hardship in numerous cases. We also discussed the possibility of raising the minimum standard which applies to all businesses, namely £1,000, to some such figure as £2,000 or £3,000, which would remove from the sphere of the E.P.T. a large number of small cases. Several members of the Committee stressed the desirability of doing something in that sphere. Lord Keynes drew attention in particular to the fact that raising the minimum standard will do a good deal to meet the difficult case of the farmers (who were not subject to the E.P.D. in the last war). He adds: 'Nothing is more certain than that their business is entirely unsuited to E.P.T. applied down to a very small standard. But the same thing applies to most cases of modest profits, the greater part of which are probably earned by personal and individual enterprise and skill and not merely as a return to capital.'

R. N. V. H.

10 February 1944

Annex: Lord Keynes on the E.P.T. post-war credit
(paragraphs 6, 7 and 10 above)

Paragraph 10. I think these considerations might reasonably weigh against action forthwith under *all* the headings preceding it collectively. But it seems to me a very insufficient argument for doing nothing at all. This would be a continuation of the practice of carrying on a taxation policy, not based on merits, but on sentimental, or, if you like, political considerations. I believe that great evil has followed from the concessions that have already been made for these reasons, much more than is commonly realised. The fact that direct taxation has now passed the point which can be justified on merits is effecting a change in the psychology of the taxpayer, which, if it is not soon reversed, may become permanent. Everyone nowadays is concerned in rearranging his affairs so as to attract as little taxation as possible, and this, as a general, universally excused phenomenon, is something new in this country. I do not think that we shall do well to continue it without mitigation for another year. Our recent discussions concerning the stimulation of post-war exports indicate an exceedingly unsatisfactory business psychology, and I fancy that existing taxation is one of the important roots of that.

I feel that this is a particularly insufficient argument against action on the lines of your paragraphs 6 and 7. Here is something which may be of importance in improving the psychological situation and will not cost the Treasury a penny, on the assumption that we are definitely going to do this sooner or later. To put it off is a pure concession to misguided sentiment. Whilst, therefore, I should be prepared to agree that action all along the line, i.e. including *all* the proposals under discussion, might be politically inadvisable in a single step, I cannot believe that this would apply to action under 6, and also possibly action under 9 at the same time, leaving 8 alone for the time being.

Finally, I think it very doubtful whether the sentiment in question really does exist at the present time with any degree of intensity worth bothering about. The evils which everyone was anxious to avoid in 1940 have been avoided successfully, and there is now no risk that they will arise. The experiences of the last war have not in fact been repeated. I fancy that public opinion is quite aware that matters have been carried too far and would strongly welcome such mild and reasonable modifications as have been under discussion. A great deal to be said for acting on the merits of the case rather than to placate supposititious and possibly non-existent, anyway misguided, sentiment.

Keynes returned to E.P.T. in the 1945 Budget discussions.

E.P.T. AND CHANGES IN STOCK VALUES

I attach a copy of a forthcoming article in the *Economic Journal*[20] since it sets out the facts of the position and offers a remedy which seems to me to be satisfactory. (Those who lack leisure will have got the substance of the matter if they will read down to about the middle of the fourth galley.) My own brief comments are the following:–

(1) A remedy has already been enacted on the lines I have been suggesting in the U.S. and in France, and, I believe, in Sweden. If we also want to remain a private enterprise country, we must not kill the goose (which is what our tax system is doing), even though it is such a goose as not to be able to explain its sufferings in an intelligible human voice. The grievance, which is stated by business in terms of a shortage of working capital, would be expressed by an economist as the result of a deprivation of real resources through the mortal blows of taxation.

(2) A complete remedy at this late date is difficult and very

[20] K. Lacey, 'Commodity Stock Values and E.P.T.', *Economic Journal*, April 1945.

expensive. We need, therefore, to consider what partial remedies are open to us. I shall assume that business is in a position to provide the Revenue with the necessary accounting facts. But, for purposes of illustration, I shall, generally speaking, avoid the complication where there is a change in the volume as well as in the price of stocks.

If prices rise during the E.P.T. period from p_1 to p_2, if the quantity of stock is q_1, and if the whole of the stock is deemed to have been turned over in the last period, so that p_2 has been paid for all end stocks, the firm will have paid in E.P.T. $q_1(p_2-p_1)$, and it will have to borrow this sum or find it from other resources in order to hold its old volume of stocks q_1 at the new price p_2.

The remedy proposed by the Revenue is that if the price falls to p_3 within a stipulated period after the end of E.P.T., the firm can recover $q_1(p_2-p_3)$. If, during this period, prices return to their pre-war level, so that $p_3 = p_1$, this does the whole trick. If prices remain up, it is worth nothing. If they rise further, the position is still worse, since income tax will continue its depredations on the increased money valuation. (Under our present tax system a sufficient price rise would put all businesses out of action.)

My remedy is to refund $q_1(p_2-p_1)$, that is to allow the firm to continue to carry its stocks at the old price. (If the quantity of stocks has fallen to q_2, then I should make an immediate refund of only $q_2(p_2-p_1)$, but allow an appropriate tax reserve to be set up to be drawn upon if the stocks rise again to q_1 within a stipulated period.)

Is there any intermediate, partial remedy?

(a) We could start the new system in respect of any accounting period which ends after 1 April 1944, but not make it retrospective, whilst retaining the Revenue's remedy in the event of prices falling.

(b) We could establish standard prices not exceeding (say) 25 per cent above pre-war, allow firms to write down their present stocks and their accruing stocks for the next five years (up to the amount of their pre-war stocks) to this figure and recover the difference from E.P.T. (or income tax); and start the new system from 1 April 1945.

(*c*) We could refund a proportion of $q_1(p_2-p_1)$, say 50 per cent.

(*d*) We might refund only the excess of $q_1(p_2-p_1)$ over the 20 per cent E.P.T. credit.

Alternative (*b*) is the one which I find most attractive.

(3) It must be remembered that this problem arises acutely under high income tax as well as under E.P.T. Thus it is important to introduce a new system from henceforward, even if we cannot make it retrospective.

(4) The present system further inflates the revenue when prices are rising and further deflates it when they fall, thus acting as a counter-stabiliser.

KEYNES

16.1.45

Chapter 6

FINANCIAL MARKET POLICY

Before the outbreak of the war, the authorities had decided to buttress their chosen interest rate policy with a careful catering to the tastes and preferences of the market.[1] They had also decided that dear money would not be the most appropriate means of attracting from the general public the real resources necessary for the prosecution of the war. Keynes played a considerable part in preparing the climate of opinion underlying these decisions.[2]

The long-term rate of interest desired by the authorities in the context of these arrangements was 3 per cent, with appropriate adjustments for small savings and short-term issues. However, the first two major issues in March and June 1940 met with a meagre response from the public. In this situation, the authorities, given their emphasis on channels of finance and their belief that bank finance was almost immediately and peculiarly inflationary, might have lost their nerve and adopted a policy of dearer money. That they did not do so was to some extent the result of the strength of their commitment to a 3 per cent war, but the official historian of wartime financial policy continues:

> More important than this, however, in giving to the authorities the nerve to persist in their borrowing principles was the increasing influence of Keynes and other economists, both in discussions directly bearing on the borrowing programme and more generally in their illumination of the fundamental causes of war inflation.[3]

On this toughening of nerve in the late summer and early autumn of 1940, no single memorandum or recorded discussion proved influential.

However, there is one memorandum from this period which demonstrates how Keynes brought his intimate knowledge of the working of financial markets to bear on the problems of war finance.

[1] However, even as late as 1939, the Treasury did not have a coherent theory of the term structure of interest rates.
[2] See *JMK*, vol. XXI. Keynes also made some contributions after the outbreak of war to public discussions of the appropriate loan policy. See above, pp. 29–31,62–4.
[3] Sayers, *Financial Policy, 1939–1945*, p. 204.

STOCK EXCHANGE EQUITIES

In the quarter ending June 30 Government securities were very stable in face of the news, falling about 2 per cent. During the same period (according to the Investors' Chronicle index) other fixed interest securities fell from 119 to 100 and industrial ordinary shares from 98 to 66. By the end of June (to which the above relates) there had been some recovery compared with the middle of the month. Moreover the above is an *average*; and when an average has fallen by about a third, it means of course that many individual securities have fallen by a half or more. At the bottom the shares of many important and highly reputed companies were selling on a 10–13 per cent yield basis after allowing for the probable incidence of 100 per cent E.P.T.

This collapse is to be attributed to the effect of very adverse news coming on the top of certain other, less inevitable, factors of which the most important were probably the following:–

(i) The greater imminence and probability of severe air raids against this country caused a belated appreciation of the fact that equity owners had no defined compensation against war damage. The uncertainty of the position led to an unwillingness to assume any new risks, with the result that aeroplane companies, for example, which were naturally supposed to be particuarly vulnerable, sold at a price which seemed to discount the destruction of all their uninsurable property without compensation (even to-day prices in this group are not much better). The hesitation of private investors was further accentuated, as always happens in such circumstances, by the apparent reluctance of professional investors (including the jobbers) to support the market; for this shook the confidence of the private investor, who was otherwise inclined to buy, in his own judgment.

The factors influencing the professional investors are given below. But apart from these temporary influences, it is difficult to see how the Stock Exchange market in equities could continue to function in the event of significant war damage. For details of war damage are not to be published, so that those in the neighbourhood will be in the possession of information which shareholders and the market generally will not have. Indeed, it might be held that even the publication of Stock Exchange quotations might furnish useful information to the enemy. For if a particular aeroplane factory, or power station or a plant of Imperial Chemicals is heavily damaged, this will become apparent in the fall of the affected shares.

It is not easy to see the solution of this problem. A more satisfactory compensation scheme would mitigate the difficulty, but would not solve it completely. I do not think that the case for a new compensation scheme can be made to depend, except secondarily, on the advantage to Stock Exchange stability. The most one can say is that a better compensation scheme might put off the day when the proposal made immediately below would be necessary. There may, therefore, be no way out except to suspend dealings in home industrial equities if and when the campaign from the air takes on a really serious aspect. This need not embrace even a majority of Stock Exchange securities;—Government and municipal securities, all overseas securities, and many fixed interest home securities could continue to be dealt in. The exact contents of the list to be suspended needs a little thinking out, since it should probably include near-equities as well as actual equities. I suggest that a list should be carefully prepared before-hand, the suspension of dealing in which could be put into force without delay if necessary.

(ii) The attitude of professional investors was considerably influenced by two other events which happened fortuitously more or less at the same time.

The first was the complete immobilisation of all American

securities. This chiefly affected the investment trusts who found themselves suddenly deprived of the use of what they had regarded as their most liquid assets. The wideness of quotations made switches within the British market impracticable, and they were not able to give out low supporting limits, as they might have done otherwise, against the prospective sales of Americans. Thus at the critical moment they found themselves suddenly deprived of buying power. This, however, was a purely temporary prohibition, imposed for special reasons, which has now been removed.

(iii) The second was of a more fundamental character.

It happened that just at that time there was a meeting with representatives of insurance institutions at which they were officially pressed to apply *all* their available liquid resources to the purchase of Government securities. This was followed up by a circular letter to all insurance offices from the Chairman of the British Insurance Association to the same general effect but leaving it ambiguous as to whether this injunction applied to their net increment of income (which would apply chiefly to life offices) or to all cash, however accruing, as, for example, from the sale or repayment of existing securities. As a result most insurance companies cancelled all their outstanding limits to buy, which happened to withdraw support from the market just at the moment when it was most needed.

Subsequently some oral assurances were given to some of the London companies which resulted in their resuming operations on a small scale. But there has been no revised elucidation in writing of the above letter which still remains the semi-official instruction. The Edinburgh companies, for example, do not know how they stand, having received no fresh guidance, and are still out of the market.

It is evident that the insurance offices want nothing more than to follow loyally the wishes of the Treasury—if only they knew what they were. It is for the Treasury to decide whether they wish the insurance offices to support the market outside Government securities (in so far as, left to themselves, they are inclined to do so, having regard to all the risks); or not. The offices can be relied on to act accordingly.

Now this raises a fundamental question. Is the purchase of non-British Government securities on the Stock Exchange disadvantageous to the Treasury's borrowing programme and something from which a whole-hearted patriot will consider it to be his duty to refrain?

This is a question of far wider concern than for the insurance offices only. If it is against the public interest for them to purchase non-Government securities, it is equally so for any private person. Indeed many private persons are already in doubt where their duty lies; and this hesitation is a contributory cause to the weakness of the market.

An extreme example of the view that any employment of funds outside Government securities is undesirable was supplied by Sir Robert Kindersley last week when he endeavoured to persuade the public over the wireless that anyone who left a large balance with his bankers was doing a thoroughly unpatriotic thing as compared with lending it to the nation for 2½% or 3%. Was Sir Robert's advice in the interests of the Treasury? Or was he chiefly interested in the propaganda value of certain statistics at the cost to the Treasury of their having to pay 2½% for funds which they would obtain otherwise at 1%?

Thus it is of real importance to clear our minds. If investment in the Stock Exchange outside Government securities is, at the best, the indulgence of a mildly vicious propensity, comparable perhaps with scrounging timber to build a summer-house or using petrol for frivolous purposes, is it advisable to keep such opportunities open? If it is unpatriotic to buy shares (and, on the other hand, patriotic, presumably, to sell them), to keep the Stock Exchange open is merely to provide an opportunity for the selfish to make a profit at the expense of more patriotic people. And in proportion as the wishes of the Treasury and a sense of duty prevail, prices will sink towards zero.

My own analysis leads to a different conclusion, as follows:–

(1) We now have *a closed market*, which is unable to obtain an increased supply of securities either from new issues within the country or from any outside source. This makes an essential difference. It means that the prices at which existing securities change hands cannot attract new issues which will compete with the Government for command over real resources. Thus from this point of view transactions in non-British Government securities are entirely harmless.

(2) Can such transactions affect unfavourably the *terms* on which the Government can borrow? If individuals are influenced to offer their resources to the Government as the only proper outlet for them, this makes it easier for the Treasury to offer terms which bear no relation to market conditions. But so long as the market remains open, a generally low level of Stock Exchange prices is bound to have *some* depressing influence on Government stocks, which it is difficult to ignore in making a new issue. The recent level of Stock Exchange prices generally has somewhat worsened, rather than otherwise, the terms on which the Treasury could expect to issue a funded loan.

(3) Our whole emphasis should be on the curtailment of consumption and not less (here our propaganda has been much less definite) on the avoidance of postponable or unessential expenditure on repairs, renewals and improvements of a capital nature. It matters a great deal if we use up resources in these ways; financial transactions which do not involve, directly or indirectly, an increased use of physical resources are quite innocent.

Thus the depression of the Stock Exchange only serves a useful purpose if it inhibits some private expenditure of the above character. It probably has some effect in this direction.

A man will be more unwilling to sell out stocks in order to maintain his accustomed standards of consumption or to maintain and improve his durable assets if they are fetching a very poor price. In ordinary times the level of Stock Exchange prices has a considerable influence on private expenditure both on consumption and on durable assets. But in present circumstances I do not believe that this factor is of decisive importance or indeed of any significant importance as an argument for keeping the Stock Exchange unduly depressed (though it is a good argument for preventing the sort of boom which occurred in the last war). Moreover it is equally an argument for keeping the gilt-edged market depressed. And if this factor is of decisive importance, it would be much better to close the Stock Exchange altogether, particularly as it is no longer needed for the purpose of absorbing new issues. To keep the Stock Exchange open and then to make as sure as possible that quotations shall be at a bankrupt level is to get the worst of all worlds.

(4) To preserve confidence and credit, and to allow the smooth completion of transactions and the winding up of debts, including the flow of funds into Government stocks, a reasonable level of Stock Exchange prices is even more important than in normal times. It is also desirable that the quotations used for the purpose of balance-sheet valuations should be in reasonable relation to real values.

(5) Depressed prices on the Stock Exchange are decidedly adverse to the collection of revenue. Death duties and stamps are the most obvious examples of this. But I am not sure that the effect on income tax through investment profits is not the most important. There are several exceptions to the general rule that capital losses and profits are not taken into account by our income tax system. Those who are reckoned as professional investors, which includes all insurance businesses (except life) and all financial businesses (except strict investment trusts) have to bring into current profits currently

399

realised profits and losses on securities. This means, when prices are very depressed, that large relief from income tax and E.P.T. can be obtained by anyone who is classified as a professional investor, not merely by outright sales but also by exchanging one depressed security for another.

I conclude that a considerable balance of advantage lies in maintaining liquidity for securities at a reasonable price-level; from which it follows that those who have the pluck in these anxious and risk ridden times to support the market in equities are performing a public service.

At any rate, the first step is for the authorities to decide whether or not they accept this conclusion. If not, then I am sure it would be better to close the Stock Exchange wholly or in part. Indeed the argument for keeping the Stock Exchange open is not *very* strong, since it no longer fulfils the function of helping to absorb new issues. A highly depressed Stock Exchange, with quotations out of relation to real values and to a cool judgment of risks, is much worse for confidence and credit than no Stock Exchange at all.

If, however, the above conclusion is accepted, then some public expression of the official view would be helpful. Nevertheless any such expression of opinion should be very carefully guarded. For the average man will not readily understand the peculiar conditions of a closed market and may easily be shocked or draw false conclusions. I suggest something on the following lines—perhaps in answer to a question in the House of Commons asking for guidance on behalf of investment institutions:–

'In the absence of any new issues (except those specially approved) and with the recent complete prohibition of the sale of foreign-owned securities in this country, there is no longer a risk of Stock Exchange transactions leading to a net absorption of funds which would otherwise flow into War Loans. Provided that individuals will economise to the utmost extent both in personal expenditure and in postponable repairs, renewals and improvements of a kind not essential to the war, the Exchequer can rely in present conditions on receiving these savings directly or indirectly. Thus provided individuals are strict in not selling securities for the purpose of maintaining their expenditure, it is in the public interest that Stock Exchange transactions should continue at prices which bear a reasonable relation to real values. Investment institutions, and others who are in a position to do so with full appreciation of the risks involved will, therefore, be performing a public service if they support the market in equities. The maintenance of the liquidity of the market at a reasonable level of values is in the interest of the Exchequer and will facilitate the financing of the war. At the same time most private individuals will be well advised in present circumstances to leave this task to those specially qualified for it, and to put all their savings into one or other of the currently issued War Loans or Savings Schemes.'

To sum up, I suggest

(1) A definite scheme of compensation against war damage,

(2) the preparation of a list of securities, transactions in which will be suspended if the campaign from the air takes on a new character,

(3) a public statement by the Chancellor for the guidance of investment institutions and others.

I doubt if much more than this is feasible or advisable, short of a much more drastic scheme whereby in effect the Government itself supports the market at a minimum level.

J. M. KEYNES

22 July 1940

Keynes's memoranda on borrowing policy throughout the war demonstrate the same intimate knowledge of financial markets. But with the exception of his suggestion for tax reserve certificates, his minutes and memoranda were perhaps more important for their cumulative effect than for their impact at their time of writing. However, some of them from the summer of 1941 onwards, which argued in favour of a more sophisticated catering to market preferences, provide an indication of Keynes's approach to wartime monetary management.

Tax reserve certificates provided the first important instance of Keynes's emphasis on catering to the tastes of the market. On 17 July 1941, while in America,[4] Keynes sent the following memorandum home to London.[5]

TAX ANTICIPATION NOTES

The attached papers describe a scheme adopted by the Treasury here which is, I think, worth looking at from our point of view.

They are, you will see, issuing notes available for direct taxes which carry a modest rate of interest if used for that purpose, but can be turned into cash at notice if not used for that purpose at the cost of forfeiting the interest. The proposal has had an exceptionally good press and has been much welcomed by the public and by business. The Treasury department here defend it (a) as a concession to the taxpayer which it is not unreasonable to allow him when taxes reach so high a level, and (b) as a means of comforting the Federal Reserve Board by improving an apparent bank credit situation. They agree that the second argument is appearances only, since the bulk of the balances used to purchase these notes would otherwise have been dormant.

There has, I believe, been a certain demand on the part of the public or, at any rate, on the part of firms for some similar concession on our part, and it would probably be popular. I suggest that it is worth considering. If the rate of interest paid is not more than the interest on bankers' deposit receipts, there is nothing lost in the interest. In our case, too,

---

[4] On this visit, see *JMK*, vol XXIII.

[5] An American Treasury scheme for special Treasury notes acceptable with interest for tax payments, or repayable in cash without interest, had been announced on 3 July.

it would improve appearances by reducing the volume of bank deposits. At the same time it would be a mild mitigation to firms suffering heavy taxation.

Moreover, apart from such minor arguments, it is well worth while giving some slight encouragement with the object of making sure that tax accruals are hoarded during the interim between accrual and payment over to the Exchequer.

The U.S. Treasury tell me (1) that they have not made these tax bills eligible for the payment of death duties. They think they will probably allow them for this later on. I see no special reason why death duties should be excluded in our case; (2) interest earned is returnable as income for tax purposes and is liable for income tax. Perhaps in our case we might allow for income tax at the standard rate in the rate of interest allowed and allow the interest accrual to be free of surtax and E.P.T.

In our own case I suggest:–

(1) There should only be one series, corresponding to the American series of higher denomination, and that there should be no limit on the amount a given individual or firm holds. Income tax is now deducted at source so predominantly that there could scarcely be much demand for the smaller series for income tax purposes. But, of course, there would be no harm in such a series if there were a demand for it.

(2) The U.S. Treasury fixed ½ per cent as appropriate to their prevailing rates of interest. In our case the appropriate rate might be 2d per month per £10, that is to say, 1 per cent per annum (or ½ if free of income tax). The table prepared by the U.S. Treasury, which is in the hands of all the local tax authorities and is, I think, printed on the back of the notes, reduces intricate calculation to a minimum. If a $25 note is purchased any time in February 1942 the purchaser pays $25.24 for it. If he turns it in to pay tax any time in November

1942, he is credited with $25.60. If he does not use it for tax purposes and turns it in ultimately for cash, he will receive his original purchase price of $25.24.

(3) The notes might be available to meet income tax, surtax, excess profit tax, etc., death duties and perhaps purchase tax.

(4) It would be a convenient method of which members of the public who wish to lend money to the government free of interest could avail themselves.

(5) We might possibly allow the interest to hold good, even if turned in for cash and not used for tax purposes, if the notes are held for a full two years. But in this case it would have to be liable for surtax and E.P.T. (It would be easy to provide that the interest was surtax-free when the notes were turned in for tax purposes, but not otherwise.)

I have discussed this with Bewley[6] and Phillips, and their comments are embodied in the text.

Sustained discussion of Keynes's suggestions awaited his return from America and the clearing up of other matters. However, by mid-September discussion was in full swing. Keynes provided a more extensive justification for his proposals in a minute dated 15 September, large portions of which went into the final Treasury memorandum for the Chancellor on the proposal.

To SIR RICHARD HOPKINS, *15 September 1941*

TAX NOTES

(copies to Lord Catto and Mr Brittain)

Mr Brittain's Note (below)[7] is very interesting and instructive. At this stage it will be more useful for me to examine the substance of the proposal on its merits and not to take up the points of administrative detail discussed by Mr Brittain, except to mention the two points following:–

[6] Thomas Kenneth Bewley (1890–1943); entered Treasury, 1913; seconded to Irish Free State Ministry of Finance, 1922–3; Financial Adviser, H.M. Embassy, Washington, 1933–9; Principal Assistant Secretary, Treasury, 1940–3.
[7] Not printed [Ed.].

(1) The proposal only overlaps to a small extent with the present arrangements for pre-paying Schedule D income tax under discount.[8] For this only covers the period between the assessment and the due date of that particular tax receipt.

(2) The proposal does not affect the distribution of tax receipts between one financial year and another, since the proceeds of the tax notes outstanding would not be brought in as tax receipts but would be treated like any other part of the floating debt.

The main argument in favour of such notes is of a window-dressing character. Nevertheless the window-dressing in question is worth appreciably more than mere appearances since it promotes order and regularity in the financial system and avoids a source of serious misunderstanding. The argument runs as follows:—

(1) Now that income tax is mainly collected at source, the proposal has very little interest for individuals apart from surtax payers. It mainly relates to companies and business undertakings paying income tax and E.P.T. on their profits.

(2) The income tax and E.P.T. payable by business accrues on the average from 9 to 18 months before it is due. Formerly many firms used to take advantage of this time-lag to accumulate the tax due appreciably later than the profits to which it is strictly related. But with high and changing taxes based on fluctuating profits this sometimes led to embarrassment; and in the last few years it has become sound accounting practice to reserve the accruing tax out of the accruing profits to which it strictly relates.

(3) This change of practice, coupled with the rise in the standard rate of tax and the addition of E.P.T., has caused an enormous increase in the sums reserved in balance sheets for future taxation, so enormous that it must greatly impress anyone who has been in the habit of reading any large number

8   Pre-payment of Schedule D income tax had been allowed since 1842. The discount available in 1941 was 2½ per cent, a level fixed in 1889. [Ed.]

of such documents. It appears to be very usual to hold a large part of the sums thus reserved as a bank deposit.

(4) The increase in the amount of the sums so held at certain times of year is so great that it may be said to have changed the character and not merely the degree of the problem. It now dominates our banking statistics and involves so large a seasonal change as to make them intelligible only with much difficulty and after conjectural adjustments. I believe that this effect is much larger than it was in the last war, because at that time Treasury bills carried so high a rate of discount that it was worth the while of large businesses to take the trouble to earn it. With the present low rate of discount, the large size of the unit (£5,000, I think) and the trouble of replacement every three months make Treasury bills more trouble than they are worth, and they are not held outside the financial system on the same scale as in the last war.

(5) In the current year income tax, surtax and E.P.T. are estimated to yield £900 million and may easily be accruing at a rate of £100 million or more ahead of this. At certain times of year the unpaid sums accrued probably exceed £500 million. The great increase in the sums held by companies against accruing taxation is, I believe, a large part of the explanation of the recent substantial increase in bank deposits which have been as follows:-

		£ million
Average	1938	2,277
Average	1939	2,248
Average	1940	2,506
End June	1941	2,946
August	1941	2,997

Now to most people these figures have a highly inflationary air, especially as national income is no longer increasing by any important amount. If (say) £200 million could be taken out of the August return by subscriptions to tax notes (and the actual subscription might easily exceed this in course of time), the position would look much better and would also be nearer the facts. There is already a disposition abroad due to various causes to exaggerate the strength of the existing inflationary tendency. It is, therefore, of real importance to exclude misleading accretions from the published figures.

(6) Tax notes at 1 per cent would probably save the Exchequer some interest. Of the £500 million additional deposits, held by the banks at the end of August 1941 compared with the average of 1940, £150 million was put into additional investments (after allowing for the increase of investments to offset the reduction in advances). Thus the bank deposits which the tax notes would replace are costing the Treasury fully 1½ per cent on the average (70 per cent at 1⅛ per cent interest and 30 per cent at 2½ per cent interest).

(7) The heavy seasonal disturbance of the banking system through tax collections in the first quarter of the calendar year would be mitigated.

(8) The healthy practice of specifically reserving against accruing taxes would receive some slight encouragement, especially if the taking up of tax notes for this purpose was furthered by propaganda and official advice. Many firms might prefer, in part at least, the complete liquidity of the tax notes to the National War Bonds to which they now subscribe because they are told it is their duty. This would be doubly to the good. For it would save interest. And, whilst in the case of individuals there may be a good deal in the Kindersley argument that it is wholesome for them to get tied up in a permanent security which they will not liquidate so readily as they would spend out of a bank deposit, it is certainly the other way round in the case of the funds of a company which will be required at no distant date to pay taxes or some other unavoidable and necessary purpose, where it is undesirable that resources which ought to be liquid would purport to be tied up.

(9) Finally I come to the *mere* window-dressing side of the proposal. I believe that the total effect of all the above on appearances would have appreciable propaganda and expository value; that it would avoid misleading statements; and that this addition to our outfit would look sensible and workmanlike.

1 per cent tax notes,

2 per cent Exchequer bonds 1945/46

2½ per cent savings bonds 1953/55

3 per cent savings bonds 1955/65

looks economical, tidy and complete, which has in itself a real value for our financial morale.

(10) To judge from American experience, the move would be popular and have a good press. It appears anti-inflationary, mitigates arguments about the serious time-lag of taxation, gives some published indication of the prevalence of a sound and highly desirable business practice, and offers some slight reward for it. I am not aware of any substantial objection on the other side. The worst that can be said of the proposal is that it is not really necessary and a bit fussy.

J. M. K.

15.9.41

He also continued throughout the discussions to provide suggestions on detailed points of practice and drafting right up to their announcement by the Chancellor on 16 December, successfully pressing for their applicability to payments in such areas as the War Damage Act but failing in the case of death duties.

Keynes's many contributions to discussions of wartime borrowing policy almost entirely post-date his appointment as a Director of the Bank of England following the death of Lord Stamp in an air raid. Three of the notes Keynes received at the time provide a good sample of the many he received.[9]

[9] The appointment was announced on 18 September, although the formal election did not occur until 8 October.

FINANCIAL MARKET POLICY

Note handed to Keynes by MONTAGU NORMAN, *on 5 September 1941*

With the goodwill and future support of the Chancellor—

J.M.K. to be invited at once to join the Court: his acceptance to be announced at the General Court on September 18th and a special election, to fill the Stamp vacancy, to be held immediately afterwards.

He would join as an ordinary Director, with the same freedom and same limitations as others.

He would be expected to break off all official or published relations with Whitehall.

But unofficially he could continue to be at the disposal of the Chancellor or Treasury. Indeed, the change in his position might be in form rather than in fact.

From GERALD SHOVE, *20 September 1941*

My dear Maynard,

Well, well, well...Another of the forts of folly fallen. What a triumph. One almost begins to believe that there is some hope for the world after all. But nobody but you could have brought it off. Take care of yourself.

Yours,
Gerald

From JOAN ROBINSON, *19 September 1941*

My dear Maynard,

I am much tickled—as you may suppose. I fear you will soon be a KCB and quite lost. But never mind, I will always say you were grand while you lasted.

Yours,
Joan

I am hoping to have some figs to send next week.

To JOAN ROBINSON, *24 September 1941*

My dear Joan,

There is life in this dog yet, and I am glad to find that you still care a fig for him. Look on me hopefully as fifth column.

Yours,
J.M.K.

Keynes's first long memorandum on loan policy came during the period after his return to America in 1941.

LOAN POLICY

1. The interim period, following on the withdrawal of the 2½% bonds, was readily accepted by the financial press on the assumption that it was merely a breathing space before something better; and it has been successful in attaining the object of unfreezing the two recent series of National War Bonds and in allowing the market, relieved of the pressure of one of the two, to resume its upward movement. But the interim must, presumably, be brought to an end within a month from now.

2. If the following premises be accepted:–

(i) that movements of ¼% in the nominal rate of interest are unpopular and inconvenient, so that there is nothing between 2½% and 3%;

(ii) that the new loan or loans must be on better terms than the old from the Treasury point of view;

(iii) that some maturity shorter than the present 3% savings bonds is necessary to satisfy the popular taste and to absorb semi-liquid resources from industry and the banking system;

(iv) that it is undesirable to crowd unduly the dates of existing maturities;

(v) that the price must be in fairly close conformity with market conditions and not try to hustle them unduly;

(vi) that it is too soon to experiment with fancy loans (I will expound the only one which attracts me in a separate paper); the conclusion follows without much room for argument. For, broadly speaking, there are only two types of issues one can propose which satisfy all these conditions, namely:– 2½% savings bonds 1953/55 at 97; 2% Exchequer bonds 1945/46 at 100.

There has been a prejudice lately against issuing a loan

below par.[10] But this is a new-fangled objection which has, so far as I can see, no real justification. Moreover if a 2¾ % issue is ruled out, we no longer have any choice. And so far as the public is concerned, an issue below par will be popular since it gives some degree of insurance against a subsequent depreciation below the issue price and a certainty of a slight eventual appreciation.

3. I suggest, therefore, the following programme:–

(a) For the savings campaign:– 3 % savings bonds 1955/65 at par, as at present; 2½ % savings bonds 1953/55 at 97.

The campaign would be limited to these, in addition to N.S.C. and defence bonds, and would not concern itself with the issues under (b) below.

(b) For the banks, the money market and business to absorb semi-liquid funds, where security of capital is important in the event of early liquidation being necessary: 2 % Exchequer bonds 1945/46 at par; 1 % tax bonds.

I am developing the proposal for tax bonds on the American model in a separate paper.

4. The only 'extras' I suggest are the following:–

(i) A simultaneous announcement that the 3 % savings bonds will be withdrawn after some stated maximum has been subscribed—say £500 million, and that thereafter no further issues will be made during the course of the war which give a gross yield to redemption of as much as 3 %.

(ii) The 2 % Exchequer bonds to be accepted in payment of death duties at par *plus* accrued interest.

(iii) Treasury deposit receipts to be transferable only into the Exchequer bonds and not into either type of savings bonds, so as to push the banks into these in so far as they further increase their holdings outside the floating debt.

---

[10] At the time issues at a discount were meeting with two objections: (a) that the discount might irrationally be regarded as a reflection on the Government's credit; (b) the implied offer of capital appreciation free of tax for the rich investor might provoke embarrassing criticism. It was the second objection which Keynes referred to here. [Ed.]

5. We need contemplate no further material change in this programme during the rest of the war. The 3% savings bonds would be withdrawn in due course as proposed above. The dates of the 2½% savings bonds and the 2% Exchequer bonds would be advanced a year from time to time, and the price of the former gradually advanced towards par (which would also allow the maturity dates to be brought forward instead of advanced, if desired) should market conditions permit.   J.M.K.

15.9.41

In the period following Keynes kept up a stream of short minutes on the terms of new issues. At first his emphasis lay in the direction of issuing irredeemable securities at 3 per cent. When this proved unsuccessful, he reverted to the idea of a long stock with redemption possible over a longer period than was normally the case. This too was unsuccessful.

However, from the summer of 1942 onwards most of his efforts were directed towards a series of issues which would attract relatively short-dated money. The first extensive development of the proposal, other than the passing reference in the September 1941 memorandum above, came in June 1942.

NATIONAL WAR BONDS

1. There is still room, I think, in spite of what Mr Brittain says, for another 2½ per cent series of slightly longer maturity. (I make out that the 3 per cent conversion, 1948/53, at 103³⁄₁₆ has a gross equivalent net redemption yield of just under 2½ per cent.) A series of 2½ per cent bonds due 1951/53 would be quite in line with the market.

2. Nevertheless, I am much attracted by Mr Brittain's suggestion in his last paragraph, namely, a short interval with nothing on offer except 3 per cent savings bonds, followed by a short term 2 per cent issue. A 2 per cent issue with a five year maturity would not really be out of line with the market (the N.W.B. 2½ per cent 1945/47 has a gross equivalent

net redemption yield of only £2 3s). Nevertheless, I think Mr Brittain is right to suggest a four-year maturity, which would leave room for a five-year maturity perhaps a bit later on.

I suggest that there is an important argument in favour of such an issue, quite apart from the saving in the rate of interest. Businesses are now acquiring rather a large volume of National War Bonds having a final date maturity from 1947 onwards. They may also hold some Conversion 2 per cents, but probably little or nothing strictly short-dated. This is liable to be a menace to the gilt-edged market after the war, when they will be liquidating these bonds freely in order to replenish their working capital. It is very important that they should have some suitable stuff to dispose of which will not depreciate the gilt-edged market generally. In so far as they hold N.W.B. of 1945/47, that, by the time they want to use it, will be short enough to do no harm. But it is not too wholesome that they should be acquiring large quantities of the current issue of N.W.B. of 1949/51. The same thing applies to the banks. Undoubtedly they will have to liquidate a large volume of their gilt-edged investments when their advances recover to a normal figure. It is important that they should have plenty of stuff falling into this category which, by the time they want to sell it, is short enough to create no market disturbance.

Thus, it seems to me a fault in the present set-up that there are so few maturities in 1944, 1945 and 1946. Indeed, none of the tap issues during the war mature in these years. Thus, I believe a four year 2 per cent bond maturing near the end of 1946 would serve a doubly useful purpose. I should like to see businesses which are acquiring temporary liquid resources having them embarked in that sort of maturity rather than war bonds not due until 1951, or, still worse, in 1953. From one point of view the Treasury is, of course, always anxious to have its maturities as distant as possible. But for the management of the gilt-edged market after the war I think it will be not less important to have a sufficient supply of relatively short stuff. The gilt-edged market can only be kept good by allowing holders to be just as liquid as they feel disposed to be. I was partly in favour of tax reserve certificates because they tended in the right direction. It is not as though, as in the last war, Treasury bills were widely held outside the banks and the money market. So I believe the technical task of keeping the gilt-edged market straight after the war will be made easier, and not more difficult, by having a sufficiency of maturities in the early years.

J.M.K.

23.6.41

He returned to the issue, again unsuccessfully, in three memoranda in October 1942. The first and third in the series are of particular interest.[11]

THE GILT-EDGED MARKET

The attached statement of stocks and yields[12] shows that the Governor's view that we have no clear year except 1946 is based on the assumption that the outstanding war bonds are always redeemed at the latest of the optional dates. It does not seem to me that one need assume this. For it will almost certainly pay the Treasury to redeem at an earlier date. Otherwise they will in effect be paying 2½ per cent on a very short loan.

If a 2 per cent issue is introduced, something to be said for not giving it a single date of redemption, though undoubtedly this would somewhat diminish its attractions. I should be inclined to call the date 1946–47. It would obviously pay the Treasury to redeem 2½ per cent war bonds ahead of the 2 per cent issue, if the optional dates of redemption overlap.

You will see from the yield table how attractive a 2 per cent

[11] The second was a commentary on a note by Sir Richard Hopkins outlining the views of the Governor of the Bank [Ed.].
[12] Not printed [Ed.].

issue would be to anyone who is not a dealer in stocks. For the purpose of a bank or similar institution it is the gross redemption yield which is relevant. The table shows that for such institutions a 2 per cent issue would barely compete with some of the existing issues. (Perhaps its attraction would have to lie in a single fixed date of redemption.) But for a private holder or an industrial business, which is not reckoned by the Revenue as a dealer in securities, it is the net redemption yield which matters. The net redemption yield on a new 2 per cent issue at par would be 1 per cent, which is nearly double the present yield on the Conversion 2 per cents, and better than the National War Bonds 1945/47, without allowing for the fact that it would be free of commission and jobbers' turn, which on such short-dated securities reduce quite significantly the yield as calculated in the table, which is reckoned on middle prices without any allowance for expenses.

KEYNES

1.10.42

LONG AND SHORT BORROWING

There seems to me to be in evidence a perceptible, though at present slight, hardening of short-dated securities against long-dated. No doubt this is partly due to what we have already discussed, namely, the relative shortage of supply of the truly short-dated compared with long-dated.

But there is, I think, already another factor at work which may increase very considerably as we get nearer to the end of the war. It is commonly held, if not as probable at any rate as possible, that the present official control of the market, by which the long-term rate of interest is kept down to 3 per cent, will weaken in post-war conditions. Just as people used to believe that the outbreak of war would be the signal for a weakening of the long-term gilt-edged market, so they now tend to believe that the outbreak of peace will have that effect.

415

Since the amount of interest one can earn in the next two or three years after deduction of tax (particularly the difference between the amount one can earn on long-dated as compared with short-dated stock) yields a negligible sinking fund against possible prospective depreciation, there is a certain move to get into short-term securities, not merely by business firms who need to be short, but also by, e.g. insurance companies, who do not expect to need the money but who are anxious to avoid possible depreciation.

If this is correct it follows that if we are to maintain a 3 per cent rate for long-dated securities for the rest of the war, we shall have to expect a steady hardening of the shorts. We can keep this within narrow bounds by meeting the market and supplying them at, e.g. a 2 per cent rate, with a particular maturity for which they have a fancy. But if we do not feed the market then I should predict that the short-term stocks will steadily appreciate in relation to the longs until it will be impossible for us to issue such a stock at so high a rate as 2 per cent without departing widely from market conditions and causing rather a shock. If, therefore, we want to avoid unduly cheap money, it is important to feed the market at the present level with a view to keeping the market round about that level before it has had time to run away from us.

23.10.42   KEYNES

In July 1943 Keynes again raised the subject as the occasion for a new tap issue again came round. Again his suggestion of a short-dated issue was not followed, nor was his suggestion under (1). However, his views regarding a 1960-70 issue accorded with the final decision of the authorities.

To H. BRITTAIN, *27 July 1943*

TAP ISSUES

There are three questions here:–

(1) Should the existing 2½ per cent N.W.B. be continued for some time yet?

(2) Should they be either supplanted or supplemented by a 2 per cent issue?

(3) Should the savings bonds be supplanted by a bond with a longer period, say, to 1965–75?

In answer to (1) I should agree that there is no reason why the 1951–53 series should not raise a much larger total than they have yet reached. In view of the difficulty of substituting in the near future a similar bond of a slightly more distant date, there certainly seems good reason for carrying on with these bonds as they stand.

In answer to (2) I have, as you know, felt for a long time past that we are rather wasting money by not having a 2 per cent loan of a maturity which the market in fact wants. A five or six year bond would take money from the 2½'s and not, I should have thought, from Treasury bills or T.D.R.'s. I should be inclined, therefore, quite soon and before the 2½'s of 51–53 had run their full course, to introduce a 2 per cent with a single date in 1949, which would probably be successful, although it would, in the first instance, slightly exceed five years. The nearer we get to the end of the war, the stronger will be the appetite for an issue with a definite, early date. The way to protect the longer-dated issues will be to satisfy this demand. The only question to my mind is whether perhaps it should not be put off for another three months. The only argument against this is a certain loss of interest in the meantime. But I hope that we may agree to issue such a bond very early in 1944 at latest. I believe that its existence will help to protect the rest of the market.

In answer to (3), my difficulty here is that I consider a 1965–75 maturity less advantageous to the Treasury than a 1960–70 maturity. For I should hope in the next twenty years to be in a position to convert every issue open to conversion to a 2½ per cent basis. I do not think that the power to keep the issue out until 1975 is a compensation for forfeiting the right to convert it until 1965. As an investor, I should certainly be willing to pay a higher price for a 1965–75 bond than for a 1960–70 bond, which in point of date is neither one thing nor the other. I should prefer, therefore, to continue the existing series of 1960–70. There is such a wide margin of dates for the conversion operation that there is no obvious reason why this issue should not reach £1,000 million, or even more, whereas at present it has not yet reached £600 million.

I agree with you that most of the subscribers would take a 1965–75 bond as readily as a 1960–70 bond. But then, as you see, I don't think that that would be to our advantage. (In fact, it only could be to our advantage if a five-year bond in 1970 was carrying a full 3 per cent rate of interest.)

Should we not clear our minds of the idea that a more distant date of redemption is always better than a nearer date? As long as twenty- or thirty-year maturities carry a higher rate than, say, ten-year maturities (the factors covering really liquid maturities are rather different), one can safely conclude that the general expectation is in favour of future rates of interest being higher than at present. We shall not have fully mastered the position until the opposite expectation prevails, namely that the future rate of interest is more likely to go down than up. When that point is reached the more distant maturities will become popular and, for example, old Consols and Redemption 3's will give a lower yield than, say, Funding 2½ per cent, which is not the case at present. As soon as the expectation prevails that the future rate of interest is more likely to be 2½ per cent than 3 per cent, then the public will seek to assure themselves of 3 per cent for as long a term of years as possible. I should be reluctant to assist them to enrich themselves in this way by giving them a stock which cannot be converted before a date more than 20 years hence.

27.7.43   KEYNES

In the end, however, the authorities turned to the shorter end of the market when they announced an issue of 1¾ per cent Exchequer bonds 1950 in November 1944.[13]

To R. H. BRAND

I was delighted to see this piece of news. For some time past I have been arguing for an issue along these lines. The Bank of England, whilst not fundamentally opposed, was, under the late Governor, inclined to put the date of issue off on the ground that the time had not yet come for it. I suppose matters have been brought to a head by the fact that the dates of maturity for the various 2½ per cent bonds are now getting rather congested. But a contributory cause may also be the fact that Catto was, I know, much more sympathetic to early developments on these lines.

I hope this will be followed up before long by reducing the Treasury bill rate to half per cent. This would have the effect

---

[13] He also raised the matter with Sir Richard Hopkins in a letter dated 6 November (*JMK*, vol. XIV). On the circumstances surrounding the issue, Sir Wilfrid Eady informed Keynes on 15 November: 'I was interested to see your little comment on the 1¾ % in your personal letter to Hoppy of the 6th. As you say the main effect was intended to be psychological, and we won the Governor over to supporting us. All the experts in the City were against us. The first result of course was a very marked increase in the investment in the 2½'s, something quite phenomenal. But so far the investment in the 1¾ has gone rather slowly, and Peppiatt* looks at me with an "I told you so" look. Brittain and I agree that the next major question is an attack on the rate for Treasuries and T.D.R.'s. The volume of T.D.R.'s is so huge that there is no need at all for us to pay 1⅛ for them. Whether we can pull off one-half for the Bills and 7/8ths for the T.D.R.'s is rather doubtful. One of the things we must consider is whether, if we do that, we should complicate our negotiations externally with the holders of sterling. You of course would say now that you would be content with the retention of a large part of the balances in Treasuries at one-half, that being a not significant rate of interest.'
* Kenneth Oswald Peppiatt (b. 1893), K.B.E., 1941; Entered Bank of England, 1911; Principal of Discount Office, 1928–34; Chief Cashier, 1934–49; Executive director, 1949–57.

of saving a very considerable amount of foreign exchange on the Treasury bills held by all the governments and banks to which we owe money. I have it in mind to write to Hoppy about all this as soon as there is time.

As regards the price of issue, I think you will find that this issue is attractive to firms wanting to keep their money liquid, which are not in a position to set off depreciation on redemption against tax liabilities. For a bank or dealer in money which can set this off, probably you are right that the earliest war bonds yield better.

The chief effect on the market would be, however, I should say, psychological, in that it confirms the policy of cheap money. According to the papers, old consols have risen a full point or more as a result. It will be very interesting to see the effect on the gilt-edged market over a wider field when the relevant copy of *The Times* arrives.

Keynes's final area of concern with regard to financial markets was the system of controls on new issues. Throughout the war, the available papers and Keynes's comments to others suggest that he had kept aloof from such matters apart from a short 1942 note on post-war capital issues control and the odd brief sarcastic comment on the occasional draft he saw. However, at the end of 1944 an occasion arose which moved him to a more active involvement.

The issue of the moment involved the control of the placing of large blocks of securities previously tightly held. To control such transactions a series of informal agreements, rather than official regulations had evolved, the most important of which for our purposes was the 'Grey Market Agreement' of 19 June 1944, whereby brokers acting for issuers might place securities with jobbers on the understanding that they would be disposed of only to institutions on an approved list. The institutions pledged themselves not to take unquoted securities, except where the raising of money was officially approved, and they agreed not to sell the securities at a discount within six months of acquisition. The same sort of arrangement applied to rights issues.

It was under these arrangements that the General Electric Company made provisions for placing two million £1 preference shares with official permission in order to repay a five-year loan from the Prudential Insurance Company. Between the time the conditions of issue received official approval and the conclusion of the transaction with a public announcement a month elapsed, owing to difficulties G.E.C. experienced in making arrangements. During this month, news of the German counter-offensive in the Ardennes led to a rise in share prices. Thus the borrowers appeared to have received worse terms than necessary; the institutions securing the shares appeared to have received very generous terms which they could quickly realise; the general run of members of the Stock Exchange saw the chance of profit apparently confined to the few; and existing G.E.C. shareholders saw they had lost a valuable first option. The upshot was a storm.

Keynes, who had previously received complaints about the working of the Grey Market Agreement, reacted strongly in two memoranda, which had the effects of preventing the Chancellor's answer to the resulting Parliamentary questions taking a negative line, and of moving it towards the reconsideration of the control given the prospective post-war situation rather than merely announcing minor changes in administrative detail.

To SIR HERBERT BRITTAIN, SIR WILFRID EADY *and* T. PADMORE, *7 January 1945*

G.E.C. NEW ISSUE

Hobson's[14] criticism does not, of course, stand by itself. Similar and more far-reaching comments have occupied the whole of the financial press, and seldom has there been so much solidarity of criticism. The attached cutting from the *Financial News*,[15] which I select from a large number because it is basically good-tempered and reasonable, is quite an interesting example. But there have been dozens printed on the same general lines, whilst I have seen nothing so far on the other side.

Personally I think the criticism is well justified and that

[14] Oscar Rudolph Hobson (1886–1961), Kt. 1955; Financial Editor, *Manchester Guardian*, 1920–9; Editor-in-Chief, *Financial News*, 1929–34; City Editor, *News Chronicle*, 1935–59.
[15] Not printed [Ed.].

there is no satisfying answer to it. But it is difficult to discuss this particular instance clearly because several issues, partly connected and partly separate, are all mixed up in the formation of the popular sentiment, namely as follows:–

(1) Few outside critics can see much sense in the underlying principle. It appears to confuse the question of new issues which, if allowed, would lead to the investment of physical resources, and new issues which merely mean a change of ownership of existing bonds. On the theory of the closed market the Capital Issues Committee is believed to dwell in the dark ages. No one knows why it should be in the public interest that only the Prudential (and a dozen or so others) should have a bite (having fixed their own terms) at attractive new issues. That an issue involving the fresh use of resources may have to be forbidden is well understood; but why, when an issue is approved or is already in existence, it is right for large institutions to acquire it, but wrong for small institutions and individuals, is not so clear.

(2) Even if there were a case for restricting the distribution of an issue, it is inconsistent, having started by placing the stuff with large institutions, to ask permission to let these institutions resell to the general public.

(3) It is suspected in City circles that the business is now becoming a serious abuse. It is in danger, the critics say, of turning into an organised ramp for the enrichment of a small number of finance houses and large institutions, which are thus enabled to collect unearned commissions and preferential opportunities of investment at the expense of the companies concerned and the general public. This feeling has been strongly confirmed by the present example, since most members of the Stock Exchange and all City journalists believe that the Prudential and others consulted gave misleading and self-interested advice to the Bank of England. The Bank seeks its advice about the terms from the leading monopolists, who alone are going to be entitled to take the issue; and the

latter naturally wish the terms to be as favourable to themselves as possible, which means, of course, unfavourable to the borrower. It is being said that the result of the present situation, by which the New Issues Committee gives a monopoly to certain large institutions, is that the latter, being put in a position to dictate their own terms as monopoly lenders, are in effect trying to recover from industry some offset against what they feel they lose by being forced to lend to the Government at 2½ per cent or 3 per cent. It is pointed out that they already maintain a sort of closed ring in mortgages of over £250,000, charging unnecessarily high rates, and now another and somewhat similar vested interest is being created. In Ministry of Information circles much more sinister stories, mentioning names, are circulating which go much beyond any justifiable comment.

(4) The Stock Exchange and the City are, just now, very much up against the decisions of the New Issues Committee apart from this particular matter. The Committee's policy is thought in many cases to lack rhyme or reason; and the grey market discussions have accentuated the lack of confidence. Some people were, therefore, on the lookout for a good opportunity to have a smack back at the Committee. The G.E.C. proposal seemed so utterly indefensible on a variety of grounds that there could not, the critics thought, be a better wicket on which to open the batting.

The Chancellor should be aware that this is the background, against which the assault on the authorities, so unanimous and (considered as Stock Exchange *versus* the Bank of England) unprecedentedly (in recent times) impudent, has been made, and apart from which it would not have been pressed home. But the real cause of the trouble is, of course, remote from much of the above. The New Issues Committee is doing nothing whatever except to administer to the best of its ability certain general principles which the Treasury have entrusted to it. The mischief is that the general principles, whatever may have been the case once, are now out of date and not applicable to the impending problems of reconversion and of some reasonable measure of market liberty. And the remedy, therefore, is to re-examine the principles.

Even though some of them may have a little more validity than I think they have, this re-examination is desirable. Control of the kind which we shall need cannot be worked in conjunction with a market which retains the desirable degree of freedom and discretion, unless *it carries conviction* as being essentially reasonable and necessary in the public interest. Regulations which do not carry conviction should be abated (even if they have some theoretical merit in some minds) unless they are really indispensable. Meanwhile the disrepute, into which capital control and direction is falling, is most dangerous for future policy. We need to work out a revised system which is at the same time acceptable and sufficient—and this should not be too difficult.

KEYNES

7.1.45

To SIR RICHARD HOPKINS, SIR WILFRID EADY *and*
SIR HERBERT BRITTAIN, *30 January 1945*

NEW ISSUES CONTROL

1. Control of the pace of new investment will remain important for some time to come. We cannot depend entirely on controls on the physical side, though these (see below § 7) will have to be predominant. I, therefore, agree with Sir H. Brittain that the machinery of the Capital Issues Committee should be retained and everything required to pass through it. I would add, however, that the sole object of such control is to prevent inflation. It is a fallacy to suppose that it assists in the smallest degree the control of the gilt-edged market and the rate of interest. This is fortunate. For, were it otherwise, the maintenance of cheap money, which, in my view,

depends on a technique which has nothing to do with capital control, would scarcely be practicable in a free market. If this conclusion is doubted, I am ready to explain it, but it would overload this particular discussion.

2. As we approach the reconversion period and large industrial issues are becoming necessary sooner or later, it will be advisable, and indeed essential, to ride the market with a much lighter rein. But I have never heard hitherto any serious general criticism of the Capital Issues Committee on the ground that it forbids new issues which ought to be allowed. Such comment as there is under this heading relates to special cases such as allowing British participation in South African mining issues (and here the objection has been made in the Treasury against the advice both of the Committee and of the Bank of England). The financial journalists and City opinion generally have given the authorities full support in this, the really important aspect of the Committee's work.

3. Practically all the attack has been directed to what should be a very secondary aspect, namely the conditions in which approved new issues and existing securities should be allowed to change hands. Most outsiders (myself included) believe that official policy on this aspect is partly fallacious, partly unnecessary and partly of a minor order of importance. I will elaborate my reasons for this in detail, if desired. But I would rather base the argument on the consideration that, even if the reasons for the present official policy have a better basis than I think they have, there are strong grounds for reconsideration unless they are also really important.

4. In the first place it is clear that, rightly or wrongly, this part of the policy fails to carry general conviction, with the result that it injures the prestige and authority of the primary aspect of control, the prestige and authority of which it will be most important to maintain (in much more difficult circumstances than now exist) during the transitional period.

Moreover, being fundamentally based (as I believe) on a fallacy, it is extremely difficult to be consistent in practice. The result is that, even in present conditions of minimum activity, a certain amount of (what seems to be) unnecessary trouble arises. For even on a committee common sense is bound to break in from time to time, whereas the Treasury officials are great sticklers for consistency and cannot approve of sporadic outbreaks of daylight. It is very undesirable to prejudice the major purpose of control by minor irritations and complications, unless the latter are really important. I do not see how anyone can seriously maintain that they are.

5. In the second place, an attempt to control in detail the conditions in which securities change hands inevitably causes the authorities, if not in fact certainly in appearance, to get mixed up in all sorts of City matters from which they had much better keep aloof. A system by which the more distinguished City groups have a preference in obtaining attractive securities, a system which tends to keep shareholders out from participating in the finance of their own concerns, a system (not to mince matters) which is based on the theory that it is proper for the Prudential to acquire a security, a prominent City house having previously gained a commission for obtaining the assent of the Prudential to take it on terms which in effect the Prudential have settled for themselves, whereas it would be wrong for John Citizen or even for the shareholders in the concern to take the stock (on the ground, I am told, that it would cause in them and others a degree of mental excitement and a dispersion of concentration from more painful matters undesirable in time of war),—all this, the attention of the public having now been prominently called to it, will not wash for long, and will merely stimulate the dangerous comment, 'Is your control really necessary?'

6. Far transcending in importance either of the above considerations is the fact that the time will soon arrive when the existing officially favoured technique for the distribution

of approved new issues will be utterly unable to handle the situation. If the Treasury were to become committed to the view that this technique was essential, they would have to eat their words unduly soon and admit that they had mistaken the shadow for the substance. For as we approach reconversion, an enormous volume of industrial issues will be required to enable industry to build up their stocks and other working capital at post-war prices, and in particular to take over and pay for stocks of materials, building and equipment, which now belong to the Government, and to finance work in progress, which the Government is now financing. Apart from any new investment, considerably more than £1,000 million will be required for such purposes. Part of this will be found from the existing cash reserves of businesses and from the banks. But the justifiable new issues may run to a few hundreds of millions.

7. It will be most inadvisable to make businesses wait until the last moment when physical supplies are available to make financial provision. Unless they can make financial provision considerably in advance of physical provision, the inevitable time-lags of converson will be prolonged by financial anxiety and uncertainty; and when the time comes, the flood of issues will be greater than the market can digest.

8. We need, therefore, to begin making plans to do exactly the opposite of what we have been aiming at hitherto. We need to nurse the market back into orderly activity and restore to it the maximum of freedom, so that it will be ready and able to carry the unprecedented burdens which are soon to be put upon it.

9. Now is the time for trying to think up a much better machinery for new issues than the very expensive and unsatisfactory devices of underwriting, newspaper publicity, stagging, short-term speculation and the like, costing 10 per cent or more for moderate-sized issues, which disfigured the City before the war. The two financial corporations under

the auspices of the Bank of England are a very fine beginning to this. But they do not cover nearly the whole ground. Instead of complaisant stonewalling on a position which will surely have to be abandoned very soon, we should be tackling this imminent task with life and vigour and invention of mind.

10. If the public issues, which are going to be necessary, are to be properly spaced out, a beginning will have to be made before long. So we need to get ready. Nevertheless there is much to be said in favour of no public announcement of a change of policy until VE-day. This will provide a pretext, as well as a reason, for dropping tacitly a good deal of red tape which, even granting that it was once in place, will soon hamper and not help. I should be against announcing a few partial, piecemeal concessions which would seem to be a response to the recent agitations, but would fail entirely to meet the real gravamen of the criticism. No harm in some immediate quiet relaxation of administrative action, but any public announcement of a change of policy should be postponed until we are ready with a comletely new pronouncement adapted to the prospects of reconversion. Nothing would be more inadvisable in my judgment than to try to bolster up an existing state of affairs, which carries no general conviction, by removing the minor inconsistency that the privileged takers of new securities must not sell at all for six months, which would merely have the effect of making the terms another screw less advantageous to the borrower.

11. Nor should the Chancellor be advised to circulate a long stonewalling rigmarole which does not attempt to meet either the lowbrow Stock Exchange complaints against their liberty of dealing or the highbrow financial journalists' contention that intellectually it is all nonsense; but merely reiterates in complaisant tones the nature of the existing provisions as though they not only were, but will be, suitable and essential.

12. If anything has to be said at all at this stage (which seems to be doubtful) it should be on much simpler and more

provisional lines. The Chancellor could say that the system we set up early in the war has not worked too badly hitherto and served us reasonably well in face of all the technical and psychological difficulties, and that he does not propose to make any radical change before the end of the war with Germany; but, of course, it is only suited to conditions in which new issues could not be approved unless in rare and exceptional cases; that we look forward to a time when firms will have to make financial provision well in advance for reconversion and for taking over assets for which at present the government has financial responsibility; that, of course, this will need quite a new set-up, the shape of which he is already taking into consideration and about which a statement will be made in due season, towards which, however, the two financial corporations lately set up under the auspices of the Bank of England constitute a valuable beginning; meanwhile let the financial world be as patient as possible towards anomalies, some of which, especially during the acute periods of the war, may indeed have had more psychological, than financial or technical, justification. This would good-temperedly avoid dogmatism either way and prepare the ground for a change when the circumstances justify it, without making any immediate partial concessions which might seem to be due to outside clamour rather than to the claims of sound reasoning (which, if it is sound, would carry much further).

13. May I take this opportunity to throw out a few preliminary suggestions of a constructive kind of how we might encourage the new issue machinery to evolve as soon as VE-day has arrived:–

(a) The control must not try to make established businesses wait until they actually need the money to pay for physical developments before making financial provision. This will merely cause uncertainty and time-lags. No harm will be done to anyone if the liquid resources of business have to lie idle for a bit until the physical possibilities can be realised. That is to say, the control should normally allow any concern to take its place in the financial queue if it is able to show that it will need increased resources in the course of reconversion and redevelopment.

(*b*) Export trades should have priority.

(*c*) There must be spacing out to prevent congestion and to suit market conditions, but the pace will have to be pretty hot—say an average of £5 million a week and perhaps more (it is difficult to judge how large a proportionate part the public new issue market will play compared with other sources of finance).

(*d*) The issue of stock to existing shareholders on attractive terms should be encouraged, though only offers strictly proportional to shareholdings should be disposable as rights (see (*e*) below), but shareholders would be entitled to have priority of application for additional stock without the power to sell rights and subject to the restriction of dealing under (*e*) below.

(*e*) Apart from the above sale of rights by shareholders (i.e. a single change of hands by the act of renouncing the allotment letter into another specified name, jobbers not counting) no Stock Exchange dealings should be allowed in partly paid stock or in any new issues until two months after allotment (which would dispose of short-term stagging).

(*f*) The aggregate expenses of issue should be subject to the approval of the Committee. Apart from this, the method of issue and distribution should be entirely unfettered, though the method should be reported formally to the Committee for their information which should have the power to prevent clear abuses.

14. After reading these, and also some other recent papers, I am left with the feeling that the bureaucracy have to beware of drifting into [a] position in which they are equally opposed

both to socialism and private enterprise—to the former because it brings in politics, and to the latter because it depends on speculation and money making. It is much sounder, *I* think, to believe in both than to thwart both.

KEYNES

30.1.45

Chapter 7

MISCELLANEOUS ACTIVITIES

It is editorially convenient to conclude this volume with an account of some of Keynes's activities in the Treasury peripheral to internal finance. Leaving the Arts Council story to another volume, three of the most interesting were war damage compensation, the nationalisation of electricity and corporate taxation.

Keynes's initial success within the Treasury was a war damage compensation scheme which he put to the Chancellor's Consultative Committee at its first meeting and helped push through to the statute book. His three earliest memoranda on the subject appear below.

WAR DAMAGE TO PROPERTY

I

The present position is, roughly, as follows:–

(1) Ships and their cargoes, stocks of commodities and materials in progress (if they are for resale and have an aggregate value of £1,000—or £200 for foodstuffs—in one ownership) are covered by government insurance schemes subject to certain exceptions.[1]

(2) Immoveable property, plant and machinery, all agricultural produce, stocks excepted from the war risks insurance scheme, motor cars and other vehicles not for resale, contents of houses and other moveable personal possessions are not covered by insurance. The owner has no *defined* or *guaranteed* rights.

(3) Nevertheless the Government have undertaken, from the public funds and at the cost of the community as a whole, to pay compensation on 'the highest scale compatible with the circumstances of the country' *after* the war.

---

[1] The latest list of exceptions (Statutory Rules and Orders 1940, no. 294) is fairly extensive.

432

(4) This compensation is to be 'in full up to a certain limit of loss, and thereafter would be graded'. The Weir Committee objected to this discrimination, to which the Government have replied that they will bear this criticism in mind when the time comes to fix the compensation payable, i.e. after the war.

(5) The value of damage done is to be assessed as soon as possible, and placed on record, on general principles which have been carefully laid down in two reports by the Committee on the Principles of Assessment of Damage, the most important of which is that the assessment is to be based on the general level of costs and prices ruling in March 1939.

(6) Generally speaking, no compensation will be paid until after the war (nor is there any guarantee of its actual amount when it is paid); and no interest on the claim will be paid in the meantime.

(7) The Government has taken discretion to deal specially with cases of hardship, but there is no indication of what kind of circumstances will constitute hardship.

(8) In cases where the immediate restoration of damage is essential to the conduct of the war, the state will advance funds for the purpose. But such advances are not capital compensation and represent a loan secured by a first charge on the property and on the ultimate compensation payable. Whether interest will be chargeable on such loans has not been stated.

II

The advantage of this scheme is that the Treasury have made no 'promise to provide an unlimited amount out of public funds for compensation'. Even the limit up to which compensation is to be paid in full has not been stated publicly. No other advantage has been claimed for it, so far as I am aware.

The disadvantages of the scheme are the following:–

(1) It is the essence of the Treasury scheme that no individual property owner should have any *definite* security. Nevertheless the Treasury is committed to the maximum ultimate compensation which the country can support. Thus the scheme combines a maximum ultimate liability with the minimum support to confidence and credit in the meantime. The Treasury has been busy, so to speak, in taking out a policy in its own favour against the risk of the end of our world,— a form of insurance which wise men generally consider to be waste of money. The current cost of taking out this policy is the risk of widespread collapse of credit and confidence during the war in the event of substantial damage. For besides those who actually suffer damage, no one will know who the next victim is to be.

No doubt it is true that, whatever promises may be made now, compensation which is greater than is compatible with the circumstances of the country after the war cannot in fact be paid. But this is equally true of the national debt and of many other obligations. It would be just as true and just as inadvisable, to advertise when issuing the new 5-year war bonds that there is no guarantee of repayment at par at the end of five years but only that the highest proportion of the capital will be repaid which is compatible with the circumstances of the country at the date of repayment.

There is nothing peculiar in this respect about compensation for war damage. It is merely one amongst many financial obligations, sacred in normal circumstances, which would have to be reconsidered, if, after the war, a large part of the property of the country had been destroyed. The Government scheme seems to be based on the idea that the country can be physically destroyed and everything else go on as usual; so that it is safe to make definite promises about the war debt if one is careful to make no definite promises about compensation for war damage. I fancy that this may be based on the notion that the potential amount of compensation for war damage is astronomically large compared with other financial obligations, a question of statistics to which I return in section III.

(2) It is characteristic of human nature to overestimate unfamiliar, unpredictable and personally catastrophic risks, Buffon named 1/10,000 as the limit beyond which probability is negligible, on the ground that a man in later middle life, whose chance of early death is thus measured, is unconcerned. Indeed the chance that many of us run of being killed in the course of a year by a road accident in the blackout is greater than this; and we are not unduly upset. Nevertheless, commenting on Buffon's principle, in a famous passage in his *Autobiography* Gibbon pointed out most truly: 'If a public lottery were drawn for the choice of an immediate victim, and if our name were inscribed on one of the ten thousand tickets, should we be perfectly easy?' This is how many people feel about risks from the air. The unfamiliarity, the acute impact on the imagination cause the risk to take on apparent dimensions larger than is strictly reasonable. In one respect this natural tendency has more practical consequences in the case of property than of persons. To most people who have decided, once for all, that it is their duty to continue doing the work to which they have been called, the personal risk is unavoidable and there is nothing to do but get used to it. But where it is a question of taking on new and, so to speak, unnecessary risks through a purchase of property or shares, it is a different matter. In actual fact the proportionate risk to property is very likely much greater than to life (i.e. the chance of 10 per cent physical destruction is greater than that of 10 per cent of the population being killed), particularly when we have learnt by experience the best precautions. But, however this may be, many people would rather stand aside than take on a new and unpredictable property risk on any reasonable terms. We have seen this phenomenon, but only

435

I think in its incipient stages, on some recent days in the Stock Exchange. The prices to which equities fell did not represent any serious attempt, however crude, to estimate the risk, and merely meant that most people were not inclined to assume new risks on any terms.

There is no way of meeting this very natural human tendency except with a general guarantee by which we are all in the same boat wherever the blow falls. It is infinitely more tolerable to lose one-tenth of one's property than to have a one-tenth chance of losing all of it. That is why the principle of insurance proves such a solace to the fearful hearts of men, and why we are forever extending the field of its operation.

Moreover we shall end in the same boat anyhow. The Treasury's principle of limited liability, the idea that we can manage to keep in the same boat if the damage is moderate, but that we must be careful to find ourselves in different boats if the damage is disastrous, is the exact opposite of the truth. If there is not much damage, it might be possible to get away with the principle that those who suffer must lump it. It is in the event of widespread damage, so that no one feels safe, that we shall all discover there is no comfort to be found except by climbing into the same boat. If and when we are seriously up against it, the present Government scheme will surely be found not worth the paper it is written on.

We simply cannot allow economic ruin (for people will regard the immediate deprivation of their income coupled with no clear understanding about the future as next door to ruin) to fall each night on a random collection of innocent persons. And what do we gain by thus spreading insecurity and panic? Nothing whatever, in view of the promises which the Treasury has already given, except in the event of a destruction of the national wealth so widespread that all commitments will have to be reconsidered. The notion that in such an event we can save the rest of the situation by bilking a large number of persons, who have had no means of protecting themselves and are entirely without fault in the matter, of 10 to 25 per cent of their claims, seems fanciful.

Moreover every sensible person is already well aware that if, at the end of the war, the money obligations of the state are out of proportion to the physical wealth of the country, one or more of the familiar methods of scaling down these money obligations, such as a capital levy or the devaluation of the currency, will have to be employed. In such an event it is obviously fair that all forms of wealth should be treated alike and particularly that there should be no discrimination between those whose property has been destroyed and those who have escaped.

The fundamental contradiction in the Government scheme lies in the fact that the safeguards provided, by which claims for war damage can be scaled down, will only take effect in circumstances, namely those of inordinately large damage, in which they will be quite unnecessary, because *all* the money commitments of the state will have to be scaled down.

(3) The Weir Report must surely be one of the most unrealistic documents ever penned. It does not devote a single sentence to considering in concrete terms the actual situation which might arise under the Government scheme in the event of severe damage. The worst practical difficulties might arise in the event of damage which is large but not very large. If the damage is very large, the interruption to the normal economic life of the community will be so great that property transactions will come to a stop in any case and the usual necessity for confidence and credit will be superseded by a state of moratorium. Our object should be to preserve confidence and credit in conditions which are not nearly bad enough to justify a general breakdown. It is in such circumstances that the present Government scheme may do irreparable damage.

Let us suppose that in the next three or six months we suffer damage amounting to somewhere between 1 and 2 per cent of the physical property in the country; or, anticipating the statistics to be given in the next section, let us say between £50 million and £150 million,—with an unknown amount still to come and impending. The higher of the two figures over the longer period is an average damage of £1 million *every night* for six months (with a holiday on Sundays!), and would represent a mighty power of damage in the eyes of the onlooker; and have a great effect on the imagination and on nervous minds, especially if a fair proportion of the whole was concentrated in certain districts. What would be the practical effect of this and of the forebodings it would arouse on confidence and credit? Yet it would be a negligible percentage of total property and only a fraction of new construction in a single normal year.

It must be remembered that, in general, the owners of the property destroyed will lose their current income entirely and irrevocably and that they will have *no security* about future compensation,—nothing which can be put into figures. Moreover it is only if those concerned are *justified* in being worried, that the Treasury safeguards have any value. If the Treasury shrinks from the risk, should not those immediately affected be afraid of it? The property in question is of the kind which is usually considered the most safe and has been accepted as security for semi-gilt-edged loans. Mortgages and building societies are in particular jeopardy. None of the insurance offices (which are largely interested in mortgages and real estates), none of the building societies would be solvent *for certain*. Since these bodies are under contract to advance or repay large amounts of cash to their members in the shape of advances or policies, surrenders for cash, and withdrawals of deposits, a point would come when a moratorium for these institutions would be their only safeguard.[2] No one could say at what point the breakdown of confidence would require

[2] In the case of building societies a limited moratorium on the withdrawal of deposits had to be enacted as early in the drama as last week.

this; but it would certainly come long before the actual danger reached a disastrous proportion of the whole. Meanwhile it would be impossible to put any definite value on an equity, and it may be assumed that the Stock Exchange would soon have to bring such transactions to an end. It is an added difficulty that the details of war damage will not be announced; so that those in the neighbourhood will know it and shareholders etc. will not. The banks, though they would not escape, would probably be much less affected than the above in actual fact; but whether their depositors could be made to understand this is not so certain. In short, an inordinate preference for cash or its near equivalent over every other form of property would be liable to develop in the popular mind.

The above would not be a favourable environment for war loans or for the collection of revenue.

And one can well ask—Cui bono?

There is also the question of the definition of 'hardship'. If a bomb falls on a cattle-shed containing a small man's five milkers, is that special hardship? If it falls on a larger man's twenty-five milkers, has that ceased to be special hardship? Surely the separate examination of every individual case with a view to determining special hardship is unworkable as soon as damage is on a large scale.

It may be argued that credit and confidence and equal treatment between one man and another are of no importance in a war. I cannot take that view. The structure of society being what it is, these things are closely bound up with morale. At any rate the view that they are of no importance is not so obvious that it can be tacitly assumed without argument as in the report of the Weir Committee.

If a change is to be made, it is obviously desirable that it should be made as soon as possible; and not *after* the breakdown of credit and the destruction of morale has already occurred.

439

I repeat that, if the worst fears are not justified, the Treasury safeguards are unnecessary; and that if they are fulfilled, even in part, the Government scheme will be unworkable and injurious.

III

One of the odd features of the Weir Report is that it does not contain any estimate or figure or discussion bearing on the *value* of the property which is excluded from insurance. There seems to run through the argument a tacit assumption that the figure would be astronomically large (the word used is 'unlimited'), that it is not of 'ascertainable dimensions', and that at any rate it is very large in relation to other government commitments. If so, this is an illusion, as the following statistics demonstrate.

The most recent and careful estimates are those of Mr H. Campion published in 1939. He did not find it practicable to work out details for any later year than 1932–4. But this does not matter much, since we are interested in discovering the order of magnitude rather than an exact figure; and it is easy to bring his figures roughly up to date by adding (say) 10 per cent or a little more, to cover the increase of wealth in the last six years.

First of all, it will be useful to give his figure for the total private property in all forms in 1932–4, which is £22,670 (±1,860) million, including the deadweight national debt. This excludes publicly owned property, which he estimates at £2,890 (±435) million, apart from armaments and roads. Thus privately owned property today probably has a value of the order of £25,000 million. This is a little less than five times our annual income when working at less than full capacity, and perhaps a little more than four times a year's income at full capacity. Most people imagine I think, that the total of accumulated wealth in a country such as England is much more than four or five times a year's annual income.

What is the value of the items included in this grand total which are vulnerable to damage from the air and are excluded from insurance under the Government scheme?

(a) The main item is, of course, houses and buildings. Mr Campion estimates the total value of property assessed under Schedule A in 1932-4 at £4,600 (±500) million. This excludes farmhouses and buildings, and the property of railways, mines, gasworks and a few similar undertakings. On the other hand, it includes the *site value* of the houses and buildings covered by it. If we deduct one-sixth for site value[3] and bring the figure up to date with some allowance for the houses and buildings excluded from Schedule A, it would seem that £4,500 million is the approximate present value of all privately owned houses and buildings. It will be noticed that this is well under one year's national income.

(b) The next important item is plant and equipment including vehicles. In 1937-8 the amount claimed for wear and tear allowances was £137 million. This suggests that £1,500 million would be an approximate figure for this item.

(c) Farmers' capital is estimated by Mr Campion at £410 (±40) million. This includes tenant right and cultivations and many scattered items of property not easily vulnerable to catastrophic risk from the air.

(d) Furniture and moveable property which does not bring in a cash income to its owner he puts at £725 (±175) million.

Altogether it would seem that the value at risk is of the order of £7,000-7,500 million.

Now it is not useful to contemplate the consequences of an entire annihilation of everything covered by this total, or even of any figure approaching 100 per cent loss for the country as a whole. The highest figure of damage conceivably compatible, even in the most disordered imagination, with the continuity of any normal financial commitments is, perhaps,

---

[3] When the taxation of site values was under discussion some years ago, rather higher estimates than this were current,—up to a fifth of total value or even greater.

25 per cent; though, in my own judgment, even this is *much* too high for our present purpose.[4] *If* such devastation were to occur covering that proportion of everything in the country wherever situated, the losses in particular districts would surely be so great as to supersede all normal arrangements. Let us, however, take 25 per cent or (say) £1,800 million.

Now none of these figures is astronomically large or even very large in relation to the existing national debt (£8,000 million) or the prospective cost of the war (say, £3,500 million a year). Moreover in view of the commitments made under the Government scheme, some substantial compensation must in fact be made, so that the saving affected by the Treasury safeguards will be much less than the whole of the loss. It would not even be easy to make out a case for scaling down a total claim for £1,800 million, especially as the compensation would have to be spread—if only for physical reasons—over a period of years, if at the same time we were proposing to carry on without scaling down a national debt which might easily by that time reach £12,000 to £15,000 million. A 33 per cent scaling down would only save the Treasury £600 million which is clearly not large in relation to the other costs of the war, being perhaps one twentieth part of the post-war national debt, and represents the national income for 5 weeks or less; or, looked at another way, the whole of the loss resulting from damage averaging £5 million every night for a year would not represent above three years' normal savings in conditions of full employment, and the saving of a 33 per cent scale-down only one year's savings.

Thus there is a very weak case for discriminating at all against those individual property owners who are so unlucky as to incur war damage; and surely no case which would justify the risks to credit, confidence and morale arising out of the present state of uncertainty.

[4]   Twenty-five per cent would represent an average damage of £5 million every night for a whole year without intermission.

Have not most people got vague estimates of these figures in their heads which are highly exaggerated? In combating exaggeration I feel myself back at the end of the last war when I was writing *The Economic Consequences of the Peace* and demonstrating the enormous exaggeration of the estimates of war damage then current. In fact, of course, the apparently vast destruction was made good more easily and more rapidly than I had ventured to forecast. Unless our defence organisation is virtually destroyed and we continue the struggle nevertheless until we are practically wiped out (in which contingency paper schemes and Treasury safeguards are not worth much) it is most unlikely that the war damage will be greater than what three or four years' normal savings can make good. Indeed, this is likely to turn out an extravagantly high estimate. But it does not mean that there is no necessity for the protection of the individual victim. On the contrary, it proves that we can undertake such protection at a cost which is not greater than we can hope to meet, if we successfully survive.

IV

Having made my plea for a drastic revision of the Government scheme, I now revert, in proposing specific amendments, to a state of Treasury-mindedness which endeavours to keep commitments down to the least possible,—at the risk of inconsistency with some of the above arguments which would require a more liberal treatment.

The great vice of the present scheme is its *vagueness*. The Treasury will not get its money's worth in promoting confidence and morale today out of the commitments it will have to meet hereafter, unless these commitments, however carefully hedged round, are *definite*. The following amendments fail in the object of not discriminating against the victims of war damage; for they make no attempt to protect them against consequential loss of profit, employment, or goodwill.

443

Some, therefore, may be of the opinion that they do not go far enough. Their purpose is to offer the minimum definite protection necessary to prevent a breakdown of confidence.

It will be better to have separate schemes for immoveable and for moveable property respectively. The former can be defined to include houses, buildings, plant and machinery which are deemed to be part of a hereditament for the purpose of rating etc. The aggregate value of immoveable property is therefore a little less than the sum of items (*a*) and (*b*) in III above, since (*b*) includes moveable plant and vehicles. Thus £6,000 million should be a fairly safe figure, leaving something over £2,000 million for moveable property (though this does not allow for all the items which might be covered by the existing war risks insurance but are in fact excluded from it).

The following proposals relate to immoveable property thus defined:–

(1) Full compensation of the assessed damage, payable at dates to be fixed subsequently in each case by the Treasury.

(2) 3 per cent interest to be paid currently on the amount due, pending payment of the capital sum. (I attach great importance to this partial maintenance of current income.)

(3) The damage to be assessed on the basis laid down by the Committee on the Principles of Assessment of Damage, particularly the principle of assuming the level of costs and prices ruling in March 1939.

(4) While it has been provided that the assessment is to be made 'as soon as possible' after it has occurred, there are likely to be serious delays if the cases to be dealt with become numerous. Pending assessment, therefore, interest should be payable on the basis of the declared value (see (5) below), subject to adjustment after the official assessment has been completed.

(5) I see no reason why this very valuable concession should not be made the occasion for raising more revenue out of

immoveable property, the owners of which would be probably only too glad to pay it as the price of the scheme as a whole. This might take the following form:–

(1) to ask every owner of immovable property to declare its value within a month, (2) to require him to pay 1 per cent per annum on the declared value for such length of time (which may be longer than the duration of the war) as the Treasury may determine, (3) to pay him interim interest in case of damage on the declared value subject to subsequent adjustment after actual assessment, (4) to pay claims on the basis of the declared value or of the assessed value, whichever is less. Generally speaking owners, if they wished to save themselves trouble, could make their declarations on the basis of the value insured against fire risks.

Such contributions should not be regarded, unless very vaguely, as in the nature of insurance premiums, since there is no genuine actuarial calculation behind them and no reason to suppose that the contributions and the claims will be equal. Nevertheless, if such contributions as the above were to be kept up for several years, they might represent a substantial contribution to the actual cost of the claims. For on the basis of the above guess as to the values involved, they would bring in a revenue of about £60 million a year. Meanwhile, since there would be no additional current outgoings these receipts except the interest on the damage done (which, being subject to income tax and surtax, is not likely to be a large net sum), most of this could be regarded as a genuine receipt to the war budgets, diminishing the financial problem correspondingly and furnishing a far from negligible contribution.

6. I understand that the present Government scheme is being administered by Inland Revenue. If damage is even moderately severe, this must in course of time put an enormous burden on them and urgent matters may fall into arrears.

I suggest that it deserves consideration whether it would

not be much better to use for the purpose the existing private organisation of the fire offices. They are a highly experienced and efficient body with offices, a large staff and organisation everywhere; and the work is exactly what they are accustomed to. Above all it is their profession to give claimants reasonable satisfaction and to leave them as happy as human nature and the circumstances of the case permit. On the other hand, to ask Inland Revenue to improvise an organisation, which may easily find itself saddled with a job considerably larger than the normal job of all the fire offices in the country put together, is asking for trouble. Having laid down the general principles, I should hand over the business, lock, stock and barrel to the administration of the fire offices and refuse (so far as the Treasury and Inland Revenue are concerned) to give the matter a minute's further thought except for the elucidation of general principles from time to time. It would be for the offices to obtain the declared values, collect the contributions, assess the damage, pay out the interest, and keep all the accounts as agents for the Treasury. Almost all the immoveable property in the country is insured with one office or another, though they often join when the schedule is a large one on the basis of agreed proportions. Each office could take the properties already insured with it, parcelling out by agreement amongst themselves the risks which they share. They would know the people they were dealing with; they could collect the war damage contribution along with the existing premiums; they have already inspected the buildings and are in possession of much relevant information; and they are up to all the tricks of uncandid claimants.

They should be asked to engage any extra staff required at their own discretion and on their own terms and to charge as near as possible what it costs them with some reasonable contribution to overheads. Subject to the laying down of a few general principles, the charges for which the offices ask should be paid without criticism. They really are responsible, efficient and patriotic people.

Do not accuse me of ceasing to be Treasury-minded in making so sensible a proposal! Why not simplify the task of government and lessen the terrific burdens on central administration? On the other hand, if this suggestion is not sensible, no harm is done, since it is quite independent of the rest of the scheme.

The treatment of moveable property might be as follows:-

(1) Compensation to be paid unconditionally and as soon as possible up to the following limited amounts as a maximum in the case of

(i) Loose plant and vehicles—£200,

(ii) farmers' stock—one year's rent of the farm,

(iii) personal possessions—the rateable value of the house containing them.

(2) Owners of every kind of moveable property to be allowed at their own option to insure values in excess of the above under the existing war risks insurance scheme. (The question, whether the existing rate of premium under this scheme, namely ¼ per cent per month or 3 per cent per annum, is not too high for the *compulsory* scheme, deserves to be examined. But this rate might remain suitable for the *voluntary* scheme where there is an opportunity for the insurer to select the risks to be covered.)

J. M. KEYNES

9 July 1940

WAR DAMAGE COMPENSATION

I

Before I attempt to answer the conundrum arising out of the fact that the assessment in certain cases will be less than the cost of restoration, I should like to complete the picture by our reading together the Government compensation scheme in the context of the Landlord and Tenant (War Damage) Act, 1939. I should be interested to know whether anyone else has already analysed these two documents, or whether

I am the first
That ever burst
Into that sunless sea.

The substance of the Landlord and Tenant Act is as follows:–

A. Leases where the rent is in excess of a ground rent.

(i) If the tenant issues a notice of retention, the lease holds good and the tenant becomes liable for the physical restoration of the property.

(ii) If the tenant issues a notice of disclaimer and the landlord accepts this, the lease is surrendered and no one is liable to restore the property.

(iii) If the tenant issues a notice of disclaimer and the landlord issues a notice to avoid disclaimer, the lease holds good and the landlord becomes liable for the physical restoration of the property.

(iv) If the tenant issues either a notice of retention or a notice of disclaimer, rent ceases to be payable pending restoration. But he has to go on paying rent unless he does one or other.

Now, under the Government scheme all this has to be settled *before* the scale of compensation ultimately payable by the Government has become known. Neither tenant nor landlord is in a position to decide where his interest lies until he knows the scale of compensation. Generally speaking, however, in view of the facts that the assessment of damage, being based on loss of market value, may be below the 1939 cost of restoration and that the actual cost of restoration hereafter may exceed the 1939 cost by an unknown amount, few people will be prepared to accept liability for the physical restoration of the property in case of total damage. One would suppose, therefore, that in the great majority of such cases the tenant will issue a notice of disclaimer and the landlord will accept this notice, i.e. the lease will be surrendered.

In the case of partial damage, however, God knows what will happen. The Committee on the Principles of Assessment

448

of Damage point out that in such cases the cost-of-restoration principle is likely to prevail against the market value principle. But there still remains the gamble as to what restoration will actually cost when the time comes. For this reason, I should be inclined to suppose that here also most leases would be surrendered.

Now this means in the majority of cases that wherever the rent payable under the lease exceeds the ground rent but falls short of a rack rent, the tenant loses irrevocably the whole of his equity in the property without hope of compensation. He can only retain his equity in the property by taking on himself the complete liability for physical restoration without knowing what it will cost him or what compensation towards the cost he will receive. This would be particularly hard in cases where his rent fell short of a rack rent because he had made improvements at his own expense.

B. Leases at a ground rent are dealt with on different principles from the above. In the case of a ground lease the procedure is for the tenant to apply to the court for permission to surrender the lease on such terms of compensation as the court may determine. In other words the ground landlord is forced to buy out the leasehold interest. The only mitigation to this is that the landlord is allowed to make a counter-offer to his tenant, the reasonableness of which the court shall take into account.

This means that every single case of a ground lease has to be separately handled by the court. It also means that the court have to decide forthwith the terms on which the ground landlord is compelled to buy out the leasehold interest or the reasonableness of the landlord's counter-proposal at a stage when all the parties concerned, including the court, are in ignorance of the scale of compensation which will be ultimately payable by the state. Thus a ground landlord may not only lose his property, but may have in addition to pay out to his ground tenant compensation based on the latter's

449

interest, whilst remaining without any security as to whether he himself will receive similar compensation from the state. Until there is some experience as to the basis on which the courts fix compensation, tenants will have no means of knowing whether or not it is in their interest to surrender the lease. Nor will landlords know what sort of counter-proposal it is reasonable to make. If the court bases its terms of compensation on the actual value of the tenant's interest in the property, then it will pay every ground tenant to surrender his lease, and every ground landlord will have to pay out compensation which is ruinous. If, on the other hand, the courts depart from that basis of compensation, what basis are they to adopt?

In the case where the ground tenant does not surrender the lease, it seems that he remains liable to pay the ground rent and neither party is liable to restore the property. There is no provision as to who, in such a case, receives the ultimate government compensation. But the fact that, in this event, the tenant would have to go on paying ground rent, without his landlord being under any liability to restore the property, seems to make it the more reasonable course in almost every case for the tenant to ask the court to allow him to surrender on terms of compensation.

The above account of what happens in the case of a ground lease deserves, if I have not made a mistake, to be deeply pondered. Does the Act mean that every leasholder at a ground rent is to be fully compensated at the ground landlord's expense? Or what? One extraordinary aspect of this part of the Act is that it assumes that the ground landlord owns the major interest in the property; whereas in the great majority of cases where the lease has more than 40 or 50 years to run, the contrary is the case.

II

I now come to your conundrum, the main relevance to which of the above is the demonstration that the relationship between the different interests involved is *not* satisfactorily solved at present. You call my attention to the fact that compensation may in certain cases be paid, not on the basis of the cost of restoration, but on the basis of the loss of market value. Hence, in such cases, the owner will be overstating his case if he puts in a declared value on the basis of the fire insurance value, which normally bears some sort of relation to the cost of restoration. Undoubtedly this means that the attention of property owners will have to be called to the fact that the value to be declared is the excess of the present market value of the property over its site value, with the result that the fire insurance value may not be appropriate. Nevertheless, some rough and ready declaration, even though it involved some slight overstatement, would not be impracticable.

In any case, this difficulty relates to the method of declaring value and to the payment of a premium, but does not relate to the principle of full compensation. It might be balanced by making the premium rather less than the 1 per cent, so that the cost of over-declaration would not be oppressive.

I cannot claim that my principle of full compensation overcomes by any means all the difficulties of the Landlord and Tenant (War Damage) Act. Since I do not propose to promise an amount equal to the actual cost of physical restoration, the Act should be guarded and qualified in this respect. On the other hand, my principle would make it very much easier so to amend the Landlord and Tenant (War Damage) Act as to make sense, because the amount of compensation would be known. If it was agreed to pay full compensation up to the amount of the assessed damage, then the Landlord and Tenant (War Damage) Act can be made

451

workable by providing that notice of retention and disclaimer need not be made until after the amount of damage has been assessed, and that the liability to restore the property resulting from a notice of retention or from a notice to avoid disclaimer shall not require an actual expenditure in excess of the assessed value of damage. The draftsman of the Landlord and Tenant Act must have believed that the government scheme provided for compensation on the basis of full cost of physical restoration; for the adjustments between the interests of the different parties are worked out on this basis.

III

On other points of detail my ideas were as follows:–

(1) The premium would be payable by the same persons as those who pay Schedule A tax and in the same proportion, the ground landlord paying his appropriate share on this basis.

(2) The 3 per cent interest pending compensation would be payable to the landlord if either a notice of retention or disclaimer had been issued so that payment of current rent had ceased; and otherwise it would be payable to the tenant.

(3) The ultimate compensation will be payable to the tenant if he has not issued a notice of disclaimer; otherwise to the landlord.

IV

Can you tell me if war damage reckons as a working expense for the purpose of income tax? If so, how is the net loss to be calculated when the scale of government compensation is unknown? If not, is it proposed to collect income tax and E.P.T. from a business which is for the time being ruined? This question is rather by the way. But it is easier to answer if it is known that the ultimate compensation will be equal to the assessed damage.

V

The tangle of the different interests involved is difficult anyhow. But I claim that my proposal, being definite, makes it easier to handle, not more difficult.

J. M. KEYNES

18 July 1940

WAR DAMAGE

On further reflection, I have little to add to my previous memorandum except the following:–

The question of making the existing Treasury undertaking *definite* should be kept separate from that of the advisability of using this opportunity to obtain a fiscal contribution from owners of real property. I remain strongly convinced that the former is essential on some such basis as I suggested,—which in fact falls considerably short of full compensation. Further examination of the Landlord and Tenant (War Damage) Act since I wrote my previous memorandum reinforces the view that the existing arrangements are unworkable unless the arrangements for compensation, whatever their scale, are definite.

I also remain of the opinion that some aid to the *income* of those who suffer damage during the period before they receive actual compensation is very desirable.

On the scale of the proposed fiscal contribution, however, I now think that the rate I previously suggested was too high; though I still think it important to impose such a contribution, and possibly for a considerable period. After considering its actual effect in certain concrete difficult cases, I agree that the burden would not infrequently be felt as oppressive especially in conjunction with the present level of Schedule A income tax. There is also the difficulty of dividing the contribution equitably between different interests in the same property in circumstances in which it is not possible to say exactly how the compensation will be divided. It is not possible to overcome this difficulty in every case but, if the contribution is not too heavy, the objection to the inequalities would be indeed a trifle compared with those likely to arise under the existing scheme.

I should, therefore, like to substitute ½ per cent for 1 per cent of the declared value. This would work out on the average at about 1s 4d in the £ on the Schedule A assessment,[5] or not much more than 1s in the £ on the gross income.

This is a broad issue to be settled on broad grounds of equity and expedience. Is it really conceivable if a particular town suffers damage of the order of £1 million that the community as a whole will not have to come to the rescue, —which they can well afford? On the other hand, an announcement of full compensation and 3 per cent meanwhile on the prescribed basis of assessment would do a very great deal for general confidence. We lose on every score if we fail to exercise imaginative foresight and act accordingly beforehand.

J. M. KEYNES

25 July 1940

The second example of Keynes's peripheral activities, electricity nationalisation, was a reflection of post-war planning. In the course of 1943 the authorities began to look again at the existing arrangements for the generation and distribution of electricity.

Since 1926, the centralised control of electricity generation had been public policy. The Central Electricity Board had undertaken the construction and operation of a national grid, had planned the development and expansion of generating resources and controlled the day-to-day operation of 'selected' stations. These 'selected' stations were, however, not owned by the Board. Nor was the distribution network which, like the 'selected' stations, was in the hands of local authorities or private enterprise.

---

[5] Capital value of the property 16 years purchase of Schedule A (on the average) *less* one-sixth (on the average) for site value.

In January 1944 the Reconstruction Committee of the War Cabinet received the report of the Sub-Committee on the Future of the Electricity Supply Industry. The Sub-Committee recommended that the ownership of selected stations, of non-selected stations providing public supplies, and of certain additional main transmission lines go to a central generating board. Below this central generating board there should be regional distribution boards and local electricity boards to manage any remaining generating plant and to distribute centrally generated supplies. The Sub-Committee also made recommendations as to the terms of acquisition of existing enterprises by the various boards, as well as a financial structure for the new system.

On 28 February 1944 the Reconstruction Committee discussed the Sub-Committee's report. It invited the Chancellor, in consultation with the Minister of Fuel and Power, to undertake a detailed review of the financial basis of the reorganisation favoured by the majority. The Committee reserved its final decision on the scheme as a whole until the Chancellor had reported.

The Treasury discussions of the proposals then began in earnest. In a paper which we cannot trace, Keynes strongly criticised the majority proposals. As the Treasury moved to modify them, Keynes weighed in with a memorandum to the Chancellor's private secretary.

To T. PADMORE, *19 May 1944*

I understand that these papers have already reached the Chancellor. I therefore send this note to you direct. But I am at the same time sending copies to the Financial Secretary, Sir B. Gilbert[6] and Mr. Brittain.

KEYNES

19 May 1944

FINANCE OF THE ELECTRICITY PROPOSALS

Whilst I am in favour of the general purpose of this scheme, I find myself in agreement with all the criticisms which the Financial Secretary has made of the financial technique actually proposed to carry it out.

[6] Bernard William Gilbert (1891–1957), K.B.E. 1943, K.C.B. 1946; entered Treasury, 1914; Joint Second Secretary, 1944–56.

I agree that in detail the new proposals are a very great improvement on the original version. Nevertheless, they are, in my judgment, such as to create some consternation in investment circles. And what is far worse than that, taken as a precedent they forge a most formidable instrument of potential confiscation in the future. It is from this point of view that I think they need the most careful consideration of the Chancellor before they are supported.

The Government is under no compulsion to nationalise this or any other industry. But if for good reasons they decide to do so, a plan which deprives the shareholders of any control of the management, withholds from them any possibility of increased return to compensate risk, and yet gives them no guarantee of income, seems a most unjust and undesirable way of reaching the desired end.

When an industry is nationalised, it is fundamental that the shareholders should be bought out. The principle that they can be left still to carry the risk but to be otherwise totally dissociated from the fortunes of the concern, is quite wrong. On this basis, it would be open to future governments to nationalise any industry on the basis of depriving shareholders of management and future increments of reward, and just leave them to collect such return from the industry as the new socialised managers chose, or found themselves able, to earn.

Are not the Treasury proposals trying to combine two entirely inconsistent aims? It is understandable that the Treasury may not wish to run the risk of having to meet losses in the electricity industry through political pressure to undertake unproductive services or sell electricity below cost. The unwillingness to assume this risk is an argument against nationalisation. But if the decision is in favour of nationalisation, then surely it is completely wrong for the Treasury to try to dissociate itself from any responsibility of loss, just as if the industry was still in private hands.

The previous example of this technique in the case of the London Transport Board has not been fortunate in its operation. That, of course, went much less far than this, since the marginal stocks were only given in return for distinctly precarious assets and not, as in this case, highly gilt-edged ones; not, indeed, that this was sufficient justification for that plan.

What yield investors would expect from the new stock it is extremely difficult to conjecture. Admittedly, there is a famine in good stocks outside those which are strictly gilt-edged. It is therefore conceivable that they might be marketed at 3½%. On the other hand, the capital involved is very large. Speaking as one who has had some experience in investing insurance and other money during the last 25 years in sound stocks, I should be most unattracted by this one and would certainly not be prepared to hold it for any less return than 4%, and not a very large holding even at that rate. If the stock is unpopular, there will be great difficulties in raising the large amount of new capital which will be required from time to time. And it will not be reasonable to raise new debt to rank in front of the existing stocks.

I see no answer to the dilemma that if there is no risk, and if the Treasury will in fact always have to stand behind this stock, then one is throwing money away by giving no guarantee; whilst if, on the other hand, there is a risk and the intention is that the shareholders should bear the brunt if necessary, then the proposals are very near to confiscation.

I would again particularly stress the danger of these proposals as a precedent, capable of application to other cases where the potential risk is very much greater than in this one, which is admittedly fairly safe as things go. There will be many proposals to nationalise industries in the years to come. Should it not be a cardinal principle that the shareholders are bought out at a fair value in government stock? Otherwise the way is wide open for confiscatory habits.

This particular scheme will be opposed, in any case, by those who object to it root and branch. Is it wise to fan these flames by a proposal so upsetting to all classes of investors and investment institutions?

KEYNES

19.5.44

Three days later, Professor Robertson echoed Keynes's doubts.

From D. H. ROBERTSON, *22 May 1944*

I had not seen these papers before, and am much disappointed to find that, in this first essay in post-war socialisation, H.M.G. are not facing the financial issue squarely, but are reverting to the bad old techniques—already employed in various forms over railways, cables and L.P.T.B.—of creating expectations which fall short of being promises, and so in the end involve *selective* robbery of those 'capitalists' who have ventured their money in what are, ex hypothesi, specially useful and important activities.

Nothing seems to me better calculated than this technique to bedevil fair consideration of the question whether this or that branch of economic activity is a suitable object of socialisation. If the public interest requires that the status of certain groups of risk-takers should be altered to that of creditors, then creditors they should be,—and thereafter only suffer such further looting, in the shape of high taxation or currency depreciation, as it may be held expedient to inflict on all members of this class. To single them out for having their property squandered in the public interest (whether real or only alleged) simply adds a reasonable ground to the many unreasonable ones which already exist for resistance to any interference with 'the existing order'.

D. H. R.

22 May 1944

The upshot was that Sir Richard Hopkins attempted to draft a memorandum to the Chancellor emphasising the two main problems as the Treasury saw them: the terms of compensation, and the form of management, especially as electricity would be a precedent for later schemes. In the course of Hopkins's drafting, Keynes commented.

To SIR RICHARD HOPKINS, *9 June 1944*

ELECTRICITY PROPOSALS

The main paragraph on page 3 of your note beginning: 'On the other hand if the advice of Lord Keynes...' implies that if the proposals at present in draft are accepted, the problem you discuss in this paragraph will not arise. I should say that the problem to which you are directing particular attention is not a consequence of accepting the criticisms of Robertson and myself, but arises anyhow. I think this paragraph ought to begin—'Whether or not the advice of Lord Keynes and Professor Robertson is followed, and the existing owners are paid out in Government stock, the Government will become the effective owners of the undertakings carried out by the boards, who are their nominees, and subject to their direction, so that the boards are merely...'

Generally speaking, I feel that the question of buying out the existing stockholders should be kept more distinct than your note keeps it, from the problem of keeping the boards independent of undue political influence. I think we ought to start off with the principle that if the shareholders are deprived of effective management they should be bought out. In this and future proposals, all sorts of different set-ups will be tried from time to time. If the principle is accepted that shareholders can be expropriated from management, and not become creditors, the way is open for the selective robbery to which Robertson has called particular attention.

If this issue is confused with the question of the right set-up for the boards, it seems to me that you are fighting a futile rearguard action against nationalisation, which cannot, in the long run, hope to succeed. I believe that the problem ought to be considered under the three following heads:–

1. It is to be expected that some industries will be, in effect, nationalised.

2. When an industry is nationalised, the existing share-

holders should be bought out for cash, or its equivalent in guaranteed bonds.

3. The problem of how to manage a nationalised industry so that the employees are not in the position of civil servants, and so as to avoid day-to-day Parliamentary criticism, is a primary problem which a committee should forthwith examine, if with particular, without exclusive, application to the electricity industry.

Trying to pretend that you can avoid the last named issue by tampering with the second principle is surely an ostrichism.

KEYNES

9 June 1944

On 19 June, Hopkins recommended to the Chancellor another committee to discuss the problems of finance and management. The Chancellor agreed on 25 June. The result was an official Committee on Public Utility Corporations under the chairmanship of Sir Alan Barlow. The other Treasury representatives were Sir Herbert Brittain and Sir Hubert Henderson. The Committee's terms of reference were:

To consider both generally and in particular relation to the electricity industry, the general structure appropriate for the running of a public utility service by a public authority in such manner as to conserve the interests of both users and taxpayers and to secure technical efficiency in the management; and within the framework of that structure the type of compensation which would be fair to existing proprietors of under-takings taken over; and to report.

The committee signed its report on 30 November 1944 and it went to the Reconstruction Committee under the Chancellor's signature on 2 December.

On his return from the Stage II negotiations with the Americans in Washington, Keynes examined the report at the request of Sir Richard Hopkins to whom he had made his doubts known orally.

To T. PADMORE, *19 December 1944*

Sir R. Hopkins suggested that I should write a note for the Chancellor on the report about public utility corporations. I have had to do so in great haste since I understand it comes up to Ministers tomorrow, though one can safely predict that it will certainly not be settled by Ministers tomorrow. I am sending copies to others concerned, but there has not been time to get their prior comments.

KEYNES

REPORT OF THE OFFICIAL COMMITTEE ON PUBLIC UTILITY CORPORATIONS

This report tackles a very difficult task, for it attempts to deal not only with the particular case of electricity but to produce general principles and a general pattern for nationalisation schemes in general. It is a remarkable achievement to have been produced in the time by officials mainly occupied in other matters. But it seems to me to be still a long way off from being fully baked or a sound basis for ministerial decisions.

It deals with three main questions:–

(1) The concept, set-up and control of a public utility corporation as being in general the right instrumentality for future schemes of nationalisation.

(2) The best accounting method of arriving at the appropriate amount of compensation payable, with special reference to the electricity industry.

(3) The mode of paying this compensation to the previous owners.

On the first question I find myself in general sympathy both with the approach and with the conclusions, though there is more one could say if one could afford to devote a good deal of time and some solid thinking to what is in its nature a most difficult and complicated problem, which raises fundamental issues of economics, political science and politics.

On the second question it is clear that the authors of the report have made their best efforts to be fair to both parties. But many matters are left in great obscurity, particularly those arising out of the change in the value of money (i.e. the

461

difference between replacement cost and the depreciated value on the basis of initial cost) and in the rate of interest since the companies were formed. I will not delay to go into details about all this. But there is one particular matter where it seems to me that the advice tendered to Ministers is unwise. The proposal is to offer local authorities an amount of compensation estimated at £50 million less than if their assets were to be valued on the same basis as is proposed in the case of private companies. Whilst Ministers are advised to do this, they are also advised to run away immediately as soon as the local authorities, as they are quite certain to do, make loud protests with good reason. Surely nothing does more to impair the authority of the Chancellor of the Exchequer and the Treasury than a try-on of this kind, which everyone knows cannot be sustained against the opposition which is certain to arise.

I pass on to the third question, which is the matter on which I have a clear view and feel no doubt that the advice of the Official Committee is dead wrong and bound to lead to all sorts of difficulties immediately and hereafter, if it were acted upon.

Their proposal is that, whilst the previous proprietors shall be wholly bought out and retain no control whatever over the policy or management of the concern, they should nevertheless be paid out in the shape of bonds which are in the nature of an equity inasmuch as the return on them is theoretically to depend on the profits of the nationalised public utility corporation. The rate payable cannot go up if the profits increase and can only go down if they fall. It is proposed to compensate the previous owners for the uncertainty thus created by giving them a higher rate of interest, which is to be measured by the market's assessment of the degree of risk involved. That is to say, bonds are to be issued at such a rate of interest as would cause them to sell at par after allowing for the measure of uncertainty created in the minds of investors.

The absurd thing is that the authors of the report see themselves that this arrangement could not possibly work if the public utility corporation were concerned with an industry involving any real measure of risk. They, therefore, propose that it is only in comparatively riskless undertakings, or that look like such, that this technique should be employed. In other words, they do not propose to use it in the only cases where, assuming it were in other respects acceptable, the Treasury could escape a future possibility of loss, and only use it in those cases where, from this point of view, it serves no object. Thus, the extra interest payable is not a reward for risk bearing in the sense of a risk arising out of the nature of the industry (though, even if it were, this would not make the method any the more justifiable), but merely to compensate the investor against a measure of uncertainty deliberately created by putting him at the mercy of future administrative and parliamentary decisions about the conduct of the industry, which he cannot control and the nature of which he cannot forecast.

A further absurdity arises in that the Committee virtually accept the suggestion that in fact the Treasury will always have to stand behind the bonds and could not allow them to go into default. Experience during the present war in the case, for example, of port stocks shows that, even when there is a public catastrophe, the public authority cannot allow default in cases like these. So that the creation of a certain measure of uncertainty requiring reward becomes even more gratuitous.

Some of the arguments against this course are the following:–

(1) An unnecessary financial burden is put either upon the industry or upon the Treasury. It is not easy to calculate the amount of this in advance, since one does not know how much extra interest the investor will demand to compensate him for the uncertainty. It is conceivable, I think, that, in the case of the electricity industry, he would be content with an extra ¼ per cent. If so, the burden would appear to work out,

capitalising the extra rate of interest, something between £50 and £100 million, according to the ultimate amount of capital which had to be raised. It is not at all obvious what you get in return for this. The position is either unfair or unnecessary. The idea apparently is that you can create some incentive towards efficiency by holding a threat over scattered investors, who have no control over efficiency whatever—a pure Gilbert and Sullivan conception.

(2) I would lay particular stress on the loophole which this general plan opens for insufficient compensation in future cases and the use of it where real risk is involved, the rate of interest being fixed arbitrarily and not in accordance with market conditions. The present Committee have hedged round their own proposals with conditions which make it quite fair to those to be compensated and only objectionable to the public interest. But if they set this precedent, they cannot prevent it being used without those qualifications which make it fair. By changes which would not be easily apparent to the general public this technique could become a most potent instrument of confiscation.

In this connection see also paragraph 28, where the Committee state that they do not include as an 'uncommercial activity' the obligation to provide services at unremunerative times, in unremunerative places or on a non-discriminatory basis. If this means that the bondholders are to suffer by a reduction in the return on their bonds the cost of future obligations of this character imposed by statute, surely it is monstrous and another loophole to confiscation. If not, what does it mean?

(3) In order to give any meaning at all to the contraption there have to be various provisions to secure that the management is under compulsion to aim solely or mainly at commercial considerations. The object seems to be to make it as difficult as possible to take account of social considerations. I doubt if this is really secured. But that seems to be

464

the object. Now this seems to me to defeat an important part of the purpose of nationalisation. Generally speaking, where only commercial considerations arise, and no other ulterior considerations whatever, there is no point in nationalising an industry. Where there is a strong case for nationalisation it is generally because the management must take account of social as well as commercial considerations.

Take the example of railways. We all agree that roads cannot be run on purely commercial considerations. Many economists believe that exactly the same thing is true of railways. In practice, railways ought to be run intermediately, with both sets of considerations in view. An important reason for nationalising railways is that they cannot be run satisfactorily without any reference to social considerations or to the costs and methods of other means of transport.

Or take the need of rural electrification. Do we want to put pressure on, that the cost of this should be, if possible, at the expense of users of industrial electrical power? This is only the right conclusion, if taxing industrial electrical power is the right source of finance for rural electricity which, in view of competitive conditions, it probably is not.

I should have supposed that the whole purpose of nationalisation is to allow considerations of general and social advantage to take their proper place in price policy.

(4) Great complications arise when new stock has to be issued and great opportunities for unfairness to the original bondholders. This does not seem to me to be satisfactorily faced.

On the other hand, the reasons in favour of this plan seem to me to be essentially *small* reasons. Those which I have discovered in the text appear to be the following:–

(i) It would give a little more variety in the investment market, especially as each board is to have its own stock (whether they are all to yield the same rate of interest I do not know). There is, of course, something in this. But one wonders if it is worth while to burden nationalised industries with large capital sums in order to tickle the palate of investors. If, for example, this plan were to be applied to the railways, the extra burden involved might be very great indeed. Presumably, however, the Committee would not think this proposal suitable for railways. Indeed, it is not really easy to think of any case which would satisfy even their own criteria apart from electricity.

(ii) It seems to be thought, that the technique proposed would protect the gilt-edged market. I could elaborate the reasons against this, but surely it is pure rubbish and a survival of ideas which we have learnt to discard completely in other contexts.

(iii) One object seems to make it as difficult as possible to take account of social considerations and to cause the industry to be carried on as nearly as possible as though it were not nationalised. But, if you feel like that, why nationalise it?

(iv) Perhaps part of the object is to protect the Treasury from having to give subsidies. This is much the same as (3) above. If so, is this not a relic of past financial orthodoxy, when it was always the business of the Treasury to oppose any conceivable social improvement or social policy, if it were likely to cost money? Is it not rather ridiculous and pure ostrichism to think that one can restore that former state of affairs through hollow devices such as this?

One feels that this report has been written by people who are in their hearts entirely against nationalisation, but, seeing that in some cases it is inevitable, are trying to save something out of the wreck (as they think it to be); and as a result get the worst of both worlds. For their little contrivance cannot conceivably retain the commercial motive of profit. They inevitably lost the admitted advantages of the profit incentive and then, instead of seeking to compensate that by social advantages, they try to make this also as difficult as possible, and use for this purpose a device which is both futile and expensive.

I am very far from being out of sympathy with what they are feeling in their hearts. I am not in favour of large-scale nationalisation. In my opinion, an industry should not be nationalised if it ought to be run solely or primarily on commercial considerations. *Ergo*, if it is nationalised, it should not be enjoined to pretend that a social purpose is out of bounds.

The right way to save something out of the wreck (which I hope it is not) seems to me to be along the lines of the other part of the report. There is great value in the proposed boards as a method of securing commercial management once the general policy is laid down. They retain some of the decentralisation of decision which is a major merit of private enterprise. There is even an element of competition, or rather a measuring rod for efficiency of management, by retaining several boards with independent financial systems. By going all out for modern accounting methods it may be possible to obtain better measuring rods of efficiency than private enterprise ever had. All this is very important, and the report makes valuable contributions to a solution on the right lines. On the other hand, the pretence of securing efficient management by putting a risk more theoretical than actual on a scattered body of investors, who will be entirely deprived of control, is phoney and is certain to be discovered as such sooner or later. Nor is it a good way of protecting the departmental interests of the Treasury to spend tens of millions in order to erect futile defences.

I understand that the dissident member of the Committee, with whom on this issue I am in agreement, was Sir Hubert Henderson. The same view was expressed by Professor Robertson. Thus all the professional economists who have been consulted take the view contrary to that of the Committee. Sir R. Hopkins raises similar doubts. I do not think that the economic section have yet been consulted. My view is that this part of the report is another Uthwatt[7], rather plausible, perhaps, at first sight, but falling to pieces under close inspection. I predict that it will land ministers, if they go in for it, in the same sort of frustration and confusion and waste of time.

KEYNES

19.12.44

When ministers met at the Reconstruction Committee on 20 December, the Minister of Fuel and Power was asked to attempt to draft the heads of a bill. In the meantime, discussion in the Treasury continued with Sir Herbert Brittain replying to Keynes and drawing forth a rejoinder from him.

From SIR HERBERT BRITTAIN, *20 December 1944*

REPORT ON PUBLIC UTILITY CORPORATIONS

I should like to make some comments on Lord Keynes's paper of yesterday's date.

Perhaps one should deal first with the main general arguments on page 4 and later pages for using state credit in the case of the electricity industry. These appear to be:

(*a*) that the Treasury can safely issue its own stock because this industry is a good risk;

(*b*) that under our proposals the present investor is 'put at the mercy of future administrative and parliamentary decisions';

(*c*) (pages 5–6) that it is futile to suppose one can create an incentive towards efficiency by giving those investors boards' stocks;

(*d*) (page 7) that in the absence of State credit we are obliged to require the management 'to aim solely or mainly at commercial considerations' and (page 8) to damp down social considerations in order (page 10) to avoid a state subsidy.

[7] The reference is to the report of a committee under Mr Justice Uthwatt on the problems of compensation and betterment in the context of town and country planning.
    Andrew Augustus Uthwatt (1879–1949), Kt. 1941, Life Peer, 1946; called to the Bar, 1904; Judge, Chancery Division, High Court, 1941–6; Lord of Appeal in Ordinary, 1946; Chairman of Expert Committee on Compensation and Betterment, 1941.

None of these arguments seems to me to be valid.

On (*a*), if it is to be an argument for the issue of a Treasury stock that the industry is a good risk, there is nothing to prevent similar issues being claimed and justified for other industries which are good risks and which could conceivably be rationalised through the adoption of the public corporation system, with consequent economies in administration and reductions of prices.

On (*b*), this suggestion is an unjustifiable exaggeration in view of our paragraphs 75 and 26.

On (*c*), we have never been guilty of such a supposition. The issue of boards' stock rather than a Treasury stock was never designed as a measure towards industrial efficiency.

On (*d*), even if state credit were used, we should surely insist on something like our proposed provisions for ensuring that the industry was run on a commercial basis, subject to what we also propose about financial assistance when works or services are carried out under special directions. One would gather, from Lord Keynes's comments, that we had altogether forgotten about social considerations, whereas such considerations (and economic) were the *raison d'être* of the special financial assistance just referred to. Despite the gibe (on page 10) at the too careful regard of the Treasury for the public purse, I cannot see why, in the present case of electricity, we should go further than we have proposed and contemplate the possibility of a *general* subsidy to an industry which is in so healthy a condition and should even better itself as a result of this reorganisation. (Incidentally, I should have thought that accusations of ridiculous orthodoxy and ostrichism in the Treasury's control of expenditure on social developments were today woefully misplaced!)

As regards the commercial aspect, even though, as Lord Keynes says on page 10, the commercial motive of profit will no longer exist, there will still be a commercial motive in the earning of interest charges and in the reduction of prices. He himself recognises on page 11—presumably even if the Treasury assumes all the boards' capital liabilities—that the system of boards is a method of securing 'commercial management', by which I assume he means management with a view to the maximum business efficiency.

The following comments may be made on more detailed points.

Page 2. I don't understand the references to the 'change in the value of money', and to the changes in interest rates. As regards the former, the existing shareholders will not have to replace the physical assets; and it would clearly be wrong to saddle the new boards *both* with a capital liability now for the higher current values *and*, when the assets have to be replaced, with the ultimate excess cost of replacing them over the accumulated depreciation provision.

As regards local authorities, Lord Keynes's reference is a parody of what we wrote in paragraph 117. The offer of the less favourable basis would not be a mere 'try-on' but would be based on the quite genuine grounds that (i) we should try to save the new boards the difference to their capital liabilities—an argument which Lord Keynes thinks very important in support of his own case on page 5—and (ii) local authorities may well have regard to the fact that they are not being squeezed in the interests of private enterprise. If they have good arguments telling the other way, we will consider them: but why should we let the other case go by default?

Page 5. As to our 'standing behind the bonds', the reference is presumably to the concluding words of paragraph 15. These were not intended as implying a continuous guarantee of the full interest on the stock, but as an indication that we should probably have to help the boards in times of special trouble—as in the cases quoted by Lord Keynes.

Page 6. I don't understand the reference to 'insufficient compensation'. I thought that the argument against board stocks implied (as regards income at least) that present shareholders were going to get too much compensation? In any case, we expressly safeguarded the merits of other cases.

As regards the possibility that the qualifications in this case may not be observed in other cases, I do not see how we are to do business if we are not allowed to treat a case like the electricity industry on its merits and on the assumption that future cases will be similarly treated on their merits.

On the question of 'uncommercial activity' our point was that even under private enterprise a public utility is expected to carry a certain amount of business which, considered by itself, is unremunerative.

Page 8. Under paragraph (4), I do not see why the issue of board stocks should mean any more opportunities for unfairness to the present shareholders than the issue of Treasury stock. Perhaps the 'great complications' can be further elaborated.

Page 9. Since, under (ii), the humble practitioners of the Treasury and the Bank of England are not vouchsafed even the crumbs of argument, no comment is possible.

H. B.

20 December 1944
(copy sent to Lord Keynes)

MISCELLANEOUS ACTIVITIES

From SIR HERBERT BRITTAIN, *1 January 1945*

ELECTRICITY—TREASURY GUARANTEES

At the meeting of the Reconstruction Committee on the 20th December, the Chancellor was asked to consider a suggestion that the Treasury should have power, on application made in special circumstances, to guarantee the stock of a regional board. One set of special circumstances which was put forward was that some regional boards might have more difficulty than others in raising money, owing to the fact that the nature of the district which they covered resulted in higher operating costs.

No doubt it is one thing to insist now that existing shareholders shall take, in exchange for their existing shares, the unguaranteed stocks of the new boards, on which, as we believe, the boards should be fully able to meet their liabilities, and that it will be another thing to persuade investors in the future to put up fresh cash for the industry on the basis now proposed. Nevertheless, if we have any confidence in that basis, it seems to me that the arguments against providing for any Treasury guarantees, as now proposed, are conclusive.

(1) The technical electricity experts have told us in the course of our discussions that the proposed 14 or so new regions have been chosen with a view to maintaining, within each board's area, pretty much the same combination of different types of districts—urban, rural, etc. If that is so, it is doubtful whether we could ever draw a clear line between those boards who could justify assistance by Treasury guarantee and those who could not. We should really be facing the possibility that sooner or later a guarantee would be available to all boards on proof of special circumstances.

(2) To announce that we think it likely that a Treasury guarantee may be necessary to finance future development of the industry would be a confession that we are doubtful whether (in some areas at least) the industry can develop on a commercial basis. That would be inconsistent with the emphasis at present being laid on the absence of risk to existing investors; it would be a poor commentary on the supposed advantages of the reorganisation; and it would raise suggestions of serious government interference in the conduct of the industry.

(3) The right course surely is to wait and see whether in fact circumstances arise which make recourse to a Treasury guarantee imperative. If the question arises, either it will be a sign that the general set-up now proposed has not worked out as we hoped and that a full review of the position of the industry is required: or it will be the result of the Government desiring to lay down some new policy for the industry which is not a paying proposition without a guarantee, in which case we should clearly avoid

471

committing ourselves to a guarantee until the policy itself can be fully weighed.

(4) It would in fact be very awkward to impose a Treasury-guaranteed stock at some future date on the financial structure which we propose to give to the new boards. After the debentures it takes over, a board will have one stock charged upon all its assets. (The annuities payable in respect of the surplus net maintainable income of the old companies will rank *pari passu* with that stock.) In the ordinary course, if a board desired subsequently to raise new capital, it would do so by successive issues of new stock—which would (if the precedent of the Central Electricity Board were followed) all rank *pari passu* with the original issue. If, however, any of these later issues were to be guaranteed by the Treasury, we should require, in the interests of the taxpayer, that the stock (and any sums paid out under the guarantee) should have a priority in front of existing stocks. Assuming that the issue were for normal development of a board's business, and not a matter of salvaging the existing assets, such priority would not be fair to the existing shareholders.

For these reasons, I think we should advise the Chancellor to ask the Reconstruction Committee to decide against any provision in the proposed electricity legislation for a Treasury guarantee in any circumstances.

H. B.

1 January 1945

To SIR RICHARD HOPKINS AND OTHERS, *6 January 1945*

ELECTRICITY—TREASURY GUARANTEES

I

As the Chancellor knows, I am a heretic on this proposal, which I believe to be unwise in substance and incapable of being successfully defended before critics. I should predict that the great majority of economists and financial journalists in the country will combine to attack it, on grounds which are unanswerable, whilst they will be aided and abetted by the much less defensible objections of local authorities, shareholders and political opponents of nationalisation. I think it is a great misfortune to make a very necessary and admirable proposal carry on its back this unnecessary load of trouble.

472

Sir H. Brittain, on the other hand, argues from the standpoint that the proposal is a very good one. He reads the minutes of the Reconstruction Committee to mean that the Committee have accepted the general financial scheme of the official committee as rightly applicable here and now, and have merely asked the Chancellor to examine the desirability of giving discretionary powers in the Act, which would allow a Treasury guarantee hereafter in special circumstances. He argues that to do this would indicate a lack of confidence that the proposals are even applicable now. He points out that a Treasury guarantee hereafter would raise awkward questions of priority, with which those who think that this is one of the arguments against the present proposal will not disagree. Finally he argues with some force that we can leave it to the future to amend the proposals in the directions proposed, if experience shows this to be necessary.

On the assumption that the plan is intrinsically a good one, Sir H. Brittain's arguments against introducing the suggested qualification have some force. But, from my point of view, the underlying assumption begs the question. I should, therefore, like to take this opportunity of arguing the matter a little further.

II

In a previous paper I have called attention to some of the questions of principle which arise. The most important of these arises out of the fact that the official committee seem to take as axiomatic what most contemporary economists would deny, namely, that a public corporation *ought* to have a price policy identical to that which characterises the private commercial enterprise. I will not attempt to carry this part of the argument further and will stick to the more technical matters directly raised by Sir H. Brittain's note. Apart from matters of principle, the above and others as well, the question whether the type of income bond which the official committee

473

proposes is the best instrument either now or hereafter largely depends in practice on how much it will cost. If the investor rather likes the plan and will take the bonds at a rate of interest not much above the gilt-edged rate, say, ¼ per cent higher, that is one thing. If, however, they want, say, 1 per cent higher, it becomes doubtful whether this technique (the main argument for which appears to be that it might exercise a wholesome psychological influence on the members of the board of the corporation) is worth while. If it were a question of 2 per cent more, perhaps no one would support it. Unfortunately, the proposal has not emerged from the official committee in a sufficiently developed form for it to be possible to answer this question. There are two types of obscurity still remaining:–

(i) It is proposed (paragraph 7(*a*) of appendix ii, page 41) that the bonds shall carry that rate in excess of the gilt-edged rate which will cause them to sell in the market at par. Thus the rate is in effect (as indeed equity requires) to be fixed by the market. It remains obscure, however, how it is proposed to discover what the appropriate rate on this basis is. At the time when the bonds are created, they are not to be issued to the market, but to the companies for ultimate distribution to their different classes of shareholders. What happens if the authorities offer 3¼ per cent bonds and the companies argue that they must carry 3⅜ per cent if they are to sell at par? Will the authorities then arrange to have them underwritten by financial houses, so that, if the companies think the interest unattractive, they can ask for cash instead, or how will it be settled?

(ii) Whatever the answer may be under (i) the appropriate rate will depend *inter alia* on the following considerations:–

(*a*) the redemption terms;

(*b*) whether there is a statutory sinking fund;

(*c*) on the instructions to the boards as to the accumulation of reserves;

(*d*) whether it is an obligation to pay the services of the bonds in advance of making reserves and other provisions and out of previous reserves and provisions, if necessary;

(*e*) the powers, if any, to borrow further sums in priority or ranking equally;

(*f*) whether the interest and the sinking funds are cumulative;

(*g*) the circumstances in which the board is entitled to ask for a Treasury subsidy before agreeing to provide a particular service or tariff;

(*h*) the precise form of the statutory duty placed on the board to earn the stipulated interest; and finally

(*i*) whether, having regard to future political prospects and the Governments likely to be in power, the investor feels that he is sufficiently secure from statutory or administrative future action to his disadvantage.

The committee cast no light on these details. But the draftsmen to whom the duty of preparing the Bill is entrusted will have to face them. These income bonds are a new kind of obligation, the character of which the Act will have to define with some precision. Until this is done, no one can say if a game (of which the rules are not yet written) is worth the candle. It will not be easy to put in black and white how far the bondholder has contractual and statutory rights and how far he is at the mercy of the efficiency of the statutory corporation, of the duties which may be laid on it hereafter by Parliament and of the future of the industry. These are not really matters for a legal draftsman.

III

The corrected minutes of the Reconstruction Committee record that their decision 'was provisional on their agreeing that a satisfactory financial scheme had been evolved for reorganisation on these lines'. Whilst some parts of the subject matter may now be ready to be handed to the Ministry of Fuel and Power for the preparation of the heads of a Bill, surely the above indicate that the financial provisions are not yet ripe for this.

Judging from the minutes of the meeting the pros and cons of the financial provisions (or at any rate, the cons) were not before ministers in any detail. Has the Economic Section been consulted? Are Ministers fully cognisant of the criticisms which are certain to be raised? Will it not save time in the end to consider somewhat more deeply at this stage an issue involving such profoundly important and very difficult questions, both of principle and practice?

Take another illustration, where further examination seems to me to be necessary. It is proposed that the main basis of compensation should be neither the market value of the shares nor replacement cost nor the value assessed as a going concern, but should be estimated, so to speak, historically, being initial cost less subsequent depreciation. Thus concerns built up when prices were high get more than those built up when prices were lower. I am not at all sure that this may not prove to be the best way out, at any rate in the case of electricity. The committee scarcely argued it. Yet this surely needs more consideration, both in this particular case and as a precedent, before it can be sensibly defended. Ministers must remember that all this will be gone through when published with a toothcomb by those who know a great deal about it and whose interests are deeply touched. Ministers will need to be on firm ground and know their case extremely well. The Bill inevitably raises matters of acute controversy. In the main, I am entirely at one with the recommendations of the official committee. I cannot emphasise too much how unwise it seems to me to be to complicate a great controversy, where they are on strong ground, with a provision in a matter of detail which is bound to be spotlighted and where, as I believe, they will get very much the worst of the argument.

KEYNES

6.1.45

Discussion continued in the Treasury throughout January. As it proceeded, opinion moved against implementing any scheme for the present. One of the reasons for delay was put by Sir Richard Hopkins on 2 February as follows:

> But Lord Keynes wishes to develop a different theory concerning the management of the gilt-edged market and we are about to enter upon a detailed discussion of his views [in the National Debt Inquiry]. That will take time.

As a result, the Chancellor agreed to a delay by communicating to the Reconstruction Committee that the Treasury could not see its way clear at present to provide a guarantee or trustee status for the securities of the proposed undertaking. There the matter rested.

Keynes's comments on post-war corporation tax had arisen earlier in response to a request from Sir Wilfrid Eady in connection with the work of the Steering Committee on Post-War Employment.

From SIR WILFRID EADY, *14 December 1943*

I should be grateful for your help on this matter.

At various stages on the Steering Committee when we have come up against the problems, particularly in the transitional period, of stimulating industrial enterprise and assisting in the re-equipment and reorganisation of industry we seem to have collided with the problem of the effect of our taxation policy upon industry. We are compelled in certain places to suggest artificial ways round the flank by subsidies, etc. Two or three of us on the Committee do not think our report would be complete without drawing very pointed attention to the general problem and before we write a page or two on the theme we want to have Gregg here next week to discuss the matter with him.

You will realise how difficult that discussion may become if Gregg, with his amazing knowledge of the taxation system and machinery, leads us from questions of principle into questions of detail, especially in the absence of Hopkins.

The Board of Trade have produced the attached note and that covers

477

some part of the field, but I want to begin if possible a little further back, to start with the proposition that, just as Customs policy has in the past been adapted to the requirements of an employment policy, so the direct taxation must be capable of such adaptation and must not count as a policy in itself but as part of the government's general policy.

At the same time I am personally impressed with the difficulties that Gregg has often adduced about altering the incidence or nature of industrial taxation suddenly so as to fit in with the 'timing' of economic stimulus. That is an improvement which might quite likely be manageable once we have got some of the principles established.

The first principle is, I think, to establish the view that nothing in the existing income tax system requires the standard rate to be applied to money put to reserves by industrial enterprise. Hopkins has often pointed out that the number of incomes which are taxed as 10s neither more nor less is a relatively small proportion of the total and he holds that we could, if we wished, make the taxation on reserves 7s 6d when the standard rate was 10s.

Gregg and others would say that 'especially favourable' treatment of undistributed profits ought only to apply within limits, and possibly subject to the purposes to which the undistributed profits are to be put within a reasonably narrow time limit.

Can you help me to state that proposition positively?

2. Can you also help me on the general question of the E.P.T. standard? Hopkins, I think, expects E.P.T. to continue after the war for a variety of reasons, including the fact that as it is at present designed it is, so to speak, a contingency reserve on which firms may call when their present favourable revenue position is altered.

Apart from the question of 80 per cent or 100 per cent or 60 per cent, what is really wrong with the standard year? There are a number of small firms who have expanded during the war and have shown themselves capable of efficient production which can claim that further expansion is impracticable without an alteration of the standard year.

3. Do you think that the Board of Trade note sufficiently brings out the problem created by the Inland Revenue's administrative definition of capital? The two incidences of which I am conscious are what seems an out-of-date treatment of depreciation allowance for buildings and, in connection with research, the problem of the pilot plant.

If there are any other leading points which you think should be included I should be glad to know them.

W. EADY

14 December 1943

Board of Trade Note

TAXATION OF INDUSTRIAL POLICY

1. An alternative to abating tax on undistributed profits might be to accelerate and extend the existing taxation allowances for capital expenditure. The relief in that case would be earned whether the expenditure was financed out of profits or capital or borrowed money.

Plant and machinery

2. At present capital expenditure on plant and machinery attracts taxation relief in the form of an annual wear and tear allowance. This allowance is more or less evenly spread over the whole life of the asset, and enables the business to recover tax on the cost of each machine plant by the end of its life.

3. An acceleration of this relief, either by granting a substantial part of it at the time when the plant is bought or by spreading the allowance over a shorter period than the full life of the plant, or perhaps, by a combination of both methods, would leave industry with more of its profits for investment in additional plant, and should provide an incentive to earlier scrapping and replacement. This proposal does not appear to present any administrative difficulties.

Buildings

4. The only tax relief at present given on buildings is a special repairs allowance for mills and factories, that is, buildings which house plant and machinery. In the absence of a wear and tear allowance such as exists for plant, the application of special relief to expenditure on buildings generally presents difficulties. But these should not be insuperable in the case of mills and factories and perhaps warehouses. The introduction of relief for this expenditure might need to be deferred until the time was ripe for its encouragement.

Capital expenditure on research

5. Expenditure on buildings and plant for research may be a special case. At present no tax relief is given (other than a repairs allowance) for the building; the plant attracts the normal wear and tear allowance. It may be that the whole of this expenditure should be allowed as a deduction from profits as and when it is incurred, subject only to its reinstatement as capital for income tax purposes if and in so far as it is afterwards diverted to other uses.

6. The granting of taxation relief for capital expenditure would not directly assist the expansion of *current* assets, that is, stocks, book debts and

479

the like. But the financing of these is a matter for the banks, and, provided a business can provide its fixed assets out of capital or profits, the finance for its current assets should be forthcoming.

BOARD OF TRADE

November 1943

Keynes replied.

To SIR WILFRID EADY, *16 December 1943*

INDUSTRIAL ENTERPRISE AND EMPLOYMENT
AND THE TAX SYSTEM

1. The first matter to clear out of the way is the spurious doctrine that the sole purpose of taxation policy is to apportion the costs of government equitably without *arrières-pensées* as to the effect of the particular method or formula in stimulating industrial enterprise and employment. If there ever was such an orthodoxy, it was abandoned many years ago. Almost everyone, whether in the Civil Service or in Parliament or amongst the general public, would be surprised, and indeed shocked, if they were to be told on high authority that this was an operative orthodoxy of government. If, however, it is not, then it is important to repudiate it and not allow it as an inhibition. Thus, you will see that I agree entirely with the fourth paragraph of your note.

2. Nevertheless, I agree that no promising proposals have yet been put forward with a view to altering the incidence or nature of industrial taxation as between one year and another so as to fit in with the timing of economic stimulus. I believe that we should give up the idea of progress along these lines. To get this out of the way would clear the road for more promising and constructive proposals.

3. You point out very truly that there is no principle of taxation requiring a uniform rate of income tax, irrespective of the way in which the taxable profits are being applied. Three alteernative proposals seem to be available:–

(*a*) to charge undistributed profits at a lower rate, whatever is done with them;

480

(*b*) to make an allowance for any capital expenditure, whether out of profits or out of borrowed money;

(*c*) to restrict the relief to profits which are 'employed in the business', i.e. there would be relief in any year on the difference compared with the previous year between the total of the reserves and the reserves employed outside the business.

I do not like (*a*) because this might operate in a deflationary manner. As the Americans, who have always partially exempted profits put to reserve, have found out, it is a mistake to encourage businesses to withhold dividends from shareholders merely for the purpose of hoarding them and not employing them in the business.

I see great difficulties in (*b*), which appears to be the Board of Trade proposal, both in its application to new business (for one could scarcely allow new businesses taxation relief corresponding to the whole of their capital, yet it would not be fair to discriminate in favour of businesses gradually increasing their capital as compared with a business which increases it once and for all) and also, as the Board of Trade point out, because there is not in the case of all businesses a clear case for preferring fixed capital to capital employed in the business in other ways.

My favourite proposal is, therefore, (*c*). In former days I should have expected the Revenue to reject this on the ground that there was no clear definition of 'money employed in the business'. Fortunately, the administration of E.P.T., where these words play a crucial part, has led the Revenue to work out a careful definition of the meaning of these words and one, so far as I know, which has proved quite acceptable to both parties. I believe, therefore, that the right compromise, which would, of course, give relief over a less wide field than (*a*) or (*b*), is to charge at a lower rate (I suggest half the standard rate) undistributed profits which are employed in the business. This would be a very substantial concession to growing and enterprising firms.

4. The principles of depreciation and obsolescence: at present, unless I misunderstand the position, fixed capital is divided into three classes:–

(i) categories not at present depreciable, of which buildings (subject to minor exceptions) and expenditure on patents, research and goodwill (I am not sure what exceptions are allowed to this) are the most important;

(ii) capital subject to an annual wear-and-tear allowance, more or less evenly spread over the whole life of the asset;

(iii) capital of a miscellaneous kind or having a short life, which need not be made subject to the annual wear-and-tear allowance but can, at the option of the taxpayer, if the Revenue agree that it is a suitable case, be charged against current working costs.

My definite suggestions are the following:–

Nothing should be left in category (i) except land and, perhaps, goodwill. It is greatly in the interest of industrial efficiency that buildings should be frequently renewed. Now that design and factory layout change frequently, it is quite fantastic to treat all buildings as virtually immortal. Category (iii) should be enlarged so as to cover anything where the proper depreciation is 20 per cent or more (you will appreciate that this is an option to the taxpayer; he could take an annual wear-and-tear allowance if he preferred). There remains the question of category (ii), which would be more extensive through gains from (i) and less extensive through gains from (iii). The minimum rate of depreciation allowance should be 2½ per cent. The standard allowance in each year appropriate to the class of capital in question should be a fixed allowance based on the initial cost and not, as at present, a diminishing allowance based on the written down cost. Where the appropriate annual allowance is greater than 15 per cent, depreciation should be allowed to continue until the item had been written off completely, any scrap value subsequently recovered being taken into profits. Where the standard rate of depreciation is less than 15 per cent, depreciation allowance should cease when the item had been brought down to 15 per cent of its initial cost, this balance being dealt with on obsolescence principles.

There should be a new classification of research expenditure according as it involves patents or not. Where patents are concerned, the writing off should be at a rate appropriate to the length of life of the patent. Where the results of research expenditure are made generally available, according to some approved formula, the firm should have the option of writing it off at once or over a period of years.

Firms should be allowed to anticipate depreciation allowances at (say) 3 per cent compound discount (3 per cent is not too low, since for practical purposes this is a rate of interest net of tax).

There remains the question of obsolescence. This should be allowed without the condition of replacement. In addition, a manufacturer should be allowed at any time to claim on the difference between the written down value and the current valuation, made by an approved valuer.

You will see that this is on the same general lines as the Board of Trade's note, but goes further and is much more specific.

5. You also ask me about the general question of the E.P.T. standard, on the assumption that E.P.T. continues at some reduced level for an appreciable time yet. You enquire in particular about what is wrong with the standard year.

At present a firm has the option of taking as its standard year either (1) 1935 or (2) 1936 or (3) the average of 1935 and 1937 or (4) the average of 1936 and 1937. You will notice that 1937 taken separately, 1938 and 1939 cannot be brought into the picture. The objection to this is that by, let us say, 1945 this standard period will be a very long time ago and may bear little relation to the current situation. In addition to that, it is limited to a very small range of years, with the result that some firms find themselves caught at a peculiarly unfortunate date. A great deal could be done, I think, by giving firms further options to take as their standard period 1937, 1938 or 1939. I believe that 1937 was originally omitted because this was thought to be rather too good a year, which would injure the yield of the tax. But in the post-war period it would not be unreasonable to allow firms to recover their 1937 prosperity. On the other hand, the year 1938 was probably excluded because it was a very good year for some armaments businesses. This was a valid reason for the war period, but is certainly not a reason for excluding 1938 in the post-war period, when it will certainly not be the armaments businesses which will be doing unduly well. Yet to include this (and also 1939) would bring the standard a very great deal more up to date.

I do not think there is much wrong with the allowance in respect of new capital. That was put right in one of the recent Finance Acts.

The remaining grievances relate to small firms, privately owned, and also perhaps, though less clearly, to new firms.

If a business is substantially owned by those who run it, the maximum remuneraton each of them can take before E.P.T. comes into force is £1,500 per annum. This, in conjunction with the very low minimum of £1,000, sets a very tight limit to the aggregate return from private businesses and partnerships with small capital. Yet it will be particularly undesirable in the post-war period to discourage such firms from any prospect of making any money on which they can build up their future. Take the following example (I may have worked out this wrong, since I am not expert in the matter. If I am wrong, it would be instructive to know the right answer). The new firm has a capital of £30,000. It is allowed 8 per cent on this, namely £2,400. It is a one-man business. He can, therefore, do a little better than the above by appealing to the minimum standard, which is £1,000, *plus* £1,500 extra to himself as a working proprietor. Assuming that £1,500 is a reasonable remuneration to him, the most he can get is £1,000 as interest and risk reward on his capital of £30,000 engaged in a new business. Thus he will do better to hire himself out to another firm and put his capital into Consols. It may be, however, that I am wrong in thinking that he cannot add the £1,500 on to the interest allowance of £2,400. If so, it is not so bad, but still extremely insufficient.

My solution would be to let small businesses off E.P.T. (incidentally, this would help farmers a great deal) by raising the minimum from £1,000 to £5,000. In addition, I should allow a deduction of £1,500 for each working proprietor before estimating the taxable profits, and I should raise the interest allowed on the amount of the capital from 8 per cent to 10 per cent. After all, this is not a question of guaranteeing a man 8 per cent or 10 per cent. It is allowing him to earn 10 per cent, if he knows how. Whilst established businesses distribute less than 10 per cent, none of them can survive and continue unless it is earning at least that amount. It is intolerable to restrict new businesses to that figure. Ten per cent seems to me to be the minimum. There might be a case in favour of 12 per cent.

In making the above suggestion I am influenced by the feeling that small, private businesses are exceedingly un-suitable to E.P.T., which was designed for quite a different sort of enterprise and, indeed, earns most of its revenue from other types of business.

I should expect that anyone thoroughly understanding the system and genuinely anxious to improve it from the above point of view could make more comprehensive and better suggestions than the above. The above suggestions are very likely open to criticism in detail, but they illustrate the object at which I suggest one ought to aim.

6. I should like to mention one other point, though per-haps it is not very relevant in this context. The late Chancellor

twice endeavoured to convince business that the E.P.T. refund was a reality. But he has only very partially succeeded. I fancy that it would greatly facilitate financial planning for the post-war period if a yet further effort could be made to produce conviction in the business world. My proposal would be to introduce a clause into the Finance Act, providing that a certificate stating the amount of E.P.T. refund should be given to businesses on the same line as deferred credits, and should be introduced into balance sheets, provided that the equivalent sum is placed to a special reserve, which cannot be drawn on for dividend or bonuses, though it would be available, of course, in the event of a liquidation. In short, it would be in the same position as the capital of a company. The objection which the Revenue made previously to a suggestion on these lines seems to me to be invalid. It was based, I believe, on the difficulties arising when an adjustment of E.P.T. already paid has to be made for one of the many reasons which may require this. But that seems to me to raise no complication at all. It will only arise when the Revenue are paying back some E.P.T. When they do that, the corresponding E.P.T. refund certificate would, of course, fall to be cancelled to an appropriate extent. That would simply be a routine part of repaying that part of E.P.T. which was repayable.

KEYNES

16.12.43

DOCUMENTS REPRODUCED
IN THIS VOLUME

Where documents come from the Public Record Office, their call numbers appear before the date.

MINUTES

DOCUMENTS REPRODUCED IN THIS VOLUME

PUBLISHED LETTERS

UNPUBLISHED LETTERS

DOCUMENTS REPRODUCED IN THIS VOLUME

ACKNOWLEDGEMENTS

The Royal Economic Society is grateful to the following for permission to reproduce material.

The British Broadcasting Corporation for the broadcasts printed on pp. 240–5 and 365–7

The Controller of Her Majesty's Stationery Office for Crown Copyright material

The Mirror Group Newspapers for the article from the *Manchester Daily Herald* on pp. 87–90

The New Republic for the article on pp. 144–155

The Radio Times Hulton Picture Library for the Frontispiece

The Times for the articles on pp. 41–51 and 74–81

The Trustees and *The Evening Standard* for the cartoons on pp. 100 and 290.

The Editors would also like to record their thanks to Professors R. S. Sayers and J. R. N. Stone for advice.

INDEX

Agriculture
labourers' wages, 41
subsidies, 232, 359–60
and wartime price policy, 5–6
Aircraft production, 188, 189, 351
companies, 394, 395
Air raids, 435
effect on price of stocks, 394, 395; on stock exchange transactions, 401
Air raid precautions (A.R.P.), 16, 42, 75
Alcoholic drinks, tax on, 379–80, 381
whisky, 156
wines and spirits, 358, 380
Aliens; and financial policy in wartime, 168–9; enemy, 162, 168, 190; non-enemy, 164
internment, 190–1
Allen, Roy George Douglas (b. 1906), statistician, Treasury, 376
'Allied Exchange Policy' (May 1940), 172–4
Allies
in World War I, 11
in World War II, 176, 178; exchange policy proposals, 173–4; plan for pooling resources, 175–6, 180
America, see United States of America
American countries, 26
Amery, L. S., 92 n
Analysis of the First Year's War Finance' (December 1940), 333, 334–7
'Note', on, by D. H. Robertson, 338–41
correspondence on, 342–50
Anderson, Sir John, Chancellor of the Exchequer (September 1943–July 1945), 423, 428, 455, 456, 472, 473, 477; sets up Committee on Public Utility Corporations, 460
memorandum to, 458
Anglo–French financial agreement, 179
proposed joint committee, 181
Argentine, 22, 175
Armaments firms, 348, 484; profit tax on, 387; rearmament programme (1937–8), 387
Armed forces, 54, 83, 148, 151, 306, 356; deferred consumption (pay) for, 50,

84, 117, 122, 147, 239–40, 278; 'output', 126
military expenditure, 150, 153
Army recruiting campaign, 256, 258, 263
Arts Council, 432
Ashton-Gwatkin, Frank Trelawney Arthur (b. 1889), Ministry of Economic Warfare, 22, 23 n 14
Attlee, Clement Richard (1883–1967), Leader of the Opposition (1935–40), Deputy Prime Minister (1942–5), 40; hostility to deferred payments plan, 97
Australia, 167
Austria, 27

Balance of payments
estimates (1940), 106, 125, 203
and domestic requirements of Budget, 218–19, 220
financing of, 127, 141, 297
limit to, 128
problem of, 'the clue to recovery', 378
also mentioned, 340–1, 343–5, 347
Balance of trade, 54, 332, 334
deterioration, 54, 125, 204; export drive to improve, 128, 129; means of financing, 160, 162, 170–1; proposed pooling of trade balances, 173, 175
Balfour of Burleigh, 7th Baron (George John Gordon Bruce, 1883–1967), 99, 328
Balogh, Thomas (b. 1905), economist, 163
Bank of England
JMK gets 'free entry' again, 158; is elected a Director (1941), 408–9
accepts policy of Monetary Committee, 159
and mobilisation of foreign resources, 168, 171, 172, 174–5, 297
and new capital issues, 422, 425, 428
Stock Exchange hostility to, 423
also mentioned, 198, 199, 331–2, 335, 346, 470
Directors of Bank, 139
Governor, see Norman, Montagu Collet

493